TRAVELLING CONCEPTS IN THE H
A ROUGH GUIDE

Travelling Concepts in the Humanities is intended as a guidebook for interdisciplinary cultural analysis in the humanities. In this challenging work, Mieke Bal analyses a variety of concepts – such as meaning, metaphor, narrative, and myth – that 'travel' from one discipline to another. To illustrate the possibilities of these concepts, she provides examples drawn from a number of disciplines, including literary criticism, art history, and visual studies. Interdisciplinarity, she argues, must seek its heuristic and methodological basis in concepts rather than in methods.

This is not only a guidebook, but also a story of adventure: we are witnesses as concepts travel into or through visual studies (or the cultural practice of art), displaying their possibilities through a series of fascinating case studies. Returning from our travels we find that the object constructed no longer is the 'thing' that we chose; it has become a living creature, embedded in new questions and considerations.

This lively, wide-ranging, and innovative study will be of interest to scholars in a variety of disciplines, including literary studies, art history, biblical studies, feminist theory, and visual and cultural studies.

MIEKE BAL teaches in the Faculty of Humanities at the University of Amsterdam, and is Andrew D. White Professor at Large at Cornell University.

TRAVELLING CONCEPTS IN THE HUMANITIES
A Rough Guide

MIEKE BAL

Green College Lectures
Green College, University of British Columbia

UNIVERSITY OF TORONTO PRESS
Toronto Buffalo London

© University of Toronto Press Incorporated 2002
Toronto Buffalo London
Printed in Canada

ISBN 0-8020-3529-9 (cloth)
ISBN 0-8020-8410-9 (paper)

Printed on acid-free paper

The name Rough Guide is a registered trademark of the publishers Rough
Guides Ltd, 62–70 Shorts Gardens, London WC2H 9AH, used here with
their consent. The publishers have no editorial connection with this publication. Rough Guide travel guides, music guides, phrasebooks, and reference
books are available at all good bookstores or at www.roughguides.com.

National Library of Canada Cataloguing in Publication Data

Bal, Mieke, 1946–
    Travelling concepts in the humanities : a rough guide

(Green College lectures)
Includes bibliographical references and index.
ISBN 0-8020-3529-9 (bound). ISBN 0-8020-8410-9 (pbk.)

1. Humanities.   2. Interdisciplinary approach to knowledge.
I. Marx-Macdonald, Sherry   II. Title   III. Series: Green College
lecture series.

AZ515.Z5B34 2002   001.3   C2002-900960-X

This book has been published with the help of a grant from Green College,
University of British Columbia.

The University of Toronto Press acknowledges the financial assistance to
its publishing program of the Canada Council for the Arts and the Ontario
Arts Council.

University of Toronto Press acknowledges the financial support for its
publishing activities of the Government of Canada through the Book
Publishing Industry Development Program (BPIDP).

To the participants of the ASCA Theory Seminar –
past, present, and future

Contents

Illustrations and Credits

Acknowledgments

This book was originally conceived as a series of lectures delivered during my stay as Cecil H. and Ida Green Visiting Professor at Green College of the University of British Columbia during November 1999. I had proposed to devote the lectures not to a single topic, but to a sustained plea for and demonstration of interdisciplinary cultural analysis through a number of case studies. The lectures enjoyed the kind of constant audience so rare at academic events. This made the discussion of the overall theme through the concrete cases all the more meaningful and productive. The round-table discussion concluding the series went on to explore the many questions raised by the lectures, but also the 'remaining questions' that addressed many profoundly unresolved moments. These questions allowed me to thicken the thread that runs through the cases, with the result that both continuity and detailed analysis could be ensured for the present book. I am deeply grateful to Richard Ericson, Principal of Green College, to the faculty and staff, and to all the students who honoured me with their attention. In particular, I thank the participants of the round-table discussion: Nancy Frelick, Alec Globe, Tineke Hellwig, Ruth Iskin, Joshua Mostow, Valerie Raoul, Rose Marie San Juan, and Lorraine Weir.

For each of the specific studies, many other people were also helpful with their critical comments and support. I deviate from custom by not naming them all. Most appear in the references. I would like to give special thanks to Sherry Marx-Macdonald, who was the first, last, and ongoing interim reader of this emerging book, and whose many perceptive comments as its editor helped shape it into a more accessible rough guide.

There is one group in particular, though, who deserves credit. It is the group who inspired me to undertake this work and who kept challenging my positions in the most friendly, constructive, and critical way: the participants of the ASCA (Amsterdam School for Cultural Analysis) Theory Seminar at the University of Amsterdam. It has been my privilege to interact with them over many years and to see their many intuitive ideas, merged with intellectual passion, grow into wonderful new PhDs and books. Not only do I devote the closing chapter to the 'spirit' of this ongoing, changing, but in some senses permanent, group, but I could think of no more appropriate dedication for the present book than the people who, in fact, made it.

TRAVELLING CONCEPTS IN THE HUMANITIES:
A ROUGH GUIDE

Introduction

This point of arrival, with talk of a performative concept of gender, is very different from the point of departure, Austin's conception of performative utterances, but to make your fortune, as the genre of the picaresque has long shown us, you have to leave home and, often, to travel a long way.

Jonathan Culler (2000: 48)

This book can be read as a rough travel guide – rough because partial, based mostly on my own travels. The research that went into it was purposefully limited to what emerged during those travels. It is a guide because it can be used in any way you like, following or wilfully ignoring any of the paths it maps or signposts. It is a rough guide because it offers suggestions and ideas for those teachers and students eager to explore the intellectual excitement of interdisciplinary cultural analysis and deal with the roadblocks and other divergences from the straight path they encounter along the way.

It is like those rough guides for cheap and handy travel because it aims to address the practical aspects of an intellectual education without excessive cost. Practical, here, refers to the practice of developing research projects for all levels of students and faculty struggling to be convincingly precise and profound yet at the same time accessible, in an age characterized by the loss of boundaries. By cost I do not mean anything economic. I mean the high costs involved in such obvious endeavours as getting the basics, reading the classics, and working through one's own methodological toolbox. It is about saving time so that the actual work gets done, without cutting corners where corners matter. It is a book against confusion and for a workable situation;

against simplification and for an enriching yet unforbidding complexity. First and foremost, though, it makes its object out of the problems of interdisciplinary cultural analysis.

The quotation from Jonathan Culler's article that is cited here as an epigraph uses the metaphor of travel. To make your fortune, you have to travel. Hazardous, exciting, and tiring, travel is needed if you are to achieve the gain of new experience. Culler's article, which traces the fortunes of the concept of the *performative*, travels first back and forth between philosophy – where the concept was first used – and literature – where it solved major problems but at the same time challenged the limitations of the philosophical proposal – then back to philosophy, on to cultural studies, and back to philosophy again. His article stands out as model for the kind of study of 'concepts as travelling' that I had in mind when I first contemplated this book. Not that this volume contains such studies. Rather, it travels on – with studies written by others – into a practice that is its real subject.

The anthropologist's work is more clearly cut out. To do anthropology, you have to choose a field, apply a method, and construct an object (Augé 1999: 1). The same holds for cultural analysis, on condition that a few words are changed to point out that the world of culture is not so easily mapped. The *field* of cultural analysis is not delimited, because the traditional delimitations must be suspended; by selecting an object, you *question* a field. Nor are its *methods* sitting in a toolbox waiting to be applied; they, too, are part of the exploration. You don't apply one method; you conduct a meeting between several, a meeting in which the object participates, so that, together, object and methods can become a new, not firmly delineated, field. This is where travel becomes the unstable ground of cultural analysis. Cultural analysis, like anthropology, does construct an object, albeit with a slightly different sense of what that object is. At first sight, the object is simpler than anthropology's: a text, a piece of music, a film, a painting. But, after returning from your travels, the object constructed turns out to no longer be the 'thing' that so fascinated you when you chose it. It has become a living creature, embedded in all the questions and considerations that the mud of your travel spattered onto it, and that surround it like a 'field.'

Culler's reference to the picaresque tradition inserts an element of fictionality into your travels. The travels proposed here do, indeed, appear like armchair trips. Perhaps they just happen on a stage: in a classroom, in a study. In this sense, then, the fictional theatricality of *mise-en-scène* subtends the metaphor of travel, as a reminder of the basis of humanist study in that large, unmanageable field called 'culture.'

The thesis on which this book is based, and of which it is both an elaboration and a defence, is extremely simple: namely, interdisciplinarity in the humanities, necessary, exciting, serious, must seek its heuristic and methodological basis in *concepts* rather than *methods*. Despite its simplicity, and its *de facto* endorsement by authors of such articles as Culler's, I am not aware of any publication that addresses its *consequences* head-on. The turn to interdisciplinarity during the 1990s was necessarily accompanied by a proliferation of such articles, and of the encyclopedias and smaller handbooks that contain them. My endeavour here, though, is to look at the *practice* of cultural analysis that these publications support.

My conviction that a concept-based methodology is crucial has grown out of my experience as a teacher. At the undergraduate level, the need for concepts has been obvious for a long time; my earlier book *Narratology* was a first response to that need. Since then, I have been increasingly involved with the development, 'from scratch,' of a great number of PhD and postdoctoral projects that were not easy to place within any one discipline. The reduction of the number of fellowships and, consequently, of class size, together with a developing interest in work that crosses disciplinary boundaries, has led to classes becoming less homogeneous. From the beginning I have experienced this change as exciting and productive – not the fellowship part, but the rest of it.

Let me sketch the situation I have been dealing with. It will be familiar to many. A philosopher, a psychoanalytic critic, a narratologist, an architectural historian, and an art historian are talking together in a seminar about, say, 'signs and ideologies.' Eager young scholars, excited, committed. The word 'subject' comes up and keeps recurring. With growing bewilderment, the first participant assumes the topic is the rise of individualism; the second sees it as the unconscious; the third, the narrator's voice; the fourth, the human confronted with space; and the fifth, the subject matter of a painting or, more sophisticatedly, the depicted figure. This could be just amusing, if only all five did not take their interpretation of 'subject,' on the sub-reflective level of obviousness, to be the only right one. They are, in their own eyes, just 'applying a method.' Not because they are selfish, stupid, or uneducated, but because their disciplinary training has never given them the opportunity, or a reason, to consider the possibility that such a simple word as 'subject' might, in fact, be a concept.

No single participant questions the other's use; each simply assumes that the other is confused, and turns off the concentration button or, in the best of cases, gets upset. Each fictive participant in this familiar drama uses the pronoun 'we' without specifying to whom it refers. The other members of the seminar who are listening just don't get it and drift off. By the time the discussants realize there is a misunderstanding, the seminar is over. It is with this situation in mind, and in the hope of remedying it a bit, that I have written this book.

The activity we conduct in the kind of setting I have just described might become a little clearer if we gave it a name. Not the name of one of the disciplines from which the participants come, but one that posits its interdisciplinary character. While trying to think of a single term to describe my own work – a question, given my excursions into different fields, that I have often been asked – I came up with the name of cultural analysis. Not literary studies, art history, philosophy, or women's studies; not theory; not even cultural studies. The latter intuitively articulated negation surprised me most of all. In the wake of women's studies, cultural studies has, in my view, been responsible for the absolutely indispensable opening up of the disciplinary structure of the humanities. By challenging methodological dogma, and elitist prejudice and value judgment, cultural studies has been uniquely instrumental in at least making the academic community aware of the conservative nature of its endeavours, if not everywhere forcing it to change. Cultural studies has, if nothing else, forced the academy to realize its collusion with an elitist white-male politics of exclusion and its subsequent intellectual closure. Everything about cultural studies that makes me not want to say that is what I do must be considered a footnote to this major acknowledgment.

Inevitably, this new inter-discipline has suffered from the unforeseeable difficulties and hardships that every pioneering activity encounters. In defying disciplinary boundaries, it has had to contend with three problems, all of which jeopardize its ongoing intellectual vigour today. For the sake of clarity, allow me to put these rather strongly and without the required nuance.

First, while one of cultural studies' major innovations has been to pay attention to a different kind of object, as a new field averse to traditional approaches it has not been successful (enough) in developing a methodology to counter the exclusionary methods of the separate disciplines. More often than not, the methods have not changed. While the object – *what* you study – has changed, the method – *how* you do it – has not. But without the admittedly rigid methodologies of the disciplines, how do you keep analysis from floundering into sheer partisanship, or from being perceived as floundering? This is the major problem of content and practice that faces us today, which in turn creates more problems, especially in teaching situations. It is this problem that will be the primary focus of this book.

Second, cultural studies has involuntarily 'helped' its opponents to deepen rather than overcome the destructive divide between *les anciens* and *les modernes*, a binary structure as old as Western culture itself. This is unfortunate, for this opposition tends to feed an oedipally based psychosocial mechanism that is unhelpful when it comes to changing predominant power structures. The problem is primarily a social one, but in the current situation, where academic jobs are scarce and hierarchies returning, it entails a tendency to a monolithic appointments policy that threatens, under the name of backlash, everything that has been accomplished. Whereas a book like this cannot change that situation at all, a recognizably responsible practice based on reflection on the problem of method may help to pave the way for a more nuanced academic environment. This forms the secondary focus of this book.

Third, the inevitable consequence of the inadequate methodology and reinforced opposition combined is even more mundane yet just as dangerous. At a time of economic crisis, the interdisciplinarity inherent to cultural studies has given university administrators a tool with which to enforce mergings and cancellations of departments that might turn out to be fatal for the broad grounding cultural studies needs.[1]

Why, then, is the idea of 'cultural analysis' helpful in seeking to remedy these three problems? By fundamentally changing the way we 'think' methodology within the different disciplines, it is possible to overcome the three major – indeed, potentially dangerous – drawbacks of cultural studies. Against the first and most important one for my project, concepts will be brought in as an alternative for the idea of

---

1 This danger is real and potentially fatal for the humanities. I have had occasion to witness it while serving on evaluation committees of postgraduate programs. This danger alone is enough to make us cautious about giving up discipline-based groupings too easily.

coverage. Within an interdisciplinary setting, coverage – of the classics, of all periods or 'centuries,' of all major theories used within a field – is no longer an option. Nor is 'sloppy scholarship.' If a different alternative can be articulated, the divide, which is the second drawback, can be lessened. The creation of a methodological common ground, all the more urgently needed as the self-evidence of coverage is challenged, is the only unified answer we can give to administrative attacks on staff. Solving the first two takes the wind out of the sails of administrators too eager to take advantage of the situation.

The political thrust of this book, then, is, first, to persuade colleagues and students that there is a way out of these predicaments, and second, to offer ideas to those trying to find their way in the labyrinthine land of a humanities without boundaries. Such a land can only unify through travel, through learning foreign languages, through encounters with others. If Europe can unify, so can the academy, and – I contend – with much less difficulty, sacrifice, and impoverishment.

The analysis part of the term 'cultural analysis' is what is at stake here. In my view the counterpart of the concepts we work with is not the systematic theory from which they are taken, although that theory matters and cannot be neglected. Nor is it the history of the concept in its philosophical or theoretical development. And it is certainly not a 'context,' whose status as text, itself in need of analysis, is largely ignored. The counterpart of any given concept is the cultural text or work or 'thing' that constitutes the *object* of analysis. No concept is meaningful for cultural analysis unless it helps us to understand the object better *on its* – the object's – *own terms*. Here, another background, or root, of the current situation in the humanities comes to the fore.

The turn to methodology mentioned earlier was partly a reaction to the cultivation of the object and its details in critical movements such as the new, literary hermeneutics in Germany, the *explication de texte* in France, and the New Criticism in the Anglo-Saxon world. The general term *close reading* is still with us, but the practice of it, I am afraid, is not. This loss is due to practical changes; in particular, to the reduction of programs. But it is also due to the loss of innocence that came with the awareness that no text yields meaning outside of the social world and cultural makeup of the reader. Nevertheless, I have often had occasion to regret the loss of analytical skills that accompanied the disenchantment with the illusion that 'the text speaks for itself.' True enough, a text does not speak for itself. We surround it, or *frame* it, before we let it speak at all. But rejecting close reading for that reason has been an unfortunate case of throwing out the baby with the bath water. For, in the tripartite relationship between student, frame, and object, the latter must still have the last word.

Whereas this sustained attention to the object is the mission of *analysis*, it also qualifies the term 'cultural analysis.' I will not define 'culture' in this book. It is well known that definitions of culture are inevitably programmatic. If 'culture' is defined as the thoughts and feelings, the moods and values of people, then 'analysis' is bound to a phenomenologically oriented approach that shuns the social that is culture's other. If subjectivity is the focus, then social interaction remains out of its scope. And if it is the mind that comprises the cultural fabric, then all we can analyse is a collection of individualities. These traditional conceptions have been abandoned or adjusted, but they continue to share the impulse to define culture in the abstract and general sense.[2] This is the area of study the social sciences focus on. It would be presumptuous to pronounce on what 'culture' is, except perhaps to say that it can only be envisioned in a plural, changing, and mobile existence.

The objects of study of the disciplines that comprise the humanities *belong* to culture but do not, together, constitute it. The qualifier 'cultural' takes the existence and importance of cultures for granted, but it does not predicate the 'analysis' on a particular conception of 'culture.' For, in distinction from, say, cultural anthropology, 'cultural analysis' does not *study* culture. 'Culture' is not its object. The qualifier *cultural* in 'cultural analysis' indicates, instead, a distinction from traditional disciplinary practice within the humanities, namely, that the various objects gleaned from the cultural world for closer scrutiny are analysed *in view of* their existence in culture. This means they are not seen as isolated jewels, but as things always-already engaged, as interlocutors, within the larger culture from which they have emerged. It also means that 'analysis' looks to issues of cultural relevance, and aims to articulate how the object contributes to cultural debates. Hence the emphasis on the object's existence in the present. It is not the artist or the author but the objects they make and 'give' to the public domain that are the 'speakers' in analytic discussion (this is argued extensively in chapter 7). For now, I wish to insist on the participation of the object in the production of meaning that 'analysis' constitutes.

2 See Wuthnow et al. (1984), an early publication that uses the term 'cultural analysis' for a description of anthropological method.

The most important consequence of this empowerment of the object is that it pleads for a qualified return to the practice of 'close reading' that has gone out of style. This book as a whole *is* that plea; it 'argues' it by demonstrating it. This is why all of the chapters – different as they are in the way they explore the possible relations between concept and object and the function they assign to the concepts – are *case studies* rather than systematic explanations of the concept concerned. Even chapter 1, where concepts are discussed in general, can be construed as a case study – of a classroom situation in which concepts are the subject matter. For their part, most of the other chapters focus on the relationship between a concept and a more recognizable cultural object.

Rethinking the use and meaning of concepts as a methodological principle is the guideline I propose in this admittedly rough guide. I have a long-standing interest in the methodological potential of concepts. My interest in concepts as a tool for – at first mainly literary – analysis even determined my intuitive selection of *narrative* as my initial area of specialization. I was 'simply' a literary scholar at the time, based in French and soon after in Comparative Literature. Barely having arrived there, I moved on to Biblical Scholarship, then to Art History. But I never truly belonged to any of these disciplines. All along, I had one foot in women's studies and another in a field called 'narratology' that had no place in the academy. From early on, I considered the theory of narrative a relevant area of study precisely because it is *not* confined to any one academic discipline. For narrative is a mode, not a genre. It is alive and active as a cultural force, not just as a kind of literature. It constitutes a major reservoir of the cultural baggage that enables us to make meaning out of a chaotic world and the incomprehensible events taking place in it. And, not to be forgotten, narrative can be used to manipulate. In short, it is a cultural force to be reckoned with.

Some readers of my earlier work may, therefore, be surprised that neither 'narrative' nor 'focalization' figures in the table of contents here. But, while these two concepts remain important, and are, in fact, good examples of *trans*disciplinary concepts (I discuss their travels through the disciplines in the first chapter a bit), I wish to avoid reiterating my earlier work. It was my fascination with narrative as a cultural force rather than as a literary genre that gave me the motivation at the time to work on narrative theory. But at some point I realized that the reason I saw narrative in this way had to do with the concept of narrative that I had unreflectively endorsed. It was through the diffuse, self-evident yet powerfully specific concept of narrative that I began to consider 'culture' in the first place.

'Narrative' is thus a transdisciplinary concept, while 'narratology,' the systematic study of the phenomenon that concept names, has been developed within the disciplinary niche of literary studies. As a result of the move towards greater interdisciplinarity, others have alleged narrative as important. One example is the narrativist movement in historiography. But as long as such movements remain efforts within one discipline, very few of its participants can take the time needed to study the theoretical work from another discipline, even if it provides them with a key concept. Narrativism has had little exposure to narratology. Simply borrowing a loose term here and there would not do the trick of interdisciplinarity. Conversely, the narratology that came to the attention of narrativists was so narrowly based on fiction that they saw little point in it for their historiographic project. This is a major setback for both.

It was this realization that set me thinking about concepts. Concepts not so much as firmly established univocal terms but as dynamic in themselves. While groping to define, provisionally and partly, what a particular concept may *mean*, we gain insight into what it can *do*. It is in the groping that the valuable work lies. This is why I have come to value concepts. The groping is a collective endeavour. Even those concepts that are tenuously established, suspended between questioning and certainty, hovering between ordinary word and theoretical tool, constitute the backbone of the interdisciplinary study of culture – primarily because of their potential *intersubjectivity*. Not because they mean the same thing for everyone, but because they don't.

Intersubjectivity is a concern that binds procedure with power and empowerment, with pedagogy and the transmittability of knowledge, with inclusiveness and exclusion. Thus it connects heuristic with methodological grounding. The power of concepts to facilitate invention cannot be thought of without the intersubjectivity of which power is a factor. Intersubjectivity itself also happens to be a good example of a flexible kind of concept that I find most helpful. Let me indicate briefly how the notion of intersubjectivity ends up in my project.

It came into currency in the humanities' part of the academy during the 1960s, when the humanities discovered the importance of methodology, beyond the discourse of criticism alone. At that time, the formative years of my academic life, a number of slogans from the philosophy of science became dogmatic guidelines for the humanities and the social sciences, both eager to emulate their more self-evidently scientific other, the natural sciences. Intersubjectivity was a key concept from 'falsification' Popper, or Daddy Methodology. It embraced a program of idealized consensus and non-ambiguity: intersubjectively defined concepts and methods were to have exactly the same meaning for all those concerned. Meanwhile, Habermas, the Lefty, promoted self-reflection, a position that also leaves its traces in this book. By reflecting on why scholars raise certain questions, choose particular methods, and arrive at specific conclusions, the interests served by scholars become part of the field of inquiry. 'Interests' is meant in the strong sense of Habermas' German word *Interesse*, meaning that you have a stake in the thing that interests you. Feyerabend the Anarchist relieved us of all worries, arguing that justification always post-dates discovery, and that the latter is as much a product of random circumstance as of methodical experiment. When that became a bit too conducive to sloppiness and methodological indifference, Kuhn made us reasonable again by proposing a social theory of scientific inquiry. His key term, 'paradigm,' indicates a set of methodological presuppositions, procedures, and applications that are so taken for granted as to become habits, both unquestioned by those on the inside and a subject of contempt, negligence, or even ignorance for those on the outside.[3] In a sense, the present book and all it stands for might also be seen in terms of a paradigm shift and, like some of my earlier work, it may receive adherence and rejection as a result. Intersubjectivity, it turned out, is limited – relative to groups, views, and consensus.

In the context of the attempts to make the humanities less philological and critical, and more scientific, humanists became interested in a methodology that stretched beyond their strict disciplinary concerns. They began to look to the philosophers of science mentioned above. Although most of us moved on from the illusions and the ill-conceived emulation, some elements of the discussions stuck. I personally took the concept of *intersubjectivity* with me and cherished it, not primarily for its promise of a clear-cut, unambiguous formulation of terms – which could at best be attempted but never achieved – but for its insistence on the democratic distribution of knowledge. Of course, Popper would turn in his grave if he saw me running with it. But to

---

3 See Popper (1972; 1982); Habermas (1972); Feyerabend (1993); and Kuhn (1962) and his response to critics (1986).

worry about that would be to fall for the argument of authority.

Instead, without abandoning disambiguation because of the impossibility of achieving it, the concept of intersubjectivity, I believe, can combine a concern for clarity with something more geared towards the social aspect of knowledge as foregrounded by Habermas. For me, it became a word again, one that I unpacked into 'inter-,' as in interdisciplinarity, international, and intercultural, and 'subjectivity,' as in Lacan, Althusser, or 'person.' I then inflected the two elements into 'narratology,' as in 'interpersonal.' From there on, 'inter-' regained a place in my methodology, but without the authority of master.

My interest was in developing concepts we could all agree on and use, or at the very least disagree on, in order to make what has been labelled 'theory' accessible to every participant in cultural analysis, both within and outside the academy. Concepts, I found over the years, are the sites of debate, awareness of difference, and tentative exchange. Agreeing doesn't mean agreeing on content, but agreeing on the basic rules of the game: if you use a concept at all, you use it in a particular way so that you can meaningfully disagree on content. That use doesn't go without saying. Intersubjectivity in this sense remains the most important standard for teaching and writing. Whatever else it does, cultural studies owes it to its principles of anti-elitism, to its firm position against exclusion of everything that is non-canonical and everyone who is not mainstream, to take this standard seriously. In the bargain, between Popper and practice, considering intersubjectivity has made me understand the difference between a word and a concept. This book is the outcome of that understanding.

In the following chapters, I present a number of cases of different forms of intercourse with and through concepts that might be useful as a rough guide for specific interdisciplinary endeavours. Do not expect an overview or list of the 'most important' concepts, or a firm definition of what each concept 'really' means or a prescription of how it should be used. The stakes of this book are both lower and higher: lower, in that I submit just one way to use a concept; higher, in that I aim to demonstrate how the variety of ways in which a concept can be brought to bear on an object makes for an analytical practice that is both open and rigorous, teachable and creative. Hopefully, the case studies offered here will open up venues for differentiated but specific uses of concepts, as sites of both methodological openness and reflection and, hence, without the loss of accountability and intersubjective communication that so often accompanies such openness. The cases are showcases of practices; and the kinds of practices at issue – not the specific concepts or their handling – are central to my argument. In each chapter, a different practice comes to the fore. Some form of travel occurs in each.

The first journey, in chapter 1, explores the entanglement and later disentanglement of concepts that partially overlap. The overlap of concepts is an inevitable consequence of their creation and subsequent adjustment within the separate disciplines. But this overlap leads to their confused and vague use in interdisciplinary work. The journey in this chapter, then, is between a variety of places: between disciplines, words, and half-baked and rigidified concepts; and between concepts and objects. I discuss the use of concepts in general, presenting the case for a particular intercourse with and through a specific number of concepts currently in use in interdisciplinary practice in the humanities. Departing from the examples I know best, narrative being too general and too obvious, I discuss briefly the relation of non-coincidence between the narratological concept of focalization and the visual studies' concepts of gaze and look.

But, while being presented and defended, it is primarily the concept of *concept* itself that serves as a first example of the kind of flexibility I have in mind. Flexibility in a sense that precludes neither a certain provisional solidity, or grounding, nor an openness to change. None of the cases in this book pronounces on the dilemma expressed in such slurs as 'rigid' versus 'sloppy.' Any field, be it disciplinary or interdisciplinary, has both valuable and shamefully poor results. This book is not a cookbook; recipes are not to be expected. Nor are prescriptions, moralizing or otherwise. If the case studies offer any guidance at all, the 'how-to' concerns the possibilities of deploying concepts in analysis, and not the analysis itself. If a metaphor does exist that might be helpful in assessing the particular use of a concept, 'elasticity' might be it, because it suggests both an unbreakable stability and a near-unlimited extendibility. 'Travel' is meant to suggest these qualities as the basis for an intellectual adventure. It is this paradoxical status of concepts that helps us to live with and through the following dilemma: that *only practice can pronounce on theoretical validity, yet without theoretical validity no practice can be evaluated*. It is practice, therefore, that remains the focus of the 'how-to' nature of this book.

After the first journey, in which the concept of concept is tracked, the second journey, in chapter 2, takes us farther from home. Its purpose is to show that it makes sense to take the trouble of learning the language of the country we are visiting. Here, the single concept of *image* is put forward, clothed in the three elements – focalization, gaze, and look – inherited from chapter 1. This chapter continues the issues already raised around the concept of concept in the preceding chapter. For the tensions between visuality and textuality remain foregrounded; as key fields of interdisciplinarity, visuality and textuality will never disappear from this book. As an emblem of the contested and exciting field of 'word and image studies,' the ambiguous word, term, or concept of image will be put in the eye of the maelstrom of related concepts that whirl around in that field, of which *metaphor* is the most conspicuously relevant. This concept is known to be dualistic in itself, for it designates the simultaneous deployment of two meanings. It will be taken and exploited in its 'literal' meaning – of 'translation.' But 'translation,' too, is dual because moving between language and visuality, between present and past.

The concept of image, although indicating the most objectified of objects in the humanities and distinct from 'text' in that it depends on a material support that is an integral part of the object, is thus, paradoxically, naturally prone to dispersal, if not dissemination. But, then, the unavoidable metaphoricity of the concept's name conjures up more metaphors, just as a streaming river can be wild but also obey the bed within which it streams. Subsequently, the journey becomes more hazardous. In fact, this chapter facilitates the dispersal of one concept in order to argue that it is precisely the plurisemic potential of the concept that enables it to serve as a tool for analysis. In view of this potential, the chapter focuses on two works of visual art – two images – both sculptures, from different historical periods. Thus the concept is also deployed to answer persistent questions about historical difference and the place of historical considerations in cultural analysis.

Chapter 3 proposes an itinerary of a different kind, one that goes back and forth between practice and theory. It starts, for the traveller from the academy, at the far side and does not quite return home, for the concept keeps shifting. Here, a concept from artistic practice – *mise-en-scène* – is deployed as a theoretical concept for cultural analysis. The use of a theatrical concept for theoretical work represents another case of methodological metaphorics. The issue at stake is the productivity of carrying over a working concept between cultural practice and theoretical reflection to produce an account of how practice 'works' in theory.

The consequence of this pondering of a conceptual metaphor, *mise-en-scène*, is then deployed more fully. While chapter 2 builds the stage on which the picaresque travel can be seen productively as fictional, theatrical, and metaphorical without losing its relevance for cultural analysis, the concept of *mise-en-scène* is singular and not prone to dispersal. We can wilfully use it metaphorically, translating it from one art – theatre – into another – installation. Indeed, the concept is used metaphorically, on objects not destined to be '*mis en scène.*' The concept's relevance for the cultural objects that might be analytically engaged is best demonstrated in this case by plurality, so a variety of objects are discussed. But they are not relegated to the subservient status of examples. Instead, each is shown to benefit from the concept and to benefit the concept's own further enrichment simultaneously.

The journey in chapter 4 reverses this perspective. It proposes a round trip between (academic) concept and (cultural) practice. Here, though, the return trip does not follow the same route as the outgoing journey. The concept of *framing*, which enjoys great currency at present but is also, and primarily, a common word, is mobilized to resolve the dilemma indicated above that binds theory and practice in a potentially deadly embrace. To strengthen the case, 'practice' here is taken quite literally. The concept travels back and forth several times between (artistic) practice and (academic) theory, and between (academic) practice and (artistic) theory. The starting point is a simple request to do a practical job; the result is a generalized position regarding the practice within which the job in question was embedded, indeed, framed. Framing and being framed, followed by confining and productive framing, are argued to be conducive to a form of analysis that respects no boundaries, not even the one between the academy and cultural life. In this chapter the concept itself is 'in practice' in the case reported.

Because the traveller might get lost if she runs into concepts that are both close and distant, the fifth chapter engages the conceptual issue of 'confusion.' Many of the complaints about the travelling use of concepts concern the 'sloppiness' with which they are alleged as labels – when the student or scholar doesn't even know their 'precise' meaning or context. I have often heard this complaint in relation to the (frequently used) concept of the *performative*. 'They don't even know who Austin is,' said a colleague whose primary concern is the 'correct' philosophical understanding of concepts. This remark set me thinking, for I agreed with his complaint that concepts are misused. But for me, the primary concern is not 'correct' but 'meaningful' use. Often concepts are invoked merely as labels. Whereas for my colleague the loss was of precision, for me it was of analytical insight. Labelling does not yield insight – but neither does precision alone.

In response to both the over-casual use of concepts as a mode of name-dropping and the noticeable rigidity concerning the 'legitimate' use of concepts, I attempt, in this chapter, to suggest a kind of productive confusion rather than precision of concepts. I pursue the question of theoretical neatness through the two concepts of *performance* and *performativity*. While obviously the two are related, they are also clearly in tension. For, while *performance* is grounded in a 'score' anterior to the actuality of the performance, *performativity* lives by the present and knows no anteriority. The tension between the two concepts has given rise to a theoretical concern about keeping them distinct. The case study here probes the possibility that such theoretical neatness comes with a price: the loss of the subtle understanding that purposeful theoretical confusion can also yield. This chapter, then, makes a plea for a certain voluntary conceptual messiness. It does so through an analysis of a work of installation art – visual and verbal, or rather, synaesthetic – that is performative by means of performance. Theatrically *mise en scène* as well as framed, the image is now shown at work in a unique performance, reiterated but never identical to itself.

The procedure advocated throughout this book – close engagement between object and concept – affects the status of concepts in an increasingly profound way. In chapter 2, I argue for the productive dispersal of concepts. In chapter 5, I offer a plea for their productive 'confusion.' Although aware that this metaphoric deployment of a concept may already stretch the tolerance of many, in chapters 6 and 7 I go even further. Since concepts no longer need to be acceptable in any way for them to be productively engaged, these chapters discuss concepts that I consider problematic for political or theoretical reasons or both. After chapter 5, the traveller will be experienced, but as easy trips are not really desirable, chapter 6 takes us into a territory we construe as exotic, a field for ethnographers – for some, perhaps, even a slightly hostile field – to explore the kind of place, people, concept we love to hate. The journey in this chapter is one that questions the tendency towards disingenuous wholesale disavowal of what, growing up, we see as the bossiness of preceding generations. The concept at stake here – *tradition* – is one of those politically problematic concepts that has almost, but not quite, fallen out of favour, perhaps rightly. It is engaged not to define it, or to prescribe the importance of what it 'covers.' For this is precisely the kind of use that thinking about the conceptual issues of concepts so productively counters. Instead, *tradition*, balancing precariously between 'word' and 'concept,' politically dangerous and productive, avoidable and inevitable, is deployed to demonstrate a practice of cultural analysis in everyday life, in an almost ethnographic endeavour that focuses on a culture I both know and cannot know: my own.

The problematic status of ethnography is not explicitly discussed, but it is one of the chapter's subtexts. The triangular relationship between analyst, concept, and object here receives a counterpart in another triangle. The analyst (myself), the concept (tradition), and the object are all inflected by the object's peculiar status. The case studied comprises the visual analysis of a tradition constructed from the vantage point of an astonished outsider – the artist-as-ethnographer. Moreover, the tradition in question is politically highly problematic. It is the basically racist (Dutch) tradition of *Zwarte Piet* (Black Peter). This study explicitly involves my own position as a member of the culture that maintains that tradition. Issues of self-reflection, moralism, and cultural critique, recurrent throughout this book, come to the fore here with greater insistence. This is necessary, because here lies the major difference between the old close reading, where the text is alleged to speak for itself; cultural studies, where, in contrast, critique is more important than the object; and the newer close reading, which is informed by both, and which I advocate in this book. The concept of *tradition*, precisely because it names such a problematic cultural process, is eminently suitable to be the third interlocutor for this exchange between three relations to the cultural object.

Chapter 7's journey also leads to the past, in fact to the source of the Nile. But here, the subject is a concept many hate to love. It is another problematic concept, but this time primarily a theoretical one, although theory and politics cannot be disentangled. I will be fighting it – and not just to be recalcitrant. The concept is *intention*, and, in the wake of that general word-concept, such notions as author or artist, or authority, including the verb 'to mean.' The continuity between 'authorship' and 'authority' is largely responsible for the legislation of meaning that constitutes the primary target of academic polemics. I have frequently argued for the bracketing of the artist in the debate on what objects 'mean.' I have often been challenged to defend my position and never been satisfied with my responses. Many arguments can be alleged in favour of anti-intentionalism. People study texts with no (known) author, such as the Hebrew Bible. Sometimes it is productive to take the position – also in the debate on 'high' and 'low' – that an artist such as Rembrandt is best considered not for his intentions but as a product of popular culture. Contemporary art can even be appointed as the subject of the production of old art in what, in my book *Quoting Caravaggio*, I have called 'preposterous history.' Chapter 2 discussed this bracketing of the artist as an issue of historical interpretation, while in this chapter the same position towards history becomes an element in the discussion of *intention*.

Here, I again allege a contemporary art work as the spokesperson for the historical object. But this case study shifts from art work to academic work. As I did in *Double Exposures*, and with the same hesitation, I make the writings of one of our colleagues the focus, if not quite the object, of analysis. The concept of *intention* is so controversial and yet so pervasively invoked that intercourse with it can only be polemical. This is the subtext of chapter 7: whereas I discourage my students from spending intellectual energy and passion on trashing others, I encourage them to conduct a productive debate. This is a skill in itself. In a discussion of *intention*, dismissing the simplistic and unreflective appeal to artistic authority is a futile exercise. In contrast, a serious discussion with a most explicit and sophisticated practitioner of the position the concept itself promotes seems more like a practical version of attempts at falsification. The 'rough' goal of this case study is to offer guidance in academic debate, as a travel back and forth between opposite positions. The issue is an academic attitude. The stake is a claim for the existence of 'cultural analysis' within the university, in complementarity with – neither merged with nor separated from – the traditional disciplines.

The journey in chapter 8 has no return ticket. There we arrive in the present, the global village, where we are bound to stay. The two concepts of *tradition* and *intention* come together there, with a new concept being proposed that embodies an intellectual attitude that fits 'cultural analysis' better than any other. Earlier on in this introduction, ethnography was put on the table as an emblem of academic travel. In chapter 8, it shows up again, in an entirely different guise, as the producer of a tenaciously problematic concept, a methodological centrepiece, and a subject position, that of the 'native informant.' But, in today's global culture, it is no longer possible to posit the idea of 'native.' Plurality, change, and displacement make any fixed position hard to sustain.

Hence, in parallel with chapter 1, a somewhat larger number of concepts are at stake but in a converse way. Whereas there the concepts served as examples, here, at the end of our travels, a cluster of concepts join forces. The limit of the concept of concept becomes visible through the multiple deployment of the rhetorical concept of personification. The figure of the 'native informant' – a person, subject, image, or character, depending on how one sees ethnographic texts – is transformed from the travelling hero of ethnography into a figure of rhetoric, a ploy to articulate conceptual continuity between the disciplines. And, whereas in chapter 7 I conduct a debate with a colleague, here the colleague and I change places, so to speak. Or, perhaps, simpler and more radically, I become her student.

In the guise of 'native informant,' the concept-figure of 'personification' is taken as the site of coherence in Gayatri Chakravorty Spivak's 1999 book *A Critique of Postcolonial Reason*. Using this as my case study, I probe the difficulties of structuring a complex argument through a conceptual character, through a figure of personhood as a sign of cultural issues that touch people. I thus reach the most precarious of concepts: 'personification.' I like the idea that this concept designates a figure on the imaginary stage where culture 'happens' – the fictional, theatrical stage. While Spivak deploys the figure of the 'native informant' to bind together the multiple strands of her book, I go on to confront that figure with the figure of the teacher – of 'cultural analysis.' Having made that travel, I end up having produced a rough guide while using it myself. The meta-concept that characterizes and guides the traveller, and the one I intend to highlight as the emblem or allegory of the endeavour of this book, I borrow from Spivak: *critical intimacy*.

Thus, by the end of this book, the travels for which it has been a rough guide have not been limited to the territories of the different disciplines in an argument against territorialism. Nor are the concepts the only ones that have travelled. The book also, and perhaps more importantly, has travelled – between intellectual positions, practices, and attitudes.

Most of the cases presented explore visual material: images, sculptures, art installations. The 'image' concept of chapter 2 remains at the core of all the others. The choice of materials is congruent with the immense interest in visuality in the humanities today. But lest this be misconstrued as an 'invasion' of art history, an 'abandonment' of the text-based disciplines, a closeted disciplinarity, or a nostalgia for high art, all of which have been imputed to me at some time or other, let me emphasize three aspects of the case studies I discuss. First, they are grounded in an ongoing complication of the concept of visuality itself. This complication involves a strong discursivity as being integral to visual images. In this respect, my analyses of visual objects consti- tute the ongoing demonstration of what I consider to be the tightest form of interdisciplinarity. Second – and therefore – the visual image is taken to stand for any cultural object, in its resistance to being reduced to any one medium. In this sense, the case studies are as much pleas for abandoning the grounds of disciplinarity as they are arguments for methodological grounding of a different kind. Hence, and third, the privileged place of visuality in this book embodies the double status of concepts in the practice of cultural analysis. While concepts are prod- ucts of philosophy and tools of analysis, they are also embodiments of the cultural practices we seek to understand through them. This circu- larity is perhaps best understood through the metaphor of travel – with a rough guide.

1

Concept

concept
– something conceived in the mind; a thought, notion
– a general idea covering many similar things derived from study of particular
  instances
Synonyms: see IDEA[1]

Departure

Concepts are the tools of intersubjectivity: they facilitate discussion on the basis of a common language. Mostly, they are considered abstract representations of an object. But, like all representations, they are neither simple nor adequate in themselves. They distort, unfix, and inflect the object. To say something *is* an image, metaphor, story, or what have you – that is, to use concepts to label something – is not a very useful act. Nor can the language of equation – 'is' – hide the interpretive choices being made. In fact, concepts are, or rather *do*, much more. If well thought through, they offer miniature theories, and in that guise, help in the analysis of objects, situations, states, and other theories.

But because they are key to intersubjective understanding, more than anything they need to be explicit, clear, and defined. In this way everyone can take them up and use them. This is not as easy as it sounds, because concepts are flexible: each is part of a framework, a systematic set of distinctions, *not* oppositions, that can sometimes be

1 This and all subsequent definitions of concepts at the beginning of chapters are selections from the entries in the *Longman Dictionary of the English Language* (1990).

bracketed or even ignored, but that can never be transgressed or contradicted without serious damage to the analysis at hand. Concepts, often precisely those words outsiders consider jargon, can be tremendously productive. If explicit, clear, and defined, they can help to articulate an understanding, convey an interpretation, check an imagination-run-wild, or enable a discussion, on the basis of common terms and in the awareness of absences and exclusions. Seen in this light, concepts are not simply labels easily replaced by more common words.

So far, this is a standard view of the methodological status of concepts. But concepts are neither fixed nor unambiguous. Although I subscribe to the above principles, the remainder of this chapter discusses what happens in the margins of this standard view. In other words, it looks at the concept of *concept* itself, not as a clear-cut methodological legislation, but as a territory to be travelled, in a spirit of adventure.

Concepts, in the first place, look like words. As Deleuze and Guattari noted in their introduction to *What Is Philosophy?*, some need etymological fancy, archaic resonance, or idiosyncratic folly to do their work; others require a Wittgensteinian family resemblance to their relatives; still others are the spitting image of ordinary words (1994: 3). 'Meaning' is a case of just such an ordinary word-concept that casually walks back and forth between semantics and intention. Because of this flexibility that makes semantics appear as intention, one of the points of the present book – and of chapter 7 in particular – is to convey the notion that the pervasive predominance of intentionalism – the conflation of meaning with the author's or artist's intention – with all its problems, is due to this unreflective conflation of words and concepts.

To say that concepts can work as shorthand theories has several consequences. Concepts are not ordinary words, even if words are used to speak (of) them. This realization should be balm to the heart of those who hate jargon. Nor are they labels. Concepts (mis)used in this way lose their working force; they are subject to fashion and quickly become meaningless. But when deployed as I think they should be – and the remainder of this book articulates, demonstrates, and justifies how that might be – concepts can become a third partner in the otherwise totally unverifiable and symbiotic interaction between critic and object. This is most useful, especially when the critic has no disciplinary tradition to fall back on and the object no canonical or historical status.

But concepts can only do this work, the methodological work that disciplinary traditions used to do, on one condition: that they are kept under scrutiny through a confrontation with, not application to, the cultural objects being examined. For these objects themselves are amenable to change and apt to illuminate historical and cultural differences. The shift in methodology I am arguing for here is founded on a particular relationship between subject and object, one that is not predicated on a vertical and binary opposition between the two. Instead, the model for this relationship is interaction, as in 'interactivity.' It is because of this potential interactivity – not because of an obsession with 'proper' usage – that every academic field, but especially one like the humanities that has so little in the way of binding traditions, can gain from taking concepts seriously.

But concepts are not fixed. They travel – between disciplines, between individual scholars, between historical periods, and between geographically dispersed academic communities. Between disciplines, their meaning, reach, and operational value differ. These processes of differing need to be assessed before, during, and after each 'trip.' The bulk of this book, and of much of my previous work, is devoted to such assessments. Between individual scholars, each user of a concept constantly wavers between unreflected assumptions and threatening misunderstandings in communication with others. The two forms of travel – group and individual – come together in past practices of scholarship. Disciplinary traditions didn't really help resolve that ambiguity, although they certainly did help scholars to *feel* secure in their use of concepts, a security that can, of course, just as easily turn deceptive. As I see it, disciplinary traditionalism and rigid attitudes towards concepts tend to go hand in hand with hostility to jargon, which, more often than not, is an anti-intellectual hostility to methodological rigour and a defence of a humanistic critical style.

Between historical periods, the meaning and use of concepts change dramatically. Take *hybridity*, for example. How did this concept from biology – implying as its 'other' an authentic or pure specimen and presuming that hybridity leads to sterility – that was current in imperialist discourse with its racist overtones, come to indicate an idealized state of postcolonial diversity? Because it travelled. Originating in nineteenth-century biology, it was first used in a racist sense. Then it changed, moving through time, to Eastern Europe, where it encountered the literary critic Mikhail Bakhtin. Travelling west again, it eventually came to play a brief but starring role in postcolonial studies, where it was taken to task for its disturbing implications, including the historical remnants of colonial epistemology.[2] Far from decrying such a long journey to a provisional dead end, I see how important such a concept is for the development and innovation of the very field that now rejects it. History – here the history of concepts and their successive networks – can be a dead weight if endorsed uncritically in the name of tradition. But it can also be an extremely powerful force that activates rather than stultifies interactive concepts.[3] Finally, concepts function differently in geographically dispersed academic communities with their different traditions. This is as true for the choice and use of concepts as for their definitions and the traditions within the different disciplines, even the newer ones like cultural studies.

All of these forms of travel render concepts flexible. It is this changeability that becomes part of their usefulness for a new methodology that is neither stultifying and rigid nor arbitrary or 'sloppy.' This book aims to demonstrate that the travelling nature of concepts is an asset rather than a liability. In the present chapter, I will discuss some of the itineraries of that travel – between departure and arrival and back again. The case serving as an example is one many will recognize: it involves the partial overlap of concepts used today in different disciplines, concepts that tend to get muddled in a mixed setting. To help the move from a muddled multidisciplinarity to a productive interdisciplinarity, such cases of partial overlap are best dealt with head-on.

Travel between Words and Concepts

In the cultural disciplines, a variety of concepts are used to frame, articulate, and specify different analyses. The most confusing ones are the over-arching concepts we tend to use as if their meanings were as clear-cut and common as those of any word in any given language. Depending on the background in which the analyst was initially trained and the cultural genre to which the object belongs, each analysis tends to take for granted a certain use of concepts. Others may not agree with that use, or may even perceive it as not being specific

2 Young (1990) opens with this point. For a recent in-depth criticism, see Spivak (1999). For a brief account, see Ashcroft et al. (1998: 118–21).

3 History and tradition, my long-term interlocutors in the kind of work this book accounts for, are the subject of reflection in my earlier book (1999a) and ch. 6 of the present volume.

enough to merit arguing about. Such confusion tends to increase with those concepts that are close to ordinary language. The concept of text will serve as a convincing example of this confusion.

A word from everyday language, self-evident in literary studies, metaphorically used in anthropology, generalized in semiotics, ambivalently circulating in art history and film studies, and shunned in musicology, the concept of text seems to ask for trouble. But it also invokes disputes and controversies that can be wonderfully stimulating if 'worked through.' If this working through fails to take place, the disputes and controversies can become sources of misunderstanding or, worse, enticements to ill-conceived partisanship, including discipline-based conservatism. There are, for example, many reasons for referring to images or films as 'texts.' Such references entail various assumptions, including the idea that images have, or produce, meaning, and that they promote such analytical activities as reading. To make a long story short, the advantage of speaking of 'visual texts' is that it reminds the analyst that lines, motifs, colours, and surfaces, like words, contribute to the production of meaning; hence, that form and meaning cannot be disentangled. Neither texts nor images yield their meanings immediately. They are not transparent, so that images, like texts, require the labour of reading.

Many fear that to speak of images as texts is to turn the image into a piece of language. But by shunning the linguistic analogy (as in many ways we should) we also engage resistance – to meaning, to analysis, and to close, detailed engagement with the object. That resistance we should, in turn, resist, or at least discuss. The concept of text helps rather than hinders such a discussion *precisely because it is controversial.* Hence its use should be encouraged, especially in areas where it is not self-evident, so that it can regain its analytical and theoretical force.[4]

But 'text' is perhaps already an example that leads too much. In its travels, it has become dirty, come to imply too much, to resist too much; hence it has become liable to deepen the divide between the enthusiasts and the sceptics. What about 'meaning,' then? No academic discipline can function without a notion of this concept. In the humanities, it is a key word. Or a key concept, perhaps? Sometimes. Let me call it a 'word-concept.' This casual use, now as word, then as concept, has two major drawbacks. One drawback of its casual use as a word is the resulting reluctance to discuss 'meaning' as an academic

---

4 For these aspects of the word-concept 'text,' see Goggin and Neef (2001).

issue. The other is its over-extended use. More often than not, scholars and students speak of 'meaning' without even specifying whether they mean (sic) intention, origin, context, or semantic content. This is normal, inevitable. Just now I couldn't avoid using the verb 'to mean' because I was unable to choose between 'intending' and 'referring.' But this confusion is largely responsible for a major problem in all the humanities. For, as a result, students are trained to say that 'the meaning of a picture' is identical either to the artist's intention, or to what its constitutive motifs originally meant, or to the contemporary audience's understanding, or to the dictionary's synonym. My suggestion here is that students ought to be trained to choose – and justify – one of the meanings of 'meaning,' and to make that choice a methodological starting point.

The concepts I discuss in this book belong, to varying degrees, to this category where ordinary and theoretical language overlap. Other concepts or sets of concepts that come to mind – which are not central to the case studies here – are history (and its relation to the present); identity and alterity; subject(ivity) and agency; hybridity and ethnicity; individual, singular, different; cognitive, scientific, and technological metaphors; medium, mode, genre, type; fact and objectivity; and last but not least, culture(s).[5] But, as I mentioned in the introduction, the project here is not to provide an overview of key concepts in cultural analysis. Others have already done that. Instead, I offer case studies as examples of a practice in which concepts are elaborated in the context where they most frequently occur: through the analysis of an object; in other words, through case studies – through samples of my own practice of cultural analysis.[6] The purpose of each chapter is not to define, discuss, or offer the history of the concept central to it. Rather, the case I try to make is for a flexible, close attention to what concepts can (help us) do. Hence, not they but the way I propose to handle them is the point. That way, I submit, is best captured by the metaphor of travel.

There is also a social aspect to the intersubjectivity that concepts create. That social aspect is my primary concern here. Concepts are, and always have been, important areas of debate. As such, they promote a measure of consensus. Not that absolute consensus is possible, or even

5 Alas, also the one I will leave alone here. For the concept of culture, a book-length study at least is needed. For just two recent examples, see Hartman (1997) and Spivak (1999).
6 On the practice of cultural analysis, see Bal, ed. (1999).

desirable, but agreement on the fact that – provisionally, tentatively, and testingly – a concept is best deployed in a specific meaning because the results can then be discussed is indispensable if we are to get out of turf-policing defensiveness. This book grew out of the conviction that in this sense concepts and the debates around them have greatly increased in importance with the advent of interdisciplinary study. The mission of concepts is vital if the social climate in the academy is to be maintained and improved, if disputes are to promote rather than preclude the production of knowledge and insight (as, alas, happens all too often). It is around concepts that I see cultural analysis achieving a consensus comparable to the paradigmatic consistency that has kept the traditional disciplines vital – albeit, simultaneously, dogmatic.[7] Rejecting dogmatism without sacrificing consistency is a way of improving the human *ambiance* while increasing the intellectual yield. For this reason I consider the discussion of concepts an alternative methodological base for 'cultural studies' or 'analysis.' My first point, then, is to plead for the centrality of conceptual reflection – for the following reasons.[8]

Concepts are never simply descriptive; they are also programmatic and normative. Hence, their use has specific effects. Nor are they stable; they are related to a tradition. But their use never has simple continuity. For 'tradition,' closer to a word that moves about, is not the same as (Kuhnian) 'paradigm,' itself a concept threatened with word-status when used too casually. 'Tradition' appeals to 'the way we always did things,' as a value. 'Paradigm' makes explicit the theses and methods that have acquired axiomatic status, so that they can be used without being constantly challenged. This rigidity is strategic and reflected. But 'tradition' does not question its tenets; hence, those tenets become dogmatic. Traditions change slowly, paradigms suddenly; the former without their inhabitants knowing it, the latter against their resistance.

---

7 Publications such as, famously, Raymond Williams' *Keywords*, and more recently, Martin Jay's rewriting of that book, *Cultural Semantics: Keywords of Our Time*, testify to the link between enhanced conceptual awareness and increasing interdisciplinarity as emerging from a cultural studies perspective. Another interesting piece of evidence for the need of this 'rough guide' is the successful volume edited by Frank Lentricchia and Thomas McLaughlin (1995). This book, explicitly designed for *literary* studies, has an entry on *performance* that appears to take one meaning of this concept so much for granted – the one that led to the art practice called 'performance art' – that it becomes the only meaning raised, much in the way my fictional students each bring in their own self-evident notions of 'subject.'

8 These reasons form a counterpart to the first paragraph of this chapter.

It is the same distinction as between subliminal change and revolution.

Concepts are also never simple. Their various aspects can be unpacked; the ramifications, traditions, and histories conflated in their current usages can be separated out and evaluated piece by piece. Concepts are hardly ever used in exactly the same sense. Hence their usages can be debated and referred back to the different traditions and schools from which they emerged, thus allowing an assessment of the validity of their implications. This would greatly help the discussion between participating disciplines. Concepts are not just tools. They raise the underlying issues of instrumentalism, realism, and nominalism, and the possibility of interaction between the analyst and the object. Precisely because they travel between ordinary words and condensed theories, concepts can trigger and facilitate reflection and debate on all levels of methodology in the humanities.

Travel between Science and Culture

Let me, then, plot the first route of our travel. Work with concepts is by no means confined to the cultural field. Although the use of concepts in the natural sciences differs from their use in the humanities, we can still learn something from their travels in and among the sciences. In the preface to her book *D'une science à l'autre*, devoted to the interdisciplinary mobility of concepts travelling between the sciences, Isabelle Stengers helpfully states the purpose of probing travelling concepts. She announces that her book seeks to explore the ways the sciences can avoid the Scylla of a false purity and disinterestedness, and the Charybdis of arbitrariness and loss of interest, both often said to threaten after the traditional ideals have been unmasked as empty pretensions. As a remedy for the pain of the loss of innocence – and the loss of neutrality and disinterestedness – her book, she continues, offers concepts. Not as a glossary, but as theoretical issues, hotly debated and apt to be misunderstood and to help the sciences along. Concepts as issues of debate. In our culture, the sciences are taken more seriously than the humanities. This deserves some attention, for that difference may not be engraved in stone.

The sciences are taken seriously in at least one of two distinct senses. The first is *de jure*, 'by right,' or 'by law': 'scientific' is what obeys the rules of scientific procedure. Concepts have a key place in the assessment of the 'lawfulness' of the sciences. Concepts are legitimate as long as they avoid the status of 'mere metaphor' or ideology, and as long as they follow the rules of scientificity in terms of demarcation of and application to an object domain. Here the epistemology is normative.

Mainstream scholarship in the humanities works implicitly with a consensual endorsement of this normativity. A humanities' light shed on this normativity is in order, for this normativity has a problem of temporal logic. The legalistic normativity proclaims beforehand what is in need of explanation and analysis. In this sense, it embodies the rhetorical figure of *proteron hysteron*: it is literally pre-posterous, putting first what in fact comes later, in terms of both temporality and causality. This figure obscures the precise relationship between time and causality. Thus untangled, the problem can be reframed productively as narratological: its founding figure is *analepsis*, the narration of what comes later, before what earlier. As a consequence, causality is rendered opaque, if not suspended.

The second way science is taken seriously is *de facto*, 'in fact,' or 'in reality': here, by contrast, 'scientific' is what is recognized as such within the social-cultural field of scientific practice. A very practical example is the institution of peer review for grant applications. In this conception, the norms of what is acceptable move, are unstable, elaborated by the same actors whose status as scientists depends on judgments about what is scientific. Here, again, narratology can clarify the issue. The epistemological problem is of a different narratological logic. It is primarily actantial not temporal.[9] The primary epistemological problem is the actantial conflation, the double role of the social actors – the practising scientists – as both subject and object of the evaluation. Numerous others follow.

Scientific communities often try to disavow the fundamental interestedness of all the actors in the outcome of the evaluation by giving priority to normative epistemology. To do this, they (must) disavow the problem that inheres in it by attributing a kind of atemporal permanence to the criteria, in the guise of universalism. But it is precisely the rhetoric of universalism, which flies in the face of everything we know about the history of science, that suggests that the *de jure* argument is, 'in fact,' as the expression goes, a *de facto* argument. For the *interest* in disinterestedness becomes blatant in the process, thus shift-

---

9 The narratological concept 'actantial' refers to positions in a fixed structure of roles that can be filled by different 'actors.' See my *Narratology* (1997b: 196–206). The concept was the structuralist elaboration, by the French linguist A.J. Greimas, of a model contrived by the Russian folklorist V. Propp in the 1930s (1966).

ing the debate irresistibly from legitimate to factual truth, from law to practice, from temporal to actantial logic. For the second epistemological problem – the actantial one, based on the illusion of a universal validity of norms – is prohibitive only so long as norms such as neutrality and disinterestedness, including the criteria by which these are established, are inscribed in stone – or, in interest.[10]

This is where concepts demonstrate their key role in the methodological discussion. They help demonstrate that this neutrality is an actual rhetorical strategy rather than just a theoretical possibility. Lack of interest is, in fact, deadly for scientific inquiry, as it also is for humanistic, or any other, inquiry. Reflection on the nature and effectivity of concepts makes this particularly obvious, because, above all, the role of concepts is *to focus interest*. As Stengers writes, the primary definition of scientific concepts is to *not* leave one indifferent, 'to implicate and impose taking a stand' (11). Once the fiction of neutrality has been cleared away, judgments still need to be made. The only remaining domain of analysis that allows us to make judgments on concepts as keys to scientificity is the social-cultural field of scientific practice. Legal, normative epistemology can only be subordinated to that practice, and, as the history of science amply demonstrates, its rules are constantly changing.

To understand the role of concepts in a practice of science whose priority over normative epistemology has now been argued, the following features of scientific concepts must be examined. According to Stengers, concepts imply an operation that involves the redefining of categories and meanings in both the phenomenal and social fields. *De facto*, concepts organize a group of phenomena, define the relevant questions to be addressed to them, and determine the meanings that can be given to observations regarding the phenomena. *De jure* – I would insist on the subordination of the second part of this problematic to the first – adequacy must be granted, hence, recognized. A concept must be recognized as adequate. This adequacy is not 'realistic'; it is not a matter of truthful representation. Instead, a concept is adequate to the extent that it produces the effective organization of the phenom-

10 The ambiguity of 'interest,' here, is purposefully left hanging. Money is often a (side) issue in the academic dynamic. Not only grants come to mind here, but also the financial earthquakes of dis- and reattributions of old master paintings, and the less obvious financial consequences of critical attention paid to a constant litany of artists who are somewhat arbitrarily included in the canon, along with their anonymous counterparts.

ena rather than offering a mere projection of the ideas and presuppositions of its advocates (11). The point of discussion in the practice of
science is, of course, to minimize the risk of taking the latter – projection – for the former – production. A certain degree of predominance
of *standpoint epistemology* is therefore inevitable.[11] Among the criteria
that tend to be applied are, for example, the requirement that the concept give a sense of providing 'authentic access to phenomena'
(Stengers 11), that the new organization be compelling, and that it
yield new and relevant information. Obviously, all of these criteria are
of a relatively subjective nature, gauging by the interest that the concept and its yield solicit. Hence, they solicit, at least partly and provisionally, a standpoint-epistemological position.

Stengers devotes a good part of her introduction to the notion that
'nomadic' concepts have the power of 'propagation,' a word she uses
to avoid conflating it with its negative element, 'propaganda.'[12] The
propagation of a concept that emerges in one field, in another field that
changes its meaning and whose meaning it, in turn, changes, constitutes the primary feature of a concept, both as asset and liability, or
risk. It is only through a constant reassessment of the power of a concept to organize phenomena in a new and relevant way that its continued productivity can be evaluated. This reorganization might be much
more visible in the natural sciences than in the cultural fields. But, even
within a single culture artefact, the reorganization of phenomena,
aspects, and elements, such as words or motifs, actors, and events,
through a concept brought to bear on that artefact, can be innovative as
well as conducive to insights relevant beyond the artefact itself. For, in
the reorganization it facilitates, a concept generates the production of
meaning.

Here, we reach a point where the natural sciences and the cultural
disciplines share a crucial methodological concern. Stengers explains
this standard by identifying two meanings of 'propagation': diffusion,
which dilutes and ends up neutralizing the phenomena, as in the propagation of heat; and epidemic propagation, where each new particle
becomes an originating agent of a propagation that does not weaken in

---

11 For a review of various epistemologies, including a critique of standpoint epistemol-
     ogy, see Alcoff and Potter (1993).
12 Averse to the currently fashionable romanticizing of nomadism, for its trivializa-
     tion of the plight of homelessness and expatriate existence, I prefer to use the meta-
     phor of 'travel,' thereby gaining in voluntariness what I lose in the sense of (mobile)
     habitat.

the process (18). 'Diffusion' is the result of an unwarranted and casual 'application' of concepts. Application, in this case, entails using concepts as labels that neither explain nor specify, but only name. Such labelling goes on when a concept emerges as fashionable, without the search for new meaning that ought to accompany its deployment taking place. I recall vividly the sudden frequency of the word 'uncanny,' for example, and, also, quite upsettingly, a certain abuse of the word 'trauma.'

I say 'word' here instead of 'concept' because, in these cases, the dilution deprives the concept of its conceptualizing force: of its capacity to distinguish and thereby to make understandable in its specificity; hence, to 'theorize' the object, which would thus further knowledge, insight, and understanding. 'Trauma,' for example, is used casually to refer to all sad experiences, whereas the concept in fact theorizes a distinctive psychic effect caused by happenings so life-shattering that the subject assaulted by them is, precisely, unable to process them *qua* experience. 'Trauma' as concept, therefore, offers a theory that the casual use of the word obliterates.[13]

'Propagation,' in the sense of contamination – and despite its negative connotations and, indeed, the fear that such a metaphor solicits – keeps the meaning of the concept constant in its precision, so that instead of diluting, it functions as a strong, well-delimiting searchlight. These two conceptual metaphors from the sciences, 'diffusion' and 'propagation,' clarify the tangled problem of the application of concepts, also for the humanities.

A final defining element of a concept is the *foundational* capacity inherent in its discovery. Enabling both a description of and experimentation with the phenomena, which in turn allow actual intervention, a new concept founds an object consisting of clearly defined categories (Stengers 29). In the humanities, the foundational capacity comes with a new articulation, entailing new emphases and a new ordering of the phenomena within the complex objects constituting the cultural field. In a somewhat grandiose interpretation, one could say that a good concept founds a scientific discipline or field. Thus, to anticipate the subsequent specialized discussions in this book, one might claim that the articulation of the concept of narrativity within the humanities and the social sciences founded the discipline of narra-

13 For a theoretical discussion of trauma, see van der Hart and van de Kolk in Caruth, ed. (1995), and van Alphen (1997).

tology. This is an inter-discipline precisely because it defines an object, a discursive modality, which is active in many different fields.

Concepts play a crucial part in the traffic between disciplines because of two consequences of their power to propagate, found, and define an object domain: they capture, in a conflation of epistemology and scientific practice, the scientificity of the methodology they ground;[14] and, moving in the opposite direction, they 'harden' the science in question by determining and restricting what counts as scientific. This can bring false comfort to those distressed by the kind of pedagogical situations described in my introduction. For, in such situations, the work in need of doing was precisely that of unhardening the concept, of de-naturalizing the self-evidence that each disciplinary group had unreflectively adopted. Discussions of an interdisciplinary nature lead neither to an 'anything goes' attitude nor to an undecidability or aporia. Instead, hardening and unhardening alternate and shift.

If interdisciplinary discussions sometimes become parochial and fussy, this is not so surprising. Such a situation is best dealt with through explicit discussion. Each participant is answerable both to his or her own disciplinary community back home and to the 'foreigners' in the country s/he visits in whose language s/he is not yet fluent. Even if a participant has already been trained in an interdisciplinary field, that field will not cover all the ground covered by all the other fields involved whose members participate in the discussion. This double answerability is a good – albeit demanding – situation.

At this juncture I wish to insist that the self-protection of the mono-disciplines is not all negative. As long as self-protection keeps its boundaries permeable, I would even consider it indispensable, both for the individual disciplines and for the endeavour of interdisciplinarity. A certain protectiveness is useful against dilution, through which universal fuzziness threatens to undermine the very means by which the concept serves analysis. The travels I outline in this book must be considered in terms of 'propagation,' not 'diffusion.' The latter, however, the more common practice, is often presented under the banner of *multi*-disciplinarity. The metaphor of travel can help to clarify the difference between interdisciplinarity and multidisciplinarity, and to show why that difference matters.

14 The word 'capture,' if not its meaning, comes from Stengers (30).

Travel between Disciplines: Looking and Language

Let me now give an example of a situation in which the propagation of a concept is potentially productive but also potentially diluting. The example consists of a cluster of neighbouring concepts: 'gaze,' 'focalization,' and 'iconicity.' These concepts are different but affiliated. They are often conflated, with disastrous results, or, alternatively, kept separate, with impoverishing results. The following reportage describes the travels through which they have gone. In this travel journal, I will give my view of what happened with these concepts in the cultural field, and move back and forth between that general development and my own intellectual itinerary.

The 'gaze' is a key concept in visual studies, one I find it important to fuss about if fuzziness is to be avoided. It is widely used in fields whose members participate in cultural studies. Norman Bryson's analysis of the life of this concept, first in art history, then in feminist and gender studies, amply demonstrates why it is worth reflecting on.[15] He rightly insists that feminism has had a decisive impact on visual studies; film studies would be nowhere near where it is today without it. In turn, film studies, especially in its extended form, which includes television and the new media, is a key area in cultural studies. The itinerary Bryson sketches is largely informed by the centrality of the concept of the gaze in all the participating disciplines. If we realize that film studies, at least in the United States, grew out of English departments, the time- and space-map becomes decidedly interesting.

The concept of the gaze has a variety of backgrounds. It is sometimes used as an equivalent of the 'look,' indicating the position of the subject doing the looking. As such, it points to a position, real or represented. It is also used in distinction from the 'look,' as a fixed and fixating, colonizing, mode of looking – a look that objectifies, appropriates, disempowers, and even, possibly, violates. In its Lacanian sense (Silverman 1996), it is most certainly very different from – if not opposed to – its more common usage as the equivalent of the 'look' or

15 See Bryson's introduction to *Looking In: The Art of Viewing*. This text, in fact, was one of the reasons I became more acutely aware of the importance of concepts. Some of the thoughts in the present chapter are developments of my remarks in the Afterword of that volume. Silverman (1996) offers an excellent, indeed, indispensable, discussion of the 'gaze' in Lacanian theory.

a specific version of it.[16] The Lacanian 'gaze' is, most succinctly, the visual order (equivalent to the symbolic order, or the visual part of that order) in which the subject is 'caught.' In this sense it is an indispensable concept through which to understand all cultural domains, including text-based ones.[17] The 'gaze' is the world looking (back) at the subject.

In its more common use – perhaps between word and concept – the 'gaze' is the 'look' that the subject casts on other people and other things. Feminism initiated the scrutiny of the gaze's objectifying thrust, especially in film studies, where the specific Lacanian sense remains important. Cultural critics, including anthropologists, have recently been interested in the use of photography in historical and ethnographic research. More broadly, the meaning-producing effects of images, including textual-rhetorical ones, have been recognized. In this type of analysis, the 'gaze' is also obviously central.[18] The objectification and the disempowering exotization of 'others' further flesh out the issues of power inequity that the concept helps lay bare. Indeed, the affiliated concepts of the other and alterity have been scrutinized for their own collusion with the imperialist forces that 'hold' the 'gaze' in this photographic and cinematic material. Enabling the analysis of non-canonical objects, such as snapshots, the concept is also helpful in allowing the boundaries between elite and larger culture to be overcome. Between all these usages, an examination of the concept itself is appropriate. Not to police it, or to prescribe a purified use for it, but to gauge its possibilities, and to either delimit or link the objects on which it has been brought to bear.

So far, in its development in the academic community, the concept of the gaze has demonstrated its flexibility and inclination to social criticism. But, for the issue of interdisciplinary methodology, it also has a more hands-on kind of relevance. For it has an affiliation with – although is not identical to – the concept of focalization in narrative theory. This is where my own involvement came in. In my early work, I struggled to adjust that concept. In fact, in narrative theory, the concept of focalization, although clearly visual in background, has been

16 See Bryson (1983) for a distinction between the 'gaze' and the 'glance' as two versions of the 'look.' For slight amendments, see Bal (1991a).
17 Ernst van Alphen's analysis of Charlotte Delbo's writings is suggestively titled 'Caught by Images' (2002).
18 See, for example, Hirsch (1997, 1999).

deployed to overcome visual strictures and the subsequent metaphorical floundering of concepts such as 'perspective' and 'point of view.'

It is precisely because the concept of focalization is *not* identical to that of the 'gaze' or the 'look' (although it has some unclear yet persistent affiliation with both these visual concepts) that it can help to clarify a vexed issue in the relationship between looking and language, between art history and literary studies. The common question for all three of these concepts is what the look of a represented (narrated or depicted) figure does to the imagination of the reader or to the look of the viewer. Let me briefly outline what is at stake here, as an example of the gain in precision and reach that concepts can offer through, not in spite of, their travel, on condition that multidisciplinary 'diffusing' yields to interdisciplinary 'propagation.'[19]

'Focalization' was the object of my first academic passion when, in the 1970s, I became a narratologist. Retrospectively, my interest in developing a more workable concept to replace what literary scholars call 'perspective' or 'point of view' was rooted in a sense of the cultural importance of vision, even in the most language-based of arts. But vision must not be understood exclusively in the technical-visual sense. In the slightly metaphorical but indispensable sense of imaginary – akin but not identical to imagination – vision tends to involve both actual looking and interpreting, including in literary reading. And, while this is a reason to recommend the verb 'reading' for the analysis of visual images, it is also a reason *not* to cast the visual out of the concept of focalization. The danger of dilution here must be carefully balanced against the impoverishment caused by an excess of conceptual essentialism.

The term 'focalization' also helped in overcoming the limitations of the linguistically inspired tools inherited from structuralism. These were based on the structure of the sentence and failed to help me account for what happens between characters in narrative, figures in image, and the readers of both. The great emphasis on conveyable and generalizable content in structuralist semantics hampered my attempts to understand how such contents were conveyed – to what effects and ends – through what can be termed 'subjectivity networks.'[20] The hypothesis that says readers *envision*, that is, create, images from tex-

19 To my embarrassment, I must fall back on my own academic history for this case.
20 For an elaboration of subjectivity networks, I must refer to my book *On Story-Telling* (1991b).

tual stimuli cuts right through semantic theory, grammar, and rhetoric, to foreground the presence and crucial importance of *images* in reading.[21] At one point, when I managed to solve a long-standing problem of biblical philology 'simply' by envisioning, instead of deciphering, the text, I savoured the great pleasure and excitement that come with 'discovery.'[22] Let me call the provisional result of this first phase of the concept-in-use dynamic 'the gaze-as-focalizer.'

The second phase goes in the opposite direction. Take 'Rembrandt,' for example. The name stands for a *text* – 'Rembrandt' as the cultural ensemble of images, dis- and re-attributed according to an expansive or purifying cultural mood – and for the discourses about the real and imaginary figure indicated by the name. The images called 'Rembrandt' are notoriously disinterested in linear perspective but also highly narrative. Moreover, many of these images are replete with issues relevant for a gender perspective – such as the nude, scenes related to rape, and myth-based history paintings in which women are being framed. For these reasons combined, 'focalization' imposes itself as an operative concept. In contrast, 'perspective' can only spell disaster. But, while narrativity may be medium-independent, the transfer of a specific concept from narrative theory – in this case, 'focalization,' which is mostly deployed in the analysis of verbal narratives – to visual texts requires the probing of its realm, its productivity, and its potential for 'propagation' versus the risk of 'dilution.'[23]

This probing is all the more important because of the double ambiguity that threatens here. Firstly, 'focalization' is a narrative inflection of imagining, interpreting, and perception that *can*, but need not, be visual 'imaging.' To conflate 'focalization' with the 'gaze' would be to return to square one, thus undoing the work of differentiation between two different modes of semiotic expression. Secondly, and conversely, the projection of narrativity on visual images is an analytic move that has great potential but is also highly specific. To put it simply: not all images are narrative, any more than all narrative acts of focalization are visual. Yet narratives and images have *envisioning* as their common form of reception. The differences and the common elements are equally important.

21 A key text remains W.J.T. Mitchell's opening chapter 'What Is an Image?' in *Iconology* (1985). The word 'envision' yields a tentative concept in Schwenger (1999).
22 This happened several times in my work on the Book of Judges (Bal 1988a).
23 Again, I must refer the reader here to the discussion in my book on the subject (1991a, ch. 4).

In my own work, the examination of the concept of focalization for use in the analysis of visual images was all the more urgent because the new area of visual imagery appears to carry traces of the same word by which the concept is known. This was a moment of truth: is focalization in narratology 'only a metaphor' borrowed from the visual? If so, does its deployment in visual analysis fall back on its literal meaning? If the latter is the case, the travel involved has failed to enrich the traveller.

Again, to make a long story short, the concept of focalization helps to articulate the look precisely through its movement. After travelling, first from the visual domain to narratology, then to the more specific analysis of visual images, focalization, having arrived at its new destination, visual analysis, has received a meaning that overlaps neither with the old visual one – focusing with a lens – nor with the new narratological one – the cluster of perception and interpretation that guides the attention through the narrative. It now indicates neither a *location* of the gaze on the picture plane, nor a *subject* of it, such as either the figure or the viewer. Instead, what becomes visible is the *movement* of the look. In that movement, the look encounters the limitations imposed by the gaze, the visual order. For the gaze dictates the limits of the figures' respective positions as holder of the objectifying and colonizing look, and disempowered object of that look. The tension between the focalizer's movement and these limitations is the true object of analysis. For it is here that structural, formal aspects of the object become meaningful, dynamic, and culturally operative: through the time-bound, changing effect of the culture that frames them.

This is an instance of a concept travelling from one discipline to another and back again. The itinerary is to be termed *inter*-disciplinary in this specific sense. To call it 'transdisciplinary' would be to presuppose its immutable rigidity, a travelling without changing; to call it 'multidisciplinary' would be to subject the fields of the two disciplines to a common analytic tool. Neither option is viable. Instead, a negotiation, a transformation, a reassessment is needed at each stage. Thanks to its narratological background, the concept of focalization imported a mobility into the visual domain that usefully and productively complemented the potential to structure envisioning that had been carried over from visual to narrative in the first phase.[24]

24 I did not even have to fall back on such notoriously fuzzy and deceptive concepts as *implied viewer*, to be coined by analogy to an implied author that is tenaciously problematic.

Travel between Concept and Object

All this sounds awfully abstract. In fact, this work on the twin concepts of gaze and focalization is entirely indebted to concrete studies that I and others have performed on specific objects, studies in which the concepts travelled between theory and the object on which they were set loose. To flesh it out a bit more, without going into the kind of detailed concreteness the following chapters offer, let me point out one particular element of the concept of focalization's travel that will help us to grasp it better. It is its 'time-travel,' its voyage through a non-linear history, which is part and parcel of conceptual mobility. In other words, the concept's history as I have lived through it at an earlier stage of my academic life. One reason why the mobility of concepts – their travelling through space, time, and disciplines – is important relates to the usefulness of understanding the affiliations, legacies, and partial recalls that play a part in their development and deployment. I have suggested this already through the example of hybridity. When developing the concept of focalization, but also at a later point in time, when studying issues around the gaze, a relationship with linguistics became necessary. Literary studies cannot do without it. For it is a feature of the object of literary studies to be linguistic.

At some point in time, linguistic inspiration came to me from a figure marginal to the structuralist movement who never openly discussed visuality: Emile Benveniste. Despite later developments in linguistics that made some of his early formulations appear 'obsolete,' the importance of Benveniste's work in the specific case of sorting out the partial overlap between concepts must be acknowledged.[25] His linguistic theory lends itself to interdisciplinary crossover in ways that inform the creation of new concepts and insights. In my discussion of the gaze and focalization here, Benveniste-inspired insights complete the rich, powerful, analytic potential of the two concepts.

Compared to Lévi-Strauss, Lacan, Foucault, Derrida, and Deleuze, to evoke a sequence of wise men, Benveniste is probably the least recognized of those French 'masters of thought' who had such a lasting impact on the humanities during the last quarter of the twentieth cen-

---

25 I put 'obsolete' in relativizing quotation marks because it is an extremely problematic notion. Relying on fashion and the judgment of 'old-fashioned,' the notion fails to account for what remains vital of a complex idea, *some* but not *all* of which has proved untenable.

tury. Acknowledging this influence is a matter of intellectual force and consistency. His work is crucial not only to understanding what Lacan did with Freud's legacy, to appreciating Derrida's deconstruction of logocentrism (the content bias), and to seeing the point of Foucault's definitions of episteme and power/knowledge.[26] His work is also key to understanding developments in analytical philosophy as they have filtered through into the study of literature and the arts in the concept of performance. Anticipating chapter 5, I will briefly outline how the popular concept of performativity and the more idiosyncratic concept of focalization come together in a further specification of the gaze/look combination.

As is well known, reference – both a verb and a noun – is secondary to deixis, the 'I-you' interaction that constitutes a referential merry-go-round.[27] Yet, it has not been one of Benveniste's *concepts* that has had the decisive influence. Rather, it is one of his basic *ideas*: the idea that subjectivity, produced through the exchange between the 'I' and the 'you,' not 'reference,' is the essence of language. I will continue with the example of the previous section and draw on the debate around focalization, in which I, too, have been engaged. I invoke this debate here to demonstrate the implications of the primacy of the 'I'/'you' interaction for theorizing through concepts. In the case of the concept of focalization, I have proposed a way of reconfiguring it that I see, retrospectively, as based on the Benvenistian idea, and that deviates from the use Gérard Genette put it to in 1972 (Eng. 1980).

Focalization is the relation between the subject and object of perception. The importance of the concept for me was that in it I found a tool to connect content – visual and narrative, such as images in movement – with communication. It enabled me to account for the subject-constituting element in discourse to which Benveniste's language theory had pointed me. It is a mistake to assume that the concept of focalization as I have advocated it can be seen as an amalgam of Genette's use and mine, as is often done in literary studies; they are in fact utterly incompatible.

26 For this concept, which underlies my interest in intersubjectivity beyond a formalist methodology à la Popper, see Spivak's chapter 'More on Power/Knowledge' in *Outside in the Teaching Machine*.

27 Benveniste's writing is utterly clear and illuminating. It has been collected in English in Benveniste (1971). Kaja Silverman is one of the few scholars who has taken Benveniste's legacy seriously. See her *Subject of Semiotics* (1983) and my review of it, reprinted in *On Meaning-Making* (1994a).

I did not know this myself when I first wrote about it. It was when writing a critical assessment of their differences and their respective methodological and political frames that I understood for the first time the formidable implications of what my seemingly slight amendments had entailed. They appear to be just fussing in the margins about a term, a piece of jargon. But the tiny (in the formal sense) differences were related to such issues as the blind acceptance of ideological power structures versus the critical analysis of them. There has been an ongoing dispute about this since then, on which I will be brief here. For Genette, a narrative can be unfocalized, thus 'neutral.' For me, this is not possible, and pretending that it is only mystifies the inevitable ideological thrust of the text. It seems worth noting that this difference, even within a single literary text, already indicates a fundamental difference of disciplinarity between Genette's literary interest and my own interest in cultural analysis.

When it came to distinguishing between the possible focalizers responsible for the description of Philéas Fogg in Jules Verne's *Around the World in Eighty Days*, the difference between Genette's 'zero focalization' and my insistence on the 'subject of focalization' turns out to relate to the possibility of overcoming the firm subject/object opposition. This difference laid bare the obliteration and facilitated the insertion of political issues, such as class, within formal or structural analysis. Perhaps most important, my version of focalization created the possibility of analysing, rather than paraphrasing and broadly categorizing, a text.[28] It seems to be a trifle, fussing over a small passage. But, in fact, this insight was entirely contingent upon the endorsement of the performative notion of meaning production in and through subjectivity, which Benveniste had initiated, without ever fussing over the concept of performativity. It decided not only the interpretation of the concept of focalization that I would go on to elaborate, but also the importance within that concept of what I have come to see as *framing*.

Framing will be discussed, and its productivity demonstrated, in chapter 4. The point here is that Benveniste's undermining of the priority of reference in favour of deixis has implications that reach beyond the limits of his own chosen discipline, into the wider domains of

---

28 This latter difference, incidentally, also defines the difference between literary analysis and typology, perhaps a useful analogue to the difference between cultural analysis and cultural studies. Genette replied to my suggestions (1983) in a manner that I found extremely unhelpful. For this discussion, see Bal (1991b).

social interaction and cultural practice, the various fields to which the humanities are devoted. If the distribution of subject positions between the (linguistic) first and second person constitutes the basis of meaning production as I and many others believe to be the case, there is no linguistic support for any form of inequity, suppression, or predominance of any one category of subjects in representation.

Undermining the subject/object opposition promoted by reference, Benveniste, in the same sweep, undermines individual authority, as well as its many models in cultural texts. To examine the inequities and authorities that undeniably structure these texts, the basis of those positions and that distribution is to be sought neither in meaning as the product of reference nor in authorial intention. Instead, meaning is produced by the pressures of the 'I' and the 'you,' who keep changing places with regard to the meanings that are liable to emerge. These pressures, far from emanating from the subjects whose linguistic position posits them as, precisely, *void of meaning*, outside of the situation of communication, instead come to them, *fill* them with meaning. This filling comes to them from the outside, from the cultural frame the pressure of which enables them to interact in the first place.

The close affiliation that remains between focalization and the gaze is thus relevant *because*, and not in spite, of the latter's ambiguity – the difference, that is, between the Lacanian gaze and the more ordinary use, synonymous with the Lacanian look. The concept of the gaze helps to assess the ideological charge of a subject-position such as the focalizer. In Verne's novel, Passepartout, bearer of the look, is the focalizer. He is the servant, and he is impressed by Philéas Fogg, his master, because he cannot withdraw from the pressure of social structure, the gaze; the description renders precisely that. Thus, the concept helps to understand how structure – Philéas' subject position – betrays ideology – class confinement – without making the subject individually responsible for it.

This is also the way the gaze-as-look and the Lacanian gaze as the visual side of the cultural, symbolic order can come together. If the Lacanian gaze produces the frame that makes meaning production possible, the unstable holder of the look, the focalizer who is now 'I,' then 'you,' must negotiate his or her position within its confines. The subject of semiosis thus lives in a dynamic situation that is neither totally subordinated to the gaze, as a somewhat paranoid interpretation of Lacan would have it, nor free to dictate meaning as the master of reference, which the subject has often been construed to be. This brings me to a final aspect of the travel of concepts in relation to objects, namely their constant commute between theory and analysis.

Throughout my work on the concepts of focalization, subjectivity, and the gaze, I came to realize, first, that analysis can never be the application of a theoretical apparatus, as I had been trained to assume. Theory is as mobile, subject to change, and embedded in historically and culturally diverse contexts as the objects on which it can be brought to bear. This is why theory – any specific theory surrounded by the protective belt of non-doubt and, hence, given dogmatic status – is in itself unfit to serve as a methodological guideline in analytical practice. Yet, and second, theory is also indispensable. Third, however, it never operates alone; it is not 'loose.' The key question that makes the case for cultural analysis, then, is the following: are theory and close analysis not the *only* testing grounds in a practice that involves both methodology and relevance? My contention is that in practising detailed analysis from a theoretical perspective, one is led to resist sweeping statements and partisanship as well as reductive classification for the sake of alleged objectivity.

Avoiding these fatal ills, which cling to both cultural studies and traditional disciplines alike, a close analysis, informed but not overruled by theory, in which concepts are the primary testing ground, works against confusing methodological tradition with dogma. It would appear that to challenge concepts that seem either obviously right or too dubious to keep using as they are, in order to revise instead of reject them, is a most responsible activity for theorists. Interestingly, concepts that don't seem to budge under the challenge may well be more problematical than those that do. Some concepts are so much taken for granted and have such generalized meaning that they fail to be helpful in actual analytic practice. This is where the issue of analysis comes in.

The three priorities of methodology implied so far – cultural processes over objects, intersubjectivity over objectivity, and concepts over theories – come together in the practice of what I have proposed to call 'cultural analysis.' As a professional theorist, it is my belief that in the field entailing the study of culture, theory can be meaningful only when it is deployed in close interaction with the objects of study to which it pertains, that is, when the objects are considered and treated as 'second persons.' It is here the methodological issues raised around concepts can be arbitrated on a basis that is neither dogmatic nor free-floating. Concepts tested in close, detailed analysis can establish a much-needed intersubjectivity, not only between the analyst and the audience but also between the analyst and the 'object.' It is in order to drive this point home that I suggest reconfiguring and reconceiving 'cultural studies' as 'cultural analysis.'

What does analysis have to do with it, and how does – here, linguistic – theory come into it? Any academic practice lives by constraints yet also needs freedom to be innovative. Negotiating the two is delicate. The rule I have adhered to, that I hold my students to, and that has been the most productive constraint I have experienced in my own practice, is to never just theorize but always to allow the object 'to speak back.' Making sweeping statements about objects, or citing them as examples, renders them dumb. Detailed analysis – where no quotation can serve as an illustration but where it will always be scrutinized in depth and detail, with a suspension of certainties – resists reduction. Even though, obviously, objects cannot speak, they can be treated with enough respect for their irreducible complexity and unyielding muteness – but not mystery – to allow them to check the thrust of an interpretation, and to divert and complicate it. This holds for objects of culture in the broadest sense, not just for objects that we call art. Thus, the objects we analyse enrich both interpretation and theory. This is how theory can change from a rigid master discourse into a live cultural object in its own right.[29] This is how we can learn from the objects that constitute our area of study. And this is why I consider them subjects.[30]

The logical consequence of this combined commitment – to theoretical perspective and concepts on the one hand and to close reading on the other – is a continuous changing of the concepts. This is yet another way in which they travel: not just between disciplines, places, and times, but also within their own conceptualization. Here, they travel,

29 This is, by now, a well-known consequence of the deconstructionist questioning of artistic 'essence.' It is by no means generally accepted, however, as George Steiner demonstrates. See Korsten (1998) for a critical analysis of Steiner's position. On the status of theory as cultural text, see Culler (1994).

30 As I have written many times – perhaps most explicitly in the Introduction to *Reading 'Rembrandt'* – the maker of an object cannot speak for it. The author's intentions, if accessible at all, do not offer direct access to meaning. In the light of what we know about the unconscious, even an alert, intellectual, and loquacious artist cannot fully know her own intentions. But nor can the maker or the analyst who claims to speak for the maker speak for the object in another sense, the sense closer to the anthropological tradition. The object is the subject's 'other' and its otherness is irreducible. Of course, in this sense the analyst can never adequately represent the object either: she can neither speak about it nor speak for it. See ch. 7 for an elaboration of this position.

under the guidance of the objects they encounter. Such internal transformation can be demonstrated by the emerging concept of visual
poetics, implying both a specification of focalization and a transformation, along the lines of the interdisciplinary travel between literary and
visual analysis, and between concept and object. The term 'visual poetics' is not a concept but an approach in which affiliated concepts such
as focalization, the gaze, and framing accrue, to become a little more
than just concepts: in fact, the skeleton of a theory.

Travel between Concepts

For precisely this reason, it can be helpful to build bridges between the
traditional disciplines and cultural analysis. Let me take Proust's
Recherche as an uncontested example. It was, after all, the central object
through which narratology was developed in the structuralist era. It
was Genette's *case*. In my attempt to sketch a visual poetics, it thus
seems only fair to take up where the main proponent of the current of
structuralist narratology left off.[31]

Two misconceptions about such a 'visual poetics' circulate, doing
great damage both to it and to the interdisciplinary study of culture in
general. First, in spite of the lofty associations that the word 'poetics'
may evoke for some, there is no connection whatsoever between visuality and 'high art,' painting, or any other recognized visual genre. Nor
is there any connection with language as a meaningful sign-system.
Second, such a 'poetics' asks for a discussion within a semiotic framework that is best begun by stating that the term 'iconic,' so often
applied to the visual in yet another misconception, cannot be adduced
for 'reading' objects either. This issue helps clarify how concepts travel
back and forth between each other.[32]

Just as focalization cannot simply be projected from narrative onto
visual images, so iconicity cannot be equated with visuality. Yet iconic-

---

31 Genette (1972) proposed the concept of focalization, which he derived from Henry
   James, through a detailed analysis of Proust. But neither Genette nor James elaborated on the consequences of that concept for an encounter between literature and
   visual images. With Proust as his case, however, Genette should have known better.
32 The use of 'iconic' for /visual/ is very widespread, even among avowed semioti-
   cians. See, for example, Louis Marin, who, in spite of his brilliance, is remarkably
   confused about iconicity (1983) and sometimes disappoints because of it (e.g. 1988).
   His posthumous volume (1993) is less focused on the ill-guided attempt to equate
   looking with speech acts, and much more profound on visual discourse as a result.

ity invariably shows up in inquiries on the contributions of the visual domain to the literary, which appears to be its systemic counterpoint. To be sure, there are well-known cases of iconicity in onomatopoeia, in visual poetry such as Apollinaire's, and in novels where a blank page hides either a crime (Robbe-Grillet's *Le voyeur*) or an immeasurable duration of sleep (Duras' *L'après-midi de Monsieur Andesmas*). But the concept is of little help when it comes to accounting for the invasion, by one sense or medium – vision, for example – of the realm of another, such as language. The thrust of semiotics is precisely to offer a media-independent perspective, not to pin down each medium to just one of its concepts. The distribution of Peircean concepts among the media kills their critical potential. If iconicity equals the visual, and symbolicity equals the literary, there is absolutely nothing to be gained from such translations.[33]

By contrast, I am interested in examining to what extent and in what ways the senses' *encounter* with the concepts can take place at the crossroad between the media – here, language – and in assessing the importance of the other medium *qua* other. This is where the example of Proust, many theorists' favourite, comes in. Proust's text is almost too good to be true as a playing field for such an inquiry. Rich in visual evocations, it is not particularly rich in icons. And the icons it does contain are often auditive rather than visual. But it is replete with visual 'takes,' as well as with reflections on what it means to look. Moreover, while it is one of the Western world's literary masterpieces, I would argue that this work deploys insights from popular culture to elaborate its poetics. Last but not least, with its intricate play with focalization, it invokes vision 'on the street,' while talking about visual art in annoy-ingly elitist and non-visual terms.

Of all these misunderstandings, the conflation of iconicity with visu-ality is perhaps the most damaging. The famous passage where Peirce defines the three categories of signs according to their *ground* – close but not identical to, because broader and less rigid than, *code* – has suffered, like various canonical examples of literary theory, from over-citing and under-reading. Yet it deserves to be quoted to remind us that there is no special affiliation between iconicity and visuality:

> An icon is a sign which would possess the character which renders it sig-
> nificant, even though its object had no existence; such as a lead pencil

33 In ch. 2, translation will be deployed otherwise.

streak as representing a geometrical line. An *index* is a sign which would, at once, lose the character which makes it a sign if its object were removed, but would not lose that character if there were no interpretant. Such, for instance, is a piece of mould with a bullet-hole in it as a sign of a shot; for without the shot there would have been no hole; but there is a hole there, whether anybody has the sense to attribute it to a shot or not. A symbol is a sign which would lose the character which renders it a sign if there were no interpretant. Such is any utterance of speech which signifies what it does only by virtue of its being understood to have that signification.[34]

In the case of the icon, it is the sign itself that possesses its ground, and far from leading to the kind of realism that informs the equation of icon with image, the definition, based as it is on resemblance, stipulates that the object – the signified or the meaning rather than the referent – does not need to be anything at all ('even though its object had no existence').

What defines the 'streak' as an icon is the fact that we give it a different name: a line. To give another example: the signature is an icon because it is self-enclosed; it owes its ontological status to nothing but itself. It is an effective sign because it enables one to *lie*, as Eco's famous definition has it (1976: 10). It is an example of the index ('a piece of mould with a bullet-hole in it as a sign of a shot; for without the shot there would have been no hole') that makes lawyers pore over a signature with a magnifying glass to assess its visual resemblance to the 'authentic' signature, the guarantee of the existential origin in the body of the person it signifies. According to Peirce, no *interpretant* is necessary for the sign to exist (although one is necessary for the sign to work as a sign).

Is iconicity bound up with resemblance, analogy, conformity? Peirce doesn't say. But it *is* a sign that possesses a quality of its meaning. In the case of a visual meaning, this can lead to resemblance if, and only if, that quality is predominantly visual, even if the sign as a whole is not.[35] The example Peirce gives is neither more nor less visual than the example of the index. But, without the existence of the object, one has

---

34 Peirce, in Innis (1984: 9–10; emphasis in text).
35 See Eco's relevant critique of the motivated signs – icon and index – (1976), which defines resemblance more on the basis of ontology than I think is warranted for Peirce.

no other standard than a *presumed* resemblance – one which is neither ontological nor total, and which does not overrule difference.

The important element in the definition of the icon is primarily its negativity, for it suspends the ontology of the object. The 'icon' is constructed or conceived by the reader, the decipherer of signs that we all are in our capacity as *homo semioticus*. In other words, what makes the notion of iconicity important for reading is not the fact that it leads to some pre-established, 'real' model, but that it produces *fiction*. It does so by both subjectivizing – à la Benveniste – and culturally framing – à la cultural studies – the object iconically signified. We would be unable to make the 'streak' signify anything if we didn't live in a cultural environment where geometry and handwriting circulate and are based on lines.[36]

Hence, the second important feature of the icon thus conceived is that it can only emerge from an underlying symbolicity. It is as a trace that the pencil leaves the 'streak' behind when it is guided by the hand that projects it. The overlap of the categories is inherent in their definitions. It is in this sense that Peirce's basic concepts can be useful to an analysis of literary visuality – of visual poetics – but only if it is reinterpreted through Benveniste's subjectivization of discourse.

Let me now draw a provisional conclusion, one that affects the status of concepts in cultural analysis. I contend that thinking about visual poetics fares better if it avoids taking definition and delimitation as its starting point. But, to avoid alienating practitioners of the various disciplines of the humanities, let me add that such a poetics works best if its primary starting point – but not outcome – remains the undeniable boundary that separates visual from linguistic utterances. The attempts to produce inter-media texts prove it, and the existence of essentially mixed-media texts such as cinema and video in no way contradicts this. Moreover, although one cannot deny the visual aspect of textuality in general – the visual act of reading – textuality still cannot be grasped at a glance. Nor is the glance self-evident as a way of apprehending the image.

The look remains the basis for the distinction between primarily spatial and primarily temporal objects, even though neither dimension can exist without the other. The difference, however, is not an ontological one. It is meaningful to activate the look only in the use of objects. Unread, a novel remains a mute object; unread, an image remains an

---

36 For a theorizing account of this aspect of iconicity, see Neef (2000).

equally mute object. Both need time and subjectivity to become semiotically active. Hence, the question of the visual within the literary – of a visual poetics – is best *not* answered by definition and delimitation, by a mode of classification that turns difference into opposition and family resemblance into hierarchical polarization. The question is not *if* literary texts can have a visual dimension, but *how* the visual writes itself, and how a literary writer can deploy visuality in his artistic project. An analysis that invokes semiotic concepts not to define but to overcome stultifying definitions, and that follows the intertwinements of the three modes of meaning-making that are never 'pure,' can contribute to a richer understanding of a poetics that is irreducible to a linguistic structure, even if it is, also, irreducibly linguistic.

Travel within the Classroom

In accordance with the above, then, I will refrain from defining my three travelling concepts, and leave it to each reader to see what she can do with the gaze, focalization, and iconicity, separately or together. Let me stop at this point, to look back a little. How would I now set up a class or a seminar session devoted to the question central to this chapter: what is a concept, and what can it do? Hesitating, as I do, to give the impression that this rough guide is meant to be prescriptive rather than descriptive, or suggestive of a teaching practice, let me nevertheless take the risk by ending this chapter with a suggestion for teaching. The status of this suggestion, I insist, is to open up rather than to close off what *might* be a class. Let's say the first part of this session would consist of the discussion presented so far. The bulk of the discussion would centre on the three affiliated, yet different, concepts located on the border of the territory of the visual. The considerations that came first in this chapter would be brought in as the need arises.

The second half of the session would consist of stepping back and considering what concepts are and do, much as a class about a particular theory would end by thinking about theory in general. I would start, then, with a confrontation. After travelling the path sketched above, the concept cluster consisting of visuality, image, the gaze, focalization, and iconicity would be held up against the introductory chapter of Deleuze and Guattari's *What Is Philosophy?* From that text I would draw the following 'beginnings,' or suggestions, for how to think concepts.

Concepts are

- signed and dated (hence, have a history)
- words (archaisms, neologisms, shot through with almost crazy etymological exercises, sketching a philosophical 'taste')
- syntactic (of a language within a language)
- constantly changing
- not given but created.

These features would be linked to the issues of visuality already discussed.

Returning to Deleuze and Guattari's suggestions, a second round of confrontation would then seem to be called for. Here, the general questions would serve less to characterize the concepts than to reassess what we have been doing to and with them. There are no simple concepts, Deleuze and Guattari say. This explains the multiplicity of their aspects and possible uses. The point of these aspects and uses continues to be to articulate, cut, and crosscut an understanding of an object *qua* cultural process. In this sense, a concept-in-use is like first-/ second-person exchange. At the same time, concepts are connected to problems; otherwise they are meaningless. Using concepts just to characterize or label an object means falling back into a practice of typology whose point is limited as well as limiting.

Meanwhile, the concepts used here, like all others, are always in a process of becoming, a process that involves developing relations with other concepts situated on the same plane (this might be an opportunity to explain the structuralist tenet about the homogeneity of planes).[37] Every concept relates back to other concepts, hence, the discussion of visuality ends up in a cluster of concepts. Yet its components are inseparable within the concept itself. As a result, a concept can be seen as a point of coincidence, a condensation, an accumulation of its own components. Hence, a concept is both absolute (ontologically) and relative (pedagogically). And, while it is syntactic, according to Deleuze and Guattari, a concept is not discursive, for it does not link propositions together (22). This may be precisely why concepts maintain the flexibility that a full-fledged theory, discursively elaborated,

---

37 Jonathan Culler's book on Saussure (1986) is one of the finest examples of explaining structuralism through a concrete case study, in this case Saussure's theory of language.

must lose. To understand, then, what our itinerary has consisted of, I would invoke the philosophers' statement that concepts are centres of vibrations, each in itself and every one in relation to all the others (23); concepts resonate rather than cohere.

By the end of the session, though, the general exhilaration about the openness of academic activity might be in need of some remedial caution. Again, Deleuze and Guattari's text is helpful. In a shorthand formulation whose usefulness parallels its common-sense recognizability, the authors characterize disciplinary tendencies when they write that from discourse, or sentences, philosophy extracts *concepts*, science extracts *prospects*, and art extracts *percepts and affects*. As the title of their book already intimated, this attributes to philosophy the task and privilege of devising and designing concepts. Indeed, Deleuze and Guattari begin (2) by stating that '[p]hilosophy is the art of forming, inventing, and fabricating concepts.'

The idiom in which their characterization of the three disciplinary domains is couched may be a bit problematic, because of the positivistic connotations of 'extracting' and the rather rigid division of labour involved. But the point is that specialization is implicitly presented as collaboration. And this collaborative element prevents specialization from being foreclosed, which it so often is. I would, therefore, consider this formulation of 'what is philosophy' to hold for the humanities as a whole. What is here described as 'science' could also be seen as a long-term motivation for academic work. And 'art' can be reconfigured as 'practice.' From this rewriting of their suggestive sentence, an attractive program for the humanities emerges. It is with such a program in mind that I end this chapter, with a survey of the theoretical implications of each of the concepts discussed in this book. The chapters grope towards sketching a totally partial and personal – but at least *concrete* – version of such a program.

Deleuze and Guattari reveal a fondness for metaphors, whose 'imaging' potential they continuously exploit. For the purposes of this book, which aims to present teaching as creative, this fondness is attractive. I will exploit it as fully as I can, mainly by putting a strong emphasis on metaphor and image on as many levels as possible. After discussing the concept of metaphor itself in terms of image in chapter 2, I practise it – by establishing a metaphorical relationship between cultural practise and theory/analysis in chapter 3, a relationship which, in turn, is reversed in chapter 4. Then, in chapter 5, I practise metaphor by untangling two affiliated and often confused concepts – 'performativity' and 'performance' – only to wilfully confuse them again, in an integrative conception of metaphor. With this I am referring to metaphor as integrative, as producing a roadmap or rhizome, a landscape or stage, unlike the monistic conception that considers the figure as a vehicle only. A conception of metaphor as image that, as the second chapter argues, can stand for a conception of language, translation, and history.

The productive potential of concepts as imaging and imaginative metaphors is further developed in the last three chapters. There, the theatrical nature of academic work comes more and more clearly to the fore. The ground for this particular image is laid in chapter 3, through the concept of *mise-en-scène*, borrowed from, precisely, theatre. This inclination to think theatrically converges with the poststructuralist, postmodernist resistance to the illusions of 'natural' and 'true' and 'authentic,' which have accrued to standards of scholarship dominated by that key concept of deception, 'objectivity.' But the alternative to that deception is not the abandonment of methodological 'rigour' (a detestable word that I use somewhat the way 'witch' was used in early feminism and 'queer' in gay thinking). In this sense the art work that will be my interlocutor in chapter 5 is theatrical. Pushing the theatrical metaphor further, into the object-domain, chapter 6, on 'tradition,' is *about* a particular tradition of a profoundly theatrical nature, yet one that cannot be disentangled from 'real life.'

Theatricality is also my tool for unsettling the dogmatic primacy, in the cultural disciplines, of 'intention.' Heedless of Barthes and Foucault, who tried so laudatorily to undermine the authority of 'author'-ity, routine research in the cultural disciplines continues to consider authorial intention the only possible check on interpretation-gone-wild. Giving up that anchor would indeed unmoor interpretation and deprive it of its standards. Having militated for a long time against this notion, which I consider to be both mistaken and damaging, I now present the argument, in chapter 7, by staging the debate I have so often longed to have. But perhaps, given the theatrical nature of academic debate, I do not occupy the position I advocate. Instead, perhaps, I propose allowing the concept of intention, with its long history that makes it almost catachrestic, to linger on stage where tradition and anti-intentionalism are still in combat.

Finally, the theatrical metaphor returns, when, in the last chapter, I take seriously, literally, and concretely, the personifying metaphor that our philosophers invoke as a figure for philosophy itself. Here, my sample seminar comes close to wondering where all this travel can possibly end up, and what position remains for a student of cultural analysis who endorses the many ambiguities and uncertainties I am promoting. Perhaps it is time to decide who these students are, and what a (future) teacher is. Deleuze and Guattari invoke a conceptual persona (*personnage conceptuel*) from Greek philosophy: the teacher. In the face of *that* tradition, I end on a figure of the teacher that is both a traditionalist and a theatrical gesture.

In philosophy, this figure is usually the lover. In her book *What Can She Know? Feminist Epistemology and the Construction of Knowledge*, Lorraine Code takes this tradition and turns it around. For Code, the concept-metaphor that best embodies her ideal is the friend, not the lover. Moreover, the conceptual persona of the friend – the model of friendship – is not embedded in a definition of philosophy but of knowledge. This definition is necessarily one that takes knowledge as provisional. If the authority of the author/artist, as well as that of the teacher, is unfixed, then the place it vacates can be occupied by *theory*. Paul de Man defined theory long ago as 'a controlled reflection on the formation of method' (1982: 4). The teacher, then, no longer holds the authority to dictate the method; her task is only to facilitate a reflection that is ongoing and interactive. Knowledge is knowing that reflection cannot be terminated. Moreover, to use Shoshana Felman's phrase, knowledge is not to learn something *about* but to learn something *from*. Knowledge, not as a substance or content 'out there' waiting to be appropriated but as the 'how-to' aspect that the subtitle of the present book indicates, bears on such learning *from* the practice of interdisciplinary cultural analysis.

Within the framework of the present book, and of Felman's description of teaching as facilitating the *condition* of knowledge (1982: 31), Code's apparently small shift from lover to friend is, at least provisionally, a way out of the philosophy/humanities misfit. Friendship is a paradigm for knowledge-production, the traditional task of the humanities, but then production as interminable process, not as preface to a product. Code lists the following features of friendship, as opposed to the lover's passion, as productive analogies for knowledge production:

– such knowledge is not achieved at once, rather it develops
– it is open to interpretation at different levels
– it admits degrees

- it changes
- subject and object positions in the process of knowledge construction are reversible
- it is a never-accomplished constant process
- the 'more-or-lessness' of this knowledge affirms the need to reserve
  and revise judgment (1991: 37–8).

This list helps to distinguish between philosophy in the narrow sense, as a discipline or potential inter-discipline, and the humanities as a more general field, 'rhizomically' organized according to a dynamic interdisciplinary *practice.*

Philosophy creates, analyses, and offers concepts. Analysis, in pursuing its goal – which is to articulate the 'best' (most effective, reliable, useful?) way to 'do,' perform, the pursuit of knowledge – puts them together with potential objects that we wish to get to know. Disciplines 'use' them, 'apply' and deploy them, in interaction with an object, in their pursuit of specialized knowledge. But, in the best of situations, this division of tasks does not imply a rigid division of people or groups of people along the lines of disciplines or departments. For such a division deprives all participants of the key to a genuine practice of *cultural analysis*: a *sensitivity to the provisional nature of concepts.* Without claiming to know it all, each participant learns to move about, travel, between these areas of activity. In our travel in this book, we will constantly negotiate these differences. We will select one path and bracket others, but eliminate none. This is the basis of interdisciplinary work.

2

Image

image
- *a representation (e.g. a statue) of a person or a thing*
- *the optical counterpart of an object produced by a lens, mirror, etc. or an electronic device; a likeness of an object produced on a photographic material*
- *exact likeness, semblance; a person who strikingly resembles another specified person*
- *a typical example of embodiment (e.g. of a quality); incarnation*
- *a mental picture of something not actually present; an impression; an idea, concept*
- *a vivid or graphic representation or description*
- FIGURE OF SPEECH; *esp. one (e.g. a metaphor or simile) involving a likeness*
- *a conception (e.g. of a person, institution, or nation) created in the minds of people, esp. the general public, often by manipulation of newspapers, television, etc. by public relations experts*

While content and language form a certain unity in the original, like a fruit and its skin, the language of the translation envelops its content like a royal robe with ample folds.

Walter Benjamin[1]

Folds, Flames, and Fire

The image of a royal robe with ample folds cannot today but evoke

---

1 'The Task of the Translator' (1968: 75). This essay, central to my argument as my primary 'philosophical object,' will henceforth be referred to by page numbers only. See also the discussion in Derrida (1982: 93–161).

that historical aesthetic and its contemporary counterpart that we associate with Gilles Deleuze (1993), with the idea of the fold. The image is thoroughly baroque. Walter Benjamin, whose work on German baroque drama has inspired extensive philosophical commentary on the baroqueness of his thought as exemplary of modernity in general, is not speaking here about art but about language.[2] Comparing the task of the translator with that of the poet, he creates a powerful image of the former's product as both rich (royal) and encompassing (ample), expansive yet enveloping.

Image: something to *see*, visible in its particularities. Image: a figure of comparison, a kind of metaphor, explicitly presented as such. Two basic meanings of the word 'image' converge here, melting to become a not-yet-concept that is both very well known in its casual use and not quite so well worked out in its conceptual sense. Benjamin's image is not reducible to 'just' a metaphor. In view of the account of the narrative concept of focalization that travelled from literary to visual studies and back again, and the opposite travel of the concept of the gaze, I would like to suspend classification, and to insist on the strictly *visual* nature of the comparants – fruit and skin, the royal robe with the ample folds. One *sees* forms and texture, even if seeing, here, in turn, solicits other senses, like smell and touch. Visual, then, but a kind of vision that is not 'pure,' not without tactile overtones. And, of course, rendered in language.[3]

The person who wrote this, Walter Benjamin, it seems safe to say, is one of those 'friends' – to use the revised metaphor for 'teacher,' as this figure has been construed from the Platonic tradition up to Deleuze and Guattari – that, as a type of teacher, has been inflected by feminist philosophy.[4] In cultural analysis today, few predecessors are more frequently quoted, alleged, discussed, or 'applied' than this figure. His words, even the more casual ones of journalistic criticism, are weighed like gold for their 'true' – that is, their intended – meaning. That is not my project here. My aim is to probe the image of the royal robe *qua* image, and from it to learn how to conceptualize the image as travel-

2 Benjamin (1977); Buci-Glucksmann (1994).
3 For a key analysis of the many senses of 'image,' see Mitchell's introductory chapter 'What Is an Image?' in his *Iconology*, a book that no one interested in understanding images and the tense relationship between visual and literary studies can afford to ignore (1985).
4 I am referring to Code's feminist revision of the teacher as 'friend,' discussed in ch. 1.

ling between visual and literary studies. The word 'metaphor' imposes itself in that in-between space where image is the meeting-place between language and vision. *Metaphor*, long regarded with suspicion by the philosophers of science and those humanist scholars who took the sciences as their model, may be the best place to look for a methodological discussion of cultural analysis in its differences from that scientific, or scientistic, model. And if the epigraph to this chapter is any indication, taking Benjamin as a friend is a good move.

The quotation comes from his essay on translation, not metaphor. That essay, in line with his more straightforwardly philosophical musings on language, takes an explicit position against the idea of translation as derivative.[5] It proposes a philosophy of language in which the translation serves not the original, but the liberation and release of its potential, which he calls 'translatability' and which is located in that which resists translation. Although his essay – somewhat embarrassingly to our postmodern taste – abounds in organic metaphors, essentialism, and a terminology of purity, the gist of his philosophy of language through translation can be seen, retrospectively, as a critique of logocentrism. The 'pure language' that translation is called upon to release in the original is – far from the core of truth of the hermeneutic tradition – located nowhere more precisely and more definitively than in the folds that envelop it. Elsewhere,[6] when describing the task of the critic, Benjamin uses equally baroque imagery to upgrade the function of the critic compared with that of the commentator (the philologist). In this case, the image is fire. Fire and fold: two images that refer language to the domain of visuality, and philosophy to the – baroque – aesthetic. Images, moreover, that are central to the work of two philosophers of our time, John Austin and Gilles Deleuze, doubtless among the most influential in the cultural disciplines to which art history belongs.

As will be recalled in chapter 5, John Austin, whose philosophy of language liberated language from the stronghold of meaning in a way

5 On Benjamin's philosophy of language, see de Certeau (1982, 1986) and Derrida (1982, 1987). These texts were discussed by de Vries (1992) in terms more focused on (Jewish) mysticism and the 'mystical postulate' than those I will use here, although, as I hint later, mysticism is not to be neglected as the bottom line of Benjamin's vision of translation. Moreover, Bernini's *Saint Teresa*, to be discussed later in this chapter, foregrounds the link between mysticism and translation on an additional allegorical level.
6 In the essay on Goethe's *Elective Affinities*, quoted by Hannah Arendt (Benjamin 1968: 5).

that resonates with Benjamin's, introduced the concept of *performativity* – today widely used and abused – into the discourse on language. For him, fire is the image of the fleeting nature of speech acts: not a semantic core, and, although it can do great damage (Butler 1997), not a thing, but a temporally circumscribed event; something, like fire, *that hovers between thing and event*. Deleuze, explicating and updating Leibniz's baroque philosophy, demonstrated that the aesthetic motif of the fold is far more than just a decorative element. Indeed, as a figure it defines a specific type of thought. A thought, it is now well known, that Benjamin exemplifies, and that connects – from within, so to speak – the seventeenth-century baroque, permeated with religion and authoritarianism, with the baroque of our time, which tries hard to be liberated from both.[7]

In this chapter, I will trace the travel between art history – a specific, albeit dominant, area of visual studies – and literary studies – a specific, albeit dominant, area of language studies – with the help of Benjamin's image of translation. I will confront Benjamin's essay on translation, as a sample of philosophical discourse, with an art-historical issue, so as to explore a few elements of the key question of the latter: how to *do* art history. Image, as a concept that points towards the visual, and its other version, metaphor, originally a philosophical and literary concept, will be the dual site of collaboration between these two humanistic disciplines.[8]

Here is my plan for the trip ahead. Somewhat simplified: the game to be played here consists of mapping the travel of the concept of image, between two disciplines – philosophy and art history – and between two historical periods – the historical baroque and the late

---

7 But that liberation is harder than we thought. See de Vries (1999) for the tenacious presence of religion in the kind of philosophy which, in Deleuze's terms, today would most definitely be qualified as 'baroque.' Needless to say, in spite of his caution in endorsing Benjamin's thoughts on language, Derrida is also a baroque thinker.

8 As Hent de Vries pointed out to me, the status of this essay of Benjamin's as 'philo-sophical' is subject to debate. However, disciplinary 'purity' is the last thing I am worried about here. Given Benjamin's status as a hot item within philosophy on the one hand and the philosophical issues his views on language broach on the other, I would feel entirely justified in using this text here as 'philosophical,' if that were my primary goal. Instead, I use it as a sample, if not of philosophy *sensu stricto*, then at least of the kind of thought that is dear to philosophers, and, I contend, is embodied in visual art when it is attended to as 'meaningful' without being a 'conveyer' of meaning, without being 'translatable.' 'Philosophy,' then, takes place *between* the two essays by Benjamin and the two sculptures I will allege here as examples of the baroque aesthetic.

twentieth-century response to it. Whether we call it 'image' or 'metaphor,' the concept at issue, along with the latter's etymological synonym, 'translation,' is tested for its capacity to raise and then solve problems of historical interpretation. To make the case as strongly as possible, I provisionally endorse that other dogmatic tenet of both art history and literary studies: the concern for aesthetics. This concern, in turn, hovers between philosophy on the one hand, and art history and literary studies on the other, and, as a concept, again, remains locked up in the field between its use as a word, where everyone claims to be in the know, and a concept, where some (philosophers) claim to know better.

Significantly, a third term – 'ecstasy' – is invoked to ec-centrally position aesthetics as the philosophical-artistic object to be understood. To make the point about concepts travelling more forcefully, I refrain from *defining* the concepts, at least in any traditional, methodologically 'responsible' way. Through this deliberate omission, I aim to foreground their vulnerability as well as their strength, to better underscore the power of their flexibility: their travelling as a heuristically productive endeavour. Instead of definitions, a trajectory is proposed.

As the journey's destination, the central term to be revised here is, simply, *history*, or 'the name of the discrepancy between intention and occurrence,' to recycle the strikingly productive definition proposed by Jonathan Culler (1988: xv). *Discrepancy*, to my mind, is a brilliant word to indicate the gap between past and present, as well as to suggest the two – or more! – sides of that gap, without prejudging the *kind* of cuts, joints, and erasures needed to make that discrepancy something we can look at and learn from. Discrepancy, then, would be the kind of vision of history that cultural analysis, as distinct from but not opposed to cultural history, would commend.

Two works of art – one from the seventeenth century, the other from the present, both considered baroque – are called upon, as a dual case to present my view of the relationship between philosophy, literary studies, and art history, with the concept of *image* at the centre. I propose this relationship as an *ecstatic form of translation*. Moreover, I will argue that this form of translation is a good example of cultural analysis because it is both ethically responsive, and, in the strict sense, where philosophy and art history blend, *aesthetic*. On the one hand, I will put forward the baroque sculptor Gianlorenzo Bernini's famous *Ecstasy of Saint Teresa*, from 1647, located in the Cornaro Chapel of the Santa Maria della Vittoria Church in Rome. This is a major object of interest for both the 'typical' art historian (Lavin 1980) and the less typical but more influential philosopher (Lacan in his Seminar 20).[9] It is in this double status that it will here serve as my historical object. On the other hand, I will propose the contemporary sculptor Louise Bourgeois' sculpture *Femme-Maison*, from 1983, not yet studied in any detail by art historians or engaged in any way by philosophers, as my theoretical object. I hasten to add that these two works will exchange functions as my argument develops.

This exchange, in fact, embodies the essence of my argument. In an anti-instrumentalist conception of theory, I contend that the relationship between philosophy, literary studies, and art history is best reframed as a relationship between history and theory – two aspects of both philosophy, and art history and literary studies – which, in turn, stands for the relationship between object and analysis.[10] But theory here is not an instrument of analysis, to be 'applied' to the art object, supposedly serving it but in fact subjecting it. Instead, it is a discourse that can be brought to bear on the object at the same time as the object can be brought to bear on *it*. For this relationship is reversible in both temporal and functional terms. The historical interpretation of objects of visual art requires a fluctuating, mobile, and irreducible tension, between past and present and between theory and history. In what I have called elsewhere a 'pre-posterous' history, historical interpretation is, by definition, a philosophical activity.[11]

The status of my sculptural objects as 'images,' that is, as objects of visual art, is equally subject to doubt. To be sure, they are clearly images; things to look at and give meaning to, to derive aesthetic connectedness from, and to characterize historically and formally. While it would be pedantic to argue about Bernini's relevance to the (art)-historical concept of *baroque*, it would not be to scrutinize his work for its implications for that concept. His work is the paradigmatic example

---

9 Mitchell and Rose (1982).

10 For the sake of convenience, I will henceforth speak only of philosophy and art history, subsuming literary studies under the latter, since both disciplines are engaged with images and aesthetics.

11 See Culler (1994) for this view of theory. On 'preposterous history,' see the introduction to my *Quoting Caravaggio* (1999a). The reverse might also be true – philosophy being by definition a historical activity – although that may be a profoundly a-philosophical response to philosophy. If I may, for a moment, challenge these disciplining conventions, I would suggest that Derrida's postmodern – and post-Holocaust – response to Benjamin suffers from a lack of historicizing within philosophy, in spite of its insistence on dating (1982: 71; 1990: 1040).

of baroque sculpture. But what can it, in turn, say about what 'baroque' is, means, and entails? Louise Bourgeois' work is a different case. For now, let me just say that, in addition to calling herself a baroque artist, Bourgeois made a sculpture called *Baroque* (1970), and one called *Homage to Bernini* (1967).

Since, for these two, totally divergent reasons, Bourgeois and Bernini can be considered exemplary of what art history calls 'baroque,' it is through their two works of *Ecstasy* and *Femme-Maison* that the concept of baroque will be considered – as both historical and philosophical. In defiance of art-historical practice, I will treat these works together, as if they had no separate existence. I will also deal with them as much theoretically-philosophically as in terms of their visual existence, or 'nature,' their status as 'images.' The relationship between the two works individually and between them and the concept of baroque will be construed in terms of translation, according to the metaphor in the epigraph to this chapter. Needless to say, the figure of the fold will be deployed as baroqueness' synecdoche.

It may seem paradoxical to begin an analysis of sculptural images with an analysis of philosophy. Yet this deceptively traditional order embodies my claim about the sculptures *qua* images. For, far from 'applying' Benjamin's text to this visual analysis, I will end up by arguing that the two sculptures, in their preposterous historical relationship, take up and enrich Benjamin's conception of translation. In this sense, by 'stating,' more emphatically than the philosopher-critic does, that translation *is* metaphor, they 'do' philosophy. At the end of our journey, the image will be conceived as such: as translation, and as metaphor.

Theses on the Philosophy of Art History

The past can be seized only as an image which flashes up at the instant when it can be recognized and is never to be seen again.

For every image of the past that is not recognized by the present as one of its own concerns threatens to disappear irretrievably.
        Walter Benjamin, 'Theses on the Philosophy of History,' V (1968: 255)

Image, recognition, disappearance: history depends, for its conditions of possibility, on the self-centred anachronism of the present. Here, Benjamin does not 'do,' produce, or perform an image, as with the royal robe of translation; he speaks directly *about* images. And what he has to say concerns their historical status. In spite of his current popularity, these words are not heeded in the academic environment, where 'the call for history' (Culler's critical term; 1988) has resounded loud and clear for decades. Especially not in art history, whose objects are images, whose primary tool (iconography) is predicated upon recognition, and whose greatest magic consists of 'disappearing' the object under the dust of words.[12]

But philosophy is a discourse in the present that, unlike historical thinking, engages past thought in the present, without reconstructing it as it allegedly was or causally explaining it. If there is a relationship between philosophy and art history, then it takes the form of a philosophy *of* art history. Such a philosophy can only be involved in recognizing – for the present, 'as one of its own concerns' – the objects of its inquiries, which flare up only for brief instants, like scenes that snapshots are unable to grasp and of which they can inscribe only a trace. The philosophical attitude I would like to propose in this chapter is not to make the best of a sad situation but rather to endorse this image of history as truly important for the present, which is, after all, our only lived temporality – a matter of life and death. Not stoic resignation but ecstatic enthusiasm is involved if we are to heed the warning that was Benjamin's last, given to us to honour – on the eve of his and enlightenment culture's suicide.

To make this proposal more concrete, I will now bring Benjamin's 'Theses' to bear, 'pre-posterously,' on a much earlier, much more practical, and much less ominous text: the introduction to his own practical piece of work, 'The Task of the Translator.' I will attempt to translate

12 The uneasiness in art history about the need for language to 'do' the discipline is a long-standing commonplace. It keeps recurring, and was recently most emphatically reiterated by Elkins (1999). This particularly wordy author produced yet more words to say that words fail. This outdated romanticism about images and their purity serves today to keep 'others' out of a field whose boundaries the words are busy policing. My uneasiness is not about the use of words for talking about images, but about the extent to which those words point to images, point out their specifics, or fail to do either. The standard art-historical discourse, which uses images as illustrations of its own arguments and whose arguments allegedly concern the images but in fact do so only tangentially, is the one I mean with this verb 'to disappear.' In line with Maaike Bleeker's comment on the Cartesian split between mind and body in terms of discursive performance, following Drew (1990), the relationship between art works and art-historical discourse could be characterized as 'dys-appearing,' provided this word is taken as the active progressive verb form (2002).

his position on the philosophy of history ('every image of the past that is not recognized by the present as one of its own concerns threatens to disappear irretrievably') into the practice it solicits. For this purpose, it is more suitable to recognize, as one of our own concerns, his ideas as a practising philosopher in the routine present of 1923 than his apocalyptic vision on the eve of his death. According to Benjamin, history, including the history of art, is neither a reconstruction of nor an identification with the past; it is a form of translation. And he invokes images to make that point.

Translation: *tra-ducere*. To conduct through, pass beyond, to the other side of a division or difference. If this etymology of translation is acceptable, it can be recognized in Benjamin's celebration of translation as liberation (80), transformation, and renewal (73), as a supplementation that produces the original rather than being subservient to it:

> Translation is so far removed from being the sterile equation of two dead languages that of all literary forms it is the one charged with the special mission of watching over the maturing process of the original language and the birth pangs of its own. (73)

It is the consequences of this philosophy of translation as a philosophy of language that I contend to be extendable to the historical interpretation of visual objects as images and that defines the relationship between philosophy and art history as I see it. The central element here, again, is travel: movement, displacement, carrying over. And, while *moving* guides us towards the realm of aesthetics, *translation*, far from helping us to confine the object, liberates it from confinement, de-centring it, and its readers, into ec-stasy. I will argue that through these moves, we get a fuller picture of what an *image* is and does.

Moving

One of the first consequences of this philosophy of translation is the principle of *dissipation*. For a revision of the concept of image outside of the essentialism that enshrined and imprisoned images, this seems important. The moment one undertakes to translate, the object translated resists containment within the 'duct,' the conduit. It attaches itself left and right, engages a single 'destiny,' and attempts the many encountered along the way. It also leaves elements behind, lost forever; hence the sense that translation is always reductive. But this dissipation is also enriching. And, in anticipation of what follows, *ec-static*. The translator endorses a loss of (linguistic) self in an activity that cannot but dissipate language.

A second consequence derives from the notion that translation traverses a *gap*, an irreducible difference between the original and its destiny in the new environment. This gap puts the discrepancy that history is, according to Culler's definition, into perspective, literally, by the work of *mise-en-abyme*.[13] The preposition 'trans-' is as deceptive as the verb 'to carry' (*ducere*). For even if translation effectuates a passage, it can never really build a bridge. The gap remains, and, even in the best of translations, the result of the act of translating manifests its scars. 'Dissipation' plus 'gap' equals infinite process, without origin or end. Translation is an ongoing activity (after a translation has been printed, its reader continues the task) and it seems important to subsume images in the field liable to be engaged in this task. And, since translation emphatically has neither origin nor end, but is a process through a dissipated field, crossing (out) gaps and hauling along history's remnants, a verb – 'translating' – not a noun, is needed here.[14]

There is an illuminating parasynonym of this Latinate word, namely its Greek version: metaphor.[15] The mere fact that these two terms are loosely etymological synonyms – if taken 'literally,' so that they yield their status as images – informs the rough guidance offered in this chapter. Whereas translation is reputed to pursue slavish adequacy and metaphor to seek innovation, they come together in a deployment of their conceptual treasures for the sake of analytical innovation. Nuances differ; literally, 'metaphor' means to carry beyond, not through; 'transference,' rather than 'translation,' if we confine the

13 This frequently invoked but seldom reflected-upon concept is deployed here to underscore the allegorical nature of the discussion. For an extensive reflection on the concept itself, see my earlier essay in *Lethal Love* (1987).

14 Benjamin's commentary on Genesis suggests as much. See his essay 'Über Sprache überhaupt und über die Sprache des Menschen,' in volume 2, 1 (1980). In his time and context, the endgame could not help but lead to 'God.' Today I would suggest multimedia and transnational practice as a good alternative. For the implications of the activity of translating within the latter, see Spivak (1999).

15 De Certeau (1982: 238) equates 'translation' with 'metamorphosis.' This is certainly justified in his context (mysticism). Strictly speaking, however, this choice is predicated on a formalist bias (*morph* means form), as well as on an unwarranted emphasis on the outcome, not the process.

former to its psychoanalytical meaning.[16] Benjamin's insistence that a translation changes the original beyond its initial state, revealing, or rather, producing the *translatability* that is its 'essence' (71), justifies the metaphor, or the image of translation as 'metaphor.' Translating as metaphoring, in Benjamin's conception of it, can be considered distorted representation. As Sigrid Weigel formulates it in her study of Benjamin, metaphor is 'translation without an original' (1996: 95). Below, I will risk decomposing these words to substantiate this claim, and use them to characterize the image as an object of a Benjaminian visual studies inquiry.

Two specific meanings of translation will be left behind here to avoid their obviousness getting in the way of the complexity of the argument. The first is the usual sense of 'passage' or 'transference' from one language into another. In Benjamin's view, this sense recedes before the supplementation of each in the service of the emergence of 'pure language' (74). But, as the *mise-en-scène* of some key problematics of art history, it cannot be overestimated. Linguistic translation successively stages the problems: of the subject – who speaks in a translation?; of context – where is the translated text or, to speak through the title of a 1992 volume (Niranjana), how can we 'site' translation?; and of moment – what is the historical position of a translated text?

But, once those consequences become clear, translation can no longer be considered as just an exchange between languages, for all these questions pertain to *any* work of historical interpretation. This is one reason why both history and philosophy are considered here as activities of translation, and why they must not only be realigned but also enmeshed. Sighting, citing, and siting translation requires an account of the literal or concrete result of each of these verbs: spectacularization, recycling, and location. This leaves straightforward translation from language to language far behind. It also invokes, through the visuality implied in these words, the notion that the object of translation is not a fixed semantic core, a *meaning*, but an image.

The second sense of 'translation' that is to be discarded concerns intermediality. My reason for bracketing this issue is strictly political. Reflection on the complex and problematic relationship between words and images tends to solicit defensiveness. The emphatic indivis-

---

16 Transference is at the heart of Shoshana Felman's psychoanalytic theory of literature or, more precisely, of reading literature (1982). There, the site of transference is, indeed, 'beyond' the text rather than 'through' it.

ibility of film and theatre notwithstanding, art historians often allege images' visuality as their essence, so as to bar literary scholars from access, under the banner of disciplinary purification (e.g. Elkins 1999). Others, nonbelievers in purity, abuse images as illustrations, in terms of the fidelity that for Benjamin (78–9) marks bad translations. They invoke images, point to them, but their discourse does not engage them *qua* image.[17] By bracketing intermediality I aim to disarm those who tend to allege that intermediality is a special, impure case of images. In contrast, as I will argue in the next chapter, I consider images a special, impure case of intermediality; but that reversal does not concern me here.

I bracket these two meanings of translation to foreground three other aspects of its meaning that allow it to become a suitable model for historical work on – as well as through – images: it is multiple (dissipating), metaphorical (transforming), and active (for a verb rather than a noun renders its 'essence,' in Benjamin's sense). In Greek, the word 'metaphor' appears on moving vans. 'Moving,' then, in all its possible meanings, may be our best bet yet.[18]

This pun would please the artist whose face is best known through the photograph Robert Mapplethorpe made of her, in which she carries a work, *Fillette*, that resembles both a French bread stick, a *baguette*, and a hyperbolic penis. This photo may serve to introduce Bourgeois, who was born in 1911 in France, and now lives and works in New York. Bourgeois the artist, the maker of images, is here, 'in' the image that she both did and did not make. She posed for it, the image made by her is in it, yet Mapplethorpe is the official maker of it (fig. 2.1). In this photo, her aging, wrinkled face smiles like that of a naughty girl. Bourgeois, the most prolific and versatile artist of the twentieth century, hard to pin down art-historically and loath to be pegged, as she currently is, as a 'token' woman/feminist artist, stands here as a theorist of the concept of image. She works so much with metaphor – so many of her works can only be understood if one takes the puns of their titles into account – that 'liberating,' 'translating,' metaphors might well be her underlying principle of coherence. Her works are images in the

17 I have written extensively on this problematic elsewhere, an argument I am reluctant to rehearse here (1991a, 1997a). Let me just add that this refusal or incapacity to engage images is in fact a feature of mainstream art-historical discourse.

18 To emphasize metaphor's active nature, but wanting to avoid confusion with the slippery activity implied in the more usual verb 'to metaphorize,' I will use, neologistically, the verb *to metaphor*.

2.1 Robert Mapplethorpe, *Portrait of Louise and Fillette*, 1982

most variegated sense, internally split between visuality and language. *Fillette* is a good case, and so is the image of her, by Mapplethorpe, where she seems to gently mock those who take images, or penises, too earnestly.

Early-modern Bernini, on the other hand, is much more earnest, at least if we believe art history. But there is room for doubt here, too, especially if we dare to look at his images through Bourgeois'. His clearly erotic representations of swooning saints make art historians feel obliged to blushingly insist on his deeply devout walk of life and on the mystical not erotic nature of the scenes he depicted. On the face of it, he doesn't poke fun at language and the body the way the postmodern Bourgeois does. Yet, Giovanni Careri, in his masterful study of Bernini's multimedia chapels, without which the present analysis could not have been written, wryly responds to that prudish distortion that shuns Bernini's sensuality by reminding us that 'in the seventeenth century the boundaries between the spirit and the senses were not drawn according to the Victorian criteria that we have inherited from the nineteenth century' (1995: 59). In the face of the conception of history that I choose to advocate, nicknamed 'preposterous,' it is certainly useful to alert my readers to the abuse, described by implication in Careri's sentence, of a truly preposterous reversal of history – from the Victorian era absorbed in our own, to the baroque past – that is used to censor and that remains unreflected. In fact, once we deploy Bourgeois' punning as a searchlight to look back 'pre-posterously,' Bernini's thresholds between registers of representation (his transitions from painting to sculpture to architecture), which are so keenly analysed by Careri, come to help us *site* the activity of translation in his *Ecstasy*.[19]

Art historians have tended to see this activity through the systematic principle of analogy that Benjamin would call 'bad translation' (72), that is based on 'resembling the meaning of the original' (78).[20] This form of translation rests on the principle of logocentrism, where meaning is the endpoint of interpretation – centripetal, transhistorically stable, and transmedial. It ignores what Benjamin defines as the 'mode' in translation – its *translatability* (70–1), and limits itself to the 'inaccurate transmission of an unessential content' (70), unessential because (only) content. It is important to note that Benjamin's remarks on translation build on his resistance to *two*, not one, conceptions of language, which *together* flesh out what logocentrism is. He opposes the idea that the 'word' coincides with the 'thing' – a vision in turn relevant for his engagement with Hebrew, where 'word' and 'thing' are both indicated by the noun *dabar*. He also opposes the idea that words convey meaning because it implies that meaning is whole, and stable enough to be the object of conveyance. As an alternative, I submit that words convey images, which are, in turn, accessible through other words and images.

It becomes possible to say this when we realize that the two concep-

19 The fact that ecstasy is the trade of the mystic, and that mysticism, in turn, is the main focus of de Vries' article on Benjamin's philosophy of language, makes the case I am building here even tighter (1992: 443).
20 Lavin (1980) interprets all levels of signification as different ways of conveying the same meaning. In the same vein, Perlove (1990) goes on to translate Careri's meaning into theological 'originals.'

tions Benjamin resists have *referentiality* in common. The first considers reference absolute, the second sees it as mediated by semantics – as meaning – yet primary. But, if meaning is unitary, whole, and stable, nothing really happens in the transition from semantics to reference. And although a sculpture or image is not a set of words, iconographic analysis in fact treats it as if it were just that. In juxtaposition to that habit, Careri proposes a more Benjaminian mode of translation, which, as the latter has it, 'lovingly and in detail incorporates the original's mode of signification' (78). In line with this injunction, Careri analyses not so much the singular meaning of singular elements as the 'multiple syntactic and semantic *modalities*' that produce that meaning and also determine its effectivity (Careri 1995: 85; emphasis added).

For my own analysis, I will take my cue from Careri's interpretation, and from his clear and convincing articulation of his method, which is a particular brand of reception theory. Through what I would call a 'preposterous' translation of Sergei Eisenstein's theory of montage in cinema, Careri, carefully avoiding the term 'baroque' so as to estrange his readers from its traditionally banal and confusing usages, qualifies Bernini's Albertoni Chapel as a *pathetic* work:

> ... in which the uniting of sensorial elements with intellectual and cognitive ones is achieved through a violent shock – by a paroxystic mounting of tension and by a series of conceptual, dimensional and chromatic leaps from each element to its opposite. (83)

He thus grounds the effectivity of what I would like to call the 'ecstatic aesthetic' not in content or textual sources – for he firmly rejects iconography as a method of translation – but in the 'tension of representation to "go outside itself"' (83). In other words, he translates what he sees, the 'original,' into something that comes to terms with, as Benjamin has it, 'the foreignness of languages' (75), defined a bit later as 'the element that does not lend itself to translation' (75). This aspect of Bernini's work, the untranslatability that defines its effect, can properly be called 'pathetic,' or, for my purposes here, *moving*. In the 'proper' sense of that word, as defined by Schaeffer (1997), then, it is the site of the 'aesthetic.' This sense of 'moving' is integral to 'image.'[21]

---

21 In his indictment of conceptual confusion concerning our intercourse with works of art as well as with the concept of work of art, Schaeffer writes: 'la plus grande entrave de l'esthétique est la théorie de l'art' ('the greatest handicap of aesthetics is art theory,' 21; my translation).

Moving House

Over a period of many years, beginning in the 1940s, Louise Bourgeois produced a great many works with the generic title *Femme-Maison*. Generic, not serial. These works form a genre not a series. Through a great diversity of media and styles, they explore the ambivalent relationship between women and (their) houses. Sometimes the woman loses her head, imprisoned as she is in her life as *femme sans/cent tête(s)*, to speak surrealistically. Sometimes she falls from a roof. Other times she escapes from the house and manages to communicate through it, using it, headless herself, as a prosthesis. How can we know if the house is an asset or a liability, a possession or a prison? And on yet other occasions she manages to climb onto the roof and proclaim her freedom, albeit dangerously.

Are these works using 'image' to make 'metaphor,' say, in the dualistic sense, translating the melancholia of the trapped woman from the realm of feeling, a sense of lifestyle, to the realm of the senses, of visibility? It is difficult to ignore the extent to which the comical absurdity of this situation coincides with the tragical absurdity of the situation in which many women were trapped at the time these works were being made. But to interpret the *Femme-Maison* pieces in this way, that is to translate them in the sense of transmitting this as their singular information content, is, as Benjamin would insist, impossible. Resisting simple metaphoricity, they stubbornly remain images, showing, for vision, what exceeds translation.

For there are at least two translations, and they are both necessary and incompatible at the same time. One translation moves from feeling, melancholia, or frustration, to visibility, through concretization: the figuration of the trapped falling into a trap, into a visible, deforming prison; but also, within the language of the title, *maîtresse de maison* becomes *femme-maison*, a literal translation of the English 'housewife.' Another retranslates what we see into language: the woman whose head gets lost in the house, because, in a moment of Bovaresque stupidity, she has lost her head, become a woman without a head.[22] This visual pun is a linguistic pun, but also a metaphoring, a transferring, from the domain of 'words' and 'images' to the domain of historicist

22 'Bovaresque' refers to the heroine of Flaubert's *Madame Bovary* (1857), who idealizes romantic love.

2.2 Louise Bourgeois, *Fallen Woman*, c. 1946–7, oil on linen

linearity (figs. 2.2 and 2.3). But the metaphor works only because the literal meaning of 'to lose one's head' continues to travel along.

Nor can we ignore the visual allusion to Max Ernst's visual pun of his generic *femme cent tête*. Suggesting another version of Ernst's work, Bourgeois can also be alleged to translate it in order to appropriate it, thus staking out her claim to a place in surrealism. Can these two translations – into a women's issue and into a surrealist pun – work together as a critique of the surrealists' sexism?[23] But, then, the metaphor of the lives of women imprisoned in their houses contradicts the act of the woman artist debating with her colleagues. Nor can we deduce from the style or content of these women's lives – their figuration or their humour – a conclusion that would make them translatable in terms of their historical moment, school, or style, just by labelling them 'surrealist.' Such labels are as confining as the houses of which – they say – women are the 'mistresses' (*maîtresses de maison*).

In fact, Bourgeois eludes academic categories, because she fights one translation with another. Actively metaphoring from one side of our categorizations to the other, her *Femme-Maison* genre offers a perspective on the constructive possibilities of translation that are generated by the impossibility of translating 'badly,' that is, in the semantic singular, informationally. She offers travel as a 'dissipating' way of accruing what one encounter on the way is reduced to trading. In the first place, the internal anachronism of the post-surrealist and post-melancholic sculpture alleged here, in the 1983 *Femme-Maison* (fig. 2.4),

23 On Ernst and the surrealists' attitudes towards gender, see Krauss (1993, 1999a).

2.3 Louise Bourgeois, *Femme-Maison*, c. 1946–7, oil on linen

2.4 Louise Bourgeois, *Femme-Maison*, 1983, marble

deconstructs from within – a spatial term to be taken literally – the attempt, inherent in art-historical methodology, to translate in such a manner. Nor can 'psychoanalysing' Bourgeois' work be helpful; she masters her own discourse on her past too well to avoid a collapse of unconscious and rhetorical material. Instead, her work lends itself singularly well to an analytical *mode* – not 'meaning' – of translation. In Jean Laplanche's terms, this mode is anti-hermeneutic (1996). Dissipating and crossing the gaps it leaves in place, that mode is ana-lytical: unbinding.

Indeed, the reason no singular meaning – either women's melancholia or surrealist jokes – can 'fit' this *Femme-Maison*, as iconographic interpretation would require, is because there is no key or code with which to do the translating. Instead, Benjaminian translation comes closer to Freudian free-associating, which is 'only the means employed for the *dissociation* of all proposed meaning' (Laplanche 1996: 7; emphasis added). For this sculpture associates its namesakes with itself, only to propose conceiving of the objects titled *Femme-Maison* not as a series but as a genre that traverses the differences between media. Therefore, the 1983 *Femme-Maison*, I contend, proposes the genre not as surrealist or feminist but, *through* the preoccupations of Bourgeois' time, as 'baroque.' This term is not a translation of the sculpture, or a code to translate it with, but an enfolding that embraces past (Bernini, religion, and sensuality) and present (Bourgeois, feminism, and surrealism), into a fold which, as Deleuze would have it, embodies baroqueness.

Here, the term 'baroque,' in its most visual sense – point of view – does not characterize the *Femme-Maison* and *Ecstasy* independently. Rather it describes the relationship between a contemporary and a historical baroque work:

> Moving from a branching of inflection, we distinguish a point that is no longer what runs along inflection, nor is it the point of inflection itself; it is the one in which the lines perpendicular to tangents meet in a state of variation. It is not exactly a point but a place, a position, a site, a 'linear focus,' a line emanating from lines. To the degree it represents variation or inflection, it can be called *point of view*. (Deleuze 1993: 19)

No; I am not proposing to classify the 1983 *Femme-Maison* as baroque, rather than as surrealist or feminist. I am invoking 'baroque' as a theoretical notion that *implies* – literally, that is, visually, in its folds – a

mode of translation, an activity of metaphoring, that resists the singular translation of one sign into another with the same meaning. The
baroqueness of Bourgeois' work is more like the royal folds of Benjamin's translation, including the folding of thought upon which
Deleuze insists, than like the decorative prettiness that is too often
associated with that historical style.

Rather than saying that, in *Femme-Maison* (1983), Bourgeois (transhistorically) translates Bernini, let's say that she addresses – dialecti-
cally, polemically, and respectfully – the way Bernini attempted to represent Teresa's ecstasy ec-statically. Without in the least imitating
Bernini, she, like him, supplements his work, ec-statically. More precisely, she examines through this sculpture the way her seventeenth-
century predecessor attempted to translate the transfiguration – itself a
form of translation in the sense of metamorphosis à la Certeau – of the
mystic. *Femme-Maison* as theoretical object houses this inquiry within
the modalities of the historical object. The issue of philosophy and art
history, then, has moved house.

Flaming

The retrospective examination I am proposing here requires 'metaphoring,' if not moving vans. Moving it from its time and place, in
Counter-Reformation chapels, Bourgeois' work metaphors baroque
sculpture, in particular Bernini's *Ecstasy* (fig. 2.5), in two ways, which
are characteristic of both works. In the first place, it integrates the
interior and exterior of the represented body. In the second, it integrates the interior and exterior of the space in which the viewer stands
in relation to that body.

This double integration suspends the very distinction between exterior and interior, as well as that between sculpture and the bodily
viewer. This integration gives yet another turn to the image as translation, a turn involving the liberalization of ecstasy. These two forms of
integration are emblematic for the state of language involved here,
called 'mystic.'

Accordingly, the case – Bernini's *Ecstasy* – is also a theoretical object,
one that articulates what critics painstakingly attempt to say. According to common art-historical lore, Bernini aimed to translate a text –
say, the Spanish mystic Teresa's description of her own ecstasy – into
sculpture. In de Certeau's conception of mysticism, Bernini was
thereby demonstrating a deep understanding of mysticism's challenge

2.5 Gianlorenzo Bernini, *Ecstasy of Saint Teresa* (detail)

to language. As Hent de Vries writes in a commentary on de Certeau's text, such an understanding involves '[formalizing] the different aspects of its writing, of its "style" or "tracing"' (1992: 449), thus producing the 'fabulous' event/experience that the mystic herself could not, precisely, 'render.' Mystical experience cannot, by definition, be 'expressed,' because in this view, it is always-already an after-effect. It comes after the shattering of language, and is situated in a void, which requires a new mode of 'speaking,' such as Bernini attempts.

That mode of speaking is a formal espousing, a tracing; and it is performative: it is a form of acting, both *theatrically* and *socially*. This view of mystic experience thus anticipates the exploration of theatricality, in chapter 3, and the bonding between performance and performativity, in chapter 5. In the perspective of the present book, these two meanings of the performative – theatrically as 'performance' and socially as 'performativity' – are the keys to the 'cultural' in 'cultural analysis.' Thus, the subject is, or attempts to be, larger than – not prior to – discourse. The performative speech act has an illocutionary force, which, according to de Vries, is a promise without the social conditions that can make promises effective speech acts.

This is why it is, by definition, also a failed or failing speech act. One is tempted to add that the necessary failure of the speech act is a function of the aporia of subjectivity that results from the mystic attitude. The subject is 'larger' than the discourse, but, far from transcending it, she cannot be prior to it, and therefore, she can only 'do' mystical experience by way of abandonment. This is the unavoidable abandonment of subjectivity – necessary for the transfiguration – through the abandonment of discourse. Bernini's work, then, is the indispensable prosthesis through which Teresa's ecstasy can come to be – pre-posterously – an after-effect.[24]

This is clearly not simply a translation of words into images. For Teresa's text itself is already an attempt at translating: the writer sought to render a bodily experience in language. *The image is the result of that effort* – provisional, failing, and de-centring. Moreover, the experience itself is a translation – a transfer – of divine love into the ecstasy of this human being, as well as of the spiritual into the corporeal. This transforming translation as such is not at all new in Western culture.

So far the philosophical discussion of mysticism has centred largely

---

24 For a commentary on the text in which Teresa attempted to render her mystical experience, see Bilinkoff (1989).

on language; specifically, on the problematic of language as 'translation' of experience. But the relevance of the Bernini/Bourgeois encounter lies in its extension of the *semiotics* of mysticism into the wider
range of human experience that it encompasses, that is, into a semiotics
of the failure of meaning production. To understand the implications
of visual ecstasy for our concept of image, Bernini's ongoing ambition
to render transformation in still marble offers an instructive pathway.
One of his earliest attempts concerns, precisely, an ontological transformation based on Ovid's story of Apollo and Daphne.

Ovid's *Metamorphoses*, a much-used model for the arts in early
modernity and invoked by de Certeau, is one of Bernini's 'sources,' if
not here, at least explicitly in one of Bernini's earlier works. The very
concept of transformation implies a program of study of the possibilities of inter- and multimedia translation. Take his famous *Daphne and
Apollo* in the Galleria Borghese: clearly, the job was difficult. At first, it
looks like a great success of triple translation: within the myth, from
myth to plastic form, and from sculpted human flesh to vegetation.
The young woman's hair, flowing in the wind because of the speed of
her flight, is transformed into rather rigid branches at the moment her
flight is stopped by the man who is pursuing her. The narrative movement rigidifies into an image that will stick forever, never aging.

But, it is at the threshold, namely, the surface, that Bernini is confronted with untranslatability. In this early work, it stops him in his
tracks; in the later *Teresa*, he challenges it by means of 'royal folds.' This
is precisely how he became a baroque sculptor. At the site where
Daphne's soft skin begins to change, translated from one materiality
into another, the laurel's bark is both fine and coarse, differentiating
and detaching itself from the soft skin at the very juncture when the
transformation ought to produce a perfect blend.[25] One could speculate on the meaning of the precise site on the female body where this

---

25 This is also the place where Apollo touches Daphne. As Andrea Bolland emphasizes,
   the sculpture explores the deceptiveness of vision and its irreconcilability with touch,
   hence, the inevitable frustration of erotic vision (2000). If I may take this opportunity
   to mark the difference between cultural analysis and art history as the 'home' discipline of the study of sculpture, it should be pointed out that Bolland's long article on
   this work pays scant attention to the visuality – including the implied discussion on
   the respective roles of the senses – and rests the near-totality of her argument on literary sources, whose relevance for the sculpture is argued through the typical specula-
   tions that Bernini 'might have read' some of these sources. I find this an instance of
   what I irreverently call art history's tendency to iconophobia.

untranslatability manifests itself. At least in the common, albeit extremely infantile, conception of femininity, this site defines her as a woman. For untranslatability is located in her genitals.[26]

But Daphne's transformation was not her own. It was, in fact, a violation and destruction of her agency. Although, according to the literary sources, she implored her divine father to destroy her beauty so as to shed her assailant – in a reaction to the threat of rape that is still often only too 'normal'! – she was 'protected' by the opposite: remaining beautiful, she lost her agency, and became the will-less instrument of Apollo; his muse.[27] In contrast, Teresa willed, according to the *volo* of the mystical postulate, her transformation. Bernini's task, therefore, became much more challenging. In accordance with the paradoxical transformation of a subject subjecting herself to loss of self, in *Teresa*, the transformation is much more radical, much more successful as metaphoring, to the extent that material layers can no longer be distinguished. There is a narrative reason for that difference. In contrast to Daphne's transformation, this one is willed – the mystical *volo* – by the subject, who is at the same time subjected to it, even if she lacks the subjectivity to carry out her will. But through the retrospective 'criticism' we see embodied in Bourgeois' work, this difference also acquires art-historical and philosophical meaning.

In a Benjaminian allegorical manner, the difference is articulated at the precise site where the folds and flames coincide. Bernini has created a sculpture that captures a moment between thing and event, as the speech act *par excellence*. As a result of her extreme, pious passion, Teresa the mystic, on her own account and in line with cliché metaphors of passionate love, is simultaneously beyond herself and burning. Her state is called 'ecstasy.' This word denotes extreme intensity but also, etymologically at least, de-centring. This last aspect tends to get ignored. But Bernini didn't ignore it, and Bourgeois reminds us of it. She does so by placing more figurative emphasis on the ambiguity

---

26 Needless to say, Freud's narratives of little boys seeing 'in a flash' the absence of the mother's penis – seeing, that is, the unseeable, absent, synecdoche of his self – set the tone for an ongoing identification of male and female identity with the genitals, a naïve mythical theory. See Bal (1994b). Laplanche says of such theories that they are 'an infantile theory of sexuality based on binary logic (plus/minus) [which] becomes a semantic theory with universalist claims' (1996: 9).

27 The classical source is Ovid's *Metamorphoses*, lines 452–567, in which the story figures as the first love story and as a story about the origin of poetry. See also Yves F.-A. Giraud (1968).

of inside and outside, which is just as important in Bernini's sculpture but can be more easily overlooked there because the arrow and the doxic interpretations of ecstasy get in the way of the work's aesthetic. Bourgeois' critical work is important, for the ec-centricity of ecstasy is, in turn, a defining feature of baroque aesthetics and baroque thought.

Moreover, here, unlike in *Daphne*, penetration does take place. The angel has already penetrated her with the arrow. According to the excerpt from her writing exhibited in the chapel, the mystic appreciates the angel's individuality.[28] He holds her garment by one of its finest folds. Andrea Bolland comments on the chiastic structure (my term, not hers) of the respective functions of 'touch' in the two sculptures:

> In the Daphne group, Apollo's left hand caresses the bark that has begun to encase and protect the chaste nymph, while in the *Ecstasy*, the angel's left hand delicately grasps a fold of the voluminous drapery that both shields and replaces Teresa's enraptured body. (2000: 324)

The remark, echoing Lavin's comment on the predominance of drapery over body (1980: 110–11), while establishing a continuity-in-difference with the *Daphne*, also foregrounds the notion that the site of *Teresa*'s baroqueness is, not surprisingly, the folds.

Beyond the banal and slightly prudish idea that the drapery would *shield* the body of her who, after all, desires to shed protection, there is, however, a more philosophical reason for this abundance. Ec-stasy knows no centre, either on the picture plane or in the fiction, in the guise of linear perspective's vanishing point. The transformation of Teresa, set on fire by the divine love that pierces her heart, emanates from the interior towards the outside, where her body's envelope, the lusciously folded drapery that iconographically marks the sculpture as baroque, equally transforms into flames. Her whole body becomes a flame: each part of it, of its cover, its surface beneath which nothing else remains, becomes a flame; fire comes to overrule previous shapes.

More than ever, the folds in Bernini's *Ecstasy* exemplify their func-

---

28 '... mas bien veo que en el cielo hay tanta diferencia de unos angelos a otros, y de otros a otros que no lo sabría decir.' This statement in the flier put out for the tourist – and as such, an object of popular culture – foregrounds the erotic nature of the figure: her smile, her head thrust backward, her powerlessly hanging hand, and her parallel foot, in front of the denuded breast of the young boy.

tion as baroque device *par excellence*, suspending the distinction between interior and exterior as they assume the shape of flames.[29] From the point of view of iconography, this is undeniable. But there is more to this metaphoring. The saint's body, although in paradoxical willing abandon, figures a will-less body that is neither standing nor reclining. In the shape of the letter 'S,' it unwillingly 'imitates' the shape of the flames sketched by the folds of her habit. It offers an *image* of that shape.

To measure the importance of this feature – of the wavering, not only between thing and event but also between inside and outside – it is useful to consider, by contrast, another commentary from our time. In his *Seminar 20*, in a desire to translate 'badly' and in contrast to what Bernini appears to be doing, Jacques Lacan reverses this totalization of the interior's exteriorization, thus cancelling the de-centring of 'ecstasy.' Seeing in it the desire to be penetrated, the psychoanalyst-philosopher relegates the mystic's heart back to its false function of centre, in order to promote the phallic interpretation that the sculpture had so superbly avoided. He thus demonstrates the blindness that comes with obsession, when he claims that Teresa's *jouissance* is a matter of her desire to be penetrated again and again (*encore*) by God, the transcendental phallus.[30]

As well as finding this a rather implausible way of eliminating the narrative dimension of the sculpture – by turning its event into a reiteration – I submit that this is a translation of Benjamin's 'bad' kind, an 'inaccurate transmission of an unessential content' (70).[31] In contrast, and through narrativity, visual representation stipulates that the mystic has already been penetrated – by the flaming arrow. Here/ now what matters is that the fire spreads throughout her entire body, *including its surface.* The ecstasy is a literalized 'ec-stasis,' according to a conception of metaphor that is neither monist nor dualist but, rather, pluralist, a conception of metaphor as activity and dissipation. The surface, the skin, participates in the fire, and in the process, loses its status as limit (of the body). Hence, the participation of the clothing. The transformation – here, transfiguration – is total.

29 Lavin (1980: 122) translates. For him, the flame-like pattern of the folds is a 'visual counterpart of her own metaphor,' so that the folds/flames seem 'not only to cover but to consume' her body.
30 See, for the relevant fragments, Mitchell and Rose, eds. (1982: 137–61).
31 Given Benjamin's opposition to a simplistic semiotic conception of language, any transmission would have to be inaccurate, any content unessential.

It is the figure of the flame that translates the baroque language, including its modality. In flame, fire 'metaphors' passion. One only has to read Racine's *Phèdre* to realize the extent to which this metaphor emerges from its own death, when it is literalized and made active again after having been abused into meaninglessness in an over-extended baroque poetry. Speaking, once again, with John Austin, the initiator of the analytical philosophy of speech acts, fire, the flame, is, precisely, the paradigmatic example of the speech act as performative: hovering between thing and event.[32] Indeed, in Bernini's work, the momentary arrest, the resolution, or the hesitation between narrative movement and arrested visuality, could not be more adequately meta-phored than by these generalized, incorporated flames. How does one translate a flame? Given the metonymic logic of narrativity, any attempt to do so consumes it. As soon as one attempts to trace its shape, one falls back onto cold marble, and the flame disappears. Ber-nini, a skilled pyrotechnical engineer, knew this. But this sculptor, who was also involved in theatre, knew as well that flames can be *mises en scène* in a hyperbolic poetics of theatre. Teresa, going up in flames, is – not coincidentally – both ecstatically mystical and hyper-theatrical, in pose, dress, and mimic.

Is it a coincidence, then, that the flame is also the image that Ben-jamin used to characterize the work of the critic as distinct from that of the philologist? In a beautiful passage, quoted by Hannah Arendt in her introduction to the *Illuminations* volume, and set in a characteristi-cally melancholic tone, Benjamin supplements Austin's emphasis on the occurrence in time of the performance of speech acts, by insisting on the present ('being alive') of the critic's activity. The image of the flame represents both the importance and the presentness of that work:

> While the former [the commentator] is left with wood and ashes as the sole objects of his analysis, the latter [the critic] is concerned only with the enigma of the flame itself: the enigma of being alive. Thus the critic inquires about the truth whose living flame goes on burning over the heavy logs of the past and the light ashes of life gone by. (5)

---

32 Speech-act theory, with its insistence on the meaning-producing effect of utterance, remains a compelling framework within which to rethink contemporary art. Austin's theory (1975) has been subject to (failed) attempts to 'normalize' it, as Shoshana Fel-man (1983) argues. For Felman, incidentally, seduction is the paradigmatic speech act. On this, see ch. 5.

The ongoing and – in Benjamin's terms – life-saving relevance of critical work demonstrates how preposterous history can be, as an alternative both to art history and to a medium-essentialist theory of art or
literature. But, thus, criticism is synonymous with translation. It is one
form that translation can take. Especially when juxtaposed to the passage quoted earlier from the 'Theses' ('every image of the past that is
not recognized by the present as one of its own concerns threatens to
disappear irretrievably'), criticism is here embodied by the modern art
work's 're-working' of Bernini's prosthetic supplementation of Teresa's
failing subjectivity. This is Bourgeois' critical intervention against
Lacan's subordination of the sculpture to a doxic and – perhaps not
coincidentally – phallogocentric commonplace. In other words, it is her
argument against 'bad translation.'

But if mysticism for most of us can be safely relegated to the baroque
age, the ecstasy that is its paroxysm cannot. The question here is how
mysticism can regain meaning from confrontation with our time. Transfiguration, including its collusion with death, is not unrelated to what
Georges Bataille called *alteration*. According to Rosalind Krauss'
account of it (1999a: 8), this concept simultaneously grasps two totally
different kinds of logic that can help to further clarify the paradox of
Benjamin's philosophy of translation.[33] The first is that of decomposition, the blurring of boundaries through matter's tendency to dissipate.
The second is what we today would call 'othering,' the logic of radical
distinction. The two meet where death decomposes the body and transforms the former subject into a soul, a ghost, a spirit; they meet, that is,
in the transfiguration that both 'melts' the body and elevates it to something else – here, in sanctity. This is why flames can so aptly replace
decomposition. But flames themselves are in movement – and in time.
The resolution of the hesitation between narrative movement and still
visuality could, therefore, not be better shaped than in this all-consum-
ing theatrical fire. By absorbing transfiguration, transformation, and
translation, this fire is an ideal example of what the concept of image
implies.

Teresa's transformation into a voluptuous fire consumed its subject
entirely, whereas Daphne's metamorphosis did not. Daphne was still
subject to a division between her inner body and her outer layer, so
that her transformation confined her to that fragmentation to which

---

33 Krauss uses Bataille's term to elaborate a concept for the analysis of surrealism
   beyond the formalist argument that considered surrealism not formally innovative.
   See Krauss (1999a: 7–8).

a subject remains condemned when exteriority and interiority are divided. Teresa, however, escapes fragmentation, division, but at the cost of her total absorption into the otherness of her desire. She relinquishes subjectivity.

The integration of Teresa's inside and outside fires can also be seen as programmatic of a sculpture that integrates 'within' the architecture that houses it. For the sculpture is integrated 'within' a chapel in which the viewer must stand in order to see it. This integration is precisely part of the challenge posed by Bernini's representation of a holy woman in the unified composition of a chapel. He pushes the inquiry into narrative sculpture as far as he can within a discussion of the unification of sculpture and architecture. But the unification remains disharmonious. Thresholds remain thresholds, mediations as well as separations. And, as if to foreground thresholds and the need for translation that they entail, on the marble fence that separates the viewer from the mystic lies, today, a small pile of sheets, with quotes, in five languages, from Teresa's writing. Here, the link, the pathway, the trajectory – the rough guide – is 'metaphoring,' as an activity of translating by means of the eye, thus transforming, producing images from one level of scale to the next and – if you're lucky – back again.

Virtuality

In her 1983 *Femme-Maison*, Bourgeois intervenes on this dual level. Bernini's integration of the interior fire with the exterior flames that were meant to affect the faithful viewers turns this playing with fire into a metaphorization of the second degree. Bourgeois responds to Bernini at the point where the latter's sculpture is integrated within the architecture her woman inhabits. More radically than Bernini, Bourgeois insists that woman and habitat are neither one nor separable. The metaphoric act – the multiple translation that supplements the untranslatability of the 'original' – happens at the threshold of these two orders of scale. But, instead of guiding you over the threshold as Bernini does, Bourgeois' *Femme-Maison* keeps its frontier closed; it is open to conquest, but not without a fight. Bernini's chapel invites the viewer into its interior. It is from this interior position that the latter is invited to *see*, from the outside – but, metaphorically, to enter, inside – the experience that consumes but also limits. The chapel thus creates a *fiction of presence.* This is how it activates what is today called 'virtuality' (Morse 1998).

Between Bernini and Bourgeois, the process of metaphoring – operated, so to speak, by the later artist – takes the form of quotation, Benjamin's ideal of writing. Bourgeois' 1983 *Femme-Maison* quotes Bernini insistently, in ways that her earlier works in this genre did not. This citational practice is not limited to a simple recycling of the figure of the fold. This piece also quotes the attempt to integrate scale and space, the entanglement of the body and its dissipation, the *volo* of the subject doing the abandoning. But, as a form of translation and criticism, Bourgeois' quotation is a response. In a project of integration pushed even further, Bourgeois translates the one level of integration – of body, skin, and dress – into the other – of sculpture and architecture.

Where Bernini pursued a double integration, Bourgeois translates Bernini's project so as to release from it what matters most: not meaning, information, a unification of diverse media and dimensions, but the tensions, thresholds, and modes of signification that both separate and integrate them. For Benjamin, this would be the 'purity' of language, *reine Sprache*. In the post-purity age that is ours, I propose, preposterously, to give Benjamin credit for having at least implied that this purity could be an origin-less, end-less multiplicity.[34] Instead of 'badly' translating it as 'pure,' this notion of the *reine Sprache* to be released by translation, is better translated as 'language as such.' For Bernini and Bourgeois, it brings us closer to a conception of the concept of image.

The image, according to Benjamin's use of it in the epigraph to this chapter, becomes, then, the 'image as such.' But this image is not 'purely' visual. On the condition that we interpret 'language' as semiosis and 'pure' as unconfined to a particular medium, Benjamin's formulation of the translator's task can help us to understand the full impact of this response, the concept of image it implies, and the preposterous history it facilitates. The issue is nothing like purity, but rather an openness owing to the liberation of language from the confinements imposed on it by conceptions of translation as 'true,' in the sense of 'faithful,' 'literal.' This is why Benjamin's theoretical images demonstrate what an image can be considered to be, and do. For such a formulation articulates how Bourgeois 'explains,' supplements, and further pursues Bernini's work – by transforming, by seeking to 'release in [her] own language that language [as such] which is under

---

34 Here I venture to take issue with Derrida as de Vries renders his thought (1992: 463).

the spell of another, to liberate the language imprisoned in a work in [her] re-creation of that work.'

To achieve this, Bourgeois speaks the language of the baroque fold and all it has implied since Deleuze's work on Leibniz. This is a visual language, but as we have already surmised from her work with titles, it is a language that resists and exceeds a 'pure' visuality that she does not accept. Bourgeois 'metaphors' that language by literalizing it. According to Deleuze's Leibniz, the fold represents infinitude by engaging the viewer's eye in a movement that has no vanishing point. The fold theorizes and embodies a relationship without a centre. In an important but enigmatic sentence, Deleuze describes the baroque response to the truth-claim of Renaissance perspective:

> Leibniz's idea about point of view as the secret of things, as focus, cryptography, or even as the determination of the indeterminate by means of ambiguous signs: *what* I am telling to you, *what* you are also thinking about, do you agree to tell *him* about *it*, provided that we know what to expect of *it*, about *her*, and that we also agree about who *he* is and who *she* is? As in a Baroque anamorphosis, only point of view provides us with answers and cases. (22)

Baroque point of view establishes a relationship between subject and object, then returns to the subject again, a subject that has been changed by that movement, and that goes back, in its new guise, to the object, only to return, yet again, to its ever-changing 'self.' Scale is one important element in this transformation.

Subjectivity and object become co-dependent, folded into each other, and this puts the subject at risk. The object whose surface is grazed by the subject of point of view may require a visual engagement that can only be called microscopic, in relation to which the subject loses his or her mastery over it. The mystic subject about to abandon her subjectivity is easier to understand in such a thought-fold. A baroque historical view of the Baroque, on the other hand, abandons the firm distinction between subject and object as well as the subordination of the former to the latter.[35]

It is within this double context of the subject/object relation in art as

---

35 Part of this paragraph is taken from my book on this subject (1999b). On the similarity and difference between baroque and romanticism in this respect, see Octavio Paz's suggestive remarks (1988: 53–4).

well as history that I would like to place Bourgeois' work on Bernini's folds, as a conceptualization of the image. These folds are Bernini's principal work on Teresa's mystical aporia. In the 1983 *Femme-Maison*, the fold envelops both the eye and the architecture in a single movement. Unlike Bernini's folds, Bourgeois' refuse any regularity. On one side, towards the bottom, the folds own up to their deception, transforming the infinitude of the surface, when the base of the sculpture turns out to be simple matter. Elsewhere the folds come forward, detaching themselves from the interior mass, betraying their banal secret of Teresa's transfiguration through reference to Daphne's detached bark.

Here and there the folds form knots, thus citing that other baroque figure (Allen 1983). By the same token, they transform the infinitude of texture into inextricable confusion, and liberation into imprisonment. The cone-shaped, sagging body refuses to be elevated into the flames of transcendence. Firmly fixed on its disk-shaped base, the body remains heavy and refuses to believe in miracles. But still, its sagging pose is as abandoning as Teresa's S-shape.

For, as far as her work suggests, Bourgeois is not deeply devout. Nor would her historical position encourage her to be so in the way Bernini's did him. In a post-Catholic culture, she is therefore able to point out that Bernini's devotion doesn't exclude the sensuality the nineteenth century has taught us to unlearn. The translation of one form into another, and the simultaneous translation of the senses, is all the more powerful, multiple, and active precisely because this housewoman is not transcendental. On top of the body, like a secular chapel, stands a skyscraper, the angular emblem of twentieth-century architecture. The gigantic body of folds together with the folds of flesh simultaneously render the mutual dependency and threat that this inextricable integration signifies. This sculpture absorbs architecture in a disillusioned but also joyful, if not ecstatic, endorsement of the materiality of body, house, and sculpture. It offers an *image* of that endorsement.

Sculpture, 'as such,' then, the site of translation, functions as Benjamin's 'pure language' or language as such, which it is the translator's task to release. The house confines women but also offers them the very mastery that imprisons and protects the body it weighs down so heavily. But to prevent us from kneeling down before tragedy in transcendental escapism, the folds, knotted around the neck of the building, are also, literally, just that: folds; fabulations or fabulous fictions of presence that flaunt their fictionality. The difference, here, is the *motif* of the image in its appearance as metaphor, according to Gérard Genette's analysis of metaphor as comparant, compared, motive, and modalizer (1972). Instead of being the common element, then, Bourgeois' metaphoring deploys difference, changing our perspective on metaphor in its wake.

Between figuration and conceptualism – yet another route for her metaphoring activity – Bourgeois winks at us, when, from a specific viewpoint, the surface full of secrets is no more than a dress, a habit, unlike Teresa's habit-turned-flames. Fabric that lovingly envelops, warms the house with its royal folds. Care, humour, comradeship, and the maternal excess that suffocates surround the architecture. The level at which this work absorbs and releases Bernini's search is the level of the most paradoxical integration, the fullest one – of the arts into the one art-as-such, pure, ideal, and non-existent, which Benjamin induces the translator to pursue.

Here, translation can no longer be traced as a one-directional passage from source to destination. It mediates in both directions, between architecture and sculpture, building and body, body and spirit, body and clothing, clothing and habitat ... And what it yields, produces, and makes visible, yet refrains from fixing, is an image.

Ecstatic Aesthetic

So where does this leave the relationship between philosophy and the historical study of the arts, if, let's say with Benjamin, we wish to be a 'critic' instead of a 'commentator'? The history part of this relationship, as I have argued on numerous occasions, can only be preposterous. Reconstructing the past 'as it really was' is impossible – if it is desirable at all. Bourgeois *translates* Bernini by transforming his work, so that after her, in the present that is ours, the baroque sculpture can never again be what it was before her intervention. That translation, I submit, is an image according to Benjamin: one that grasps the image from the past, which 'can be seized only as an image which flashes up at the instant when it can be recognized and is never to be seen again.' Thus, Bourgeois saved Bernini's *Ecstasy* for our time. How urgent this is! 'For every image of the past that is not recognized by the present as one of its own concerns threatens to disappear irretrievably.' An image in the full sense – literary metaphor or graphic visible 'text' – can only exist culturally if it is 'recognized by the present as one of its own concerns.' The concept of image, thus conceived, is an object for cultural analysis, of which art history can be a branch but not a master. So much for the history aspect of the image.

The art part of the image also has a tenacious bias to shed. That bias is, of course, the misconception of representation as imitation, as mirroring. It is best conceived of – translated into – *translation* according to Benjamin. But on one condition only. The philosophy part of its analysis must heed Richard Rorty's injunction to rigorously turn away from the representational obsession to be a mirror of nature (1979). It is this obsession with mirroring that underlies the idea of history as reconstruction, just as it underlies the logocentric conception of translation, and of art. Such an obsession can only remain locked up either in illusionary projection or tautological conflation, thus barring the liberation of language into 'language as such.'

Michael Baxandall's superb tautology provides an excellent example of this obsession, with mirroring as the only possibility for the historical reading of images: 'The specific interest of the visual arts is visual' (1991: 67). This line demonstrates what his chapter argues: that the language of artspeak can only be indirect, a crudely inadequate approximation. Baxandall characterizes the art historian's discourse as ostensive, oblique, and linear. This is as good as any formulation of the kind of translation that Benjamin sought to ban. Since the advent of poststructuralist critique, we know that the language that constitutes the matter of all texts cannot be described according to the Saussurian axiom, which suggested a one signifier/one signified equation. Language may unfold in linear fashion, but that unfolding in no way accounts for the multiple significations construed along the way that sometimes fall into dust before the end of the sentence. Meaning cannot be atomized; nor is it simply accumulative. Hence, putting one word after another may have the semblance of linearity, but producing meaning does not.

To bring Baxandall's analysis of art discourse to bear on my own analysis of the triple relationship between Benjamin, Bourgeois, and Bernini, the following self-reflective assessment is in order. I will happily admit that I haven't succeeded in adequately evoking the visual nature of the objects under discussion. Nor did I try. But nor have I managed to write ostensively, as Baxandall claims art history must. The photographs that 'illustrate' this argument – it is unnecessary to insist on the inadequacy of the notion of illustration! – do not provide enough visuality to enable my readers to see what I saw, when, some time ago, I took notes for my description of Bourgeois' sculpture, my translation of it. My language was indirect, in accordance with the nature of language. It was also linear. But, at the same time, it circled around, avoiding an imaginary centre. Perhaps surprisingly, perhaps not, Bourgeois' work itself presents the inadequacy not only of descriptive language, but of the very idea of a 'literal' translation between images and words. It does this not so much because language is linear but rather because, in the 'purity' released by the translation – its dissipation – visuality 'as such' is temporal. The time it takes to see Bourgeois' sculpture, and to see Bernini's sculpture through it, prevents any unification of objects. Bourgeois' sculpture cannot be unified in either of the specific 'languages' – the Catholic baroque or the post-modern baroque – by way of the mind of the person – here, me – who would subsequently wish to describe it. If words fail images, then it is not because images are beyond meaning, but because meaning is always-already dissipated by the translation that attempts to grasp it. Because, that is, meaning is itself ecstatic.

Teresa's flaming soul moves outward, not inward. Bourgeois' body that envelops the house, that secular chapel, insists on it, against Lacan. We know, since Freud, that man – neither man nor woman – is not master in his own house, any more than the *maîtresse de maison*, with a hundred heads or none, is. The theoretical metaphoring that *Femme-Maison* (1983) performs is to show – to perform, theatrically and socially, not to state – that the image is not master in its own house either: its meanings cannot be confined, ceaselessly escaping any attempts to grasp them. Even in his own textbook of translation, *The Interpretation of Dreams*, Freud explicitly cautions his readers against 'reading off the page,' that is, against translating symbols and figures. Even if he, too, sometimes falls for the allure of content. But this happened only later, after he had been pressured to adapt his work a bit more to the intellectual styles of the day. As Laplanche rightly remarked, up to the first edition of 1900, *The Interpretation of Dreams* contained no reading code for the 'bad' translation of dreams, no reductive, summarizing hermeneutic. The commentary on Irma's dream, so centrally important to the theory as a whole, is what Laplanche calls a 'de-translation' (1996: 7).

But do not misunderstand this reference to an anti-hermeneutic as a plea for refusing to interpret, a yielding to a vague metaphysical belief in the uniqueness of art; or, even, as a plea for a disabused endorsement of undecidability. Semantic indetermination is not the same as infinitude. Nor is endlessness. Even though each interpretive step takes place at a crossroads and therefore must leave behind other possibilities, each step is nevertheless concretely derived from a material aspect or element of the image. My reference to Freud's caution concerns something altogether different.

British psychoanalyst Christopher Bollas speaks of the *unthought known* (1987). I will have more to say about this text in relation to its theatricalization of the dream in the next few chapters. In the meantime, the concept seems suitable enough to deploy, simultaneously, in the face of works like *Ecstasy* and *Femme-Maison*, the act of interpretation on the one hand, and the refusal of that form of interpretation that is like 'bad' translation on the other; a precise equation that admits to no more than the stingy exchange of one signifier for another. The concept of the *unthought known* refers to what the senses sense, of which one has a sense but which rational thought can only encircle, not translate into a singular meaning. Such translation would be its death, for the work would cease to operate on the multiplicity of levels – rational and affective, theoretical and visual – that are required for it to continue to be recognized by the present 'as one of its own concerns' lest it 'threaten[s] to disappear irretrievably.' Translation is best understood, then, as metaphoring: the dynamic act of *doing* – of forming – metaphor on the basis of a motive, defined not as similarity or as common ground between comparant and compared, but as difference.

Bourgeois' house-chapel offers the kind of metaphoring that preserves the unthought known between rational interpretation and strong, sitable, sightable, and citable affectivity, that has content but not fixed content; a house in which, indeed, the ego is not master. In the end, then, following the preceding remarks on the image as translation, I submit that Freud's enigmatic penultimate sentence of the third of his *New Introductory Lectures*, 'Wo Es war soll Ich werden,' is best left untranslated (XXII: 80). Even Lacan, notoriously hostile to reductive translation but unable to resist trying it, came up with a number of 'good' alternatives to the 'bad' French translation, which reduces it to a one-sided moral imperative: 'le Moi doit déloger le Ça.'[36] Lacan tried his hand – and failed; his translations, each on their own account, were 'bad.' Laplanche's insistence that psychoanalysis, *qua* analysis or

36 For an excellent critical commentary, including Lacan's alternative translations, see Bowie (1987: 122–3).

unbinding, opposes translation is in line with Benjamin's view of translation. Neither of them mentions – but perhaps Bourgeois implies it – that there is, in fact, a philosophical reason for this lack of mastery.

Should it surprise us that, during the travel of the concept of image between philosophy and the historical interpretation of texts and art works, we reach a point where image teaches us about analysis, teaches us about that activity that we used to conceive of as mastery of images? It shouldn't. For that role reversal is characteristic of cultural analysis as a whole. But then, since the concept travels and won't stop for more than a night or two, we needn't worry that it will master us or our academic work – for the lesson is provisional and the teacher is friendly.

Beyond the philosophy of language, this travel reaches into the realm of ethics. For a question remains, if Bourgeois' *Femme-Maison* is to be meaningfully brought to bear on Bernini's *Ecstasy*: what does it mean that the central meaning of Teresa's mystical experience has been set aside by the later artist? In other words, that ec-stasy has been made ec-static? My phrasing announces the answer, but let me spell it out anyway. Translation – hence, also, image-as-translation – has a philosophical force to it, all the more so since it is an event suitable for a particular occasion. In his essay on the problem of translation in philosophy, Lawrence Venuti (1996: 30) insists, like Benjamin, that 'faithful' translation, in the smooth sense of catering to the target audience, is 'bad.' For it is an appropriation that obscures the 'remainder,' the Benjaminian 'untranslatable'; the remainder, the untranslatable, or – between philosophy and visuality – perhaps, the 'unthought known' that we forget to know.[37]

A translation, in Venuti's eyes, 'should not be seen as good, unless it signifies the linguistic and cultural difference of that text for domestic constituencies.' A translation must not be invisible.[38] He argues that the ethical value of this difference resides in alerting the reader to a process of domestication that has taken place in the translating, on its behalf, but also at the source text's expense. Hence, the ethics of trans-

---

37 Venuti speaks of 'domestic,' whereas I prefer the term 'target' for the audience of the translation. The term 'remainder,' which refers to all that gets lost in translation, is taken by Venuti from Lecercle (1990).
38 Venuti's argument can be claimed to shed ethical light on that other problem of translation where the seams are better left visible: realism.

lation consists in preventing that process from 'slipping into a whole-sale assimilation to dominant domestic values.' This is how his overt subject matter – specifically philosophical translation – shifts. He continues:

> The best philosophical translating is itself philosophical, in forming a concept of the foreign text based on an assessment of the domestic scene. But the concept ought to be defamiliarizing, not based on a ratification of that scene. (1996: 30)[39]

This view would not wish Teresa's ecstasy, the key element of the source text, to become invisible in the new work. But the point that no such ecstasy would be acceptable – aesthetically as well as socially, or perhaps even ethically – in the target world, for today, that is, must also remain visible. For, nor should her ecstasy become so idiosyncratic that an unwarranted 'othering' of a past religiosity would result. The 'conceptually dense text' – Venuti's term for philosophical texts under translation – must be made intelligible, yet remain, in its foreignness, informative as well as provocative, that is, *performative*. Clearly, Benjamin would agree with this injunction, to both dissipate and release the text's otherness but not to keep it an outsider to the target culture. For the latter must be able to estrange itself from its own assumptions, so that the automatic othering of what comes at it from its outside can be replaced by a negotiation.

Instead of either *erasing* or *othering* ecstasy, Bourgeois' sculpture *updates* it, to save its relevance under the banner of pre-posteriority. The desire of the subject, in her abandonment of subjectivity, to experience decentring may have been sacrificed in the negotiation. But instead of the ongoing quest to understand ecstasy in terms of the mystical postulate concerning *volo* (I desire), the decanting that results, and that Bernini has so lovingly supplemented with his own narratorial subjectivity, is very much present in the modern work. Teresa's first-person text, after thematizing her loss of self, needed a prosthetic 'third-person' to be visually told. In Bourgeois' version, her dissipation may appear less desirable. But then, who ever said mystic ecstasy, desired as it may have been by its historical practitioners, is in itself desirable?

---

39 For more elaboration of this point, see also Venuti (1994, 1995).

Perhaps giving up the self, as mystics did in early modernity – and housewives did under the influence of romantic love, and surrealists under the influence of psychoanalysis, drugs, and philosophy – provided a great experience of ec-stasy in *their* respective times. The loss of self, as has been argued in different contexts, has great benefits. Provided, that is, that the subject can distinguish between ego and consciousness, so that 'ego-ism,' or self-centred selfishness, yields to awareness of the subject's place in culture: performing – relationally.[40]

At the end of the day – and at the end of this inquiry – the point of the aesthetic issue is aesthetic again. But the aesthetic is no longer most characteristically embodied by a lone man in black at the sea.[41] Rather, what we have here is a woman abandoning her subjectivity and her discourse, for better or for worse, but, at the same time, *housing* whoever wishes to be touched. She houses us, not in the hastily translated mode fantasized by Lacan, but in the untranslatable, multiple senses that this word harbours, and for whose *remainder* we can read the sculptures. Unlike Kant's rational man, or Friedrich's monk, the subject thus housed refrains from overcoming the unhinging experience of awe. The aesthetic thrill is not one of a barely sustained threat to one's subjectivity.

As a result of the metaphoring, we can see how the subject, if it survives the flames, remains ec-static. This is how Bourgeois, through Bernini, through Teresa, *metaphors*, performs, cultural translation. She deploys her visual language as a translation that releases 'language as such,' and she conceptualizes such 'language' as wilfully in the margin – as ec-static – in an act of endorsing the limitations of rationality in favour of greater inclusion. It may include the remainder, the untranslatable, or – between philosophy and visuality – perhaps, the 'unthought known' that we forget to know; from that sideways position, sited on the edge, perhaps more is in store. And it may not. Bourgeois doesn't say. Bernini can't know. Teresa can't tell. We'll see.[42]

40 Loss of self can be beneficial, precisely in terms of overcoming cultural prejudice. Loss of self, abandonment – in other words, ec-stasy – becomes a tool for heteropathic identification. See Bersani (1989) and van Alphen (1992) on loss of self, and Silverman (1996) on heteropathic identification.

41 As the Kantian example of the sublime, Caspar David Friedrich's painting. Spivak (1999, ch. 1) offers an unsettling account of the restrictions pertaining to Kantian sublimity. Reasoning from art to morality, she thus gives a welcome counterpart to the more usual argument (Crowther 1989). See my final chapter.

42 This chapter is a spin-off from a portion of my book on Louise Bourgeois (2001a).

3

Mise-en-scène

mise-en-scène
- *the arrangement of actors, props, and scenery on a stage in a theatrical production*
- *the environment or setting in which something takes place*

I often find that although I am working on an idea without knowing
exactly what it is I think, I am engaged in thinking an idea struggling to
have me think it.

Christopher Bollas (1987: 10)

Setting the Stage

Let's see, then. This chapter is about just that kind of seeing, visual and
imaginative – as food for thought. The kind of thought-seeing that the
concept of image and its bond with metaphor have allowed me to
articulate. I see it as a cultural practice of art beyond what traditional
art history and philosophy can recognize. Far from discussing ideas in
language, Bernini's Teresa and Bourgeois' winking house-woman put
ideas out for us to see, and to connect with, as our own 'unthought
known.' Between private dream and public scene, the image happens.
Known yet outside our thought, the image, in whatever medium or
shape, launches a travel in the area between subject and collective,
which, for want of a better word, we call 'culture.'

The theatricality of Bernini and Bourgeois is part of that intellectual-
affective yield. It is also a domain where narrativity and visuality
are not in opposition. In this chapter, I propose to continue taking

theatricality extremely seriously – as a 'form,' 'medium,' or 'practice' (none of these words is adequate) in which the object of cultural analysis performs a meeting between (aesthetic) art(ifice) and (social) reality. The travelling concept here, mobilized metaphorically in the travel between all these false polarities, is the one that summarizes what theatricality most essentially is: *mise-en-scène.*

Though metaphorical, imaginative, and, indeed, 'imaging,' this concept, as my book advocates, is to be taken very, very seriously methodologically. Let's suppose, for a moment, that *mise-en-scène* is this: the materialization of a text – word and score – in a form accessible for public, collective reception; a mediation between a play and the multiple public, each individual in it; an artistic organization of the space in which the play is set; an arranging of a limited and delimited section of real time and space. As a result of all this arranging, a differently delimited section of fictional time and space can accommodate the fictional activities of the actors, performing their roles to build a plot.

The subject of this activity – the (stage) director – makes a work of art. Her tools: time, space, light. Her activities: the projection of dramatic and musical writing into a particular *chronotopos*; co-ordination; the highlighting of some meanings over others; a keying of text and score in between performers and public. Sometimes 'totalizing'; always, to use a term I prefer, *mise-en-pièce(s)*. I am just plucking this from dictionaries of theatre terms.[1] Or, to speak with Hans-Thiess Lehmann, a mediation from *logos* to landscape.[2] The activity of *mise-en-scène* makes for a revolutionary intervention, turning words leading to the formation of abstract meanings that are caught in a centripetal cultural tragedy, into a spectacle receptive to the turmoil of liberated meanings, variously attached to concrete, visible, and audible phenomena and signs. What can the point of a concept like *mise-en-scène* be for cultural analysis?

Borrowed from theatre, *mise-en-scène* indicates the overall artistic activity whose results will shelter and foster the performance, which, by definition, is unique. But, as we saw in the previous chapter and as I will argue at length in chapter 5, if performance is to be taken seriously, it is best considered in its intertwinement with performativity. The

---

1 Mostly from Pavis (1998: 361–8).
2 Lehmann (1997a). I prefer to leave undecided – indeed, insist on the undecidability of – the distinction between phenomenology and semiotics implied in this formulation, which is mine, not Lehmann's.

choice of *mise-en-scène* as a concept worth probing here is not random. In its mobility and in the change over time that it includes, *mise-en-scène* fits nicely as a metaphor for travel.

Indeed, it is easy to grasp how it travels. By foregrounding it, I continue the cheerful and disabused disbelief in 'true,' 'faithful,' or 'adequate' translation, or in 'literal' knowledge, set forth in the previous chapter. Looking back to the *Femme-Maison*, the case I was able to make for this merrily critical revision of Bernini's ecstatic woman depended on the centrality of *mise-en-scène* in both works. Already there, performance and representation come together in performativity. The ecstatically busy woman is the object of representation for Bernini. This representation can only work thanks to the performativity that characterizes it. At the same time, that performativity undermines the possibility of representation. The sculptor's earnest attempt to 'render' Teresa's ecstasy notwithstanding, the woman and her painful pleasure lie exposed, laid bare, fixed for eternity before the viewers, who can only enact their role of responsive theatre-goers. The chapel won't work otherwise. As the represented members of the donor family, keenly looking at Teresa from their benches, emblematically prescribe, the chapel is a theatre, *sensu stricto*. What happens on centre-stage is barely imaginable in a chapel, although that may be exactly where the onlookers are. They look, and imagine the ecstasy.

It is thus – through heteropathic identification, or identification outside oneself – that the mystic is empowered to 'have' the mystic experience. This enactment by the audience, this performance in performativity, is the only way the art work can actually not only be but also *do*, work. In this sense, art *is* theatre, or it is not. As a properly passive figure *mise-en-scène*, Teresa partakes of an arrangement of space that Bernini organized, to bring her score – her writing – to artistic life, in the present of viewing. This presentness was foregrounded by the *Femme-Maison*, which 'imaged,' in the sense that it 'metaphored,' Bernini's effort into the present, together with the subjectivity now no longer condemned to passivity.

Thus, as both case studies in this section will propose, rather than standing for a disingenuous, inauthentic subjectivity that parades as authentic, theatricality is the subject's production, its *staging*. In this sense the concept of *mise-en-scène* sets the stage for the performance of performativity, and, in turn, for the staging of subjectivity. Such stagings will be foregrounded in an experimental exhibition in chapter 4, where the concept travels from theory to practice, just as in the present chapter it travels from practice to theory. Then, in chapter 5, the travel from theory to practice and back to theory again will become a bit of a roller-coaster ride. For, far from being a worldly activity that adds a margin of pleasure to 'serious' life, the theatricality that *mise-en-scène* entails is perhaps the most profound manifestation of the cultural life that exists between private and public, or between individual and collective subjectivity. At least, this is what I attempt to argue through the interdisciplinary deployment of this working concept. A working concept is thus set to work in – so as to set the stage for – the academic endeavour that this book is – roughly – trying to guide.

Without trying to define *mise-en-scène*, I start from the premise that it is what the people practising it make of it. Thus, the elements mentioned above suffice to circumscribe it, and to fill it with practical and semiotic meaning. *Mise-en-scène* is a working concept – a concept to work with and a concept that works – neither fixed and theorized nor slippery as a word, according to how I distinguished words from concepts in chapter 1. My purpose is to look at how such a working concept can serve a *cultural* analysis by making more specific, more material, more practical sense of objects in their social life. The resulting insights mediate between cultural practice, the specific object of cultural analysis, and a cultural theory that enables students to make tentative generalizations. They allow the generalizations to be made, importantly, without impoverishing the cultural reality on which they are based.

This methodological need to preserve the rich complexity of an object seen as dynamic practice in a gesture of generalizing reflects, is an image of, the subject that recurs throughout these case studies. For, at the centre or core of the discussion is, once again, the status, position, and self-realization of the subject.

Staging Death

In this case study, flames continue to occupy centre stage. At the end of Wagner's *Götterdämmerung*, *mise-en-scène* in 1999 by Pierre Audi in Amsterdam's Muziektheater, Brünnhilde's immolation was staged, or signified, by means of an enormous piece of deep red fabric that was kept in motion throughout the scene, waving as if in the wind. This, supposedly, meant 'flames,' in a postmodern aesthetic that wavered between exuberance and non-realistic representation. The colour was so bright and so deep and the motion so turbulent that the meaning

3.1 Brünnhilde's immolation, from Wagner's *Götterdämmerung*, as staged by Pierre Audi in Amsterdam's Muziektheater in 1999

/flames/ was overtaken by the sheer sense of visual captivation, perhaps best called 'beauty.' This was more than just a theatrical ploy to suggest a meaning – fire – without resorting to real flames, as, incidentally, had been done earlier in the same performance cycle. Clearly, it was not a *pis-aller*, a solution to an otherwise insurmountable technical problem, but a positive choice for staging the spectacular final scene spectacularly, an artistic contribution to a collectively made masterpiece (fig. 3.1).

In other words, the waving fabric was more spectacular than real fire could ever have been. It was deployed, literally, to turn an event into a spectacle. In its spectacular form, it was a *displacement* of affect from the stage to the audience. Semiotically, the fabric did this by transforming flames, an emblematic index, into, first, iconic signification (fabric plus movement 'look[ed] like' flames),[3] then, into another level of indexicality, in which the sign acquires a visual power that displaces the entire scene from representation to presentation, from story to aesthetic.[4] At this point, the fabula recedes into sheer pre-text, a mere prop, and *mise-en-scène* takes over.[5]

It is as if Brünnhilde's diegetic death is a trifle, just another opportunity to do something different, dream-like, to the spectator's senses; to turn, in fact, story-telling into a matter of affect. Through this affect Brünnhilde does not die – in the fiction; instead, she dies, literally, *on us*. The figure on stage performs an affect that *touches* the audience, giving them death.[6] Rather than denoting flames, the waving fabric connotes a new sense of 'total art,' obeying Wagner's ideal if not his particular concretization, to the extent that visual and auditive pleasures merge so radically that one stops differentiating between the senses. This is not about Brünnhilde's death; it is about the spectator's engagement with the scene; a challenge to the fourth wall, to the limit between two worlds. But, unlike what the traditional terminology of the fourth wall suggests, the world encroaching upon the spectator's space is not the fictional one of the Germanic gods. It is the world of visuality itself. The stage becomes the site of a visual transgression upon the space normally reserved for fiction and music.[7]

Totally immersed in this wondrous synaesthetic experience, it was only later that I realized that the challenge had been even more radical than that. Vision, based on a certain distance between eye and object, is contaminated by, or emulates, the bodily proximity of music, that sense of hearing based on the actual penetration of sound into the ear of the listener. Vision becomes 'like' hearing in this precise sense. The mediating element between the two senses is the tactile attraction of

3 In a Peircean semiotic view, smoke is a classical example of the category of signs called 'index.' For a concise fragment from Peirce's extensive writings, in which the three major categories of icon, index, and symbol are defined, see Peirce (1984).
4 For the precise meaning of aesthetics as binding the senses, see Schaeffer (1997).
5 For the term 'fabula' and all other narratological terms occurring in this book, I must refer to my introductory book on the subject (1997b).
6 See Derrida (1999) for the implications of the French phrase *donner la mort*.
7 In spite of opera's similarity to theatre, this is not an obvious result, for opera's investment in the 'willing suspension of disbelief' is diverted to music. Consider, for a disenchanting example in the same performance cycle, the closing scene of *Siegfried*, in which an overweight Siegfried rolls on top of Sieglinde, a scene that would have been better left in the dark.

the waving, shining fabric, whose depth of colour emanates a softness to the touch that is as sexy as a smooth skin. The acoustic element in opera is emphatically an integral element of this effect. For this reason, the concept of *mise-en-scène* as deployed in this chapter is specified as 'operatic,' or synaesthetic. This is not to be taken literally, as an emphasis on sound, although in several of the works discussed, sound is tremendously important. Sometimes, however, a work's synaesthetic quality resides precisely in its deployment of the most silent of media: written words. Taking 'operatic' from Brünnhilde's death here and bringing it to bear elsewhere, moving from metaphoring to tentative generalization through the concept of *mise-en-scène*, the latter concept becomes enriched by a synaesthesia that already inheres in it, but that is now more strongly foregrounded. The qualifier 'operatic,' indeed, serves as a truly Derridean supplement.

Audi's inventive *mise-en-scène*, emphatically contemporary yet, in this bodily sense, profoundly baroque, ties in with the work I have been doing on contemporary responses to visual art from the baroque, of which the previous chapter gave a sense. The preposterous relationship between Bourgeois and Bernini stands for that problematic. In an earlier study, I foregrounded baroque painting, using Caravaggio as my emblematic artist. Here, the red fabric waving on stage and so intensely 'colouring' my perception of the music and the voice, affected me with the same sense of absorption as Caravaggio's paintings, because of the mobile interaction between the infinitely small and the endlessly large, which is characteristic of the fold according to Deleuze's Leibniz. Contemporary visual art often leans on baroque art in this respect, offering a supplement to it, a critical commentary.

This recycling of baroque visual thought in Audi's staging can be made to resonate with a deployment of *mise-en-scène* in installation art. Consider, for example, Beverly Semmes' *Red Dress* (1992), a piece of installation art that is as much indebted to baroque painting and its exuberant deployment of colour as it is to baroque sculpture and its engaging folds (fig. 3.2). Spilling out of a femininity-foregrounding dress that is suspended on a coat hanger, then carefully and beautifully spreading out over the gallery floor so as to become an installation, this work is a sheer-endless display of the same kind of soft, shiny red fabric as surrounded Brünnhilde when she sang and died. Here, too, the beauty-as-affect, or affect-as-beauty, is produced by a shift in meaning production between the poles of aesthetics and sex. The dress, though feminine, is not beautiful; nor does it foreground the

3.2 Beverly Semmes, *Red Dress*, 1992, velvet, wood, and metal

imaginary wearer's beauty. For, more specifically, its meaning is not so much femininity as femininity-in-training. Its shape – the tiny collar with its rounded corners, the short sleeves – has the bourgeois girl's upbringing in an anti-sexy-yet-girlish ideology written all over it. From the dress on the hanger to the rich fabric on the floor that spills directly out of the dress, the displacement from bourgeois prettiness to imaginary richness and beauty operates on the same double shift of semiotic modes as Brünnhilde's satin death.[8]

Here, too, the transformation of representation encroaches upon the space of the viewer, transforming the visual discourse from third-person story into first-/second-person interaction. The 'third-person' story of a girl growing into her sexuality, both in continuity with and resistance to her upbringing and training as 'woman,' becomes both an invitation and a resistance. In the installation in which I saw this dress-

8 This work is beautifully reproduced and discussed, within the concern with beauty that was the theme of the exhibition, in Benezra and Viso (1999: 73).

work, the Hirshhorn show *Regarding Beauty*, in Washington, DC, in 1999 (and this installation-specificity is why this work was, precisely, a *mise-en-scène*), this is literally true. The dress-work was displayed in a transitional space located between one larger room and another, and the excessive 'skirt' came so close to the area where the viewer walked that one tended to worry about stepping on it. This slight anxiety and its material trigger matter in ways that together embody the work's aesthetic program. 'Beauty,' the theme of the Washington show, was shown to be problematic through the intertwinement of the three ways in which walking on the dress – and thus transgressing the taboo posed by 'beauty' – would have been offensive yet imaginarily inevitable.

In the first place, walking on the dress would have been like walking on the imaginary girl, whose clumsy, adolescent, or debutante body was suggested by the dull, prim-and-proper shape of the top part of the dress, by the wearable section of the installation. It would have been like using her as a doormat, literally. The same doormat position, the installation implied, which this kind of dress has in store for its wearers.

Secondly, walking on the fabric would have endangered its beauty. And this is prohibited, as the 'do-not-touch-the-work-of-art' signs in galleries remind us. By the same token, this taboo on endangering beauty stands for the taboo on touching 'pretty girls,' in a culture which, to various degrees, denies girls' self-determination by the violent appropriations of their bodies by their legal guardians. Thus, the very expanse of the fabric stands guard over the girl's virginity. This sexualized aesthetic taboo is tantalizingly at odds with the desire to touch that this baroque aesthetics carries on its sleeve.

Thirdly, walking on the fabric would have felt like a contamination. Contamination is the strong, material element of a literalized sense-binding aesthetic, or synaesthetic. The point, then, would be that this contamination, which also emanates its appeal due to the richness of the fabric, involves the viewer retrospectively in the history of the imaginary girl wearing the dress. The point of contamination is that touch is not a singular event. Leaving traces in both bodies, touch, in this 'contaminative' view, refuses to go away. Thus this work of Semmes invokes a sense of danger, of risk; the risk that theatre, according to the Aristotelian-Freudian conception of catharsis, does not leave the viewer unaltered. The excess of the fabric and the difficulty of avoiding walking on it thus make a statement. They speak as a *theoreti-*

cal object, further enhancing the aspect of *mise-en-scène* that turns the latter into a key, or key-concept, from which to theorize cultural practice.

The transition between dress and skirt, between the clumsy debutante, overdressed in her mother's and milieu's taste, and her adult, chosen, but still pre-programed sexuality, is marked, in the *mise-en-scène*, by a barely noticeable indexical sign that spills over into symbolic and iconic meaning production. Where the fabric reaches the floor, the line swirls to the right (from the viewer's perspective), in a literalized distortion of 'straight' shape. Moreover, the fabric, just before extending into excess, also narrows there. Like a traditional Chinese woman with bound feet, the girl, before going out into her own life, is grabbed by feet that preclude walking comfortably.[9] High heels, that Western version of bound feet, are close at hand for the iconic imagination. And finally, if the body, here, splits into two – girl and woman, clumsy and exuberant, restrained and sexual – that distortion is also the transition where the girl's feet become the new woman's neck. The narrowing of the fabric's width, then, at the moment of freeing the girl, grabs the woman by the neck, scarring because scaring her with the history of her previous self as the fabric's strangulation.

Here, another death of the subject is being staged. And through Semmes' installation, the traditional association of red – with passion, blood, fire, and (violent) death (tragically updated by the actuality of death through blood-diseases such as AIDS) – casts a gendered shadow over the beauty of Brünnhilde's closing aria.

For their complex meaning production, both Brünnhilde's red death and Semmes' girl-woman rely on the history of aesthetics at one of its key moments, the one to which this aesthetic appeals and replies: baroque aesthetics. Caravaggio's *John the Baptist*, on which I wrote extensively in *Quoting Caravaggio*, not coincidentally also immerses a body within a red fabric, thus drawing in the viewer eager to touch the body. The latter work, for me, resonates with both the overlayering of girlhood onto womanhood, in Semmes' installation, and the synaesthetic of Audi's staging, which updated Wagner's in a profound engagement with both *it* and the present. Hence, an appeal to a sensuous cultural memory was part of the effect of both Audi's and Semmes' productions.[10]

9 On bound feet, see Kristeva (1986).
10 Cultural memory is an important, recently developed concept in cultural analysis. See Bal, Crewe, and Spitzer (eds.), 1999.

This similarity of effect, properly called *subjective* – it affects, indeed changes, the viewer's subjectivity – raises relevant questions for a cultural analysis interested in understanding the dynamic between collective and individual subjectivity. As I attempt to unfold *mise-en-scène* as a concept for such an analysis, the similarity of effect between Audi, Semmes, and Caravaggio leaves me with the question of what this strong effect has to do with the *staging* of subjectivity. The mediating term, I wish to submit here, is 'dream.'

Dreaming Subjectivity

In spite of everything that has been thought out between 1900 and 2000, it is still Freud's *Traumdeutung* that makes staging subjectivity – as a mediation between private/public and individual/collective – plausible. Not because psychoanalysis must remain the uniquely privileged theory of subjectivity, but because it is the domain of dreams that I am attracted to when I think about what *mise-en-scène* does to subjectivity. To put it another way: I am interested in the way *mise-en-scène*, as artistic practice, can be brought into more than just a metaphorical connection with what Jean Laplanche and Jean-Baptiste Pontalis take as their starting point for a revisionist inquiry into fantasy: the imaginary self-production as 'private theatre.'[11] As Samuel Weber, among others, has argued, among the different mechanisms of censorship in the dream, the important but difficult concept of 'considerations of representability' (*Rücksicht auf Darstellbarkeit*) is both a visualizing device and a tool for making the resulting image 'public,' that is, readable.[12]

Having started with a public event, an opera performance, and moving on here to another piece of installation art, I aim, therefore, to challenge the element 'private' in Laplanche and Pontalis' phrase.[13]

---

11 The authors refer to Freud and Breuer's study of Anna O. in their seminal article, reworked and republished, on fantasy (1985: 11).

12 The title of Weber's book invokes these two aspects in the ambiguity of the noun 'legend,' indicating not only the legendary status of Freud but also the mythical, hence public, and historical status of dreams on the one hand, and the legend's readability – the legend as directions for decoding – on the other.

13 Opera performance is central to the deployment of the concept of *mise-en-scène* in cultural analysis because of the two features of synaesthetics and temporal transience; installation art as conceived here foregrounds the two through a slow-down. Installation, while still transient, is temporally more extended; it is up to the viewer, not

My goal is to probe the potential of the concept of *mise-en-scène* as a tool for a kind of cultural analysis that can overcome the still-open gap between social and psychoanalytical criticism, and between public and private concerns. To this effect, and with Brünnhilde's public death in mind, I would like to look at what dreams, as they transform words into images, can tell us about staging, and what staging can tell us about dreams.

Here is the case. One day, a woman in her mid-thirties, a busy professional, married with two children, had a dream. Neither she nor anyone else appeared in it. The dream was simply a landscape: a beach illuminated by a blistering sun. The colours of the sand, the blue sky, and the turquoise-blue sea were intense compared with the colour of the real North Sea beach where she normally went, but otherwise, nothing indicated this was a different beach. There was a flag, bright green, with nuances of dark turquoise, and of yellow, orange, and perhaps red; each colour occupied its own field in the horizontally divided flag. Waving majestically in the breeze, the flag came closer, slowly taking over the field of vision. It kept moving.

This was the second dream of the woman in a few days' time in which colour intensity and sand played the leading roles. In her earlier one, she had dreamt of dunes, also in an intense sandy colour, bordered with waving, greyish-green dune grass. There, the sand had suddenly started to move, lifted by the wind, coming closer to the picture plane before settling into the slow-down movement typical of dreams. At that point the dreamer realized the sand would engulf her, but it was not at all frightening. It was vaguely exciting, and she was holding her breath – although again, she didn't appear in the dream.

In both dreams, the dreamer herself was not a character. The stage was empty of human presence.[14] Nor was she the director. In both, upon waking, she sensed that the dream was meant for her, and that it was good. The first dream had left her breathless and stimulated; the second had made her feel happy, and slightly anxious.

---

the work, to decide about the duration of the contact between work and receiver. In this context, music itself is not taken into consideration. For more on the relationship between music in opera and the construction of subjectivity, see Michael P. Steinberg's book on this subject, to which the present analysis is complementary (forthcoming).

14 This de-personalized stage provides one legend, among several, which I refer to as 'moving stains,' in my discussion of James Coleman's *Photograph*. See ch. 5.

After the first dream, she quickly realized it was giving her advice. The relevant day-rest (*Tagesreste*) was not hard to find. She was teaching a class at the time, a group of extremely bright and enthusiastic students with whom she had great interaction, as if they were real, intimate friends. The session she was preparing when she had the dream concerned an introduction to psychoanalysis as literary theory. The class had been very enthusiastic up to that point, but this week's topic had annoyed the two women preparing a presentation for it. They harboured the usual resistance to psychoanalysis. The dream, empty of subjects, was cautioning her to take the students' resistance seriously. The sand, she felt, was a danger, but one she could cope with, a coping that would enrich her. The intensity of the sand and the colours of the grass stood for the gratifyingly high quality of the course, and motivated her to be careful to maintain the high level. The dream was the empty stage of the as-yet empty time slot of the class, and was welcoming, not rejecting, her.

The second dream occurred a day after an exceptionally painful meeting between faculty and students, in which the teacher had been accused by a colleague of being a traitor for agreeing with the students' protest on some political issue. During the meeting, she had sat facing a row of students, one of whom was wearing a white shirt with vividly coloured stripes. The student had been looking at her with concern and sympathy. It didn't take the dreamer long – although it scared the wits out of her – to realize that the colour fields of the flag corresponded with those of the young man's shirt. In coming forward, the colours, as a metonym for the man, meant literally that he was coming on to her, although his 'real' behaviour indicated nothing of the sort. More frightening still, the happy tones of the dream indicated to her that she welcomed his advances. The dream revealed something. It used synaesthetic sense impressions *as well as linguistic wordplay* to perform its revelation.[15]

These dreams are here theoretical objects through which to connect *mise-en-scène* with psychoanalysis. I will discuss discipline, as the science of the 'unthought known,' later in this chapter as a field that supplies the image of *mise-en-scène* with a *raison d'être* beyond theatre alone. But let me emphasize right away, with reference to the two

---

15 I am emphasizing, of course, the elements that recur in Freud's *Interpretation of Dreams*. In that book, incidentally, the actual analyses of dreams begin with a *mise-en-scène*. Freud is careful to *locate* his day-rests.

dreams here, that this extension does not imply an invasion of the disciplinary study of theatre, opera, and other scenically grounded cultural expressions by psychoanalytically based interpretations. Nor does it entail a theoretical imposition on artistic practices. Instead, the travel here goes in the opposite direction. I am arguing for a travel of the concept of *mise-en-scène* from practice to theory, or from artistic practice to academic analysis. I am maintaining, therefore, that *mise-en-scène*, usually conceived of as a theatrical issue of dramaturgy and performance production, can be taken as a *theoretical concept*, as a tool, for the semiotic analysis of cultural practices outside of theatre and opera. As a concept, *mise-en-scène* provides an *internal* connection between narrative, still, visual imagery, and psychoanalysis, the latter of which is seen here as the theory *par excellence* of the formation of subjectivity but in need of a cultural basis beyond the individual. I will suggest that it can be useful – indeed, revealing – to speak of an *aesthetic of mise-en-scène* in enabling us to understand specific effects in a great variety of semiotic practices, ranging from everyday life to high art.

What makes *mise-en-scène* so specific that it becomes useful in such a role, as concept travelling between practice and theory? The two dreams of our young woman help spell this out. They were stages set for the semiotic benefit of the dreamer. Their revealing effect – in both cases, actually of great help in the two decisions the dreamer subsequently made – turned them into signifying events. More specifically, the meanings they were able to produce depended on a mapping of relationships that were different from the ones implied in the traditional communication model, where a sender conveys meaning to a receiver, who is presumably passive. In these dreams, something altogether different happens. While, as a dreamer, the woman was absent *on* the scene, it was *her* subjectivity that was staged *in* – and as a result, changed *by* – the dreams. This effect was produced by a semiotic that can only be analysed in terms of *mise-en-scène*. What can this mean? How, specifically, can the notion of *mise-en-scène* be a helpful analytical tool in a practice of cultural analysis that focuses on the intellectual understanding of meaning production by aesthetic means?

Neither of the dreams seemed particularly spectacular at first, except for their *affect of spectacular intensity;* nor did they harbour a clear narrativity. No events took place, no characters appeared. And – to return from dream to opera – although in Audi's oversized red fabric Brünnhilde was both present and singing her last aria, I would be willing to consider that, in that case, the character as such – the event of her death – had also receded offstage before drowning in satin flames.

But, unlike in Audi's rendering of Wagner's opera, our dreamer was not the director; she was only the spectator. There was no plot, at least not one recognizable as such, because it was not culturally encoded according to one of Barthes' codes, for example, the 'proairetic' code in *S/Z*. This idiosyncratic term refers to acquired cultural models within which spectators, readers, or listeners integrate details so as to form coherent plot sequences, such as 'falling in love,' 'growing up,' 'hold-up,' or 'train robbery.'[16]

Narrativity junkies such as myself might overlook the profound narrativity of these two dreams and consider the spectacle itself only a stage set, a prelude to the narrative to come. Only colours and sensations 'happened,' moved, moved her. Yet the importance of the colours was *signified* by their intensity, as was the affective impact. Literal, physical movement signified figurative, emotional movement, in the way metaphors have been literalized in baroque and contemporary literature. Racine, in *Phèdre*, literalizes the baroque cliché *feu*, fire, for passion, by making it consume and kill the protagonist. Marguerite Duras literalizes metaphors in conjunction with punning, e.g. *mer/mère* in *Agatha*; the suicide follows the passage of the 'coupeur d'eau' in 'Le coupeur d'eau,' who cuts off the female protagonist from the water indispensable to life.[17] Both writers thus *visualize* their language the way dreamers do. They offer words-as-concepts: words that merge their old abstract meanings into new, concrete, visual ones, to form a concept that is rather like a theoretical object. This transformation of words into images can, of course, also happen between one text and another, or between a linguistic text and a graphic text.[18] It is in a plea for this category of conceptualization that I would offer *mise-en-scène* as an analytical tool. To mark the difference between such strongly concrete concepts, or rather their concretizing use, and more abstract ones, but also to emphasize the concrete quality of all concepts, I propose the term 'conceptual metaphor.'[19]

16 See Barthes (1975b); for a clear and quick introduction to Barthes, see Culler (1983: 84). The last two examples are meant to remind the reader of the historical specificity of such stock plot elements.

17 On this aspect of Duras' work, see Biezenbos (1995).

18 In this sense, as I argued in ch. 2, Bernini literalizes Saint Teresa's metaphor of fire from her description of her ecstasy. He then visualizes the fire in iconic shapes that turn the folds of her dress into signs of flames. See, for an elaboration, Bal (2001a).

19 For an extensive argument in favour of this use, see Reynolds (2000).

The movement in the two dreams, then, stood for, signified, affect on the dreamer, through *movement* as sign and *literalization* as code. And the absent subject undergoing the affect was like the non-indifferent spectator, whose subjectivity was staged in a risky interface between fiction and psychic reality. These two elements make these dreams specific cases of *mise-en-scène*. Moving forward, the props – the sand in the first dream, the flag in the second – produced the only movement. That movement distinguished the *tableau* from a still image, say, from a painting or a photograph. In traditional terminology, this could be called the incipient narrativity of the scenes.

With *mise-en-scène* as our theoretical concept, and Brünnhilde's staged death as our theoretical object, we can see how the narrativity is not just incipient but fully deployed. The landscape was both stage and figure, that is, *actant*, albeit not an anthropomorphic one.[20] But the movement, both literal and figurative, duplicated the narrativity as impact on the onlooker, in both dreams coming so close that it was on the verge of overwhelming the dreamer, nearly, but not quite, pulling her inside the occurrence. Enough to let her subjectivity be influenced, not enough to violently attack it. In this sense, these were poststructuralist dreams – say, Lacanian – and a bit more.[21]

In fact, the dreamer was acutely aware of the telling quality of her dreams. She wasn't doing the telling; she was its addressee. But more than that: it was also telling her, not only as indirect, but also as direct object, and this, again, in the two senses that *mimeisthai*'s object, *mimesis*, indicates perforce.[22] The dreams were literally telling her something, with insistence. But whereas they did not explicitly tell – they were in the business of showing, according to the old opposition between telling and showing – neither did they *only* show. There was no fourth wall between stage and onlooker. She felt very strongly implicated, although there was no moment when she stepped out on stage. The dream 'told' her something by 'showing' something else,

---

20 A structuralist concept at the core, 'actant' refers to a class of figures standing in a fixed relationship to the function or predicate that defines a plot. The possibility of a narrativity structured through non-anthropomorphic actants is, precisely, the point of Greimas' concept. See, in particular, his concrete lesson on the application of his theory (1976).

21 As a shortcut here, see Silverman's brilliant study on the subject (1996), a revision and extension of Lacan's notion of subjectivity as culturally framed.

22 All the secrets of the enigmatic concept of *mimesis*, which has led so many critics astray, are revealed and resolved in Dupont-Roc and Lallot's twenty pages of brilliant commentary (1980: 43–63).

something about and regarding her.[23] And, the site of the encounter between the two semiotic acts of telling and showing, the site of impact – what Aristotle would have called *catharsis* – invisible in the dream, was located in *the body of the dreamer*. Hence the strong visual sensation of the colours, the excitement, the happiness she felt at being 'impacted,' so to speak.

There were no rebus-like riddles, no image-words to 'translate' in the dreams, only sensations. The dreams were *doing*, acting, performing. But doesn't performing need a subject designated to *do* the act? Christopher Bollas' 'unthought known' seems to offer an analogy to this performance in the following explanation of that phrase, which serves as the epigraph to this chapter: 'I often find that although I am working on an idea without knowing exactly what it is I think, I am engaged in thinking an idea struggling to have me think it.'[24] The point I would like to extend here to the theoretical value of *mise-en-scène*, including the passive voice of that phrase, is the complete merging of subject into object, and of object – props, things – into subjects acting, and acting subjects.

I will now explore this further through a number of works that reveal different aspects of this complex structure. To further emphasize the travelling of our concept, these works have all been chosen from the domain 'officially' classified as the visual arts, rather than from theatre or opera, in which *mise-en-scène*, in this conceptual sense, takes the place of, say, the paintbrush. To reiterate our concept's itinerary: from theatrical practice, it has moved to academic analysis, specifically connecting cultural theory with psychoanalysis. There it has been enriched with theoretical elements drawn from the provisional conflation of *mise-en-scène*, as an elaborate and highly sophisticated artistic practice, with dreams, as unconscious happenings. Now, with its accumulated baggage, it will travel to an artistic practice of an entirely different kind, visual, without a verbal component, and, mostly, still; a practice where no human actors occupy centre stage, and where things, mute but really not so mute, do the work of meaning production. In the following works, but in ways with different theoretical consequences, things act, the subject undergoes the action, and the power of the object achieves a dreamlike quality, which is, none-

23 For the importance of the double sense of regarding as 'looking at' and 'concerning,' see Didi-Huberman (1992).
24 See Bollas (1987: 10).

3.3 Bill Viola, *The Sleep of Reason*, 1988, video/sound installation

theless, the result of conscious – if not necessarily aware – artistic agency.

The Sleep of Reason

The first work is closer than the subsequent ones to theatrical *mise-en-scène*, but even so, it is not 'really' a play staged. American video artist Bill Viola's video installation *The Sleep of Reason* (1988) shows a TV monitor on a chest standing against the far wall of a room in which the viewer is invited to stand. On one side is a vase of flowers, on the other, a cosy bedside lamp and an alarm clock. The set-up has connotations of a bedroom without a bed, or, alternatively – or perhaps simultaneously – an altar without religious paraphernalia (figs. 3.3 and 3.4).

On the monitor, the viewer sees the head of a sleeping man. Immo-

3.4 Bill Viola, *The Sleep of Reason*, 1988, video/sound installation

bile, mostly. Watching him sleep makes the viewer feel uneasy. He sleeps, encased in the small, shiny image of the monitor, as if to emphasize that this is not an actor on stage. As the uninvited witness of sleep's vulnerability and its similarity to death, the viewer seems to gain more control over the man's most private world than is warranted.[25] Another uneasiness comes from the temporal dilation: watching a sleeping head on a pillow is no big thrill. Hence the double uneasiness prevents the kind of self-righteousness that, in resistance to voyeurism, comes so dangerously close to a puritanism based on visual essentialism.[26] Here, the viewer feels bad on both counts – for

25 Here, incidentally, already, the public encroaches upon the private domain. Western culture is full of myths of the – gender-specific! – dangers of sleep. Just think of the myths of Judith, Samson and Delilah, Jael killing Sisera, and the like. See, for this, my account of the exhibition around Judith that I curated (ch. 4).
26 It is primarily in opposition to such visual essentialism – the source, also, of iconophobia – that I wrote my study *Reading Rembrandt* (1991).

her own transgression and for the sleeper's boring hold over her. An equality of sorts.

The installation demonstrates, in terms of temporality, the fine line between theatre and visual art. Neither theatrical nor sculptural, the image is too still to captivate, yet its time frame is also too imposing for the viewer to feel free to leave when it suits her. The stillness of the image begins to wear the viewer out when, suddenly, a loud noise interrupts it. The light goes off and the monitor goes black. Flashes of huge and frightening images appear on all the walls of the room: roaring sea water, a fluttering white owl, gigantic crawling ants. But only very briefly. Then the room returns to stillness, to the sleeper on the screen.

Clearly – to my mind perhaps a bit too clearly – the images represent dream images, nightmares, flashes of a frightening nightlife. They are frightening even though we cannot really see what they are and hence, why they scare us. They are very short yet every bit as frustrating as the lengthy periods of still sleep. The viewer is denied the opportunity of grasping the images, of making sense of them. They are noisy, overwhelmingly so, visually and acoustically. And, since they are projected on the walls surrounding the viewer, the latter is pulled inside them, as if being imprisoned in someone else's dream.

As a teacher of cultural analysis, Viola here stages what it means to be inside someone else's dream. The dream stands for the unthought known. It is analogous to what happens when one lets down one's guard and becomes absorbed in the red fabric of Brünnhilde's undoing. Viola's installation does this so literally, so concretely, that his piece becomes a theoretical allegory rather than a theoretical object.[27] It helps make this point clearly. In this sense, though, the two dreams of my anonymous young woman are more 'artistic' – more like an image in the revised sense elaborated in chapter 2 – than this overt staging of dream life. What remains implicit in her dreams – the viewer/dreamer who is affected by the stage – is made central in Viola's piece, where the viewer must stand in the middle of the room to see anything at all. The *mise-en-scène* is the construction of the viewer's central place in the boring, bourgeois bedroom that could be anyone's. Utter solitude in total anonymity.

---

27 The distinction matters. To put it more strongly than perhaps Viola's piece deserves, the former is didactic, 'explaining' the known; the latter is complex and offers insight into the 'unthought known.' But it does much more than that and cannot be reduced to its theoretical meanings, however complex they may be.

Thus, Viola's installation stages the image – dynamic, multifaceted, deploying its activity between subject and sociality – of the viewer.

Let me now set this work in contrast to another piece of installation art. Whereas Viola is a video artist, Ann Veronica Janssens, the Belgian representative at the 1999 Venice Biennale, is more difficult to place in terms of genre or media. She calls herself a sculptor and likes to see her works as 'interventions.' She used this latter ploy – the immersion of the viewer *on*, or rather, *in* the stage – as the almost exasperatingly exclusive *mise-en-scène*, when she created a work for that occasion that consisted merely of mist (fig. 3.5).[28] The mist, the air in the room thus made white and opaque, had several very strong effects, all of which contribute to our understanding of the equation *mise- en-scène* = dream, an analogy that serves the purpose of theorizing the image as staged as a concept for analysis. First, it cushioned the visual as well as the auditive sensations that the togetherness of the visitors, unacquainted with each other inside the room, would otherwise produce. Thus, each viewer was protected from the other viewers by a layer, an envelope, which made the others seem part of the cast; people you wouldn't talk to because you arrived there by chance, a spectator stumbling onto a stage. Second, it made the space unreal, literally dream-like, a space of which the edges and ceilings were not really visible, could only be guessed. Third, the crystal-clear sound of the child's voice on tape – the second element, in addition to the mist, that the artist had constructed – cut through the mist and reached the viewer's body as if not hindered by the cushioning. This combining of limited visibility and isolated, over-clear hearing seems like a hyperbolic version of Brünnhilde's death.

Whereas in Viola's installation the viewer is ushered into someone else's dream, the images and the images' affective values of which were predetermined, in Janssens' mist work the dream, although not thematically suggested at all, happens to the viewer, who also gets to determine its specifics. She puts the viewer on stage to allow experiencing a dream 'of one's own.'[29] The status of this stage-*qua*-dream was

28 Although the mist is the piece, so to speak, in Venice there was also an acoustic intervention. Elsewhere (e.g. in Lisbon in 1998), the piece consisted only of mist. See my analysis of this and other works by the same artist (Janssens 1999).

29 The reference to Virginia Woolf's famous essay, a feminist manifesto, is here meant to remind us of the political importance of bridging the gap between private and public at the deepest possible level. For Woolf and a different bridge between private and public – thought and rhetoric – see Lord (1999), on which more in ch. 8.

3.5 Ann Veronica Janssens, *Installation with Mist and Sound*, 1999

pre-scripted, but its plot, images, and affective impact were left to the viewer to flesh out.

In Venice, with the usual crowdedness of the Biennale – and unlike in my experience of a version of this same installation in Lisbon, where I happened to be alone in the work – each visitor was cushioned from the intercourse with the anonymous others who were also present in the pavilion but blurred by the mist. This almost accidental situation nicely sums up the tension between individual and social 'dreaming.' The mist, sharpening one's sense perceptions while blurring the resulting images, also stages a resolution of that tension. It softens the intrusion of others, simultaneously softening the isolation of real aloneness.

Janssens' implied stage directions put the viewer in the position of dreamer. At the same time they give the viewer the task of constructing the narrative whose plot has as-yet to be produced. In this sense – of the openness of the narrative content combined with the stringent parameters of narrativity – Janssens' work with mist contrasts with Viola's semanticization of dreams through the pre-scripted cultural icons of nightmare and desire.[30] Yet, although Brünnhilde's undoing into red fabric is an utterly public event of an exuberantly figurative nature, its status as a staging of subjectivity is closer to Janssens' abstract mist than to Viola's concrete dreams. I like to see Janssens' mist installation as the result of a thinking-through, in a practice that is as theoretically relevant as can be, of this aesthetic of *mise-en-scène*, where staging is, by definition, staging the viewer as a subject immersed in culture. Now, the viewer *is* the image.

Dreaming Space

I am aware of the risks of psychoanalytic thought, and hasten to mention those parts of it that I feel should be discarded. The point I wish to foreground through my next *mise-en-scène* as theoretical object concerns the caution against the pitfalls of psychoanalytic criticism as ineradicably connected to biography. The following work uniquely demonstrates this. Elsewhere than in Viola's and Janssens' positions, but involved in the same experiment of staging subjectivity, I would like to place a couple of works by Louise Bourgeois, an artist who suf-

---

30 In this sense, Viola's dream images are emblems of what Barthes, in *S/Z*, would call the 'proairetic code.' See fn. 16.

fers more than others from over-semanticization, largely due to the kind of 'anteriority narratives' I have dismissed elsewhere as the 'sloth' of art history.[31] I am thinking of her installation, *Spider* (1997), part of a recent series of works called *Cells* that explicitly create isolated and isolating environments. In her own commentary on another piece from the same period, *Twosome* (1992), Bourgeois mentions the kind of psychodrama that is involved in dreaming, along with considerations of sculpture and theatre that characterize *mise-en-scène*:

> A twosome is a closed world. Two people constitute an environment, one person alone is an object. An object doesn't relate to anything unless you make it relate, it has a solitary, poor and pathetic quality. As soon as you get concerned with the other person it becomes an environment, which involves not only you, who are contained, but also the container. It is very important to me that people be able to go around the piece. Then they become part of the environment – although in some ways it is not an environment but the relation of two cells. Installation is really a form between sculpture and theatre, and this bothers me.[32]

Let us not speculate on why this mix should bother Bourgeois. I am not interested in intention. But I am interested in her statement's theoretical meaning. 'It is very important to me that people be able to go around the piece.' This definition of sculpture complements Janssens' image, where the piece goes around the people. Bourgeois conceives of the confrontation between a single subject and an environment as a confrontation that turns the single individual into a subject. Being not-alone, in other words, is a requirement for subjectivity. In the social sense we know this to be true.[33] In the aesthetic sense that I am trying to theorize here, it is also true. Here lies the social significance of *mise-en-scène*, and hence its importance as a revised conception of image and as a conceptual tool in cultural analysis.

As concrete, material, and public, as soliciting a receptivity to dreaming, fantasy, and the willing suspension of disbelief, staging reconciles the private and the public without diminishing the powerful 'specialization' of either. In other words, the dreaming that occurs on, or through, the stage, in the examples of *mise-en-scène* discussed so far,

31 See both my article (1999b) and my book on the subject (2001a).
32 Louise Bourgeois, *Writings* 210, quoted by Potts (1999: 45).
33 As well as in the linguistic sense, as Benveniste argued. See ch. 1.

3.6 Louise Bourgeois, *Spider*, 1997, steel and mixed media

is both extremely private and extremely public – to the mutual benefit of both dimensions of subjective existence.[34]

It is my thesis that *mise-en-scène* can produce subjectivity in this *interactive* sense. If this is true, then the stage must be the 'other' in relation to whom Bourgeois' 'twosome' can emerge. I will return to this later, apropos of the two dreams, where the subject is, precisely, *not* on stage. There, it is as if the environment alone suffices to stage subjectivity.

Bourgeois, in fact, creates precisely such an environment in her installations of the *Cells* series. In *Spider* (1997, fig. 3.6), a gigantic spi-

34 I insist on this to avoid the misunderstanding that I am advocating a return to individualism, 'to the right' of Viola's work, so to speak. To phrase it differently: doing justice to 'the private' or to the individual dimension of subjectivity is a political issue. But, as the problematic aspects of identity politics have unwittingly demonstrated, this can only be politically effective on condition that the dimension of 'the public' is equally fully involved. Hence the symbolic significance of *mise-en-scène* for my argument.

der hovers over a cage whose door stands ajar. Inside is a chair. The chair in the cage is quite ordinary, like a director's, but it is made to look historical, almost like a throne, because of the fabric thrown over it. The historicity of that fabric, fragments of ancient tapestry fallen into ruins, both helps and hampers the connotation of regal presence, of a throne as subject. Historicity is inherent in the institution of royalty as such. But that mythical regalness implies a luxurious richness, which the ruinous fabric, thrown over the chair in almost sloppy fashion, contradicts. Hence the chair looks like a throne, but not 'really.' So the historicizing look is theatrical, overtly presented as fake; just a layer. Emphatically theatrical, the chair, at the same time, is the environment to which the viewer as subject is invited. More succinctly: the viewer, the producer of dream stories, inhabits the *Cell*. The dream images and the stories, in turn, are the performances of which this chair, this prop, is only the trigger. Inside is the stage of the cellular drama, with no apparent director, like our young woman's dreams. There is only an empty director's chair. The stories evoked by the different figurative fragments – the spider herself, the chair/throne, the half-open cage – constitute the cells that grow and pullulate, producing unpredictable shapes, destroying the unity, and emptying out of the centre. But these stories can only live inside those spaces, inside *Spider*'s cage, if they are given life – time, subjectivity, body – from the outside. For, 'outside' means from the public side of culture's fundamental interactivity.

But, lest my point be taken too literally – stage as physical stage – let me complicate the issue further. Although requiring some form of spatial materiality, this function of *mise-en-scène* as embodying the other in relation to whom subjectivity becomes possible can in turn be given active shape – *staged* – by figurative means such as characters. These are stand-ins, not for narrative actants but for the stage on which subjectivity, itself the actant, can come to be. This, at least, is how I read the Dutch sculptor Michel Huisman's enigmatic, tender, vulnerable, and rudimentary figures of walking birds, in his exhibition *Garden, Night, and Farewell*.[35]

In this extraordinary ensemble of drawings and moving sculptures, Huisman stages relationality and environment as defined by Bour-

---

35 For a presentation, and excellent photographs, of Huisman's extraordinary work, see Huisman (1998). Like all installation art, though, and especially since many of the works are moving machines, the book is a poor substitute.

geois. The garden is the site of enigma and protection, of unlimited worlds, yet also the sole possession of the subject enclosed within it. The cultural-historical reference of this installation and its title is to the topos of the *hortus conclusus*. Like Racine's *feu*, Duras' *coupeur d'eau*, and Teresa/Bernini's flames, Huisman's garden both literalizes – and thus reactivates – the cultural cliché and its history, and – also – contests it. In particular, the installation contests the garden's closedness in the face of the colonizing art required to achieve that closedness. It also contests the connotation of safety, since the immanent threshold between tenderness and violence that characterizes the installation in all of its pieces relentlessly instils in the viewer a contagious sense of vulnerability.[36] This work, I submit, revises the history of the topos of the *hortus conclusus* by appointing space as the director that stages subjectivity.

Night is to time what garden is to space: enclosure, enigma, and the possibility of encounters unthinkable at other moments. Farewell is the dangerous and exciting moment of transition and/or ambiguity, as staged by Huisman's wind-up wooden bird, *Surrendering Bird* (1999) – which, if wound up, *resists* surrender. Or by the strange birds, whose songs become opera music. Or by the large creature clumsily walking and carrying a torch. Or by the two birds sadly trying to communicate; trying, but failing, to share gifts (fig. 3.7).

Subjectivity *ex Machina*

Like a stage, Huisman's sculptures contain machinery. When exhibited, Huisman's vulnerable creatures, made as machines, cannot be manipulated. Their machinery cannot be made to work, so that, from moving sculptures, they become still objects. But no; this is not what happens. Instead – and this is why I allege them here as witnesses to the function of *mise-en-scène* for staging subjectivity – captions on the museum wall simply and dryly explain how the machines work. They stage subjectivity in the sense of *mise-en-pièce(s)* of text into landscape beyond *logos*. The sad gift-giving, and its refusal, for example, has the following caption:[37]

---

36 For references to *hortus conclusus* and other cultural topoi, such as *bouquet, paradise*, and *locus amoenus*, see Becker (1988, esp. 7).

37 This is, however, one of the few pieces that actually do work; since they are built in a glass-covered box, these birds are less vulnerable than the larger pieces that are out in the open. My account is based on the exhibition that was held in the Stedelijk Museum, Amsterdam, Winter 1999–2000.

3.7 Michel Huisman, *No. 43* (gift-giving), 1990, acrylic on wood, steel, brass, electronics, and mechanisms

43. After pushing the black button the following occurs: the bird on the right lifts – a little askew – his head, until he looks at the other bird. Then he slowly pushes the parcel to the bird opposite him. The latter refuses; sluggishly shakes his head. Right away the bird with the parcel lowers his head again and takes the 'present' back.

As the photograph here can only obliquely hint, the heart-wrenching sadness of this scene is visually embodied in the clumsy fabrication of the joints between the head and the body, the shape of the shoulders, and the tiny light bulb between the two birds. In contrast to the pathos of the sculpture itself, of the movement, and of the represented scene, the caption first reads like stage directions: dry, but specifying pose and attitude. Yet the verbs used – lifts his head until he looks at the other bird; refuses; lowers his head; takes the present back – although unadorned by narrative ploys, hold the same sadness as the visual machine conveys. Thus, through visualized narrativity, the axis turns by ninety degrees, from sideways, third-person narrative, into first-/second-person address.

Whereas in this piece text and spectacle converge, in most of the others in the show text replaces an invisible spectacle. Enigmatically, these works appear to be only temporarily broken down, so that the viewer tends to read the rather long texts, positioned at unorthodox and unhelpful heights that make them hard to read. One such piece, early on in the show, is an illusionistically executed sculpture of a man dressed in black – as deceptive as a Madame Tussaud wax figure – wearing a gigantic mask in the shape of a bird's head (fig. 3.8). Its caption reads as follows:

47. Not visible from the outside there is a diorama on the inside, which can be seen by anyone who places this work on his head; a three-dimensional woodscape is painted on eleven sheets of glass positioned one behind the other and on a translucent exterior. From a built-in sound source, bird sounds can be heard. This 'wood' is hermetically sealed from the outside world. The spectator's breath is removed through a pipe system.
Niet aanraken s.v.p. / do not touch

The description is tantalizing. How can we know if it speaks the truth when we are denied access to the 'woodscape' inside the bird's head? We don't hear anything, so why promise us music? The detail about

3.8 Michel Huisman, *No. 47* (concealed diorama), 1991, acrylic glass, silk paper, wood, latex, steel, aluminium, outlet pipe, electronics

the spectator's breath, while hilariously irrelevant, holds up the fiction – the fiction of reality, that is.[38] It removes the last resistance to the suspension of disbelief, clearing the space for a hallucinatory wish-fulfilment.[39] Between the large sculpture and the back-breakingly positioned text, what is staged, then, is a sensuously produced *invisibility*. This is no iconophobic refusal of the sense-appeal of vision; on the contrary, there is a 'working-through' of this appeal – through its denial.

For this reason, I interpret the captions' positioning of playing hard to get, not as stage directions, which they ostensibly are, but as the narrative compensation that collapses the viewer with the character, with the figure on stage, or rather, in terms of Brünnhilde's flaming fabric, with the figuration. In other words, this positioning functions like the dangerous proximity of Semmes' *Red Dress* to the space where the public walks with dirty shoes; or like the folds in Caravaggio's red mantle on John the Baptist's appealing body.[40] This is demonstrated again in another part of the installation.

Near a chair on the back of which hangs the portrait of a boy, on a level so low it breaks your back to read it *unless you are a small boy yourself*, the caption tells us (fig. 3.9):

> 42. Although this figure displays all the external characteristics of a chair, it is not meant to be sat on; this seat has already been occupied by the boy who, though absent, is depicted on the back of the chair. This portrait is also visible in the dark by means of a light bulb placed behind it. In the 'seat' many dozens of holes have been drilled through which a built-in light bulb causes as many light spots.[41]

The passive voice used here produces, in a linguistic dimension, an emptying out of the chair of the very subjectivity that, perversely, by counterpoint, is at stake here. Whereas the caption laboriously states that the chair is not meant to be sat on, and whereas this is obviously

---

38 This is a good case for the notion that 'realism' is, primarily, perhaps exclusively, a rhetoric. Barthes' concept of the 'effect of the real' remains an adequate term to convey this point.
39 See ch. 3 of Freud's *Interpretation of Dreams*.
40 Elsewhere, I have developed the concept of second-person narrative to account for this concreteness of, here, mere captions, and there, ostensibly abstract art, apropos of the paintings of David Reed (see Bal 1999a, ch. 6).
41 Significantly, a photograph of this work reveals practically nothing of the effect I am describing. See fig. 3.9.

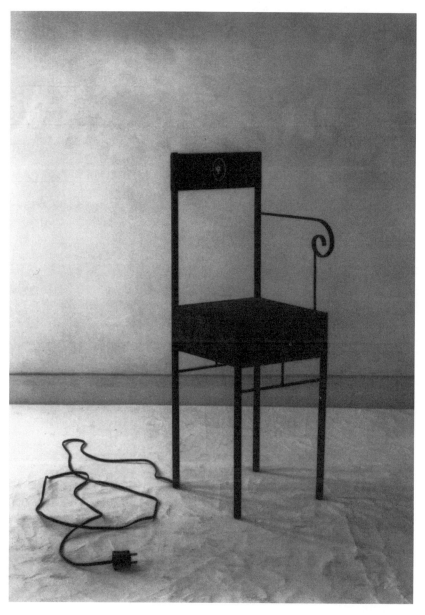

3.9 Michel Huisman, *No. 42* (chair with child), 1990, oil paint on wood, steel, transparent devotional shield, electronics

true in the material sense, the imaginary result of the use of the passive voice is to welcome the viewer after all. While constructing its occupant (the boy), the text thus also simultaneously constructs an imaginary place for the viewer, by means of what Paul de Man would have called the 'rhetorization of grammar,' the deployment of grammar for rhetorical use.[42]

On the level of content, the caption continues to do its rhetorical work. For example, the promise of tiny star-like light spots on the chair's seat could easily have been fulfilled; clearly, *not* fulfilling promises is the work's point. Similarly, a light illuminating the boy's face from behind would have made his portrait invisible rather than visible. Yet, while I, as a spectator, bent over to read the caption, none of this occurred to me. Instead, the desire to see was irresistibly provoked, produced, in the body. It was this desire that drew me into the small boy's place. This identification 'outside myself,' what Kaja Silverman has termed *heteropathic*, is what constitutes, I submit, the staging of subjectivity.

Such heteropathic identification can be, and often is, socially productive, in that it wrenches the subject outside of herself, enticing her to go out and meet the other on their ground. It is through the convergence of the descriptive, quasi-technical text, read in a bodily-uncomfortable position, with the memorial representation of a boy long-gone whom I had never seen before, that, I felt, the retrospective possibility of 'becoming' was *mise-en-scène* – in the utterly private fantasy, set in the utterly public arena of museum space.

In *The Pleasure of the Text*, Barthes uses the word 'seduction' in virtually the same sense when he calls seduction 'the staging of an appearance-disappearance' (1975a: 19). Huisman uses the dialectic between visibility and invisibility to seduce the viewer into a kind of surrender. Moreover, in her brilliant revision of Austin's theory of performativity as it had been watered down since it was first conceived, Shoshana Felman uses the speech act of seduction as her key example, as her theoretical object. Confronted with the gendered violence that lies so closely contiguous to seduction, I argued, in *Death and Dissymmetry* (1988a), that the starring role of this example is a bit frivolous, optimistic, lighthearted. Taking my lesson from both Semmes' installation and, through this, Huisman's profound yet playful sadness, I am

---

42 See the opening chapter of de Man's *Allegories of Reading*.

inclined, now, not to reject seduction as a key example but rather to revise the meaning of the speech act of seduction itself. Without prejudging the sweet, violent, or bittersweet implications of such an act, I see it here as the *mise-en-scène* of the moment when subjectivity emerges within social interaction. Appearing and disappearing is also the right phrase to characterize theatricality; a shorthand or minimal summary of staging.

It now becomes possible to grasp the meaning of the title of Huisman's show. The garden is the enclosed space of the 'private theatre' of fantasy. The night is the realm of dreaming, where reality – signified by the imaginary, proper functioning of machines – is no longer the confining parameter of the stage. The farewell to concrete, represented reality, instead of cutting off possibilities, is the beginning of a subjectivity that can now be staged, now that the obstacles that precluded that staging have been removed. The invisibility of night, like the dark that encloses the spectator in the cinema, theatre, or opera, facilitates heteropathic identification, for which the text mediates. And that – Huisman's theoretical object says, by means of the double modesty of the birds and their clumsy, imperfect execution – is the only kind of identification that opens up the rigidity of our subjectivity and the private/public binary on which traditional notions of subjectivity are predicated. As a result, the aesthetic experience – the sensuous incorporation of what happens on stage – can actually enrich and transform us.

Imaging Moving

So far, I have tried to treat separately those elements of *mise-en-scène* that turn it into a conceptual tool, in an attempt to understand how artists can offer effective forms of an aesthetic of staging subjectivity beyond the private/public divide. These elements are bound up with unorthodox forms of narrativity as well as with unusual forms of visuality. Both narrative and visual coherence are rejected. In all cases, representation gives way to presentation. In linguistic terms, third-person discourse recedes in favour of first/second-person interactivity.

In the two dreams as well as the art works, literal movement is either staged or implied, standing, in all cases, for the figurative sense of *moving* as affect. To probe the complex and paradoxical implications of this affective aesthetic, I will discuss, later, in chapter 5, how, in James Coleman's installation *Photograph*, all of these elements bind – in the chemical sense[43] – to form a *mise-en-scène* 'which is not/one.'[44] Here, I am concerned primarily with the way in which a theory of dreams – psychoanalytically based and hence primarily geared towards the private domain of the individual – is fundamentally a theory of staging. The artifice of dream*work* in this kind *of mise-en-scène* provides the installations with a dreamlike quality that wrenches the visitors out of their confinement within the drab reality of everyday life. These are *images*, and *mise-en-scène* is their primary mode of operation.

Christopher Bollas claims that the dreamer is positioned in the dream, in relation to the stage, its director, and its actors, props, time-frame and what-have-you, in ways that make the term 'aesthetic' operative without an excessive appeal to metaphoricity, at least in the traditional sense of that term. Later on, I will engage Bollas' theory of dreams in more detail. Suffice it to say here that in his theatricalization of the dream, Bollas phrases his theory using all the terms I have brought to bear on *mise-en-scène*:

> I regard the dream as a *fiction* constructed by a *unique aesthetic*: the *transformation* of the *subject* into his *thought*, specifically, the placing of the self *into* an allegory of desire and dread that is *fashioned* by the ego. (Bollas 1987: 64; emphasis added)

His insistence that the ego, not the subject, 'directs' the play has specific relevance in the context of a discussion on *mise-en-scène*. The ego is, indeed, 'other' to the subject. This alone makes subjectivity theatrical. The subject cannot take hold of, grasp, or confine the ego. We can now see, in a somewhat more literal sense, how and why the sleeper is both the subject of the dreams – the dreamer as well as the subject-matter – and emphatically not the dreams' subject: not its narrator, its director, or its writer/painter. This reworked theory, incidentally, offers strong support to the anti-intentionalist position as more adequate for the practice of, specifically, *cultural* analysis.

As an artistic practice, *mise-en-scène* is one of many techniques that engages the viewer in an aesthetic experience. In this sense, it is a specialized artistic field, requiring training, skills, and talent. As a concept,

---

43 The chemical domain offers a nice frame for the deceptively simple title of this work, *Photograph*.

44 The allusion to Luce Irigaray's *Ce sexe qui n'est pas/un*, which in turn alludes to Simone de Beauvoir's *Deuxième sexe*, is not to suggest a direct relationship between Coleman's installation and this feminist intertext.

it refers to something more adequately indicated as a cultural practice. This practice involves us every day, but more acutely so in confrontation with situations that frame-freeze, so to speak, the *mise-en-scène* itself, as a cultural moment in which routine is slowed down, self-awareness is increased, and satisfaction is gained from going outside ourselves. Theatricality, offering a fictional realm of experiment and dreaming precisely because of its artificiality, remains a productive frame to think cultural practice as a social binding of subjects whose subjectivity remains unassaulted. It offers interactive images of that binding.

In different ways, all the artists whose installations I have foregrounded attempt to yield power over their creations to the viewer, in a generous endorsement of the wilful suspension of authority that is required by the staging of subjectivity in a cultural merging of individuality. Viola staged the cultural amid the private, overwhelming our sense of self with images of others. Janssens' viewers stumbled on stage and were confronted with a solitude in unreality that nevertheless refused to sever the link – with those vague, misty others and with spatial otherness – that the mist hides and shows. Bourgeois' psychodrama is staged in a theatre of temporal distance, where props trigger the viewer to participate. Far from indulging in mere autobiography, her 'autotopographic' installations are places where *mise-en-scène* itself embodies the other, in relation to whom subjectivity becomes possible. Huisman's characters shape the stage but not as actants. They shape the stage which is itself the actant – the turning point of the action. His theatrical machines, including their captions that stand in for the machinery, thus function as a theoretical object that yields a theory of the subject as theatrically produced; a subject *ex machina*.

At the end of this itinerary, then, the full cultural importance of *mise-en-scène* as a staging of subjectivity is itself the object being staged. This is how a concept taken from a specialized practice becomes a searchlight that illuminates what is powerfully *cultural* about the practices we study. At the beginning of this chapter, I wrote that *mise-en-scène* is a materialization of text in a form that is accessible for a public, collective reception; a mediation between a play and the multiple public – to which I added: each individual in it. I would now like to rehearse that earlier, specialized, and practice-oriented definition as if it were a theory of dreams.

The artistic organization of the space in which the play is set – the dream itself – arranges a limited and delimited section of *real* time and space (read: time and space that belong inalienably to the subject, and to which the subject inalienably belongs) so that a differently delimited section of fictional time and space can accommodate the fictional activities of the 'actors' – in the cases studied here, props and the stage itself – performing their roles to build a plot.

Which discipline should house this kind of analysis? Art history, the warden of installation art? Or theatre studies, whose practitioners know the specialized language and the practice's history? 'House' as noun evokes the world of privacy into which the subject is born, only to be thrust out into the world so that he or she can live. Inevitably, both disciplines must be involved. So, of course, must psychoanalysis, film studies, and literary studies. But the reflection, leaning on the practice, will always spill over, from the house into that larger world that we call, for the lack of a more precise term, culture. No 'natural' house, then, but a public stage where subjects can meet.

On stage, and between stage and audience, the roles of player and director are shuttled back and forth. Perhaps, and perhaps not, the viewer can grasp some element or aspect of the subjectivity being put forth in that unsettling setting. No one is master in 'his' own house, wrote Freud, famously, in his over-interpreted phrase. But I am not interested in adding to that interpretive activity. I propose to take this image-metaphor at face value, so that Bourgeois' house-woman and the visitors of Janssens' mist installation can be the recipients of Huisman's bird's gift. For perhaps that sad gift, refused by the bird's other, is no other than the *id* that dislodged the self-confident, Cartesian subject from the Freudian house. *Mise-en-scène* as a cultural activity and artistic practice offers us a conceptual tool with which to both endorse the consequences of this negativity wholeheartedly and enjoy the 'beauty' of its ongoing probing in the various *mises-en-scène* that the various art practices of our culture offer. This is a post-humanist view of subjectivity, but one that reaffirms the subject's importance; one that, in a post-baroque sense, believes in miracles – as long as these can come up with a subject *ex machina*.

4

Framing

frame (n):
- *something composed of parts fitted together and joined*
- *a structure composed of constructional members (e.g. girders or beams) that gives shape or strength (e.g. to a building)*
- *an open case or structure made for admitting, enclosing, or supporting something*
- *a limiting, typical, or appropriate set of circumstances; an event that forms the background for the action of a novel or play*
- *(infl) a frame-up*

The Matter with Context

Together with image then, *mise-en-scène* – a concept from an art practice many perceive as 'merely' artificial, pleasurable, lighthearted – will remain a basis for the further travels in this book. As we now know, image, in its revised conception as an event in the present, is, by definition, *mise-en-scène*. By putting image thus made 'theatrical' at the heart of cultural analysis, I aim to foreground several important aspects of how 'cultural objects' are viewed. The practice of cultural analysis being explored in this book thus becomes inflected, or tainted, with fictionality. Something of that same constructionist, *ex machina* inclination is at stake in this chapter. As in chapter 3, a particularly promising concept will be brought to bear on a specific cultural practice, so as to further flesh out what a cultural-analytical conception of 'image' might entail.

Another important feature that has accrued to our starting point of image is the tight bond between analysis and the cultural practice to which it pertains. This is why, with *mise-en-scène*, I put forward a concept from artistic practice – carrying it over from one art form to another, whereby its analytical capacities came to stand out – then made it operational in analysis. In the present chapter, instead of taking a concept from one cultural practice to bear on another as a theoretical searchlight, the opposite itinerary will be followed. Here, a theoretical concept, popular in the humanities and so far not taken up by cultural practice, will be deployed as a tool in one such practice. Together, chapters 3 and 4 will show that the bond between theory and practice is as inextricable as it is productive for both. And so the concept of *image*, now *mise en scène*, takes on still more baggage.

As is well known, the concept of *framing* has been productively put to use in cultural analysis as an alternative to the older concept of context.[1] The change here has not been one of terminology but of implications. And these are major. I am not sure they have always been fully endorsed, even by those who deploy the new concept together with its Derridean overtones. But my focus here is not to rehearse at length the arguments in favour of *framing* over *context*. Rather it is to argue for a specific *use* of each concept individually, that is, for a specific kind of cultural analysis as a form of material practice. To this end, I will debate neither the new concept's philosophical meanings nor its more or less loyal usages. Instead, I will briefly summarize three arguments in favour of its use over context as a way of framing my own discussion of *framing*.

The first argument pertains to *context*. *Context*, or rather, the self-evident, non-conceptual kind of data referred to as context, is often invoked for the interpretation of cultural artefacts such as art works, in order to uncover their meaning. In effect, though, its deployment serves to confuse *explaining* with *interpreting*, or, as Thomas Pavel once described it, origin with articulation (1984).[2] This confusion is a left-

---

1 One of the most influential formulations of this concept, usefully succinct, is Jonathan Culler's 'Author's Preface' to his volume *Framing the Sign* (1988). As one of my students remarked with disappointment, the preface is great but the essays hardly use the concept at all. This, I pointed out, is not true. They barely *name* it, hence, they don't use it in the sense of citing it, but the *practice* of it is pervasive throughout the essays. This absence of the term in the presence of the activity is perhaps what characterizes 'framing' most importantly.

2 Pavel was talking more specifically about psychoanalytic interpretation. I find it quite significant that those who look down on psychoanalysis for precisely this reason don't see how other, more 'positive,' 'verifiable' methods induce the same confusion.

over from the positivist era in the humanities, when the humanistic disciplines attempted to update themselves by emulating the sciences, mostly social. The ambition to explain, not merely interpret, was inherent in that emulation. With this confusion, and in any endeavour of an interpretive, analytical nature, a whole range of presuppositions becomes important, whereby the term 'context' loses both its specificity and its grounding. The perspective becomes unacknowlegedly deterministic. The unavowed motivation for the interpretation – indeed, the analytical passion – becomes entangled in a conflation of origin, cause, and intention.

These three forms of beginning, while betraying an ontological nostalgia, in turn import a confusion of metaphysics, logic, and psychology. This nostalgia is masochistic, since the first, metaphysics, is largely irrelevant, the second unattainable, and the third unknowable. I will not speculate on why this masochism persists, why it is even passionately defended, or why the status of its leading questions remains undiscussably dogmatic. But I will contend that if the confusion and the passion are cleared away, the humanist with interdisciplinary interests can pursue a much more exciting project, an analytical interpretation that avoids paraphrasis, projection, and paradigmatic confinement, and that opens up a practice of cultural analysis that endorses its function as cultural mediation.[3]

The second argument in favour of *framing* becomes clear from the simple facts of language. Context is primarily a noun that refers to something static. It is a 'thing,' a collection of data whose factuality is no longer in doubt once its sources are deemed reliable. 'Data' means 'given,' as if context brings its own meanings. The need to interpret these data, mostly only acknowledged once the need arises, is too easily overlooked. The act of framing, however, produces an event. This verb form, as important as the noun that indicates its product, is primarily an activity. Hence, it is performed by an agent who is responsible, accountable, for his or her acts.[4]

Furthermore, in a regress that might, in principle at least, be infinite, the agent of framing is framed in turn. In this way, the attempt to account for one's own acts of framing is doubled. First, one makes

3 A specific form of beginning – the position of the author and the role of authorial intention – will be the subject of a separate case study in ch. 7.
4 This may be perceived as a burden by some – the scholar, after all, may become subject to what can be perceived as a form of policing – but I will argue that this accountability is also liberating. Not to speak of the much more frightening, because 'lawless,' policing that goes on in the name of methodological obviousness, or dogma.

explicit what one brings to bear on the object of analysis: why, on what grounds, and to what effect. Then one attempts to account for one's own position as an object of framing, for the 'laws' to which one submits. This double self-reflection, it seems, might help solve the problems of an unreconstructed contextualism as well as of a moralistic and naïve self-reflexivity à la early Habermas.

The third argument in favour of framing is the involvement of *time* in interpretation and analysis. 'Framing' as a verb form points to process. Process both requires time and fills time. It is a factor of *sequence* and *duration*. And where there is duration, change occurs: differences emerge over time. This is where history, inevitably and importantly, participates in any act of interpretation or analysis. One way of taking this simple fact through to its consequences is to enforce a reversed perspective on historical thinking, starting with and in the present. This is one distinction between cultural analysis and history, but a distinction, obviously, that does not free the one from entanglement with the other.

An important consequence of framing having its roots in time is the unstable position of knowledge itself. This might seem to lead to an epistemic aporia, since knowledge itself loses its fixed grounding. But, as I contend in this chapter, a full endorsement of this instability can also produce a different kind of grounding, a grounding of a practical kind. Thus the case I present here, allegorically, begins and ends with a material practice. That practice, in turn, reaches out to cultural analysis, claiming to participate fully in the academic practices whose object it would otherwise, powerlessly, remain. Here, the object, an image *mise en scène*, is put under pressure; its meaning is multiplied, its material existence set up as troubled. In other words, my object is *framed*. What does that entail?

Framing, as a concept, has become so 'in' since Derrida's discussion of Kant's *Third Critique* in *La vérité en peinture* that it seems useful to avoid philosophical partisanship, in the disciplinary as well as deconstructivist sense. I will do this by first invoking that treasure-house of common speak: the dictionary. Suspending philosophy, then, I will provisionally turn this concept into a word again. Before it can become a workable concept – a tool for cultural analysis rather than a philosophical issue – the life of the word in language matters. Longman's variety of definitions quoted at the beginning of this chapter, for example, present themselves here – within the frame of the previous chapter and the shadow it casts over the remainder of this book – as the technical or abstract underworld, the underpinnings, the machinery that holds the *mise-en-scène* in place. If *mise-en-scène* is what we see, framing is what happens before the spectacle is presented.

The deployment of this word as a concept asks for a relationship with the particular analytical practices called 'disciplines.' This is why philosophy, the discipline that develops concepts, is sometimes called an inter-discipline. It is also why philosophy was one of the points on the map in the first case study, just as history – the history of art – is in this one. A concept, moreover, bears on an object, a cultural 'thing': a text, an image, a sculpture, a piece of music, a film; or, as is the case here, a collection of things framed to form an exhibition. The verb form 'framing' – provisionally distinguished from the noun 'frame' – solicits the question of its object. But, as a verb, it also predicates that object, not in the abstract void of theoretical reflection, but in time, space, aspect; it *frames* it. Thus, all by itself, even on the level of the word alone, 'framing' questions the object-status of the objects studied in the cultural disciplines. This questioning results in a repositioning of the object as alive, in ways that have to do with the 'social life of things' rather than with a metaphysical hypostasizing of objects or a rhetorical strategy of personification.[5] It also results in the status of image – rather than text – as the most characteristic, indeed, paradigmatic, kind of cultural object, provided we continue to see it as living its life in the present and the ways we frame it as provisional.

For a productive, fundamentally interdisciplinary deployment of *framing*, even within a domain – art – usually perceived as a monodiscipline, I must connect this chapter to some of my earlier work. In *Double Exposures*, I considered the *life of objects* in their *present tense*, as well as how they come to produce meaning. That work is usually classified as museum studies though it might just as well have been called semantics, anthropology, or, to use my own favourite term, cultural analysis. On no account, though, can it be unproblematically assimilated into art history, for it challenged rather than endorsed the historical that defines that discipline, foregrounding, instead, the slippery but crucial 'now-time' of art objects seen as (Benjaminian) *images*. But it did solicit art history. As a discipline, the latter was invited to reconsider its key terms and methods as being porously continuous with the other disciplinary and interdisciplinary fields that host my work. This invita-

5 The phrase 'the social life of things' refers to the volume edited by Arjun Appadurai (1986).

tion on my part fitted into my ongoing argument on the nature of interdisciplinarity, as non-indifferent to disciplinarity.[6]

But, as I observed later, an interaction and experience with the practice that was the object of study was lacking in *Double Exposures*. This was unfortunate, because the possible convergence of academic and practical agency constitutes a great challenge. The second 'discipline,' if that word may be applied in this context, that my interdisciplinarity solicits is, then, not academic but practical 'art history.' Positing that the study of practices in art museums pertains to two disciplines, not one – that is, separating art history from its 'natural' affiliation with museums – constituted the primary severance that made the case studies in my earlier book *inter*-disciplinary. I will perform the same severance in this chapter by going on a field trip to better understand the object of study. The relationship between analysis and practice – first opened up, then negotiated – constitutes the area where *framing* might emerge as a concept that helps to define the parameters of interdisciplinarity in a radical sense.

Theorizing Practice

The standard response to academic critiques of museums is that a museum is a place of praxis confined by material constraints. The practical nature of museum work is summarized by the fact that, as I have often been told, *a show is not a book*. This is true in a way that is important for the present chapter. It is also the reason why, in *Double Exposures*, I construed *shows*, *not* art works, as my object of analysis. Shows, seen again as actions described by the verb 'to show,' and *taking place* in a specific timeplace; transient, fugitive, but culturally active, existing as dormant things until brought to life by visitors. Shows, in this sense, are instances of *mise-en-scène*. Hence, it is in this way – as a practice, as *mise-en-scène* – that we do, or should, construct museums and the exhibitions taking place in them as objects of examination. Except that I do not accept the opposition to theory – or, more generally, academic analysis – implicit in this allegation of praxis.

I also resist the fact that this praxis is based on a number of other

---

6 This point was made clearer to me by a short argument in favour of a *transdisciplinary* approach (one that is, in contrast, wilfully indifferent to disciplinarity) that appeared in the introduction to Nico Beger's book (2001). On the specific importance of non-indifference, see my article (2000).

assumptions, all of which are part of it, and hence, of our object of analysis, which, for this case study, is *museum practice in its troubled relationship to art theory and history.* For example, it is quite commonly assumed by museum professionals that their research ought to be reflected in their presentation, whereby the show becomes a simplified version of the results of their research.[7] This conflation of art history and museum practice remains unreflected, and disentangling the two through the concept of framing – a concept recognized by art history, under the guise of context, as being of near-exclusive relevance – is the primary mode of travel in this chapter. These same professionals also frequently assume that the research thus presented must be *historical*, and that historical inquiry is necessarily and exclusively based on questions of intention, faction, factual environment, affiliation, and patronage. History, in this limited sense, becomes the characteristic site for the confusions that the concept of context entails – and that the alternative concept, *framing*, can be called upon to remedy.

These assumptions do two things to participants in an exhibition, framing them on specific models: they turn the public into a unified clone of the curator, and because, in spite of his appeal to praxis, the curator sees himself as a scholar, they make the public expect him to be just that.[8] This leads to a conflation of theory, or history, and practice, of the art historian and the curator, and of the subject of framing – say, the curator – and the addressees, the members of the public. Visitors are, in fact, so frequently confronted with this practice that looking at shows from the vantage point of such assumptions has become the cultural habit or unreflected frame that museum practice imposes. But curators don't always have enough time to be 'good' scholars. Nor does 'the public' have anything more than a vague, ideal existence as a unified body of disciplined citizens.

All of these concerns came together for me in 1998 when I was asked by the Museum Boijmans Van Beuningen in Rotterdam to curate the presentation of a newly acquired, early seventeenth-century non-canonical painting to the public. It was an object of 'old art' not yet framed – not part of the canon, or of the glorious Golden Age, or by any famous artist – that I was asked, precisely, to frame. To make an

---

7 This, incidentally, is a practice that makes a show out of a book.
8 I am limiting myself here to the curator of 'old' or 'foreign' art or objects – objects that only yield their meanings through mediation. In contrast, the curator of contemporary art often tends to construe him- or herself as (a clone of) the artist.

image, in the full sense, out of a dead object. The invitation gave me the precious opportunity to test if, and how, revisionist presentations are possible in practice. In this chapter, I will report on that experiment so as to 'work through' the theoretical questions and methodological issues related to *framing objects*. My hope is that framing will become convincing as an indispensable complement to image, and that it will account for the way the latter has been *mise en scène*. Framing here is presented as one of those concepts that is methodologically reasonable and responsible precisely because it opens up rather than shuts down possibilities of analysis across the divisions of disciplines that defensively claim to 'own' certain categories of objects.

I am interested in the phenomenon of exhibition as an object of cultural analysis. How is the following interaction between theory and practice different from museum studies? Among many other relevant studies in this discipline, I will mention three. Sherman and Rogoff's collective volume, *Museum Culture*, is especially interested in the institutionalizing aspects that make objects appear as 'naturally' ordered within national, historical, and stylistic discursive structures (1994). Greenberg, Ferguson, and Nairne's *Thinking about Exhibitions* (1996) shows a particular interest in shows as a form of catering, as a flirt with the public. Didier Maleuvre's *Museum Memories* (1999) makes the most of Kantian-Derridean reflections on the frame, insisting with Proust that an art work – and, by extension, an exhibition – is a form of quotation. All three studies acknowledge in one way or another that showing is a form of framing. But none focuses on the consequences of this fact, or orients framing as a concept to bear on the object of study, other than to suggestively indict the framing that goes on in exhibitions. The present analysis is meant to fill that gap, so as to make a case for the productive use of the concept of framing *in the very process of its formation through deployment*.

Underlying this work, but kept implicit, is Derrida's rich text on the frame as parergon, as a kind of supplement to the work that it is also part of; in other words, the frame is the link between work and world, not the cut between them, however hard it tries to be just that cut. This meaning of framing, in turn, frames my project – to cut or sever, then re-link, art history and museum practice – allegorically here. The new link, through a reflexive deployment of framing, will be mutual: not a dictate of one discipline cloned (but in a watered-down version) into the other, but a movement back and forth from which both emerge changed. A travel, in other words, where the travellers meet halfway, travel together for a while, then return home again enriched.

Derrida's text brings us closer to framing as a concept. But, given his repeated caution against the very idea of concepts, it would be an abuse to declare the word's concept status off-hand.[9] Instead, that caution against rigidifying must be taken along in our baggage. And, I am sensitive to the meaning of 'framing' as 'to set up.' 'Framing' cannot become a concept if it doesn't travel through the practice it was called upon to help structure. This is how a concept theorized a practice, and, as we will see, a practice theorized a concept.

On Being Set Up[10]

One of the first things I had to deal with in undertaking this project was to unravel the meaning of framing as 'to set up.' One is always set up; the pressures on objects to produce certain meanings also affect the subjects assigning the meanings. What I earlier called 'policing,' by dogma, paradigm, or discipline, is part of this set-up. But in museums there are many other factors, including material constraints, finances, or other contingencies. In museum environments, the object is put under pressure, its meaning multiplied, its material existence set up as troubled. This meant that my object was going to be *framed*, inevitably. I was already set up, both by my own intuitive responses to the painting – in turn heavily framed by my background knowledge and persuasions – and by the demands of the museum's curator, the space, and the work itself. At least six kinds of set-up were at work on me from the very beginning. Let me spell out these frames.

The painting in question was *Judith Shows Holophernes' Head to the People of Bethulia* (1605), by Gerrit Pieterszoon Sweelinck (fig. 4.1). The chief curator of old art at Boijmans had invited me to do the presentation because of my interest in the topic of the painting – the biblical story of Judith – and its traditional interpretations. I had published on *Judith* – both the biblical text and paintings 'of' or 'after' it, themselves, in fact, recreations of it. I was therefore able to answer questions that the people working in the museum had faced before they studied the painting. Questions such as 'What's that older woman doing there?' or 'Why is she putting his head in a sack?'; their framing questions. They

9 See *Writing and Difference*, in which *différance* is declared a non-concept.
10 For an interesting commentary on this project, see Denaci (2001).

4.1 Gerrit Pietersz Sweelinck, *Judith Shows Holophernes' Head to the People of Bethulia*, 1605, oil on canvas

were also intuitive questions that people tend to forget once they know more, but that members of the public might have too. The museum's reason for approaching me was thus my first frame in the sense of set-up. It was going to entail working against the expectation that I do a thematic presentation.

Before seeing the painting itself, I already had two ideas about it from seeing a black-and-white photograph. Neither idea had much to do with the topic that led to the invitation. The two words that popped into my head and that became my primary frames – to be cherished as a shield to the set-ups – were 'ambition' and 'portraiture.' The former came from a sense that the painting was a patchwork of a variety of meticulously executed genres meant to show off the artist's skills. This internal variety was not so much responsible for disrupting the work's unity – as connoisseurial response would have it – as for changing its nature. The latter, 'portraiture,' came from my intuitive response to the three faces – of Judith, of her maidservant, and of Holophernes.

To my utter dismay, these two notions also showed up in the page that Carel van Mander devoted to Sweelinck in his famous *Schilderboeck* (1604). I was blown away by this confrontation with 'historical evidence.' I was going to have to deal with it, and this could not be by ignoring it or proposing it as the 'truth' about the painting. This second framing as 'set-up,' then, consisted of a confrontation. Whereas my eagerness to accept the invitation had been motivated by the desire to mark my difference from art history, all the evidence drew me towards doing just that: using such historical evidence. My answer was to resist establishing a direct phone line between historical documentation and the work of art. The 'evidence' turned me into a reluctant art historian. Indeed, studying the painting in the restoration workshop only deepened my sense that ambition and portraiture were crucial to this painting, which was the last thing I wanted.[11]

A third set-up came from working with the curator. This is an altogether different activity to analysing his work after the fact, and certainly to analysing it from a theoretical perspective. In this case, I knew there were going to be confining parameters, and there were. One was the curator's interest in presenting the painting in conjunction with other acquisitions the museum had made over the years, acquisitions

---

11 The time spent in the restoration workshop, a near-first for me, was utterly wonderful. I thank Annetje Boersma, the restorer, and Jeroen Giltay, the curator, for their hospitality.

that revealed a sustained effort to collect early seventeenth-century paintings from the age that is, precisely, not (yet) 'golden.' This made sense from his perspective and I decided to accept it early on, even if at that point I regretted that it made it more difficult to focus on the Judith theme.

As it turned out, it was ultimately a very constructive frame. In fact, the curator's-wish-as-set-up saved me from the temptation to make the show thematic. Since thematics so often seems to be the sole alternative to monographic shows and so easily becomes totally ahistorical, I was reluctant to endorse it, even though there was pressure to do so from others in the museum. Moreover, although the curator's wish posed the problem of how to unify the show (a problem that, in the end, may not quite have been resolved), it also brought to the fore the museum's self-reflexivity regarding its own policy. This, in turn, added a dimension to the experiment it may not otherwise have had. Which goes to show that set-ups are not always, not only, negative forces.

A fourth framing condition of a material order was that the presentation had to be done using the means at hand: the collection. There was no money available for loans, and, in any event, no time to get them. I was not allowed to drill holes or make other changes in the walls of the designated room, and, owing to lighting restrictions, the prints and drawings could not be exhibited in the same room as the paintings. Significantly, at this juncture, the restrictive, potentially negative, meaning of framing – in these four set-ups – keyed into the positive one, which was to provide frames of reference with which to read the painting. As a result of being framed as in set up, I got the idea to frame the painting *by making framing itself its overall frame.* I emphasize this moment of the formation of the concept for the show because it was the moment when *framing* stood at the edge between 'word' and 'concept,' which was also precisely the moment when it was being considered as a tool for practical intervention.

My experiment now involved investigating how to understand the multiple and contradictory connections between the 'work of art' and the way we (can) frame it, so that I could construct a *mise-en-scène* that would *work.* The principle of multiplicity demanded a break with the way museums fabricate itineraries, by turning rooms into paths, using the logic of sequence, most frequently a chronological one. It required replacing this traditional walk with a different kind of travel.

The fifth frame I had to deal with reflected a problem that undermines most museums' art-historical dogma. In the case of a painting by an artist who has very few works to his name and is relatively unknown – routinely typecast as a 'minor' artist – neither a monographic exhibition nor a period show is a helpful frame. The former because of lack of material; the latter because it condemns the little bit there is to 'minor' status. In this case, overruled by considerations of canonicity, Sweelinck's work would have been subordinated to that of his master, Cornelis van Haarlem, or of his superiors; aesthetic judgment would have made the work virtually invisible. Contrary to the claim of Kant-inspired aesthetic theory, aesthetics in this sense does not entail *severing* the work from interests or politics, but is in itself a political practice – of exclusion.[12]

The sixth frame was the tension between my wish to foreground framing by offering a plurality of frames, and the need to present a unified product that visitors could recognize as such. These concurrent needs to de-centre and re-centre kept the conception of the presentation on the verge of contradiction. It was these two gestures, of de-centring and re-centring, of un-framing and re-framing, that became the foundation of my work on the show.

First, and paradoxically, for someone averse to notions of 'masterpiece,' I decided to make the painting absolutely central, by exhibiting it on a bright red screen (fig. 4.2). By staging it in this way, I hoped to turn an object into an image, in the full sense of that concept. The colour was meant to enhance the painting's centrality and tie in with its bloody theme, to be a frame in the most material sense of the word, but, in that capacity, already spilling over from the material into the symbolic. But this centring was to be a frame neither of canonization nor of phoney delimitation. Instead of surrounding the painting with other works on the basis of historical or thematic similarities, I made different frames for it. In between these different frames, the work itself was going to serve less as a centre than as a key that opened up each frame like a gearshift. This centring was, in fact, the show's work against a fixed itinerary.

Second, I gave the presentation a title other than that of the painting. It became 'Moordwijven!/Lady Killers!' In the way that some words can also mean their opposite, the Dutch word *moordwijven*, literally 'murder-women,' puns on 'murderous women' and 'terrific women,' or 'women to die for.' The word is, in fact, untranslatable. Neverthe-

---

12 This problem, incidentally, is not solved by ignoring it. I will return to this issue later.

4.2 Screen with Sweelinck's *Judith* and other paintings; foreground: display case with seventeenth-century Dutch household goods

less, what it became in English – 'Lady Killers,' without a hyphen – while blurring gender, retains the ambiguity. This gender-blurring in fact came in handy, because it added an aspect lacking in the Dutch title: the English title suggests that the biblical killer-women kill because there are men out there who kill first, a nuance that seemed appropriate in the context.

These two centring gestures were necessary to avoid a confusing effect on the visitors. They were my framing gestures against the six set-ups. According to my experiment, visitors were to be introduced to Sweelinck's painting in a variety of ways simultaneously. Instead of passively consuming the *mise-en-scène*, they could thus stage their subjectivity through it. My purpose, even if I had to program a limited number of choices, was to suggest that each viewer had a choice between many different frames, depending on his or her own interests. But earlier experiments have demonstrated that the public, framed as it is beforehand by cultural habit, is disoriented when the usual 'technology of the series' (Tony Bennett) is lacking.[13]

13 See Bennett (1995).

On Setting Up

I will now describe the various frames I constructed for the painting through the visual organization and captions. The presentation was to be held in Room 4 of the museum, which was about 13 metres long and 7.70 metres wide. Adjacent to that room was a small transitional area leading to the next room, which I wanted to use for the prints and drawings. In the centre of the right wall of Room 4 was the opening to Room 3, which left the wall divided into two sections of 5.5 metres each. The screen on which Sweelinck's painting, and its generic relatives, hung – its *visual analysis* – was to be placed about 1 metre in front of the opening to Room 5, located behind it, so as to diminish the light in the makeshift print cabinet while leaving the space in front of it accessible.

On the 2.10-metre-wide wall to the left of the entrance to Room 4, a panel with introductory text was placed. This text was designed to present the multiplicity of framings as an explanation for the visual organization. It was meant to serve as a table of contents, or menu, for the show. It is reproduced here:

Lady Killers!
Gerrit Pietersz. Sweelinck, *Judith Shows Holophernes' Head to the People of Bethulia*, 1605

The museum was recently able to purchase this important painting with support from the Museum Boijmans Van Beuningen Foundation. It is an important work for several reasons: it reflects a consistent acquisition policy; it is the creation of an ambitious, experimental artist; and it depicts one of a series of mythical stories about power struggles between men and women. Moreover, it fits in well with an unusual series of prints and drawings in the collection devoted to the same theme, which raises the issue not only of sexual relations but also of the challenge of visually representing interacting bodies. The Judith theme also frequently appears in objects of the Applied Arts section. Decapitation divides the head from the body as well as visually depriving the person of his individuality. Might a line be drawn from dissection to composition, and, specifically, from decapitation to portraiture?

Beneath this text, at a distance of one metre from the wall, I put a display case, which housed seven household utensils on which Judith and other biblical heroines were depicted. Because such objects, especially in the context of paintings, are easily overlooked, they were accompanied by more extensive captions than the paintings.[14]

The other paintings from the collection were displayed in the traditional manner, side by side on the long left wall, with enough space between them so that each could be viewed in isolation. This modernist mode of hanging fitted the content of this section – it was, precisely, its frame – which was based on the traditional preoccupation of art museums.[15] At the beginning of the wall, a general caption indicated the frame that was applied here, mentioning other acquisitions made by the museum during the preceding decade, all works by Haarlem-based masters. This was the show's 'memory' of the kind of framing that was being relinquished. It was the site of reflection – implicit, because 'a show is not a book' – on this show's difference. By putting the greater masters, especially Sweelinck's own master, on a side wall away from the central screen, the minor status of Sweelinck was both acknowledged and undermined.

Of all the paintings, only Speckaert's of *Jael and Sisera* was given an individual caption (fig. 4.3). Hung closest to the new work but on the opposite wall, this painting most obviously invited comparison with it. Its caption read:

> With her sensual mouth, looser hair and bare leg, Jael is much more sensually depicted than Sweelinck's Judith. There is more narrative movement in this painting; the story isn't finished yet.

The final sentence here shifts from a descriptive to a more overtly interpretive framing. The description was an unofficial quote from the curator's comments, which I took as representative of a 'first sight' obviousness.

'Story' has a double meaning: the diegetic story, in which Jael's act of showing is showing off and putting the other(s) to shame, and the interpretive story, which implies there will be more to say about the painting than this semi-pornographic comment suggests. My hope was that the comparison might invite the viewers to consider the two

---

14 These captions were written by the curator of the department of applied arts, Alexandra van Dongen, who also identified the objects at my request.

15 In fact, visitors inevitably entered the show via other rooms of the department of old art, where this aesthetic is systematically applied.

4.3 Hans Speckaert, *Jael and Sisera*, c. 1576, oil on canvas

paintings not in terms of their relative aesthetic merit but as two different modes of visually dealing with narrative subjects. This somewhat
didactic caption was offered as a counter-frame to the most obvious
frame of all, the one the curators relished: the theme of castration.

Paradoxically perhaps, the central section of the leaflet was titled
'*Judith* as master-piece,' the hyphen being introduced to suggest the
somewhat different meaning of the phrase, as derived from van
Mander's quote, where he cites Sweelinck as having said that he'd
rather be 'A good painter [...] than a great monarch.' And, also, to foreground the meaning of 'masterpiece' in Dutch, where the word also

refers, literally, to the 'exam' work a painter had to produce for admittance into the guild, as, precisely, a *master* of his craft. The application of the problematic term 'masterpiece' was meant to trigger reflection on it, since this category was not at all self-evident for the painting in question.

The following text, which is from the information leaflet, not a caption, pertained to the artist's ambition:[16]

> The narrative subject makes the work a historical piece. In the background, at the right, a rugged mountain landscape is depicted in which we see soldiers and two figures from behind. The two figures could be the fleeing Judith and her maid. The still life of wine, bread and olives – a choice that refers to Christ's Last Supper – gave the painter the opportunity to render several different textures very distinctly. However simple the meal, the glass of the precious Venetian jug with the drop of wine still in it rivals the glass that appears in sumptuous still lives. The exquisite depiction of all kinds of materials was doubtless part of the artist's ambition. This is further suggested by the sword, in which his signature, engraved as if in bas-relief, becomes part of the fictive world being shown to us. The jewels on Judith's richly decorated robe, the poses of all three 'actors' and the landscape that functions as a decor emphasize the theatrical element of the work. This element had already been introduced by the curtain, as was often the case in seventeenth-century domestic scenes. Unlike in Speckaert's *Jael*, no action is established here. Instead, it is as if the actors are accepting applause at the end of a performance.

The centring screen was both the most complex and the most paradoxical frame I constructed: the painting itself was the frame that spilt over onto the surrounding works that had been brought together on a variety of grounds; the screen was, after all, about the internal variety of the painting. That screen, with its two wings, was placed just before the two short walls that led up to the transitional print cabinet. The works on these sections of the walls were thus half hidden from the visitors as they entered the room.[17]

The wall to the right of the centring screen was made to look crowded,

---

16 Also, it was a patchwork made from drafts written by the department's curator (and purchaser of the painting), the restorer, and myself.

17 This was primarily a device to avoid full lighting. But it worked very well in producing an ambiance of intimacy for the prints and drawings.

with six portraits of women in it, all from the first half of the century, some oval, and, many, stylistically as well as canon-wise, totally unrelated (fig. 4.4). Only one caption accompanied this ensemble:

> Whether it is men or women who are depicted, the stately poses and dignified attire of the well-to-do middle classes make these portraits into conventional status symbols. The similarities between such portraits can conceal the true nature of the portrait genre, which was to record the unique face of the individual. Because of this, the similarity between the two women in Sweelinck's *Judith* acquires a powerful significance.

A small sign identified the painters, the sitters, and the dates, for those interested in such facts.

Where the women's portraits served, literally, as a backdrop to the main work, I placed four paintings closer to the Sweelinck, on the wings of the screen, to foreground the different genres represented within the painting. Here, I had to contend with 'historical evidence.' In his *Schilderboeck*, van Mander reports Sweelinck's own words about his ambition, albeit in indirect discourse. These words were put on the screen in large print above the painting: '... *a good painter rather than a great monarch.*' The point was not to ignore this evidence, or to give it more status *as evidence* than such indirect, gossipy reporting warrants (this is why I avoided historicizing lettering, choosing a modern typeface instead). Nor did I want to infuse the centrality of the painting with more canonizing intentionalism. The challenge, here, was to avoid one frame, intentionalism, while doing justice both to the 'implied artist' as the figure who performed this ambition in his 'master-piece,' and to his contemporary critic, who acknowledged the ambition and clearly found it relevant. I could only reconcile this quote with my overall project – to de-centre, un-frame the painting through multiplying frames – *because*, on all accounts, it was difficult to envisage as a masterpiece in the modern sense. This, in itself, obviously, implies an unwarranted aesthetic judgment on which, I hoped, the visitors would be led to reflect.

But reflection alone is not enough.[18] The historical 'effect of the real'

18 This was the error Habermas made in his somewhat idealistic program of *Knowledge and Human Interest* (1968). It becomes most clear in his chapter on Freud, where he ignores Freud's own insistence that insight alone is not enough. Felman's article on teaching, cited earlier (1983), offers an excellent antidote to this problem in Habermas.

4.4 Portraits of women (left to right):
Jan Antonisz van Ravesteyn, *Portrait of a Woman*, 1631, oil on canvas; Jacob Gerritsz Cuyp, *Portrait of Cornelia van Wesel*, 1639, oil on canvas; Jacob I. Willemsz Delff, *Portrait of Baertje van Adrichem*, 1593, oil on canvas; Bartholomeus van der Helst, *Portrait of a Woman*, 1646, oil on canvas; Bernardus Zwaerdecroon, *Portrait of a Woman*, c. 1645–54, oil on canvas; Paulus Moreelse, *Portrait of a Young Woman*, 1615, oil on canvas

that such quotes produce has a 'historicist' purpose. The notion of ambition – a word I used in the information leaflet but not on the wall – has a contemporary resonance today, whereas 'masterpiece' is completely naturalized. By drawing attention to the ambition of the artist, who, by all accounts, would not be considered important by traditional art historians and art critics, I meant to enable the viewers to frame the work with empathy. Thus, by mentioning Sweelinck's ambition rather than by glorifying great art or putting the painting at a historical distance, I was trying to help them identify with the artist, across time. Those who wished it could have what one historian has called a 'historical experience' – emphatically not based on a conflation of past and present.[19] As Didier Maleuvre argued about the historicity of things in his 1999 book *Museum Memories*,

> To be historical, an object must have seceded from time: it cannot be one with its temporal becoming. The historical object is therefore one that belongs neither to its original setting – from which it has been singled out – nor to the present – in which it resists assimilation. (58–9)

The historical experience consists of living through the caesura that inheres in the historical:

> The historical is the stuff of the past which, by being remembered in the present, desists from being in the present: it is what cannot be reconstituted in the present. (59)

Here, the *frame*, precisely, separates, acknowledges the separation, and thus *links* present to past. This experience infuses subjects in the present with the temporal density that 'history' provides. In this sense, framing, as the act of living through that caesura, becomes *a practical concept*. As a first step towards articulating the kind of concept it can be for cultural analysis, then, this handling of historical 'evidence' to allow for the possibility of historical experience exemplifies the point of a concept in, or as, practice.

But the mere notion of ambition would be too abstract, too general, to truly facilitate a historical experience, or, in this case, to frame the painting. The painting's ambition seemed not simply to be its desire to excel. Instead, it took a specific turn, embodied in its attempt to excel *in*

19 See Ankersmit (1993).

many genres. This aspect provided a frame through which to read the painting on its own terms, while at the same time keying it into a historical experience based on empathy. Incidentally, and this constituted part of its private charm for me, the painting's specific ambition thus became emblematic for interdisciplinarity in practice – within the practice of painting. This particular ambition was visually reinforced by surrounding the work with other paintings from the museum's collection in which these genres were represented. These paintings, again, were not selected for their canonical status or aesthetic quality, but because they could help to explain Sweelinck's work, just as his work honoured those genres; glosses or visual footnotes rather than stylistic commentaries. This multiple-genre frame seemed all the more attractive as it allowed the viewers to realize for themselves not only *that* genres in painting differ, but also *which* genres they might individually find most interesting.

The four genres – domestic interior, still life, landscape, portrait – differed all the more dramatically because they were put unusually close together. This central section thus became the centre of the stage; it foregrounded the fact that exhibitions are *mises en scène*. It was, in fact, only after the installation was completed that I realized to what extent the combination was a frame-breaker. Only one of these visual footnotes had a caption, the one whose connection to the Sweelinck was the least obvious, and thus the most in need of translation, since it relied more on iconographic tradition than on visual display alone. It was Gerard Dou's *Young Woman*, exemplifying the genre of the domestic interior:

> The curtain in the Sweelinck shows that Judith has bravely dared to enter Holophernes' 'domestic sphere.' In this domestic scene by Gerard Dou, the intimate world is again separated from the rest of the space by a curtain. The two curtains also add a theatrical dimension element to the depiction, whereby the demonstration of moral values and the interpretation of behaviour become more important.

The rather traditional genre painting by Dou was given a frame that doubled its meaning, gave it more 'depth.' But in the same move, the Dou sent the viewer back to the *Judith*, where the curtain was not so obvious, and the meaning 'domesticity' could easily be overlooked.

This seems as good a moment as any to reflect on captions *per se*. For captions, within museum practice, function like keys or shifters between visual and textual information, and between what the viewer is given and the curator has done. They are the sites of the learning that is meant to turn the viewer into an admirer and emulator of the curator-as-scholar.

Given this traditional role of captions and the ensuing expectations, it seemed to me they had to be de-naturalized. The decision to furnish some but not all of the works in the show with captions was in itself an important part of my endeavour to de-frame by providing multiple frames. In general, I supplied information only in those cases where it was most needed, such as for those barely readable, out-of-context, household objects. But I also hoped that the apparent randomness of the distribution of captions would entice visitors to read them. Because they would not always be where one might expect to find them, they could not become part of the wallpaper, hence easily overlooked. I was also reluctant to emphasize obvious meanings, loath to underestimate viewers, or to turn the show into a book after all. In particular, I refrained from commenting on the most revealing visual footnote.

The work I am referring to was one of the two loans it was possible to include. It was another – perhaps the only other – important work by Sweelinck: a portrait of his brother, the famous composer and musician who achieved greater fame than he did. More to trigger reflection and to shock than to suggest psychoanalytic associations as a sub-frame, I placed this portrait right next to Holophernes' head, with its undeniably similar features – the same apparently broken nose, the same receding hairline. I will return to the (un)fortunate brother below. But to frame that return, a few words are needed on an issue I can no longer postpone: thematics.

The Trouble with Thematics

Clearly, presenting a *Judith* without paying attention to the most obvious of frames, the thematic one, would be disingenuous and beside the point. Visitors would expect it, and might quickly lose interest if it were to be artificially avoided. Seeing, after all, as has often been emphasized, is as much based on recognition as it is on perception.[20]

20 'Appelons *percept* plutôt que perception un aspect ainsi composé, retenu, mémorielle-ment consolidé. Je ne perçois que par ce dont je veux me souvenir' (my translation: 'Let's call percept rather than perception, an aspect that is thus composed and retained, hence, consolidated by memory. I perceive only that which I care to remem-ber'). See Jacques and Leutrat (1998: 37).

But, as I suggested earlier, three traps lurk here: the predictably misogynistic interpretation of the theme, the ahistorical reification of any theme, and the visual tedium of repetition.

My attempt was to exploit the thematic frame by blowing it up from the inside, so to speak. This was done in several ways concurrently. The thematic part of the show was divided into two sections: the prints and drawings, and the paintings. Wishing, at all costs, to avoid the kind of thematics that surround castration anxiety or more general misogynistic fantasy, and forced by the limitations of the collection – but then, wholeheartedly – I presented the paintings in terms of ambiguity, not concentrating on powerful women, the famous lady killers, but on a variety of power relations between women and men; *lady*-killers confronting lady *killers*.

This section ran so counter to the expectation of a thematic presentation that I had more extensive captions accompany it.[21] I quote these first:

Frans Floris, *Lucretia*, 1519–20
A woman as the victim of the power struggle between men. She was raped and took her own life to save her (or her husband's?) honour. It is painful that such a sad story is often used as an excuse to paint nude women.[22]

Next was *Faun and Nymph* (1540–50), from the School of Titian. Its caption read as follows:

Not every rape ends in stories of such total victimization as that of Lucretia. Although the faun has a firm grip on her, it does not look as if their union will be a peaceful one.

Although visually almost redundant in the face of the fury that pulls

---

21 The small size of the show as a whole, hence, also of this section, made this extensive deployment of captions more palatable than it might otherwise have been.

22 If you wonder what a *Lucretia*, of all subjects, was doing in the thematic section on lady killers, you have an excellent point. The curator cited this painting first, while we were brainstorming on thematically related works in the collection. That's why it was included. It seemed outrageous, and, therefore perhaps for that reason alone, important to juxtapose this painting to the others. This is another example of a potentially confining frame that, once turned around, became utterly productive. But this incongruity also required the potentially slightly moralizing last sentence of this caption.

the faun's hair and screams loudly, this caption triggered resistance from some viewers with whom I visited the show. Interestingly for the present discussion, the painting's visuality was simply overruled by the literary pre-text when one viewer exclaimed: 'But you don't understand! Fauns and nymphs were just frolicking in the meadows, rape was not an issue!' I found this a revealing case of iconographic anti-visualism parading as historical knowledge. What does the phrase 'were just frolicking' mean? Frolicking in the historical past or in some writer's fantasy? The prefacing remark 'you don't understand!' is formulaic in this kind of argumentation.

Then came Michael Sweerts' *Sleeping Old Man and Girl*, c. 1650, which contrasted dramatically with the furious nymph:

> Sleep makes men vulnerable, as Holophernes' fate showed. The girl looks at him but her look is difficult to interpret. Within the framework of this presentation, one might wonder: is she going to play a trick on him or lovingly care for him? The painting provides no answer.

This ambiguous painting (fig. 4.5), infused with ambivalent mood, was the hinge in this small series. It clashed both with the victim paintings (*Lucretia*) and with the resistance paintings (*Faun and Nymph*), as well as with the subsequent history paintings on biblical episodes, if only by virtue of its generic allegiance to genre painting. Next to it came a few biblical works in which women trick men, but either unsuccessfully or for the men's own benefit, as in Lucas van Leyden's *Potiphar's Wife Shows Joseph's Coat*, and an anonymous Flemish work, from c. 1520, titled *Lot and His Daughters*. Inserting the Sweerts here was, among other strategies, also an attempt to make genre painting less frivolous.[23] But it was also the most effective demonstration of the power of framing. In its 'proper' context, this image would have been tautologic: a man sleeping, a girl watching over him. The uncanny, almost spooky suspense that came in merely because of its insertion between a furious nymph and depictions of women tricksters was the exclusive effect of the juxtaposition. Interestingly, those viewers I interviewed did find the suspense quite convincing.

---

23 My awareness of the ambiguities and social relevance of genre painting owes a great debt to the work of Nanette Salomon. See e.g. her book on Jacob Duck (1998) and her analysis of Vermeer (1999). An important collection of her essays is forthcoming (in press).

4.5 Michael Sweerts, *Sleeping Old Man and Girl*, c. 1650, oil on canvas

Note that there was not a single other Judith in this section, not even a Jael, Delilah, or other classical lady killer. The one *Jael*, the Speckaert already mentioned, was close by, on the same wall, but on the other side of the opening to the next room. On the one hand, this absence of the central theme was a result of the absence of such works from the collection (the frame as set-up); on the other hand, it helped me to avoid over-emphasizing the facile thematic aspect (the set-up turned productive). However, the ambiguities might easily have got lost on viewers keen on connecting this frame with the subject of the painting. Looking meaningfully relies so heavily on recognition that simply avoiding stereotypical modalities of looking by repressing their triggers would have been both futile and a demonstration of contempt for viewers' habits. To recall the Judith subject while simultaneously undercutting its centrality, two interventions were needed. First, Speckaert's *Jael*, one of the works selected from the collection, was moved from the left wall to be closer to the thematic section. Second, in the small section to the left of the entrance, I added a number of colour photographs of other *Judith* paintings as well as one drawing, all related to Sweelinck's representation of the theme in specific ways and thus countering thematic conflation (fig. 4.6).

The two most famous *Judith Beheading Holophernes* paintings, by Artemesia Gentileschi and Caravaggio, included in these photographic reproductions, were perhaps most likely to confront the viewers with certain barely conscious feelings, such as horror or admiration for a job well done (the Gentileschi), or with contradictory feelings like surprise and identification, evoked when the face of the decapitated figure turns out to be a self-portrait (the Caravaggio), feelings that enhance the Sweelinck in unexpected ways. These irreverent photographic copies were also meant to shock viewers into realizing the difference between imagery as such and the material work of the actual activity of painting, to reflect on what matters to them – the work as image or the work as thing. To foreground this question without didactic emphasis, the photograph of the drawing was also considerably smaller than the photographic reproductions of the paintings. The deceptive similarity in format and size with the slides used in art-history classes came to haunt this display.

There was also a case with two small bronze sculptures, both of Samson. One showed Delilah cutting Samson's hair. This work added to the thematic analysis the important element of motherly care expressed in the tender gesture. This is so frequently part of Delilah represen-

4.6 Photographs of famous *Judith* paintings (left to right):
Jan de Braij, *Judith and Holophernes*, 1659, oil on canvas; Caravaggio, *Judith and Holophernes*, 1598–9, oil on canvas; Artemisia Gentlieschi, *Judith and Holophernes*, 1620, oil on canvas; Rembrandt, *Judith and Holophernes*, drawing; Pordenone, *Judith Holding the Head of Holophernes*, oil on canvas

tations that the outrage in commentaries about the 'treacherous' lady killer stands in stark contrast to the *visual* representations. The other bronze was responsible for another aspect of the thematic that is seldom discussed: the homosocial frame within which these women do their killing. Often, and most clearly in the case of Samson, the women accused of treacherous behaviour act under constraint by men. Seeing the corporeal togetherness of the fighting men in the sculpture of *Samson Wrestling with a Philistine*, one might wonder about what Eve Sedgwick calls, in her *Epistemology of the Closet*, the fine line between being a man's man and being interested in men (1990) (fig. 4.7).

But what could I do now to re-frame the now un-framed theme? Like the Samson story, the story of Judith is often depicted in art. These stories are frames in themselves, even as they are also being framed. Their stories have great dramatic potential. Their combination of beauty and virtue presents a challenge to the subtle painter. Moreover,

4.7 Pierino da Vinci, *Samson Wrestling with a Philistine*, bronze, date unknown

4.8 Gerrit Pietersz Sweelinck, *Judith Shows Holophernes' Head to the People of Bethulia*, 1605, oil on canvas. Detail: heads of Judith and servant juxtaposed

the story of Judith juxtaposes two loyalties: Judith saves her people but is a threatening figure to men. As usual, the older woman, Judith's maid, is important for introducing nuances. In many representations, she is depicted as a 'madam,' something given sexual expression in the form of the younger woman. This is why such a female figure is often placed next to Delilah, although the Bible gives no cause for this. In more subtle works, by being contrasted with the older woman, the heroine is depicted as beautiful, attractive, and hence, indirectly, sexual.

But Sweelinck is more subtle still (fig. 4.8). He has the women resemble each other. This suggests cooperation, without an emphasis on sexual 'weapons.' Hence, one of the strongest traditional frames – the over-emphasis on Judith's sexuality as killing – is pushed to the background. In keeping with the biblical frame but displacing the emphasis as it has been placed through tradition, he makes his Judith look away virtuously. The older woman, on the other hand, by virtue of the resemblance, loses her traditional frame of madam or proprietor of a brothel. Instead, she represents Judith to the viewer; she looks us straight in the eye and thus assumes responsibility for our response to the event. The tension between virtue and the use of sexuality as a weapon is thus dramatically presented to the viewer, but, importantly, *without the theme itself* – without a representation of it. This is a dramatic alteration of the framing. It shifts broad thematics to restricted thematics, in the same way it shifts 'third-person' narrative to 'first-/ second-person' dialogue, constative to performative visual language, and, in the wake of that shift, meaning to force.

At this juncture, it seemed to me that it would be useful to broaden the biblical frame by comparing the case of Judith with that of Jael, represented in the nearby Speckaert. The story of Judith is similar to the subject of Speckaert's *Jael and Sisera*, a canonical Old Testament theme (Judges 4 and 5). The Canaanite general Sisera suppresses the people of Israel, after which Barak defeats his army; Sisera flees on foot; Jael entices him into her tent and intoxicates him; while he sleeps, she hammers a tent peg into his temple.[24]

Here, too, a beautiful heroine takes action, saving her people through ruse and sex appeal. In this story, unlike in Judith's, no mention is made of her virtue. In biblical interpretation, this 'gap' led to a flourish of interpretive leaps, from depicting her as a virtual prostitute to rendering her as a discarded 'old hag.' Accordingly, painters framed her in ways that fit the theme, that is, in accordance with traditional interpretations of lady killers. Hence, she is rather voluptuous in Speckaert's rendering. We are shown the moment when Jael is proudly about to show her prey to Barak, the man in charge who was unable to achieve the same victory. A double triumph, therefore, of one woman over two men, and, in a certain sense, a theatrical performance *mise en scène within* the story. Unlike in the Sweelinck, where the women are taken out of diegetic time to address the public, here the play is still on.

Theoretically, by now, viewers would have spent some time in the exhibition room. Through the various framings, the foundation would have been laid for a more integrated comparison that related the stories to their cultural life, the popularity of the stories to the tensions depicted between men and women, and the various traditions of

24 See my book (1988b) on this story and its implications for the methodology of interdisciplinary study.

depiction to the paintings and objects on display. The following question, then, was broached in the information leaflet.

Why is the story of the beautiful – or deadly – heroine so popular that it is often depicted, and even tangibly present, on household utensils, whereby housewives and maids are confronted with it on a daily basis? Like the different stories of Samson (totally defeated by Delilah because she managed to fiddle the secret of his exceptional powers out of him – his hair that had never been cut) and of Jael, this story of Judith is one of those popular myths in which the power struggle between men and women ends in favour of 'the weak(er) sex.' These stories stand next to, or opposite, other stories that have also frequently been depicted, in which women are the victims of (sexual) violence, as when Lucretia was raped and, to save her or her husband's honour, committed suicide. Susannah (in the book of Daniel) barely escapes the same fate: she resists the threats of her two attackers and is saved from death by stoning by the young Daniel, who separates the two Elders and is thus able to catch them out on their contradictions.

The most important aspect of the thematic frame thus became the *variety* of such tensions, not the uniform focus on dangerous women. For me, this was the key to making this show *work*: not repeating what one already knows (or thinks one knows), but drawing upon other knowledge to increase insight into more varied relations. It would have been a mistake to explain such stories simply as those of victims, of women's wickedness, or of a carnivalesque upside-down world in which women get the upper hand. Instead, they belong, together with more ambiguous and ambivalent stories, to a series of stories about women, men, and power. This combination of history and genre paintings, displayed under the heading of thematics, thus opened up the traditional cliché, acknowledging its cultural power and contingency, its historical persistence, and the possibility of questioning it. From a self-evident and confining frame, thematics thus became a theoretical frame.

This, then, is also the moment when the concept of frame/framing itself, already set up as a tool for bridging practice and reflection, seemed to move away from being merely an object of play and challenge to almost become a concept in the philosophical sense as outlined in chapter 1. As both noun and verb, this concept is now able to *join* two of their meanings. The thematic treatment, I submit, displayed 'something composed of parts fitted together and joining' (one of the items in the Longman's list), in order to come up with 'a structure composed of constructional members that give shape or strength.' The cultural coherence suggested in the second definition of 'frame' does more than just show up, so to speak. It reassures, in its acceptance of the reality of such a frame, while at the same time unsettling, by means of insisting on its constructedness.

Framing, as a verb, becomes visible in the same move. 'To plan, work out; to give expression to; to formulate; to shape; construct, draw up' is precisely what the viewer, in the act of reading the thematic section, sees himself doing. This construction is confining ('to enclose (as if) in a frame') so that the final meaning of framing, 'to concoct or devise (a criminal charge) falsely,' starts to come into sight.[25] With the pieces of this patchwork of common meanings, then, the material for a workable concept is put on the table.

To strengthen the emerging concept of frame as a methodological standard, its bearing on what is most centrally involved in the cultural practice under scrutiny – *vision* – was inherently addressed by the dynamic handling of thematics. For a one-sided reading often deprives one of what the depiction visually 'reveals,' that is, the meanings the visual frame is able to produce. Many depictions in which the story on which they are based points in one direction visually suggest the other side of the same story. Thanks to the depiction itself, we see that the other side was embodied in the original story from the beginning: the languid nymph, about to be raped by a powerful faun, emerges as a raging Fury; the lethal Delilah and the murderous Jael and Judith sometimes appear more like caring mothers worrying about their children. If we look back at biblical texts, which would seem to have been so inappropriately interpreted, we see instead that the depiction reveals a new – and until then unseen – side of these texts.

The feelings and loyalties dealt with in such stories are indeed ambivalent. The vulnerability of the drunken or sleeping man can be seen as a rendering of the more common insight that men do not have all the power; that women cannot be totally subjugated; that uncertainty and

---

25 I am not at all claiming a real, enforced self-reflection as part of what actually happens to viewers. What I am setting up here is a model for a post-Habermassian form of self-reflection conducted through enjoyment, based neither on humiliation of cultural participants – their assumed stupidity or 'criminality' – nor on the presumed innocence of their participation. Hence, they become more responsible in the face of the modalities of their acts of looking, and thus empowered by this increase in activity.

vulnerability always also influence relationships. Given the traditional associations with the Judith theme, this unfixed, because heterogeneous, thematic frame was very important for my own thinking about gender, but it was also the frame most liable to be perceived as lacking in unity. Equally important, though, was the focus on the pre-eminence of visual story-telling as more than, and different from, illustration. The photographs, which I hoped would entice viewers to look back at the Sweelinck and thus undermine the linearity of the presentation, were also meant to counter this risk of dispersal. But I also welcomed the practical need to make do with photographs instead of originals, as a way of countering reducing the works from the collection, including the Sweelinck, to inferior versions of greater masterpieces.

As it turned out, the drawbacks of thematics that I mentioned earlier – the predictably misogynistic interpretation of the theme, the ahistorical reification of any theme, and the visual tedium of repetition – could all be countered through a different way of dealing with thematics. The method I used in the exhibition was to deploy narrativity. The theme was first unfixed by being set against a narrative, for example, of the abuse of women as a ground for women's killings. It was further unfixed through the interaction between the viewer and the images that resulted from the difficulty of connecting the juxtaposed works in the first place. As a result, the viewer had little choice but to construct his own narrative. With the theme unfixed in this way, the doxic status of the story, which everyone knows well enough to think they know it, itself raised the issue of that knowledge and its sources. As a result, the literary pre-text became a partner in what was a dynamic reading exercize instead of an immutable origin. Thus revised, mobilized, in the double sense, thematics became a productive frame after all.

The Cutting Edge

As I mentioned earlier, the makeshift print cabinet had to be isolated from the room where the paintings were displayed because of light restrictions. Again, this was a constraint I was able to put to good use. The screen with the Sweelinck and four footnotes turned its back to the prints and drawings. To pull in the graphic section, I had the side walls of the cabinet and the back of the screen painted in the same red colour as the front of the screen. Moreover, since the walls were too small to accommodate the whole selection, some of the drawings and prints were hung on the back of the screen.

In line with suggestions made by Julia Kristeva in her exhibition *Vision capitales* at the Louvre (1998) but not fully elaborated there, I wanted to frame the object with the intimate connection between beheading and portraiture.[26] I now wanted to theorize in more general terms the fine portrait of Holophernes in the new acquisition, already foregrounded by the juxtaposition with the portrait of Sweelinck's famous brother. But to make that point, a more general aspect of the depiction of the human body needed to be explored. This could be called the humanistic frame as compared to the anatomical one. On the one hand, interacting bodies pose the problem of delimitation. What makes an individual body, as opposed to the mass of lines and planes that suggest bodies embracing or killing each other? This issue of the humanistic individual, which framed the show historically, also foregrounded the artistic question of representing three-dimensional bodies, in (inter-)action, on a two-dimensional plane. Lines, as the left-hand side of the print cabinet suggested, are not so much devices for separating as devices for linking, sometimes beyond recognition. In this sense, lines are similar to frames.

On the right-hand wall of the cabinet, another issue of visual representation – human individual existence through anatomy – framed the painting. This issue, part of which was also put forward in Kristeva's exhibition, concerns the different ways in which the individual subject is not whole. The sleeping body displays a vulnerability that seems to visually raise the question of whether sleep doesn't invite the kind of killing actions the biblical heroines represent. Is sleep a state of suspension of being, so that killing someone in his sleep is not 'really,' not morally, killing? The question of individual wholeness is also raised by decapitation as such. For is a body without a head still a human being?

Within the framework of such questions, thematic coherence yields to thematic analysis where, in line with Naomi Schor's 'restricted thematics' (1985), the threat of semantic reification is countered with meta-representational or poetological analysis. Accordingly, the result was a display of works that connected with each other through the presence of several of these issues of representation, regardless of whether they were 'about' lady killers. And, given the practical frame

---

26 See Kristeva (1998). This idea had been advanced earlier by Daniel Arasse (1987). For a critical analysis of the place of the 'cut' in this exhibition, see Denaci (2001).

as set-up, the left-hand wall was (while the right-hand wall wasn't) bound to the thematic unity of lady killers. The two walls of the prints and drawings were connected by my favourite quote from the biblical story. On the left, over the works, were the words 'Look! there lies Holophernes ...'; on the right: '... and his head is missing!'

'A head apart': this section explored the move from dissection to composition. Such stories about women's victory, and such experiments in depicting individual limbs, vulnerable sleeping figures, and heads without bodies, recurred in numerous prints and drawings in the collection. A beautiful series by Lucas van Leyden depicted no less than three of the popular biblical 'lady killers': Jael, Delilah, and Salome. In Ferdinand Bol's drawing of *Tamar and Amnon*, the other side of the story was revealed: the man rapes the woman, who has been lured with a trick.

Anatomy was an important learning tool for artists. By dissecting the human body, they got to know it so well that they were able to render it as a whole on paper or canvas. In many drawings and prints, artists were clearly experimenting with individual body parts. Drawings often show separate body parts, such as ears, hands, and legs. Strikingly, the head is often missing. It is as if the face, the most important part of the human anatomy, is better studied and mastered on its own.

This principle adds another very different reason to the uncertainties and ambivalences about the balance of power between the sexes, through which the popularity of the stories of decapitating women might be explained. Unlike the impersonal, separate body part or the headless body, the decapitated head stands for the essence and limits of the individual. One print, in which a portrait by Hollar, of the Italian painter Giorgione, shows Giorgione proudly holding John the Baptist's decapitated head in his hand, emphatically exposed this principle (fig. 4.9).

At this point, I wanted to attempt a final, encompassing act of framing. I wanted to invite viewers to retrace their steps and take a second look at the Sweelinck painting, perhaps even at the entire room. The act of viewing itself, in its modality of public viewing in the bodily dynamic of moving about a gallery, became the object of the act of framing. A push to abandon the linearity of museum visits was given, in a daring, perhaps dubious, frame presented as open to reflection and decision. On the back of the screen, in the middle and surrounded by several particularly remarkable prints and drawings, I placed a

VERO RITRATTO DE GIORGONE DE CASTEL FRANCO
da luy fatto come lo celebra il libro del VASARI

W. Hollar fecit ex Collectione Iohannis et Iacobi van Veerle. 1650.   F. van den Wyngaerde excudit.

4.9 Wenceslaus Hollar, *Giorgione with the Head of John the Baptist*, 1650, etching

drawing by Sweelinck, a depiction of Saint Luke at the easel. This striking sketch showed the same jaw, cheekbone, and eyebrows that made
the two women in the painting so alike (fig. 4.10).

Looked at with this in mind, Sweelinck's *Judith* became even more
surprising. Could it be a coincidence that the unusual shape of the face
of both Judith and the older woman who resembles her – the promi-
nent cheekbones and the distinct jaw – was also found in the face in
this sketch? Seen in this light, it is striking that Holophernes' head resonates in Sweelinck's most beautiful portrait: that of his brother, who
achieved greater fame.

This last sentence, which leads back to the painting and its two primary features – ambition and portraiture – risks reintroducing relative
canonicity and aesthetic judgment. But I also wished to connect with
preoccupations that I could be sure would be entertained by visitors
and that would thus frame their act of viewing. This point is congenial
with the point, made earlier, about historical experience. It made no
sense to expect people to come into the exhibition space with blank,
empty minds. Framed as visitors invariably are by traditional discourses on art, it seemed more meaningful to me to take such considerations into account – by putting them into a relativist and multisemic
perspective – than to ignore their important influence.

Visually, this connection between the less successful brother, here in
charge and at the centre but disguised as a woman, and the more
famous one, who ends up decapitated but then, also, beautifully por-
trayed, is supposedly based solely on the visual imprint in the memory
of the visitor, of the striking, strong features of the two murderous
women, now projected over the faint, barely readable sketch. But, as
the next chapter will make clear, memory is integral to looking. This is
another way in which looking is bound up with time – other than the
actual time needed for the optical travelling over the visual plane.
Bathing in the blood-red colour of the ground, the sketch and the
painting may or may not have anything at all to do with each other.
For the benefit of the most 'profound' frame – the one where the thematic choices of the painting are linked to the psychological makeup of
the painter – it seemed crucial to make framing work as both an act
and a concept, to 'speak' only by means of retrospective connotation,
not through actualized, explicit, denotative speech. In other words,
putting the sketch next to the painting would have meant the ruination
of what framing can mean, be, and do.

4.10 Gerrit Pietersz Sweelinck, *The Artist as Saint Luke at the Easel*, pen and brown ink

Visual Literacy

With the experimental presentation of Sweelinck's *Judith*, I was not out to probe the concept of framing, although with this retrospective account of it I do. Instead, the project was one of cultural practice; an experiment of travel between theory and analysis, in which framing had already been helpful, and a practice in which framing, although practised all the time, remained in the darkness of sheer habit. In that practice, I attempted to 'do,' perform, framing – to deploy the word-concept and make it work. In other words, I tried to make the most of that most obnoxious of notions, the *work of art*. A notion that isolates and hypostatizes the object as majestically primary to all dealings with it, this phrase was to be taken back to its etymology: work, labour, through – almost by accident – 'art.' I was trying to confront the numerous visitors who might wander into that room of the museum with a different encounter with art, one that *concerns* the people who inhabit today's society, one that *shocks* them into looking at old masters not as venerated yet antiquated remnants of the past, but as something that belongs to a present that entertains a lively relationship with its past. I had one point to make for the practice, and another to make for the theory.

As an intervention in currently hotly debated controversies, my point for the practice was that there are different ways of working in museums that can simultaneously increase both enjoyment and visual literacy. These ways do not reproduce, in vulgarized form, the historical scholarship conducted by museum professionals; they connect art to social and cultural life without moralizing, and they bring objects to life and life to bear on the objects otherwise so easily severed from what preoccupies the culture around them. What is usually called 'a work of art' is ultimately an object, a thing that works, that occupies, in our culture, just such a position – of a key between itself and the world, and vice versa. Such a thing is, in the fullest sense of the term, an image.

The point for the theory came directly out of that practice of the image. It concerns a framing act that has remained implicit so far. The separate print cabinet, whose separation was enforced by the material conditions of light, but which was emphasized and connected to the main room by the red walls, was purposefully made to appear overcrowded. The curator of the prints and drawings department shuddered when he saw the hanging, and said explicitly that he hated it. That was fine by me, for it confirmed the effect of the strategy at stake. My goal was to increase the anti-aesthetic by hanging the works deliberately close together. It became more difficult to look at and enjoy each image for its own sake, in the pose of connoisseur. The images came to stand in each other's way. The restlessness that this crowded anti-aesthetic entailed encouraged a kind of intimacy that clashes with museum aesthetic. What I envisioned was the intimacy of private collections and, given the subject matter of entangled male and female bodies, this intimacy was to invoke a semi-pornographic sense of power. But the hyperbolic density of the hanging also made that power more conscious, hence, unenjoyable.

One way of explaining this double-edged intimacy through juxtaposition is to refer to Régis Michel's brilliant exhibition at the Louvre in 2000 and its catalogue titled *Posséder et détruire: stratégies sexuelles dans l'art d'occident*. Sweelinck's *Judith* as a painting would cut a poor figure in that context. But framed *in terms of* – a phrase meant literally – drawings and prints, as in Michel's show in the lower recesses of the Louvre, whose upper floors contain masterpieces of Western art, the painting's conventional framing as a depiction of a *femme fatale* falls away as a shameful memory of other times, of framings that no one today would consciously wish to endorse.[27] This final moment, then, in which the confrontation with the shameful secrets of 'dirty old men' is invoked with a de-moralizing wink, was also, necessarily, the moment where the itinerary-as-frame has to be countered by a circularity of movement, and – in my exhibition – the viewer sent back to the bright red screen on the other side, with a refreshed *Judith*, a paltry master-piece from the un-glorious period, that could now be admired, interpreted, or simply looked at in any way the individual viewer wanted. Full and empty, the de-framed and re-framed painting was now its own exhibition, showing what today's cultural agents can do: perform, not offer, reflections. The theoretical point that came forward is this: framing adds baggage to the staged image because it is *performed*. Framing, in fact, is a form of performance. To perform, in an activity of *mise-en-scène* that straddles the imaginary divide between private and public, and between individual and collective realms of being and living: this is the mission of cultural institutions like museums. It is also the work of art, and of the artists that make art. The next chapter, while still engaging theatricality, will be devoted to the travelling concept that probes what that 'doing' is: the word-concept 'performing.'

27 See Michel (2000) for an account of this show.

5

Performance and Performativity

performance
- *the execution of an action; something accomplished; a deed, feat*
- *the fulfilment of a claim, promise, etc.*
- *a presentation to an audience of a (character in a) play, a piece of music, etc.*
performative
- *an expression that serves to effect a transaction or that constitutes the performance of the specified act by virtue of its utterance*

For the bar separating the two symbols is itself more than a symbol: it is the pictorial enactment of a necessary and irremovable cleavage between them.

Malcolm Bowie (1987: 110)

Words

In the spring of 2000, during a stay in Paris that allowed me more time than usual to stroll around the pleasant areas of that city and visit galleries, I saw an installation by Irish artist James Coleman, titled *Photograph*. It consisted of a slide presentation lasting nineteen minutes, and was accompanied by a young woman's voice declaiming poetic text. The show took place in the dark. The images filled the entire wall. No benches or chairs were available. Yet I was nailed to the ground. It was one of those rare but significant moments when I felt completely engaged, drawn in, exhilarated, and 'taken over' by a work of contemporary art.

The slides were superbly composed colour photographs of schoolchildren of adolescent age. Most were set inside a school building, some outside on the playground. Inside, the children were involved in some kind of rehearsal, of a play or dance. Outside, one girl appeared to be washing a white wall. Most showed one or two children, in bust-length portraits. In some, you could see a group in the background. Meanwhile, the voice continued to declaim lines that bore no obvious relationship to the images. Although, sometimes I hesitated: perhaps they did, after all?

I don't quite know what it was that riveted me, but I felt unable to leave the dark room. It wasn't knowledge. Nor was it a sense of standing opposite an object of study. I knew nothing of this artist's work, nor was I knowledgeable enough to understand the implications of the use of the medium of a slide installation in an age of electronic media. I think, initially, it was the deeply touching contrast between the ordinariness of the photographed situations and the extraordinary brilliance of the images that kept me in the gallery. It seemed that an important cultural statement was being made, a position proposed that made 'art' seem incredibly important. Each time the nineteen minutes was over, I told myself: 'One more time.' Soon afterwards, I became sensitized – because of the repeated seeing – to the theatricality of the children's poses in relation to the narrative setting. That setting was a rehearsal for a performance. Theatre and riveting beauty: might they have an intrinsic relationship to each other? And was that the installation's 'message'? This was when my academic identity kicked in, and I began to think about what it means to 'perform' a play or dance in an age of the theoretical over-extension of the concept of the *performative*.

Supposedly, the schoolchildren were rehearsing for a one-time event, as school performances tend to be. What were they doing in these still photographs, eternalized in poses with such a profoundly rehearsed look about them? Performance, for me, was just a word, performativity a theoretical concept. Performance – the unique execution of a work – is of a different order from performativity, an aspect of a word that *does* what it says. Hence, performance is *not* to performativity what matter is to materiality, the concrete to the abstract, or the object term to the theoretical term. Although derived from the same verb, 'to perform,' as soon as they become concepts the two words are no longer connected. So, I thought, let's not confuse them.

But keeping them apart isn't easy either, as my own attempts proved. Performance – playing a role, dancing, singing, executing a piece of music – is unthinkable without memory. How can one play a part, a role, without memorizing the part or score, without rehearsing the gestures, facial expressions, and diction that fit the role, make it available for understanding? Even improvization requires memorization of the structure that sustains it. Performance connects the past of the writing to the present of the experience of the work. So why, then, is performance art considered a break with predictability and put forward as unique in its performativity? Moreover, if memory itself is, by definition, a re-enactment, and in that sense, performative, the two are connected, after all. So what's the difference?

Performativity, at least in Austin's conception of it, is allegedly the unique occurrence of an act in the here-and-now. In speech-act theory, it is the moment when known words detach themselves from both their sleep in dictionaries and people's linguistic competence, to be launched as weapons or seductions, exercizing their weight, striking force, and charm in the present only, between singular subjects. Here, memory would only stand in the way of the success of performing, to be swatted away like a fly. But as we have learned since then, performativity misses its effectivity if the act is not cushioned in a culture that remembers what that act can do. In the face of Coleman's installation, I sensed a great difference between the two terms. As soon as I tried to put my finger on it, it melted. So how to avoid both confusion and the 'binary terror' that overstretches difference?[1]

In this chapter, I wish to connect the strong sensation I had in that gallery in Paris to my academic investment in the clarity of concepts. I want to overcome confusion as well as binary terror, to understand what this installation can tell us about the connection between these two much-used concepts and the implications of that connection for a cultural aesthetic socially important for today. Both terms have gained great currency in cultural studies. The need to keep distinguishing them seems obvious. But theoretical neatness takes as much of a toll as the messiness of confusion. Here, I will attempt to deploy the two concepts to bring to the surface what remains hidden as long as they are kept separate. I will begin with a discussion of the common-sense 'use-value' of both: the interaction between performance, on the one hand, as the skilled and thoughtful production of, say, a spectacle based on the memorization of a score by performers, and performativ-

1 'Binary terror' is the term Rebecca Schneider uses to theorize the many ways performance art made the body explicit (1997: 12–42).

ity, on the other, as 'the act itself,' in a unique present, where memory plays its tricks. Among memory's toys a particularly relevant one is time. Time is where subjectivity is produced: over time, in time, with time. While theoretical in thrust, the argument I seek to make, in all its simplicity, is contradictory to theorizing as such, for it opposes objectifying discourse and the very possibility of 'theory' as distinct from 'practice.'

A concept in interaction with a practice: this is how I framed 'framing' in the previous chapter. Another kind of practice will be invoked here to propose another way of dealing with concepts: the practice of theorizing.[2] Again, then, our concepts' travel takes place in the exciting area between practice and theory, but in a messier way, with many trips back and forth and much lingering along the way. In between, the causal, common-sense usages of the concepts in their identity as words become part of our baggage. To start from within the messy domain where art practice, theory, and common speak interact, three kinds of acts are staged in this chapter: performance, performativity, and memory. The concepts of performance and performativity are mobilized to account for memory. The possibility of accounting for memory is, then, taken to be decisive for what the two concepts can mean. In symmetry to the previous chapter, the cut or severance between the two concepts, again a prelude to their new linkage, occurs not between theory and practice but within theory seen *as* practice.

But, as Malcolm Bowie wrote about the Lacanian bar between signifier and signified, this severance, this bar 'separating the two symbols is itself more than a symbol: it is the pictorial enactment of a necessary and irremovable cleavage between them.' Irreducible, like Lacan's bar, this severance, enacted in any separate discussion of the two concepts, produces a conceptual abyss that is both necessary and untenable. As I will argue below, if maintained, this abyss keeps conceptions of recent and contemporary performance based on improvisation naïve, and conceptions of performativity, philosophical but analytically unhelpful. The recent 'memory' boom and the awareness that memory itself is a form of performativity call for a bridge between the two concepts. To put it somewhat irreverently, the issue under discussion is the need to mess up the two concepts. I will do this through their confrontation with memory.

2 This formulation is a reference to Keith Moxey's book, *The Practice of Theory*.

On Messiness

Both concepts have already been extensively generalized, deprived of their theoretical neatness, and brought to bear on a great variety of cultural practices. Jonathan Culler traces the travel of the concept of the performative from philosophy in the 1950s, through literature in the 1980s, to gender studies in the 1990s, and back to philosophy today (2000). During this journey, performativity – of a rather special *category* of words allowing special utterances that 'do' rather than state things – became, first, generalized, to stand for an *aspect* of any utterance: that aspect of an utterance as act. Generalizing further on the basis of the *iterability* on which all language-use depends, not performativity but its 'standard' other – constativity – became a special case of generalized performativity.

But, generalization, itself a useful way of unfixing rigid categories by stretching their boundaries, calls for new orderings. The next step – already in Austin's founding text – was to analyse the always potentially performative utterances into aspects. This move, from categorization to analysis of each item, is representative of the move from a scientistic to an analytic approach to culture. In the case of performativity, the analytical use of the concept facilitated a shift in focus, from the illocutionary act of performing speaking to the perlocutionary act of achieving the speech act, of securing its effect. This shift makes it possible to extend the domain of the performative from language, one category of cultural phenomena, to all sorts of events that happen because someone does them, in the cultural domain.

For the purposes of this chapter, the decisive move in this double shift (from category to analytical concept and from agency to effect) has been Derrida's insistence on the citationality that enables and surrounds each speech act. Austin explicitly excluded literature from the analysis because literary speech acts are not 'serious.' Derrida, on the other hand, by shifting the focus from the speaker's intention to the social conventions that guarantee the very possibility of performing speech acts, made the iterability or citationality of any language-use the standard, thereby subordinating individual intention to social convention.[3] From an originating, founding act performed by a willing,

---

3 See Austin (1975), Derrida (1988), and Butler (1990, 1993).

intentional subject, performativity becomes the instance of an endless process of repetition; a repetition involving similarity and difference, and therefore relativizing and enabling social change and subjects' interventions, in other words, agency.

But, back to words. Although the 'natural' noun to indicate the occurrence of performativity is *performance*, this noun has developed into a concept in an entirely different context. The home of the word *performance* is not philosophy of language, but aesthetics. Most commonly, a performance is the execution of a range of 'artistic making and doing' (Alperson 1998: 464). As a word, we use it frequently. We talk about performances – of a concert, opera, or play – for which we buy a ticket, and we praise or criticize a performance by an actor or musician. The travel this concept has undertaken is from a criticism of cultural events in non-academic reviews to a specialized art form that foregrounded the incidental, non-iterable, one-time event over the durable work of art: performance art.

Although both terms are often used and discussed, and a tendency to use them interchangeably points to the theoretical 'fashion' enjoyed by the idea of the performative, they are rarely used together. The 1996 edition of *The Dictionary of Art* has an extensive entry on 'Performance Art,' defined in the opening line as 'descriptive terms applied to "live" presentations by artists' (Goldberg 1996: 403). Nothing on performativity here. Although the focus of the dictionary is visual art, it still astonishes. This absence points to the traditionalist view in the field of art history, weary of 'theory.' In the recent *Encyclopedia of Aesthetics*, 'Performance' and 'Performance Art' are discussed extensively. 'Performativity,' again, is absent. Here, the absence is more unsettling. It reflects the visual bias of the encyclopedia's undertaking; 'aesthetics' is clearly conceived as mainly the field of the visual arts, and art history as its academic spokesperson. In this respect, an even more striking omission of performativity is perhaps in Lentricchia and McLaughlin's influential volume *Critical Terms for Literary Study* (1995). Although literary studies as a discipline has contributed greatly to thinking about 'performativity' (the term originates from the philosophy of literature's medium, language), this volume devotes a whole essay to performance, but nothing to performativity. That essay (Sayre 1995) moves from a common-sense definition of performance as word, along the lines I have followed above, to a discussion of performance art, of its bond with theatricality, then ends on the benefits of the concept of *performance* to, essentially, poetry, when it is read aloud. A great deal of the essay is devoted to voice.[4]

Conversely, most publications on performativity, of which there are many, say nothing about performance. In fact, performance became an interdisciplinary academic area of analysis at the very moment when the distinction began to lose its neatness, a neatness that was achieved, mainly, through mutual exclusion.[5] But the combined discussion of both tends to remain limited to an unreflected interchange. Culler mentions performance briefly when he evokes the misunderstanding in the reception of Butler's performative theory of gender (1990), which took that theory as implying a theatrical performance (Culler 2000: 59). Critics were outraged by the idea that gender is something you can easily shed. Butler addressed that misconception emphatically in her next book (1993) and explained the difference between gender in terms of performance and performativity. The difference, significantly, hinges on the crux Culler so effectively identified in the shift achieved by Derrida, from intention and singularity to convention and iterability. As will become clear in chapter 7, this shift undermines the individualistic, voluntaristic assumptions of intentionalism. Austin's insistence on intention and seriousness as the conditions of the collapse of speech and action in speech-act theory maintains these assumptions.

As a prelude to the discussion of *intention*, let me point out how the very separation of the two concepts of *performance* and *performativity* performs, so to speak, a reconfirmation of intention – and this, as I will argue in this chapter, at the expense of 'giving voice.' But, whereas performativity, thanks to its travels back and forth between philosophy and literary or cultural studies, has at least been a key to breaking open the dogma of intentionalism because of its need to incorporate citationality, performance, while stuck in the aesthetic of judgments of beauty, has not travelled far enough to meet its sibling and join the efforts to undermine the individualist ideology that subtends both concepts.

Sayre's essay on performance hinges on the opening, not the closing, of the text, the play, the score, through the voice that performs it. Given the role of voice in Coleman's installation, this is an important point.

---

4 To actual, speaking voice, not to the metaphorical use of the concept of voice in grammar. On issues pertaining to the latter usage as well as the narratological category of 'voice,' see Bal (2001c).
5 The journal *Performance Studies* betokens this moment. Primarily devoted to performance, it often publishes papers in which performativity is also discussed.

But voice, there, is 'with' the images, although the relationship between the two is not at all clear. Performance, in Sayre's view, becomes liberation from a dead and authoritative score. But, crucially, the absence, in Sayre's considerations, of performativity and the paradoxes pertaining to that concept results in a failure to address the key issue of citationality. The clearly posed images of children in Coleman's work, in contrast, bring this issue emphatically to the foreground, as does the declamatory, theatrical tone of the voice. Sayre's claim that performance stages, and thereby brings about, a new, transformed subjectivity implies a no less problematic appeal to a unique subjectivity defined as intentional. In my plea for another 'confusion,' I invoke the argument in Sayre's article. Recurrent throughout the present book but specifically in this chapter is my call to both give up intentionalism and 'give voice' to subjectivity – but differently. The image framed as theatricalized, *mise en scène*, will turn out to be the site of this cultural generosity. 'Giving voice' thus becomes the act where performance and performativity interact without merging.

Sayre's argument runs as follows. The pluralization brought about by the need to perform each time anew is first evoked as a factor of singularity. His opening lines state that performance is an act 'which occurs on a given occasion, in a particular place.' Artistic performance is further defined 'by its status as the *single* occurrence of a *repeatable and preexisting* text or score' (91; emphasis added). The contrast between stable, citable pre-text and transforming performance was traditionally taken to imply a hierarchy between the primary art work and the derivative performance. Sayre rightly insists on the reversal of this hierarchy, performed, so to speak, by performance art as it developed as a movement in the visual arts in the late 1960s and the 1970s. His essay thus ends with a celebration of the transformative power of performance as a key to art and literature: 'In these terms, finally, performance can be defined as an activity that generates transformations, as the reintegration of art with what is "outside" it, an "opening up" of "the field"' (103). But because this pluralization and the transformations it affords are not connected to citationality and the *cultural grounding* – a case of memory – on which this aspect of performativity insists, Sayre bypasses the critical potential of his concept, and hence, remains descriptive. This limitation stems from his repetition of a fallacious opposition that characterized the artistic movement he is describing.

Just as performance art as a movement failed to complete its radical mission, so Sayre's comment fails to shed intentionality. He thus demonstrates that a separate treatment of performance – without explicit considerations of the concept's relation to performativity – can only go halfway: only as far as a reversal, not a deconstruction, of the hierarchy. Quoting a performance artist of the late 1960s, he endorses the opposition inherent in that art to a certain kind of fictional, realistic theatre in which actors believably play at being someone other than themselves. This opposition involves the opposition between an enactment and 'the act itself' (96). An oppositional but illusory pretension of directness in time, place, and subjectivity is the result. The relation to a pre-text is severed in favour of a unique event, 'something else each time' (96). 'Each time': moments of uniqueness, as if time were not sticky, as if original acts were possible out of the blue; as if, in other words, the acting subject can be a genuine master-creator after all. The primary problem of such a conception of performance is its abstraction from a more complex sense of temporality, the one that can only be understood against a background of citationality *as* cultural memory. The analysis that follows here is offered to argue that the key aspects of the two concepts at hand, performance and performativity, are indispensable to making each other effective as analytical tools.

Memory as Mediation

Instead of rehearsing the insistence on citationality so effectively broached by others, I will step back one more time into the messiness of concepts, and use 'memory' to argue that performance and performativity must not be treated separately. Coleman's installation proposes memory as a precious mediation between individual and social life, a cultural tool that helps 'give voice' to subjects often neglected and ignored. Memory is not as theoretical as a concept; on the contrary, it is a common word we use all the time. Only recently has it been widely theorized within the cultural field.[6] The reason I bring it into

6 Memory was an important cultural element in the romantic period, as it fed the emerging nationalism of the time. In the recent academic context, memory used to be a prisoner of the disciplines of psychology and philosophy. Only when sociologists became interested in it did something like a collective memory become thinkable there (Halbwachs 1992). Recent publications, such as Huyssen's *Twilight Memories* (1995) and Hartman's *The Longest Shadow* (1996), are part of a flurry of new reflections within interdisciplinary cultural analysis. Much of this work is motivated by the turning point in Holocaust remembrance, marked by its fiftieth anniversary, and much of the Holocaust remembrance work is inspired by rereadings of Walter Benjamin. See, also, the collection edited by Bal, Crewe, and Spitzer.

5.1 James Coleman, *Photograph*, 1998–9, projected images with synchronized audio narration

this discussion is because of its entanglement with time. Memory concerns the past and happens in the present. Thus it can stand for the complex relationship between cultural analysis and history. The elements of present and past in memory are what specifically distinguish performance and performativity.

To probe the aspects and subtleties, the implications and consequences of this argument, I will engage closely with a single art work, Coleman's *Photograph*, which, itself, is a performative performance – a performance of performativity (figs. 5.1 and 5.2). Here, as in chapter 3, I take up an art work for its potential to theorize. But, unlike in the earlier practise of *mise-en-scène*, here the work stays in its place, while the concepts travel, move back and forth, between theory and work. To practise theorizing, we travel to the outskirts of Dublin, to a secondary school in a working-class neighbourhood, the setting of Coleman's images.

In spite of the deceptively simple technology used in this installation, *Photograph* offers an utterly rich sensuality beyond synaesthetic, to the extent that the senses, while each emphatically clear, can

5.2 James Coleman, *Photograph*, 1998–9, projected images with synchronized audio narration

ultimately no longer be distinguished.[7] The voice is theatrical and historical, the discourse romantic and interior. The diction is imposing and moving, and binds theatricality with poetic rhythm, rhyme, and content. That is, unless your entrance happens to coincide with the beginning of the installation, which is unlikely. In that case, you hear only breathing, sighing, and see slowly emerging blurred-looking stains on the screen.

Just white. Not white as in 'black-and-white,' although a gut-reading of the work's title, *Photograph*, might suggest this. But white as in the spectrum, where all colours merge into white. And white as in baroque thought, where white consists of foam decomposed into a thousand tiny convex mirrors, each engaging the viewer in a different, complete world. White, as in bright, light, and Might. And, finally, white as in the name of Hayden White, who changed contemporary history-

7 For an account of the technology and an exploration of the meanings it produces, see Rosalind Krauss' rich, if in the end somewhat formalistic, analysis of *Photograph* (1999b).

writing by infusing it with the need for self-reflection and theoretical analysis of what we do when we write about the past.[8]

This opening-up of 'white' points to the first way in which *Photograph* is a theoretical object. Many other ways will follow, to the point that *Photograph* theorizes our concepts beyond the academic articulations of their meaning, status, and relations. In addition to performance, performativity, and the mediating term 'memory,' then, this chapter brings in another concept that is itself methodological, a 'meta-concept,' so to speak. For the chapter practises a different kind of theory-practice bond through a different concept carried along in this discussion, the concept of *theoretical object*. Through this concept, often invoked but usually not thoroughly theorized, I establish once more the subject of this book, as a rough guide to a moving practice of cultural analysis. The travel here takes place between different sites of 'theory,' where signposts such as concept-terms guide the traveller not away from the adventure but away from the hasty highway, to further travel in a more complex network of pathways. Again, but with more emphasis, I advocate a kind of theorizing that is dynamic, that leads not to a conclusion of knowledge-as-possession but to an ongoing discovery of ignorance (of certainty, neatness, closure), which I see as key to a productive theorizing beyond the theory-practice divide. That is, I wish to heed Gayatri Spivak's severe, metaphorically phrased comment, to which I will return in the final chapter: 'The conventional highway of a politically correct single issue is merely the shortest distance between two signposted exits' (1999: 197).

Remembering the etymology of the word 'theory' as seeing-through, theorizing, then – by reflecting on the relations between performance and performativity through memory – begins with looking. The beginning of Coleman's work is hospitable to such a beginning. It opens up the concept of image beyond its multiple aspects discussed so far. The opening sequence of non-figurative stains puts the problematic of memory on the table in relation to image. Right away, memory turns out to be multilayered, overdetermined, disunified, and emphatically 'cultural' – as in the oxymoron 'cultural memory,' for *Photograph*'s beginning, with an image that is unreadable, solicits memory without foreclosing the past it acts upon.

Evidence for this open solicitation is the variety of domains invoked,

---

8 On 'white' in baroque thought, see Deleuze (1993) and ch. 2 of Bal (1999a).

and their connections to the subjects and their preoccupations. A photographic historian, like Rosalind Krauss, for example, is compelled to read them as a reference to a memory of early photography, helped, of course, by the installation's title. Having just written a book on baroque art, my own inevitable association is with Caravaggio's foaming whites, hence, with colour. Colours, colour fields, coloured objects, and subjects emerge in my memory.[9] Others might fleetingly recall such idiosyncratic little facts as this or that person called 'White,' or be painfully reminded of racial whiteness, clean linen, or hospital garb, or of angels, or AIDS, and all there is in between.[10] The point of these stains, or rather the performativity of these images-without-image, is that they make you think of something, something that is culturally embedded, so that the sequence of the subsequent images will confirm or infirm this association.

Memory as stage director. I mean this quite specifically, if not literally, in the sense that the *mise-en-scène* is predicated upon, 'directed' by, memory. This is what makes a viewer a performer. But a viewer can only be a performer if performance is taken, here, in the double theoretical sense. The viewer plays the part scripted by the work to the extent that he or she acts, responds to the perlocutionary address of the work, which reaches out, over time, from the past of the work's making into the present of viewing. The viewer is the agent of performance. But, at the same time, the play performed by the viewer is not pre-scripted, prescribed, for the white images refuse to articulate. Seeing cannot be referential. Only seeing-through, seeing-in, seeing in some absolute sense, is possible. Yet the act that constitutes the performativity of this seeing is not free, not contingent only on the associations produced by the viewer's memory alone, for, paradoxically, the white images direct the memory work. Thus, the work denies both the illusory directness of performance art as the act itself and the intentional mastery of performativity in its pre-Derridean sense. The first (non-)images of white in Coleman's work, while enticing us to associ-

---

9 This comment anticipates the role of colour in a case discussed in ch. 6.

10 On the unreflected power of an unmarked but always remembered racial whiteness, see Dyer (1997, esp. the introduction). For me, the multiple remembrance solicited by 'white' evoked an important association with Ann Veronica Janssens' mist installation, in the 1999 Venice Biennale. See my commentary in Janssens (1999).

ate, in the same move relentlessly undercut all attempts to fill them with private, incidental, and direct memory thoughts.

On Clarity

While the viewer performs the inarticulate act of looking, glued to an image of nothing, the relationship between words and images that underlies theatre comes to the fore as the bridge between performance and performativity. For, performing memory in ways I will return to in a moment, the voice begins before the moment when these ostensibly non-figurative images yield to crystal-clear figurative ones. The short-term retrospective effect of this sudden transition is astounding. For the clarity, in fact, has not increased. What seem to be blurs at first sight are images, as clear as the ones following. Meanwhile, the voice continues to read what had already begun 'during' the unreadable images: untraceable snippets of a timeless, perhaps contemporary, discourse, immediately recognizable as 'romantic' without being recognizable as specific quotations. Word for word, slowly, clearly, but unfathomably, the voice says, or rather, I hear: '*In its bright stillness present though far / would she smile ...*'[11] The bright – white but not quite – stains that look like blurs – but not quite – almost but not quite suggest a body; no, a face; no, neither. But, while my failed attempts to give meaning to the shapes linger on my retina and the unreadable images linger on the figurative images they recall – through my memories – or produce, the point of this 'dialectic of seeing' staged through this 'optical unconscious' slowly dawns on me.[12]

The point here has to do with the double meaning of the verb 'moving.' Its productive ambiguity stages the theoretical point I am trying to make in this chapter about performance meeting performativity on the site, and under the direction, of memory. Physical movement is lit-

11 In this and other quotations from the text read in the installation, I am reduced to quoting from memory. Below, I will try to interpret the artist's declining to give access to the written text, even for the sake of correct transcription, as a crucial element of the work itself. Since the text as well as the impossibility of transcribing, tracing, and, indeed, 'authorizing' it – hence, also, my inevitable misquotings – are part of the work, I present the snippets of text in italics. I take full responsibility for these snippets, which I do not 'own' but which I cannot ascribe to the work-as-object either.

12 The first phrase in quotation marks refers to Buck-Morss' study of Walter Benjamin's *Passagenwerk* (1989), the second to Benjamin's concept of optical unconscious. On the latter concept, see Hirsch (1997).

eralized, has become a conceptualizing metaphor of moving as affect. For the non-figurative images, evoking stains in the surrealist sense, move, are the only moving images in the installation.[13] But it is not they that move; it is the technical apparatus, the computer-directed timer, the projection itself. The movement of the non-figurative images caused by dissolving through time is acoustically out of sync with the sound of the slides dropping, the fan, the carousel, the voice. The a-chrony, or rather the 'heterochrony,' produced between the words and the images, the voice and the machine-sound, with the non-figurative and the figurative images remaining mutually present within one another, is congenial to theatrical attempts in contemporary *mise-en-scène* to produce apparently empty time.[14]

Heterochrony, the rhythm of the installation, characterizes memory. In this sense, too, this installation is a theoretical object. It *'theorizes' memory by offering a figuration of it as heterochrony*. Apart from the three sequences of white images, most of the installation consists of the projection of still, bright, colour photographs of, mainly, schoolgirls involved in rehearsing for a costumed dance – for the performance of an indeterminate script. This theme, if I may call it that, is, of course, extremely relevant for the tension – the indispensable relation and the irredeemable incompatibility – between performance and performativity. Performance in its ordinary sense of rehearsed play is, clearly, not to be forgotten. I will argue, throughout this analysis, that this tension, in the utterly concrete case of these schoolchildren, urges us to reconsider the dogma of intentionalism and the related issue of voice. Voice, that is, as the power to speak, to 'do' performativity; a power fraught with its culturally unequal distribution. But that is the future. For now, against the non-figurative images that mobilize memory by their refusal to represent it, the voice offers an acoustic *mise-en-scène*.

Like Rorschach stains, these sequences give up some of their openness-to-interpretation through the quasi-institutional framing imposed by the voice. Thus, the voice's framing of the images prefigures the subsequent figurative images by suggesting that figuration itself is a limitation. This is a third sense in which this work 'theorizes.' The old discussion of the relative powers of visual and linguistic art is dragged along here, but by no means on the same terms. While I will return to

13 On the concept of the stain as a representation of 'l'*informe*' as a surrealist heritage, see Bois and Krauss (1997).
14 See Lehmann (1997b).

this issue later, for now what matters is that the voice emphatically declaiming the verses, although clearly that of a young actress, is also no one's. This fundamental anonymity is the motor of the performance of subjectivity, in the double sense of the term. The anonymity, combined with the voice's 'feeling' and the words' personal but not private meanings, literally *stages* subjectivity. Artificial because theatrical, subjectivity is staged here outside the individualistic heroism of intention.

The voice's very theatricality makes the voice and its acoustic performance anonymous and, in this sense, non-figurative. The reading is slow. The pace embodies – although no body can claim it – its theatrical exteriority as a statement against any realistic interpretation. Neither the schoolgirls, who would have spoken faster or shouted or laughed, nor the poet-artist, who stays rigorously out of the picture, can be the target of the viewer's irresistible tendency to attribute this voice. As a consequence, the time the voice occupies is itself a performance of no-voice, a critique of all the connotations of personal specificity that have culturally accrued to the notion of voice. The voice, as a mould, trace, even part, of the body of the unique person who speaks, is told off by this voice-over, which, for this reason precisely, cannot be called that, for it does not dominate the images, has no power *over* them.

Nor does the voice dominate its own identity. A less theatricalized voice can be recognized; hence, this disguising of it through theatricalization, exteriorization, and heterochrony is an act of protesting, of wilfully frustrating the policing of identity through a recognizable and unique voice.[15] The voice's performance as theoretical object offers a critique of the cultural conception of subjectivity as unique by undermining both the individualism – implicitly denounced as illusory – and the control – implicitly denounced as imprisoning. The time-consuming reading this voice performs takes it out of such subjectivity and emphatically produces 'theatre,' turning it from performativity into performance. Something happens in this transition, and memory is the act that makes it happen.[16] This would seem to be the enactment of a theoretical position against the illusory 'act itself,'

---

15 For the numerous aspects of 'voice,' one might consult the recent book edited by Saleci and Žižek (1996). Voice is also a concept in narratology, where it refers to the implicit or explicit 'first person' of discourse.

16 On memory as act, as activity with its own liability laws, see Bal, Crewe, and Spitzer, eds. (1999).

the immediacy claimed by performance art, even if, at the same time, the power to act is claimed for memory. Memory is no longer passive, but active, an enactment or re-enactment; not something that happens to us but something we *do* – perform performatively.

Together with the romantic nature of what she is reading – which pushes 'quotation' into your face even though the words, like the voice, are impossible to trace to specific sources – I hear or think I hear words that sound romantic. Those that keep turning in my mind are those that speak to me; other viewers will recall other words. I feel addressed when I hear, or rather, feel, such words as: '*My friend, where art thou, day by day ...*' Breathing. Sighs. '*Oh faithful sister and friend / wouldest thou following of these lines ... shrouded ... wouldest thou read ... the fluttering of my breath and joy and woe beneath ...*' I know I am misquoting, just as the poet-artist cannot but misquote romantic poetry. We know from Borges' short story 'Pierre Menard, Author of Don Quixote' that we cannot preserve, in self-identical permanence, a discourse that only lingers in our memory. For memory is doomed to anachronism. But its fundamental anachronistic nature is not a consequence of a failure to produce 'the truth' of the elements of the past. For, after all, performance in the first word-sense is possible.

But in its re-emergence, each snippet from the past is torn off from its fabric. Memory cannot transport its time frame. For this reason, so Coleman's work 'reasons,' the attempt to recall, trace, place in the fabric of past discourses what we read or hear in the present is an act of memory that colludes with such acts of distortion as lying, pretending, and cheating. As I transcribe what I hear, stitching words into the new fabric of my analysis, I perpetrate these crimes, adding yet another layer to the de-authorizing acts of the artist. Deploying an emphatically theatrical voice, disguising its personhood, and betraying its refusal to have the person's identity policed, Coleman, the visual artist, the maker of images, drives this point home with words and sounds together. But he is a visual artist, and hence, these words and sounds in non-harmonious interaction also act *with* images. Not *on* or *over* them. Image – metaphored and staged, framed and performed – now comes to absorb the realm of the acoustic.

The poetry is as romantic as it is contemporary. Like insistent, continuous stage directions, this version of romanticism scripts rather than writes. It picks up the graffiti of our cultural memory, the personalized, interiorized experiences whose subject, irredeemably lost in time as well as in the anonymity of cultural voice, we cannot know. What I hear can be no more than scraps, shards from a past I cannot master but from which I cannot rid myself either.[17] Subjective and anonymous, here cultural memory bridges the gap between private and public. The cultural memory of romanticism as we remember it today is doubled by romanticism's discourse on cultural memory. This most subjectivizing moment of Western literature – the moment that has bound the very genre, or mode, of poetry to subjectivity – in fact questions what it also puts before its readers.

Flowing in and out of personal discourse, wavering between first-/ second-person interactivity and third-person narrative, the romantic discourse that *Photograph* proposes, in its guise as theoretical object and contra commonplace views of romanticism, is, in fact, primarily, insistently, and effectively, anti-individualistic.[18] Because of this commitment against individualism, it explores and probes the nature of subjectivity, through the double sense of the notion performance/performativity. The subject is situated between private, where it goes mad with loneliness, and public, where it drowns in alienation. Coleman's work 're-stages' this philosophy of subjectivity with the prefix 're-,' involving repetition and reply, quotation and criticism, theorizing and thinking through.

One of the ways, as theoretical and (syn-)aesthetic object, that *Photograph* does this is through the interactivity between word, sound, and image, each figurative and non-figurative in its own right. To re-stage this emergence of the subject between private and public is to make present the cultural memory that shaped contemporary society. The work, thus, shows that presence. But the verb 'showing' falls short of what is at stake. For if memory is acting, then staging the occurrence of such acts is performing – as in performativity – by means of a performance. This performance consists of the cultural situation in which all participants are necessarily enacting such acts. Showing, that is, can no longer be conceived of as a spectacle 'in the third-person present,' set before us on a stage and separated from us by a fourth wall. This is why, in a minimal account, performance, according to *Photograph*,

---

17 For a theoretical account of 'scraps' of discourse, elaborated through a discussion of the phrases in this function of scraps that constitute the literary production of the Dutch writer and visual artist Armando, see van Alphen (1997: 123–45 and 176–90; 2000).

18 See Chase (1986, esp. chs. 1 and 2) for a discussion of the tensions within romantic discourse.

requires performativity, a requirement that becomes obvious as soon as memory is foregrounded.

Sound, the physical aspect of the voice that relentlessly casts out the grammatical use of the word 'voice' as metaphorical, is involved in this profound thinking through, by means of appropriation-and-disappropriation of a romantic discourse undone from its written fixity and subsequent authorial naming. Coleman uses clarity of voice as well as childhood to open up representation. Here the voice offers an effective counterpoint to the authoritative voice present in omniscient and distant ('third-person') narration. The question 'who is speaking?,' so central to narratological analysis, falls flat, and with it, the concept of voice as equivalent to the concept of the narrator in narratology.[19] Its metaphorical nature is criticized here for its individualistic and heroic implications, which commonplace views of romanticism as the emotional outbursts of a lyrical subject have culturally established. Instead of the heroic voice of the lone poet, the theatrical voice of declamation merges with the alleged consciousness of the children soon to be filling the screen. When I hear '... *late but not in vain* ...,' I do not know if 'late' refers to romanticism or to the images finally yielding figures, or to my realization that it is up to me to perform the irrelevance of who I am.

The words 'not in vain,' with their double negativity, console me for a wound being inflicted only now, whose victim and accomplice I am wilfully condemned to be; the wound of anachronistic loss, of the irremediable lateness of any act of memory. Wilfully, for I decide to stay and perform. Condemned, for I can only do this if touched, moved, by performativity. Between the individual will and the system of language, these words are either performative or not, as I perform – do the performance of – this scrap of discourse.

As figures of inarticulation, Coleman's non-figurative stains dissolve the boundaries between self and other just as they dissolve those between body and the complex thought-feeling-emotion inadequately called 'mind.' But, they 'say,' this suspension of figurativity is not the opposite of clarity. Figurativity may instead be clarity's enemy. Figures perhaps distract from clarity of vision, as identification of

---

19 Needless to say, as a narratologist I stand corrected here. I thus experience in my own work how Coleman's work of art, once approached as a theoretical object, has real theoretical impact. Some consequences for narratology have been assessed in Bal (2001c).

authorship distracts from meaningful language use, from performativity in performance – by interposing between viewer and image triggers of such distorting acts of memory as iconographic recognition. This is a second contribution of this work as theoretical object to a thinking-through of memory.

But clarity is not only a matter of visuality in its limited aesthetic sense. If I may briefly mention yet another association that I had (even if Coleman in all likelihood did not intend to invoke it), there is an even more polemical, insistently political, aspect to this complex tension-in-integration of word and image on the borderline between figuration and non-figuration. I am referring to the association not with the whiteness of these images, which is, after all, quite deceptive and 'impure,' but with the insistent use of non-figurative single-colour images in art works by two of Coleman's – now deceased – contemporaries. As criminologist Alison Young argued, in a brilliant lecture on the use of monochromatic anti-figuration in the work of visual artist Felix Gonzalez-Torres and filmmaker Derek Jarman, there is an important need to resist images conjured up by cultural framings.[20]

Young discussed the work of these two artists, both of whom died of AIDS, in 1996 and 1994 respectively, within the framework of a few horrendous legal cases of 'gay bashing' in Australia. The cases involved the murder of men by other men who alleged a fear of homosexual 'assault' by 'possibly HIV-infected' men.[21] Through a close reading of some of the legal documentation, Young demonstrated that these murders could be downgraded to manslaughter simply because the *images* conjured up by the defendants were congruent with those the written texts of law facilitated. The elements of the testimony merged images of threat, abuse, illness, and death into a visual scene within which murder became self-defence, even though the victims, dead and hence unable to counter these images, were not proven to be HIV-positive or even homosexual. Fantasies became frozen images on a screen, simulacra of mental images always-already present, the

---

20 Alison Young, 'Into the Blue: The Image Written on Law.' Lecture at the 'Languages and Laws' conference organized by Peter Hutchings for the International Law and Literature Association, Sydney, Australia, July 2000. Young's lecture was one of two involving detailed analyses of these cases, the other being given by Dirk Meure, 'Homosexual Panic in the High Court: A Discourse Analysis of Green v R.'

21 I put in quotation marks those discursive elements that convinced the judges that the murderers were genuinely afraid.

ready-mades of homophobic panic.[22] The defendants' visual language, which identified gay sex with abuse, illness, contamination, and, indirectly, murder, constituted a visual anti-portrait of the dead men. The judgment that sanctions this use of figurativity was based on the desire to make the object of the law visible. Young called the visualizing effect of legal texts and their use in court *a legal aesthetics of appearance*.

We don't have to limit the issue broached in Young's lecture to the domain of the law *sensu stricto* to see that such an aesthetics of appearance calls for some caution. This aesthetics demands a cautionary framing of the subsequent appearance of figurative photographs in Coleman's work, of children deprived of the culturally authoritative voice that the work claims for them. Both Gonzalez-Torres and Jarman privilege the colour *blue* to provide such a framing. The former created works consisting of stacks of blue-wrapped candies, or blue sheets of paper, which the viewer was invited to take with her. Thus the object – candy, paper – is always in the process of diminishing, disappearing, but the viewer takes some with him to defer imminent death. In another work, blue curtains (separating the sick room from the world of health) move again, in the double sense of the word.

Jarman, too, deployed blue, in his non-figurative film *Blue*. The total absence of any figurative visual element in this film welcomes the narratives of the voice that fill the blue screen, in an interaction between visuality and hearing/language similar to that of Coleman's opening sequence and twice-recurring visual 'refrain.' Jarman's narratives, like Gonzalez-Torres' giving away bits of the works, provide the anti-idolatry of their work with a consoling synaesthetic. In rejecting the moving image, the two artists propose a plea to integrate the other senses into the experience of visuality. In Jarman's case, the narratives create landscapes of memories for the images that can no longer be seen. It is this narrow band between association and memory, the threat to the individual and the comforting presence of performing viewers, that makes the non-figurative monochrome an effective frame for a revision of vision, as beyond idolatry, visual purism, and representational banality alike.

In *Photograph*, the preface to the sequences of figurative images as well as the twice recurrent interruption of that sequence by the similarly moving white monochromes, works like a sharp comment, a cri-

22 For a relevant discussion of the simulacrum in this merging of discourse and image, see Durham (1998).

tique of a visual culture impregnated with realism, and especially, with a sloppy confidence in photography, which represses the imaginary nature of looking; its nature, that is, of 'theorizing' or looking-through. As I will argue, this framing performs the indispensable work required to 'give voice' to children who are framed as being deprived of voice.

Drawn by the succession of moving non-figurative stains and still figures to reconsider figuration and 'abstraction' (a word now so inadequate) as well as temporal succession and the discreteness of successive moments, I think back to the work that preceded *Photograph*, Coleman's *Connemara Landscape* (1980), which one passes in this installation before descending into the dark room of *Photograph*. Here, no sound, no movement, no words are used. Like an internal cultural memory, this work, consisting of an enigmatic image of projected lines, is non-figurative, although its title doesn't yield to the opposition with figuration. Tenaciously unreadable, it is in precarious and ultimately untenable opposition not only with the figurative images of the schoolgirls, but also with the stains, which seem blurs again in comparison with these sharp lines.

Girls without Voice

The non-figurative images, or stains, available for projection, offset against but also staged by the clear voice, give way to a photograph of two girls – equally clear. The bright colours, it now seems, are already inside the white that embodies the full spectrum of possible colours in the stains that precede and announce them. Perhaps their forms, their bodies are too? And what do these girls – fixed in an image that on all counts can only be qualified with that awkward, memory-laden word 'beauty' – do to that voice that is filling my head and body with a discourse that is not mine? The inevitable question of the relationship between words and images, a question so precariously situated between academic and artistic disciplines and so inadequately theorized, is here staged in its most crucial situation. The words fill the images, the images give body to the words. One of the many performances of this relationship itself – consisting of an entanglement, each 'mode' (to avoid the wrong word 'medium') sticking to the other but not in symmetry or harmony – is to sharpen the predicament of children who are not quite given a voice because they are not listened to. This predicament is made acute by means of an old voice, a learned one: the poetry, the stuff we learned at school. Through this 'schooling,' they are empowered to speak.

This is an important, complex issue that I cannot do justice to here. It is subliminally put on the table by Coleman's visual and verbal allusions to chalk, which invoke Brecht's appropriation of an ancient Chinese text, in the *Caucasian Chalk Circle*. The issue *Photograph* foregrounds from the Chinese, then German, allegory, is the position of the child. The child in the Chinese legend doesn't talk at all; Brecht's child babbles unintelligibly. In reference, and in opposition to this silencing, the children in *Photograph* are positioned on the threshold of empowerment. In and out of personalizing visual discourse, the children, who are the 'main characters,' are together, but do not make visual contact. Their eyes face inward, making perhaps more contact with the diffuse anonymous lines that are being read by the voice without visible body but whose body we hear in the breathing, just as we hear the mechanical body of the projection when the slides click into place and that sound collides with words like '... *the hush of hearts that beat.*'

Retrospectively, the still photographs of the live schoolgirls fill the 'blurred,' 'abstract' (all terms fail the critic here) yet moving images with meanings that, while remaining just as unreadable, are contiguous to 'heart.' Ultimately, the words can neither be quoted nor attributed. But they *can* be 'seen' in their interaction with the children, who perform not the words themselves but their meaning and performativity. For the children are literally without speech; instead, through the poetry, they are spoken *with*. Not *over*, as in a bossy voice-over; not *about*, as in a third-person narrative that represents at the cost of the absence, the representational death of the represented object; not *to*, as in the perpetual subject of the speech acts of ordering, promising, threatening, and seducing. But *with*, thanks to the merging of performance and performativity that cultural memory, once it is mobilized, can afford. On condition that it, too, is deployed as an act – not as an immediate, direct act (if such a thing were possible at all) but as a fundamentally mediated one based on citation.

Jarman's *Blue* fills the cobalt-blue screen with narratives, but these are, importantly, not unified. Coleman's white and the figurative images framed by it are filled with non-narrative discourse. This, again, is a polemical act through which the work functions as theoretical object. For, among memory's many tricks, the illusion of narrative coherence is primary. Narrative's presence, its performances, and its performativity – in short, its presence as a cultural force that affects the lives of subjects – cannot be overestimated. It is both an indispensable tool and a dangerous weapon. In this installation, narrativity imposes itself yet is held at bay. The stain-like dissolves move but don't yield story. The girls imply story but don't move. The sequence imposes moments that follow in each other's wake, but refuses to allow the relentless punctuality of rhythm and mechanical order to coincide with any chronology of events. No events come to disturb the breathtaking stillness of the photographs, so still that we can't imagine the noisiness a school space emanates. The contrast between this noisiness and the perfect stillness of the photographs, enhanced by the perfection of their execution, emphasizes the paradoxical status of the children as acting, performing, without speaking.

They do not have voices. Yet by acting out the re-presentation, the exteriorization of the discourse we hear, they appropriate it, in the performativity – the act-aspect – of their performance – the rehearsed aspect – 'on the stage.' Visual stillness entails acoustic silence, entails the whiteness of a clarity of vision that no figuration disturbs, a whiteness that leaves all possibilities open; all colours, all light, all sound, all meanings. The injunction I hear when the voice says something like '... *of white of light that I must tell ...*' is also my own doing. Who is speaking? The question can no more be answered than ignored. This puts the voice onto a different ontological level, one that the concept of performance alone cannot satisfy.

But it is not the level of the bossy narrator of classical narrative. Even in its rare moments of third-person narrative voice unconnected to images, the classical voice is far away. I cannot answer the question 'Who is speaking?' at the same time as I am absorbing the sonority of the words. Classical, realist narrative has accustomed us to the absence of voice, in all senses of the term. Its narrator is 'invisible,' and divine ('Olympic'). No sounds, no staged subjectivity. An authority the stronger the more it is invisible, holding the strings of figures and events, the make-believe of a world whose otherness is obscured by the assertion of its description. The voice of classical, realist narrative – that narrative mode so pervasive and predominant that everything else is perceived in terms of deviance from it – produces narratives that can be illustrated by images subjected to a role of abject subordination. Ultimately, Coleman's intricate theorizing of the staging of subjectivity takes the relationship between words and images as the site, or stage, where this power struggle between semiotic 'media' is overcome, in favour of an equality that, in turn, allegorizes the equality claimed for children in the images.

The allusion to Brecht's restaging of the Chinese myth of the Caucasian chalk circle, discreet as it is (no mention of it occurs, only the materiality of chalk and the sound 'lime'), takes different forms. It is there perhaps – in the intricate combination of verbal and visual allusions to Brecht's work – that the *theoretical* claim of Coleman's work is performed with the greatest precision. In itself, recalling a text emblematic of political theatre as well as the recycling inherent in language use, the act of recycling 'claims' the voice that both the Chinese and German texts deny the child. When two of the children in the images stand – in a 'post-dialogue' pose that compresses the time of speaking and the time of absorbing what was said – in the stairwell of their school, I hear words in search of a speaker that sound like '... *brief rest, a glance, free from lips or lime of marbled memories that forced him from that spot* ...' Here, too, I am unable to reconstruct the fabula of the events. But lips invoke the possibility of speaking as well as the right to be heard, while lime suggests that the lips are represented, drawn, in the lime of the chalk circle. Meanwhile, metaphors, like marbled memories, evoke scrambled scraps – a scrap that the word 'lime,' precisely, is, in the same way as the graffiti, written with lime, overwritten by the school's cleaning crew, and restored by one of the children, are scraps. The *word* lime thus overdetermines the importance of the conjunction of memory, voice, and writing, the stuff of narrative. The mournful tone of memory subjectivizes the narrative voice, infusing it with the compassion incompatible with the model of objectifying history-writing that held the realistic narrator in its spell. For both the mesmerizing voice and what it utters are so close to the image as to seem inner and other at the same time in relation to it.

The word 'lime,' in its conjunction with 'marbled memories' and its visual counterpart the graffiti, is one small but crucial element that requires, for its memory work to happen, the conflation of performance and performativity. The voice and its discourse are simultaneously being performed in the present, performatively, and helplessly, irretrievably lost in the past, of which they present a performance, through the diffuse, anonymous, collective memory. A chalk circle circles around in that present memory. But the allusion is not confined to words. Memory is emblazoned on the image, when the main character tries to clean the graffiti from the school's outer wall.

Visual graffiti now become visual metaphors of the verbal graffiti performed by the voice(not)-over, uttering sonorous words that resist grammar and meaning while speaking of what I see.

The image of the girl outdoors, following the third sequence of stains, is *about* graffiti while also *performing* graffiti. Her bright, beautiful colours stand out against the equally bright white wall, on which encrusted lime has left unreadable traces of past voices; unreadable, because the girl stands in front of them, her figuration overwriting them, as her hand holds the brush with which she meant to eliminate the chalk that overwrote this wild discourse. What makes the – literally – veiled, overpainted voices unreadable is the school's neatness, against which the girl's brush positions her revolt. In terms of Brecht's play, and its voices from the past, she aims to wash away the chalk that imprisons the child. But the brush not only stands for the act of erasure that it metonymically signifies. It also figures the intent of this girl to speak – hence, her visualized voice.

Memory as mediator between performance and performativity operates on a mixture of temporalities. Through this combination of discourse and voice, word and image, present and past, none of which, however, ever blur or merge, in spite of the deceptive promise of the stains-figuring-blurs that open and puncture the sequence like a refrain, the installation performs the staging of subjectivity most acutely, almost painfully, through the timing of memorization in short bits. The refrain-like placing of the stains sticks to the lyric qualities of the text and voice, in their joint efforts to hold narrativity at bay, this time by foregrounding narrative's other – lyrical poetry.

One gets an inkling of this when, on their third occurrence, the stains, towards the bottom of the screen, seem to be contaminated by the bright orange of the main character's sweatshirt that we saw a while earlier. And, incredibly, after such a long interval, a liminally remnant visual memory now reveals that already in the opening sequence of stains, there is an orange sheen shimmering through the white, which was succeeded by the girl in her orange sweatshirt. Perhaps that colour didn't affect me consciously then. It does now, since the stain carries the memory of it in the sequence's retrospective narrative intervention. That touch of orange in the bright white is for me the performance of the performative punctum – in Barthes' sense – that pierces the work's beauty, to allow an overwhelming sublimity to invade all domains of the work, simultaneously but without merging. Aesthetics without synaesthetic – until that orange stain.

Performing Repetition

Could it be, then, that the stains *are* the girl, that they already contain her form in their refusal of figuration, so that, undistracted by figuration, trained to see clarity in its purity, we see her photograph better? Better, that is, than photography has trained us to see with its culture of the snapshot, of quick fixes, in both senses of the phrase, helping the further acculturation of amnesia that fearfully fascinated Benjamin? In trying to answer this question – it remains obtusely unanswerable – one feels compelled to stay for another round of the cycle, another nineteen minutes. Here, the poetry – not the reality of it but the model – performs, in its visual guise of stains, the performance through performativity. The compulsion to repeat, to use a Freudian phrase, also makes this work profoundly different from theatre as predicated upon the fourth wall, from classical narrative, or from films that have 'The End' inscribed in them.

Visually, too, this work of images flaunts its theatricality, thus imposing reflection on performance as role-playing. Theatricality is both its theme and its mode. But its very thematic presence also changes the theoretical status of thematics. For, in all its promise of narrativity, no story is enacted. The theme's presence emphasizes its own status as self-reflexivity, much in line with Naomi Schor's analysis of 'restricted thematics' in Flaubert's *Madame Bovary* (1985). The schoolgirls preparing for the rehearsal wear makeshift costumes that irresistibly evoke *commedia dell'arte*. This tradition is the systematic other of romantic poetry, which, as commonplace has it, idolizes personal expression, whereas *commedia dell'arte* is formulaic, as its stock masks and costumes suggest.

Theatricality, ostensibly subjectivity's other, is Coleman's reply, his critical addition, to this view. Here, also, I will argue in the end, lies this work's rigorously contemporary aesthetic. Coleman makes romanticism's performance of subjectivity into a poetry that wavers between and encompasses the private and the public. The performance thus makes bridges between the personal and the political available again, to a time that is in need of a critique of cynical reason: on the side of the cynical, 'pure' performance, theatricality staged for delight, amusement, or brief outside sentiment; on the side of the romantic, 'pure' performativity, affect, doing something to arouse strong feeling. Beyond both, the personal *is* political, and that particular memory permeates this work qua work, this object in its guise of agent. The memory of 'the personal is political' – of the 1960s, of performance art with its deceptive claim to directness, of the revival of Brechtian theatre as theatre supposedly without the fourth wall – is an active ingredient of the work's striking force at the end of the twentieth century. Thus the polemical conflation of performance and performativity in the recall of two cultural moments of illusion articulates what it means to say: that memory is an act – and that, as such, it is, by definition, *cultural* memory.

For to perform this recall of the 1960s is not performance-only. The theoretical point of *Photograph* is also what protects it against a simplified notion of performance as play-acting. Performance is neither just the repetition of a script, nor direct, unmediated performativity. The relationship to the past that is performed here is one that recognizes the impossibility of the disavowal and refusal of what is irremediably in the present. Therefore, this performance that queries performativity (the 'lime' episode), as an act of memory, like the other acts in it, is responding to the 1960s with critical intimacy.[23] The theatricality embodied, enacted, and thematized is at the same time a critical response, a denial of performance art and political theatre's claim to be more 'real,' a critique of the unrelenting claims of realism in the history of our culture, and an endorsement of theatre as a form that, by virtue of its artificiality, is the most authentic one possible, and thus the site of a paradoxically utopian cultural agency.

This potential of theatricality depends on the relation between romantic discourse, with its claim to authenticity, and its quoted status and the compulsion to quote it. *Photograph*'s reply resides, aesthetically, in the fact that the theatrical quality of the discourse-cum-voice embodies the contrast between critical rejection and inevitable complicity within itself. The content – at first hearing, a romanticism, out of joint, perhaps, with contemporary sensibility – supports and is sustained by verses that rhyme and words that alliterate, thus foregrounding its quality as sound: '... *veiled voices ... that might mingle ...*' I may be hearing it wrong, I must be, but the compulsion to 'quote' is too strong to resist; relentlessly, this installation keeps me alert to my complicity. But do these phonetic repetitions recall, in a literal, sonoric sense, that

23 I borrow this phrase from Spivak (1999), who uses it to characterize her attitude towards Kant and other writers with whom she critically engages. The concept implies productive complicity. See ch. 8.

the past – unknown and audible, yet out of hearing ('veiled voices') – must perform in the future, when the clarity of distinctiveness is lost ('might mingle')?

But then, within the historically specific polemical recall of performance art and theatre, the theatricality underlying the theory of subjectivity put forward in this work as theoretical object remains relentlessly foregrounded. The activity that holds together the tenuous fabula of the sequence, the rehearsal, is itself a theatrical event. Moreover, each slide's image presents the children in emphatically artificial poses, their bodies' stillness doubling-up with the stillness of the images, constructed with as much artifice as surrealist photographs except that the montage occurs between frames, not within frames.[24] This is paradoxical, like the *tableaux vivants* that Benjamin H.D. Buchloh evokes apropos of Coleman's work: stills from life, instead of life from stills.[25] Poses, like a glossy fashion magazine without the fashion. Poses, instead, for heteropathic identification; two portraits, bust-length, in precise recall of the tradition of portraiture so fraught with political problems; pristine, beautiful, isolated as if sanctified, while I hear this: '*I stood beloved, in recant from the light.*'[26] Love must be performed, hence, the (romantic?) 'I' is necessary. But the child cannot speak. Her portrait says 'I'; its beauty, its insertion within the tradition that it appropriates for those it had excluded, in recant from the light, the inward looking eyes – they all say 'I' in the children's claim to speech.

The accumulated acts of memory performed in and by this installation are both nourishing and burdening for the viewer, who must participate in their performativity. All allusions to the stage culminate as the final sequence of the installation approaches, in which the preparations for the rehearsal – again, a doubling-up of anticipation of a never-realized fullness of the performance – are set against the backdrop of a stage. Drawing on all the media he deploys, including the mechanics of the slide projection, the carousels, the automatic equal

---

24 This entails a radical innovation that Krauss calls the 'invention of the medium' of the slide tape.

25 Buchloh (1999) does not develop the paradox of *tableaux vivants*. Instead, he links the historicity of the genre with memory.

26 The concept 'heteropathic identification' (derived from Kaja Silverman's highly relevant study, 1996) is further discussed in ch. 6. On the politics of portraiture and the visual polemic against it in contemporary art, see van Alphen (1996); also further discussed in ch. 6.

timing, the zoom lenses, and the sound recording, not to forget the writing in its de-individualized guise of scripting, Coleman 'writes' his meanings indirectly, through contrast, so that they are never caught in the trap of univalent denotation. *Against* a stage, not *on* it. A stage, that is, as a theoretical object in its own right, a self-reflexive theme, not an element of, or occasion for, narrative.

The curtain remains rigorously closed. Its high position suggests it is out of reach for the children. Instead, the work ends on a sigh, in the dark. Sound, bodily but 'abstract,' begins and ends the piece. Just before the closing sighs and breathing (when did I hear '... *a breathless pause* ...'?), the text joins the image, at least in its reference to space. The space of the theatre so loaded with memory is the last image I see while hearing – perhaps – the performance of a word/image interaction that resists 'illustration.' The last words do not rhyme, but they contain inner rhyme: '... *lives entwined with other lives* ...,' and that inner rhyme is signified in the word 'echo': '... *in an echo of a crowded hall, sounds* ...,' an echo, in turn, performed in the repetition of this last word: '... *sounds of how all things shall speak and quicken.*'

In between, the stage is as shabby as the everyday world of the city: graffiti on the wall, an overturned chair, a corner of the stairwell. Not a stage that accommodates fiction. At least, not the kind of fiction – escapist, fantastic, surrealist – that disavows fiction's bond to the reality from which it emerges and within which it is embedded and stitched. Yet the possibility of fictionality as the willing suspension of disbelief – as willing, that is, as the mystical *volo* that defines Teresa's paradoxical theatricality – is constantly present: in the voice, the discourse; in the costumes, the poses; and in the inward-looking gazes of the children who 'never' communicate, with each other or with the viewer.[27] Interiorizing, though, their gazes are not closed. And this is, precisely, how they offer the possibility of, indeed, facilitate the performance of, subjectivity as the origin and goal of their performance.

27 In this regard, I will, in a moment, nuance or complicate Krauss' concept of *double face-out* for this work (1999b: 18–19). While it is true, and remarkable, that the children do not look at each other and that their faces are often turned outward, their gazes do not really look outward; rather they join the voice in being *interior*. The closest the children's faces come to looking at the viewer is in one of the early images, where the children are busy with make-up (again, a literalized metaphor for make-believe) and one of them seems to look out; but she is looking in a mirror. The viewer as mirror, then. Is there a clearer case to be made for the necessary conflation of performance and performativity?

There is another way the stage is evoked while being kept tantaliz-ingly at a distance. The figurative slides have a central character, a girl who appears in most but not all of the images. Sometimes she is just in the background; if it weren't for the fact that you become used to see-ing her, you wouldn't even go and look for her in the group images. But now you do. What does this mean? Is she or isn't she the main character of the play? Well, precisely; there is no play, only veiled voices from the past that suggest a play through an appeal to our cul-tural memory. In a compelling injunction to perform the act of mem-ory, the art work dangerously detaches our 'second-personhood' from its reassuring self-evident support of pastness. And what do you do when you search the screen for her face? In one sense, I submit, you scrutinize time. The time of your own life-time construction of your subjectivity.[28]

This is the meaning of the allusion to that comic-strip device, also practised in the photo-novel, which Krauss, referring to Barthes, calls the 'double face-out.' This device is used, in the popular genres from which it derives, to collapse time. The looking of the character/actor outside the frame carries the memory of an earlier exchange in a post-dialogue reflectiveness. *Photograph* has three ways of emphasizing the borrowing from popular genres and of marking its performative dis-tance from the double face-out by convoking memory. As Krauss con-tends, *Photograph* foregrounds this device as an alternative to narrative meaning-making through the discrepancy between narrative, diegetic communication and the children's poses and facial expressions. Refus-ing, that is, to be the object of (third-person) narration, the children insist on staging their own subjectivity, each individually. The device, to the extent that it collapses time, carries the memory of what pre-cedes it. But, unlike the popular genres, memory concerns not just what was said and can be answered or acted upon, but what that which was said (or not said) does to the other's subjectivity. In this sense, the almost-double-face-out teases out, from Austin's theory of performativity, the *dangers* of performing speech acts. Not marriage – Austin's happy example – but, say, deceit, sacrifice, or, indeed, silenc-ing are potentially key speech acts.

To further emphasize the silence that holds the primary figures in its spell (or chalk circle), Coleman places tableaux of talking children in

---

28 The issue I am invoking only obliquely here will be discussed at length in the next chapter.

the background of some frames. This visual device, which, because of its conventional nature and the realism that comes with it, stages conversation within the photo-novel, would immediately overrule the silence, which is why the children are not quite looking out. Therefore, the reminiscence of the double face-out also undermines the device's complete deployment. This is another instance of what it means, in a practice of cultural analysis such as this work embodies, to perform the relation of the art work's present to its cultural past – or perhaps, here, its cultural other, the popular genre – through critical intimacy.

As a result, the refusal to look the viewer in the face, except in the latter's role as mirror, foregrounds the performativity of the act of viewing. For, the act of looking in, that is, of looking out of the viewing space into the diegetic space, is bound to fail. It is as if the boundary between the two spaces is a chalk circle that cannot be maintained without sacrificing both. The children remain forever still, forever balancing on the rope, or circle, that marks their subjectivity as staged: artifice, impossibly torn from the conventions on which it remains grounded. The near-deployment of a well-known device from popular culture, then, drives the point home that the memory of cultural conventions can be neither shed nor fully endorsed.

In this respect, both age and occupation resonate strongly with the issue of performative performance. It is no coincidence that these children, indexical for future generations, are young adolescents. Standing still, with bodies in between stages of development (which makes their gender sometimes hard to read), in a social setting in between milieus, and in the drab reality of everyday life ready to leap into the fiction of dance, they hold time itself at bay. We must first perform our act of memory. Thus they make a clearing that is better suited than any real stage to the performance of a subjectivity that is just like this work: clear and individual yet built up of veiled voices from the past; scripted by Coleman yet not written, only written down, by him. The artist's endeavour is to 'give voice' rather than record voices; to unveil rather than to rewrite. To give voice, so that the voices may be integrated into the viewer's performative performance of the children's potential speech.

Performing Performance

And so they can, finally, be heard. These girls are perhaps dreaming up their future while performing their pre-assigned roles in the present.

The girl who, on one slide, teases you into searching for her among her classmates functions like the visual space, the stage, of dreams. She 'speaks' visually in the hypothetical past-future, like some of the words spoken – but not by her (or by the artist). Drawing the viewer in, her presence-in-absence, or her unnoticeable presence, also saddles the viewer with a role in the play, gives the viewer some say in its plot and performance. And this, according to the text by Christopher Bollas already cited in chapter 3, is how the dreamer is positioned in the dream.

As I have indicated, in his psychoanalytical account of the dream, Bollas uses all the terms my analysis has been probing: 'I regard the dream as a *fiction* constructed by a unique *aesthetic*: the *transformation* of the *subject* into his thought, specifically, the placing of the self into an *allegory* of desire and dread that is fashioned by the *ego*' (1987: 64; emphasis added). Using the terminology of theatre, he articulates the nature of the aesthetic involved by insisting that the ego, not the subject, directs the play. This makes sense as long as we understand that the ego is defined as being somehow 'other' to the subject, out of the latter's grasp. Hence, the sleeper is both the subject of the dreams, metonymically bound to them, and the non-subject of them. The sleeper 'speaks' the dream, but as its voice, performing it without controlling it, in an interdiscursivity rigorously distinct from intertextuality. For the quotation has no source, no writer. Instead, the viewer stands in as an understudy, to take over the role assigned to the subject by the dream's director. To describe the viewer's part, then, the full meaning of performance – as in theatre – must be realized.

Here, one assumes, the director is not the ego (Bollas' term) of the sleeper, but that of the maker of the art work. The director-alias-dreamer is subsequently shaped, like the dreamer's ego, by individual disposition, but also by the logic of cultural framing. The role of the viewer is not to be the sleeper, but to stand on the stage where the dream images make their disturbing appearance. In this installation, Coleman yields power over his creation to the viewer, in a generous endorsement of the wilful suspension of authority required by the performance of subjectivity. This performance, in turn, can only be felicitous if it occurs in a cultural merging of individuality. And this can only happen – only be performed, successfully, theatrically – if the full meaning of performativity in the philosophical sense is realized. For Coleman yields another, major share of the creative power to the children who are enacting subjectivity – with the viewer's sustaining help.

In this conflation of performance and performativity, which calls upon the long traditions of *commedia dell'arte* and romantic poetry that each bring in their own class-bound utopias, and which, moreover, requires the institution of school to give the children a voice, memory is the crucial element. It is the motor of both activities and the factor that makes the event social. But, at the same time, memory as a concept is contaminated by the stickiness that binds performance and performativity. For it, too, needs performing. To conclude, let me allege once more that 'other' of romantic poetry to substantiate this point. Through all the layers of memory staged by Coleman in a variety of creative, metaphorical, and sensuous acts, the viewer, in his performance of memory, is given – and saddled with – agency.

This happens because forgetting is as much an act as remembering is. The viewer who declines to recall, say, *commedia dell'arte* refuses to grant these adolescent girls – categorial objects of contempt in elite, 'adult' culture, and, incidentally, alleged consumers of photoromances – the prestigious tradition according to which they set themselves free, from artists, viewers, and their social world alike, to perform (in) the lingua franca of the imagination.[29] By the same token, such an act of forgetting deprives the subjects of their most conspicuous visual work: the improvised nature of their poses; the popular clothing, costumes, settings; the public exposure of their personae; the stock characters; the simple scenario; the wishes and desires of the 'common people' they enact, and the words spoken off screen as if kept behind masks; the shifting sense of reality (Pirandello); the transformation of (elite) stardom into group work. All of these features of *commedia dell'arte*, which provide these working-class girls with glamour, can be either bestowed or withheld, according to the viewer's performative acts of memory.[30]

The viewer who allows herself to be seduced into this play accepts to perform the work, and hence, to serve the staging of the children's subjectivity. Acknowledging the way these children have been culturally silenced, like the child in *The Caucasian Chalk Circle* who never speaks, a viewer willing to perform such acts of memory bestows, finally, a voice on them that can only function if it is sustained by memory. In

---

29 See Fisher (1992) on *commedia dell'arte*, and p. 9 in particular, for this phrase.
30 This social need for memory acts has a pendant in what Fabian, in the context of ethnography, calls 'remembering the other' (1999), a phrase given theoretical weight through Silverman's discussion of it (1996).

one of the frames set in the dance hall, the 'main character,' or she whom I took to be that, has her arm in front of her body. In the background, two other girls move their arms, so that we might safely assume, realistically, that this is what she is so intensely involved in. But realism appropriates, colonizes. Instead, bizarrely, the girl, turning her back on the others and her face in our direction, is looking intently at her arm. Clad in a scrap of *commedia* costume, her arm is also posed as if to stave off the viewer. Meanwhile, she seems to be looking at her watch. Is she biding her time before taking over the stage of the adult world and ruling it, when her subjectivity has been formed and ours has faded?

Theatricality, ostensibly subjectivity's other: this is where contemporary culture has an opportunity to celebrate subjectivity as an authenticity of a different kind, where difference is neither ignored, for the erasure of otherness, nor hypostasized, for a boxing in of people in categories that confine them. I have argued that Coleman's piece deploys his art to 'argue' that those whom we overlook are beautiful and what they have to say matters. His work gives voice, so that voices may be integrated into the viewer's performative performance of the children's potential speech. This brings us back to our ongoing endeavour of fleshing out the image. The image is now present as historical translation, *mise en scène*, framed, and performed. The performance as such is endowed with performative power because the viewer, struck by that power, is compelled to perform through and with the performers. This artificial, contrived performativity that compels participation in the performance is the source of a renewed authenticity, put forward as beautiful in a culture replete with false claims to an authenticity based on myths of origin and tired of 'beauty.'

Post-script

Ma'am, is she reading Shakespeare? Can you explain the narrative to me? How much longer will it last? These are three of the many questions I set myself up to be asked as I stand in the dark taking notes. The people who ask me these questions are troubled by the connections they cannot make, the coherence they cannot project, the memories they cannot place; by the pain their bodies feel from standing too long. The decision not to offer places to sit – even that is part of the work's performativity. It places the work beyond synaesthesia. The viewer's body must participate in the performance, to start with, through the disharmonious yet inseparable acts of hearing and seeing – simultaneously but heterochronically conducted. But, more importantly, the viewer's body is involved as a whole, because the aesthetically mobilized senses are also bothered by discomfort. This bodily involvement counters the age-old mind-body split.

The solicitation that emanates from the standing position, and thus the only possible one, involves the full participation of all the senses: along with visual and acoustic pleasure, also fatigue, perhaps even pain or the semi-comfort of sitting down on the gallery floor that makes you feel like a schoolgirl. The children, after all, are also standing, tiring themselves through physical effort. This inclusion of the viewers' physical state into the work's performance not only gives them voice but also constitutes a subliminal element of performativity.[31] By extension, it comments on the self-evidence of the traditional red-velvet chairs in theatres. The similarity between the figures and viewers in terms of bodily comfort or strain is not a simple, mimetic attempt to promote realism. The similarity is not in the representation, but in the performance itself, on both sides of the screen.

The children on the screen *do* work – all kinds of work, but that work is always overlayered by (theatrical) performance replete with cultural, bodily memories. Unlike in classical theatre, here there are no soft chairs in the dark to relieve the viewers of the task of co-performing. Re-staging (again in the multiple senses of 're-') the performance/performativity in the theatre of the gallery, this work *involves* the viewers, so that, far from being put into the position of imitating, they are put into one of sympathetic complicity. Like the reticence to hand over words that must slowly be conquered – always imperfectly because subjectively – the inducement to stand does its work through time.

Time is an odd player here. The last question voiced by the audience is, I find, the most profound one. The first time I saw *Photograph*, I, too, found it long, slow. The more I saw it, the more it sped up, became faster, as it became more heavily burdened with memories. The ever-changing pace denaturalized that most naturalized of cultural conventions: time, pace, linearity. The last time I saw it, which was the very last showing before the installation was dismantled, I knew

31 This is further confirmed by other decisions by this artist regarding the viewers' position. In his work *So different ... and yet*, for example, a chaise-longue in front of the projection enabled viewers to feel free to stretch out and recline, as the performer does on a mostly invisible chaise-longue.

that for me, it was going to leave the present, and become part of the past. That time I found it excruciatingly fast, nightmarish almost; it refused to stop for me. This is when I realized that memory is the greatest cheater of all. For, as I was finally endorsing my task of performing it, it performed me, dragging me along, in the pace of a time I could neither stop nor follow. This was the work's own double face-out, its *heterochrony of the other*. And, like the people asking me their questions, I went away, dragging my feet, full of unanswered questions.

That, I think now, is the definition of subjectivity that *Photograph* proposes. To make the 'argument' for it, it performs it. And its performativity hits home. Home, after a travel to the past and back, to the 'other' and back, so that time and subjectivity are mixed up by means of the messy mix of performance and performativity. For memory – cultural memory, personal memory, which is always, also, cultural – needs them both. Perhaps, then, performance is a translation of performativity; it makes the latter audible, effective, a translation that, as was argued in chapter 2, is a metaphor of the kind no cultural practice can do without.

In the present chapter, the insistence on theatricality in cultural analysis has been foregrounded and thematized through a work that I selected to perform as theoretical object. Indeed, from the vantage point of Coleman's installation, the images that come to us through metaphorical translations, or through translations of metaphors, as in the ecstatic relationship between Bourgeois' *Femme-Maison* and Bernini's *Ecstasy*, become specifically and poignantly theatrical. Such theatricality is not poignant because of the necessary problematization of a naïve intentionalism implied in the mystical *volo*, through an emphasis on the will-abandoning body. It is poignantly engaging because of the impossibility it entails of deciding between a dystopic and a utopian view of the theatrical collapse of performativity into performance. It is this undecidability that Coleman's work not only demonstrates and endorses, but also sacrifices and transcends – in order to give voice.

Giving voice to the silenced children is *Photograph*'s ostensive performative performance. But, once we realize the function of the complex weaving in and out of personal discourse in relation to this endowment on the one hand, and of the near-double-face-outs that are the visual equivalent of this unmastering subjectivity on the other, the work's final proposition as theoretical object for cultural analysis comes to the fore. Two opposed connotations of romantic discourse are the players on this last theoretical stage. One concerns performance as performativity, the other, performativity as performance.

The first connotation concerns an obsession with subjectivity. The children need it, are entitled to it, and are all but denied it, as the hope (utopian) and rejects (catastrophic) of elite culture. In response to this connotation, *Photograph* mobilizes the staging of subjectivity as a way of building and giving agency. It does this by foregrounding, in all the ways I have presented, the *performativity of performance*. But, unlike performance art and theatre a few decades ago, this connotation of romantic poetry is not allowed to be a form of intentionalism and mastery, as the other, more traditional connotation would have it. There is no romantic genius anywhere to be seen. This is one way the shabby costumes become meaningful. But the rehearsal scenes also foreground this aspect of the *performance aspect of performativity*. Rehearsal, repetition, not the glamorous performance, is the tool that undermines the romantic claim to artistic greatness. For, the *mise-en-scène* of rehearsal says, performance is not, cannot be, unique. It consists of repeating a score that it can never approximate. Simulacrum as form, then, becomes the performativity of simulacrum.

To foreground agency, the artist must relinquish it. This is how the twin concepts discussed in this chapter, having travelled back and forth, settle for remaining Siamese twins. One and two, stuck together at the hip but not merged. Sacrifice is involved, whereby I maintain – after all – my insistence that sacrifice, not marriage or seduction, is the most theoretically interesting kind of speech act. But, through my travel between a school in northern Dublin – the stage of the narrative – and an art gallery in Paris – the stage of my performance of performativity – sacrifice has given up its immutable anchoring in power and scapegoating. Against the sacrifice of children in struggles of competition, as in the Caucasian Chalk Circle or the story of Jephta's daughter where I first brought it up, sacrifice can consist – more gratifyingly, for the pleasure it gives; more justly, for the distribution of agency it allows; and more enrichingly, for the heteropathic experiences it facilitates – of *yielding*.

Some public, cultural theatres are more inviting than others to perform such acts of sacrifice as emblematic speech act. But the arts are not the privileged theatre for experimenting and experiencing the pleasure of such acts. For most of the readers of this book, the theatre of everyday life will be more customary. Each of the last three chapters here will stage travelling concepts in one such theatre. The home, the academic forum, and the classroom will be the places where forms of yielding become possible – with the help of travelling concepts. Two very traditional and widely cherished concepts followed by an unorthodox one will be taken on a trip. In all three cases, performativity and its performance aspect operate – or should I say, perform – together.

6

Tradition

tradition
- *the handing down of information, beliefs, and customs by word of mouth or by example from one generation to another*
- *an inherited pattern of thought or action (e.g. a religious practice or a social custom); a convention or set of conventions associated with or representative of an individual, group, or period* <the title poem represents a complete break with nineteenth-century ~ – F.R. Leavis>
- *cultural continuity in social attitudes and institutions*

The ultimate uncertainty of the past makes us all the more anxious to validate that things were as reputed. To gain assurance that yesterday was as substantial as today we saturate ourselves with bygone reliquary details, reaffirming memory and history in tangible format.

David Lowenthal (1985: 191)

Whoever has approved this idea of order ... will not find it preposterous that the past should be altered by the present as much as the present is directed by the past.

T.S. Eliot (1975 [1919])

Concept or Ideology?

They dance, jump about, play the fool. Colourful, festive, full of surprises, they turn boring, grey, early-winter days into a period of partying. They knock on windows, while inside, near the hearth, children sing the season's songs. Sometimes, without anyone leaving the room, the door opens a notch and a handful of candies are thrown in. They used to threaten and shake their birch branches, but these days they mainly reassure kids by giving them candy. Reassurance is called for. This alone is what deserves attention. Fascination and reassurance – hence, a play with anxiety – are what underlie the Dutch *Sinterklaas* and *Zwarte Piet* (Black Peter) tradition. It is a tradition that seems to me to be a typical cultural configuration of sentiments towards 'race' and other differences among people as they are instilled in children.

The Zwarte Piet tradition, which serves as my case study here, has astounded many who were not brought up with it. Over a period of years, the British photographer Anna Fox came to the Netherlands to make portraits of these figures playing the black-faced fools. Her photographs explore the multiple ambiguities of that need for reassurance. As a quasi-ethnographer, she selected for her fieldwork a country close to hers, yet utterly foreign with respect to this particular tradition, which has been maintained for so long against all odds. This position of the artist-observer, hovering between closeness and utter foreignness, where the customary sense of 'the exotic' is replaced with a sense of astonished understanding, comes close to being a revision – not a rejection – of that academic tradition akin to cultural analysis, namely ethnography.[1] Ethnography studies traditions. Fox photographed this one. Her photo series is both subject and object of analysis in this chapter. While this series is the star, I cast a few paintings by Velázquez, Regnault, and Aptekar in supporting roles.

As images, instances of visual art in a performance of cultural analysis as critical pursuit, Fox's photographs derive their striking power from the way their maker succeeds in conveying the ambiguities inherent in the tradition.[2] But, in making her intervention, Fox deploys another tradition, this time from 'high art' instead of 'popular culture': that of the portrait. This double engagement with tradition turns her photographic project into another instance of the theory-practice intertwinement I have been putting forward so far. In this sense, her project is parallel to Coleman's play with the inextricable bond between – yet not collapse of – performance and performativity in chapter 5; to Bourgeois' activity of making images as transhistorical translation in

---

1 For commentary on an earlier – and radically different – kind of 'ethnographic' art, see Foster (1995). For a critical assessment and analysis of the work by an artist closer to Fox, see van Alphen (2001).

2 See Langeler (1994) for a historical study of the Zwarte Piet tradition.

chapter 3; and arguably, also, to the exhibition around but emphatically not *on* the Judith theme in chapter 4. For Fox, too, makes cultural objects that propose by visual means an intervention akin to what academics would do if they were aiming to conduct an explicit cultural critique. Her ensemble of Zwarte Piet photographs takes our notion of 'image' even further. Here, *mise-en-scène*, framed and framing, performing (the tradition as well as the analysis of it) and performative (striking the viewer), image comes to embody cultural analysis itself, as a powerful form of critique that overcomes the gap between academic and artistic work.

As I will argue below, Fox's work revitalizes the concept of *tradition*. As an instance of working with or through a particular tradition, it can be seen as propping itself up on a modified interpretation of T.S. Eliot's reflections on tradition in art.[3] But, I will also argue, her work probes, in an anti-traditionalist attitude or vision, what tradition in general is and does. Travelling between high art and popular culture but without endorsing the separation between these two overlapping domains, her photographic series will be our guide in this chapter. For it facilitates understanding yet another 'travel' of concepts, the one between the subject of analysis (the artist, but also the academic looking at the art) and the analytic work itself, as well as the place of the relevant concept in that analytic work.

For when it comes to justifying the work that humanists do to the world at large, tradition is involved in each and every piece of academic work, along with either a self-evident alibi or a bone of contention. By choosing the concept of tradition as the focus of this chapter, I aim to shed the instrumental handiness of concepts. *Tradition* is not a 'tool' for analysis. It is not a mini-theory that helps us to understand the artistic object. It is more like an ideology. Concepts have this dubious aspect to them. Here, by foregrounding one concept easily recognized as problematic in itself, I hope to demonstrate an intercourse with it that refrains from taking anything for granted. I also aim to eliminate from cultural analysis the still-rampant Althusserian idea that critical analysis can stand outside its object of critique.[4]

Two different kinds of tradition are played off against each other in these portraits. The first is the tradition of and from which Eliot speaks

3 See Eliot (1975 [1919]).
4 On the ideological aspect of concepts, see Donald Davidson's 'On the Very Idea of a Conceptual Schema' (1984).

in his famous paper, which laid the ground for a consideration of works of art on their own terms through an activity called 'close reading.' The second is the seemingly 'natural,' common-sense 'way things always were' – which is, as often as not, 'invented.'[5]

Eliot posed a dialectic between tradition – as in, say, poetic, romantic, baroque, or Western – and the individual contributions and creations artists make within traditions. The dialectic is that between originality, the dominant aesthetic in Eliot's days, and imitation or emulation. Several consequences of Eliot's view have since been rightly criticized and rejected. One is the idea that within that dialectic, literary texts should be read primarily in terms of their originality, and that, when read closely, they will yield their uniqueness and thus gain an autonomy from all other, contextual aspects, one of which is the author, whose 'individual talent' makes the text. We no longer believe that works of art can be considered out of context, that they can 'speak for themselves.' Moreover, although the New Criticism, whose founder Eliot was, has firmly rejected what was called 'the intentional fallacy,' the appeal to authorial intention has never ceased to haunt criticism.

Tradition, moreover, is one of those word-concepts that, like 'text' or 'culture,' is used in ordinary discourse as well as analytical, critical commentary. It also often has political agendas inscribed in it. This situation has methodological implications that I will spell out below. Here and in the following two chapters, I aim to make a stronger case than has been made thus far for the acknowledgment and endorsement of the position of the subject of cultural analysis – say, the academic student of culture – within the field under scrutiny. To get a clear grip on what such a word-concept can mean for a cultural analysis that does not allege for itself an illusory meta-critical distance but that stays self-consciously within the cultural realm under examination, I will suspend judgment, yielding to the cultural field that is also the target of critique, and raise questions rather than supply answers. The tradition I want to examine, and from which I cannot disentangle myself, is that of Zwarte Piet.

The Past Is a Foreign Country

Zwarte Piet triggers my oldest memory of fear. While during the rest of the year the house I grew up in was a safe haven into which, at the

5 See Hobsbawm and Ranger (1993).

onset of darkness, I quickly fled to escape the growing shadows of strangers on the street, in late November and early December that haven was visited by spooks that I never saw but who left their traces: candy, a warning note, a slightly misplaced shoe. I knew who they were, and that they were benign. Their presence was thrilling, a promise of mystery, candy, presents. But somehow, they scared me, and that spoiled the fun, the security, the confidence. I was afraid to pass the basement door on my way to the kitchen, afraid to go upstairs during the day. It took half a lifetime for me to stop looking under my bed before daring to lie on it.

Perhaps the inevitable anguish that defines the life of a small child was simply channelled – hence, held in check – by the traditional visit of Zwarte Piet, thus liberating me from it for the rest of the year.[6] Channelled, yes; specialized. And there, of course, lies the problem, the tradition that is today's embarrassment. For in the small, all-white town where I grew up, the black-faced clowns – in charge of gauging good and evil and challenging the closure of the family by pouncing on windows, handing out sweets, and knowing everything about our daily sins – marked my first encounter with racial difference, in the guise of a scary masquerade.[7]

Dutch society, like all societies, has traditions, some of which bring an embarrassed blush to your cheeks. The Easter bunny brings Easter eggs, brightly coloured, hidden in the garden. The 'pagan' Christmas tree looms over the tiny figurines representing the story of the birth of Jesus. And, during that part of the year when American children are trying to overcome their fear of darkness brought on by the gloom of the shortening days and the increasing cold, by dressing up and going out at Halloween, the Dutch are preparing for the annual visit of Sinterklaas.

All traffic in Amsterdam is stopped on the day the long-haired, white-bearded Bishop of Toledo sails into that city, past the Saint Nicholas Church, named after him, the patron saint of Amsterdam. On

---

6 This would be analogous to the function attributed to fairy-tales by Bruno Bettelheim in a well-known argument of the Freudian kind (1976). Here, I would like to be both more specific than Bettelheim and more critical of his one-sided interpretation of the ongoing use of cultural traditions in education.

7 This Dutch tradition is here analysed in its specific idiosyncrasies; that is not to say, however, that it is the only tradition of black-facing. For an altogether different tradition of this kind, see Rogin (1996).

that same afternoon in late November, he simultaneously enters all Dutch cities on a white horse, surrounded by servants, black-faced fools, many of whom are young, white women, who jump about handing out candy from a burlap sack to dutiful children, shaking their birch branches to frighten the naughty. The very bad children might be put into the sack after it is empty and taken back to Toledo, only to be returned to their families the following year. I was bad, but never that bad – apparently.

This tradition is not the kind Eliot had in mind. It belongs, rather, to what is perhaps best exemplified by the 1983 collective volume *The Invention of Tradition*, whose programmatic title has triggered a flurry of criticism of the concept of and appeal to tradition, a critique that, by now, has itself become a tradition.[8] The traditions targeted in that book's critical essays are primarily cultural rather than strictly artistic. This makes the polemic all the more urgent. In the case study here, the widely cultural and narrowly artistic domains come together, as the artist probes, borrows, the guise of an ethnographer, only to mess up the neatness of her 'field.'

In *The Invention of Tradition*, the argument goes that traditions are conservative by nature and have no basis in cultural reality. They are artificially maintained, serve dubious political purposes, and suppress alternative traditions. Rather than being traces of a past to be cherished with nostalgic longing, traditions are inventions, fictions of continuity necessary for a conception of history as development or progress. A critique of traditions along these lines is frequently heard in more progressive cultural circles, including academic ones. The Dutch Zwarte Piet tradition most certainly qualifies for such a critique.

Much of this critique of tradition is justified, and it should be made continuously, especially as long as mainstream traditions are privileged over alternative ones. Traditions that promote group formation and identity can be dubious when structured on an inside/outside binary, especially when celebrated by the dominant groups in a social environment. But they cannot be dismissed so easily when faced with the evident need of – *traditionally!* – marginalized groups in danger of cultural dispersal to promote social cohesion. And, whereas the roots of traditions are not always where their advocates claim them to be – hence, the accusation of their fictitious status, as 'invented' – the

8 See, again, Hobsbawm and Ranger (1983).

attempt to eliminate or privatize traditions is, in many cases, illusory, idealistic, or, worse, as oppressive as the tradition itself.[9]

That the Zwarte Piet tradition is the product of invention seems obvious. Perhaps not quite, or not *only*, because – as Hobsbawm and Ranger point out and condemn – governmental and other powers use tradition to manipulate people's memories, but, my guess is, *also* because of that. It turns out not to be so easy to recover the interests underlying the invention or its agents. But children live it, they don't question it, and thus the tradition shapes their minds. In answer to my typical child's question 'Where does all this come from?,' I received a number of different replies. It was rumoured that the Bishop of Toledo had once rescued children from being cooked in a huge cauldron. This was true: the evidence was engraved in stone, in a relief on the church named after him near the Central Station in Amsterdam. His fondness for children gave him eternal life. Each year he came back, to *our* country, to *our* town, to celebrate *his* birthday by giving *us* children presents. I was very lucky to live in the very place he visited. We only had to answer his questions when he came to our school, and sing for him. His golden book contained a record of how good and bad we had been during the year.

And, then, less benign if only because of their looks, Zwarte Piet: all the saint's servants are called by the same generic name. Many in one? Three versions of the story explained his/their blackness. The coexistence of the diverging explanations helped accommodate incongruities. The clowns, dressed in colourful fool's garb, were Moors, I was told, who accompanied the bishop from Spain, where they had been ever since the Moors came from Africa to fight the Christians. They were veritable athletes, prancing on roofs and climbing down chimneys. Or, in another version of the story, they weren't Moors at all; they had become black from the chimney soot; 'even though you're black as soot ...,' we used to sing. That explained the smudges, the white hairlines, the white behind the ears that we began to notice as we grew from toddlers into primary-school children.

9 Fox's work can be seen within the British tradition of critiquing tradition, including that of black modernism, of which she may well have been aware when undertaking this project. For an excellent commentary on such issues, including that of different conceptions of time and 'time travel' in black modernisms and postmodernisms, see Paul Gilroy (1993). Given my project in this chapter, to perform a cultural analysis focused explicitly on my own culture, I refrain from addressing this context.

No more questions asked; none answered. The symbolism of white equals good, black equals evil, was not spoken aloud; we just sang 'even though.' The song continued, I don't remember quite how, but probably with something hair-raising like 'in your heart, I know you're good.' But this thing about fighting Christians didn't bode well for their backgrounds. Perhaps they were once devils and had become benign daredevils through the salvaging influence of the saint. That was the third explanation of their blackness. A confused and confusing explanation, it remained implicit, providing just that touch of moralism that was needed to produce the right sentiment in children. And, precisely because that sentiment was tinted with morality – more strongly, than, say, the American Santa Claus tradition is – both race and class, and less explicitly, gender, remained subject to a taxonomy of values inhibiting true equality. Black equals evil, equals devil, come what may. So much for the moralizing, educational background of the tradition. Who invented it, and for what purpose? For it's still here, now.

On the rare occasions when I saw a black person, I said, or at least thought: a Zwarte Piet who missed the boat and has to spend the year here. Poor guy! Even if the guy was a girl. The irony of the fantasy never struck me. During the years when I 'believed in Sinterklaas' – up to the age of seven or eight – I never spoke to a black person, nor did one ever come to our house. None of the students at school were black; but, then, none were boys either. By the time I saw through the masks – the line between the black face and the white hairline, the piece of string that attached Sinterklaas' beard, the day the golden staff made of cardboard broke – I felt the sadness of broken dreams.

Even then, I vaguely sensed that my childhood was about to end. One complex knot of sentiments replaced another, equally theatrical, speaking to the ambitions of a girl growing up. Soon *I* might be asked to be Zwarte Piet. If only I weren't so clumsy with my body, growing faster than I could gracefully handle, I could be legit as a tomboy! In a convoluted way, for me, as a white girl, black also connoted freedom (fig. 6.1).

Like all European societies, Dutch society has changed. Today it is not as easy to play the black-faced fool to a crowd of racially and ethnically mixed Amsterdamers, facing descendants of the very people who, long ago, in a colonialist past, inspired the tradition that now slaps them in the face (then, it did worse). Bolder and less fearful than I was then, today's white Dutch children of kindergarten age, although

6.1 Family snapshot with Zwarte Piet

surrounded by black children, persistently call out 'hi Zwarte Piet' to black people they meet on the street, not realizing, of course, how it might feel to hear that greeting several times a day.

Then a historical moment came and went. I was a young mother, trying to raise my children as best I could, in a culture where 'black' was no longer so exceptional. Aware of the problematic nature of this particular tradition, one year the Dutch tried to allow the Zwarte Piets to paint their faces red, blue, or green. It was a crucial moment – and it failed. Nobody liked it. Now they're black again. Too bad. An opportunity to continue a tradition but adapt it to changing times – out the window, down the drain. Perhaps this was too acute a confrontation with the inventedness of the tradition to allow the acceptance of its reinvention. The last time I checked, in December 1999, the policemen in Amsterdam still conscientiously held back traffic so that black-faced fools could impress Dutch kids.

Of course – I thought as I wrote this chapter – today no culture would invent such a racist tradition. I hope. But my critical reader did not agree, and I fear he may be right.[10] This tradition is particularly troublesome because 'sophisticated,' with racism being worked over by classism (Zwarte Piets are servants) and sexism (they are feminized). The clownish behaviour even flirts with the traditional question raised in the sixteenth century, and again in the eighteenth, and then right up to the time of abolition, of whether blacks were quite human. No relativizations of the deeply racist ideology that underlies this tradition are possible. So why are the Dutch still so attached to it?[11]

I have a hypothesis, a tentative one that probably explains only part of that attachment. Let me speak in the 'we' form here.[12] We know only

---

10 I thank Darby English for this and other comments on an earlier draft. He commented that no culture would invent such a blatantly *typological* tradition of racism; the racism would be different in form only.

11 The Dutch don't deal easily with racism in their own culture. In 1990 an exhibition of racist imagery was mounted in the Tropenmuseum in Amsterdam. Black people hated it: why did they again have to be confronted with this offensive stuff? White people hated it too: a girl in a banana skirt, is that racism? See Nederveen Pieterse (1990).

12 The politics of 'we' is a problem that remains tenaciously difficult to resolve (Torgovnick, 1994). Here, I use 'we' to mark my position of inevitable collusion, which I hope, inevitably, leads to the kind of productive complicity that Spivak advocates throughout her work (e.g. 1999).

too well that this tradition is problematic. It flaunts its infraction of the sacred rule of our time: watch thy step, thou shalt be careful, tolerant, broadminded, non-discriminating, in short, *good*, regarding race, class, and gender. Although the Dutch tend to poke fun at North American moralism, dismissing it as 'political correctness,' I perceive Dutch culture as profoundly moralistic, *especially* in its more progressive corners. Perhaps, I suppose, it is precisely the deeply moralist, hence condescending, aspect of present-day Dutch liberalism that demands the preservation of this awkward tradition.[13] It is like a multi-purpose language-game.

Do I want the tradition to be abolished? Of course I do, but that might not be an effective way of dealing with the remnant racism in Dutch culture. It might help the 'aboriginal' Dutch such as myself, more than it would today's mixed culture. I don't think it would be good to abolish it in a single, swift gesture of erasure. What I suggest is that this painful, unacceptable tradition is needed just a bit longer, to allow a continued questioning of the psychological ideology that underlies its critical alternative. In what is all too eagerly called 'a postcolonial society,' political parties of dubious principles may fight lost battles to close frontiers, but even they would not dare to come up with a public figure such as Zwarte Piet. Maintaining an old tradition is a different story.

It remains a headache for the schoolteachers who have to tell the stories, explain the history, and answer the questions of children each of whom relates differently to the tradition, to the past from which it came, to the representations it embodies, and to the sentiments it promotes. Young parents today try to prevent their children believing in the story that my parents so earnestly wished to instil. More likely than not, their children have friends of colour or are coloured themselves. But, letting go of an old tradition, invented as it obviously has been: no way!

It's just as bizarre as the performance of Mozart's *Magic Flute* in the open-air theatre of Santa Fe. There, aboriginal Americans in the audience watched singers dressed up as Indians, feather headdresses and all, while looking out over the plains their ancestors had once hunted and where their grandparents had grown up, on the 'rez.' It's as bizarre as when 'aboriginal' Dutch see Muslim women being kept in

13 Incidentally, this is also largely how I see US culture as far as I know it. But there are differences, which I will not address here – particularly in the degree of explicitness with which such issues as I am discussing here can be raised.

their place as they walk, headscarf and all, a few steps behind their men; and as bizarre as it seemed to 'aboriginal' straights when they saw gay displays on boats, for which traffic was also stopped, during the 1998 Gay Games in Amsterdam. For weeks afterwards, readers wrote to the papers about it, but when it actually happened, the population came out in full force to greet the event. It was one of those moments when Dutch culture lived up to its liberal reputation a bit more than usual. That tradition, also invented, must stay. But it, too, must be examined, and its subterranean rhizomatic connections with Zwarte Piet and other contradictory behaviour, analysed.[14]

Cultural relativism then? No. The situation is just different when the game is being played by the 'qualitative' (i.e. predominant) majority, who plays it because it proves its 'aboriginal' rights. True, true, Zwarte Piet is and remains a deeply problematic tradition; there are no two ways about it. That's obvious. It has all the flaws: it is fictitious, oppressive, and conservative. But it is here that Anna Fox's photographs, as works of art to be close-read, come in. As a productive alternative to abolishing the tradition, to trashing it, Fox's series engages this tradition from the vantage point of artistic traditions of an altogether different kind.

For her photographs are not obvious. They neither naturalize, endorse, nor indict the Zwarte Piet tradition; nor do they dismiss it offhand, showing how awkward it looks to her British eye. For there is no easy way for nationals of any Western country to point the finger at their neighbour's racism without a good dose of self-reflection. In the end, Fox's is *not* a classical ethnographic project. It only uses ethnography as a third tradition, to question the self/other structure that ethnographers of the keenest sort have themselves questioned.

In looking at this photo series of the Zwarte Piet tradition, I would like to take a seemingly conservative view, retrieving some of the elements of Eliot's New Critical program that have been lost but shouldn't have been. I think the most valuable contribution of New Criticism has been its admittedly naïve focus on the text itself. This

---

14 Needless to say, the use of the term 'aboriginal' in this paragraph is meant ironically, but, like all irony, it also has a 'serious' meaning. I object to current usages of the binary 'allochthonic' versus 'autochthonic,' to keep distinguishing recent migrants from all others in European countries. In light of that use, it seems helpful to critically appropriate a term that keeps 'real' aboriginals in subordinate or at least exceptional positions.

aspect of New Criticism – the close reading of tradition-bound works but without assuming that art is autonomous – remains valuable, and has been lost. Recovering it, and thus bringing renewed attention to the tradition in relation to which the works signify, is my methodological guideline in my discussion of Fox's photographs. The close reading of works of art, freed of a naïve belief in the autonomy of art and enriched by the additional attention to the kind of intertextual relations to which embedding traditions also belong, is a most valuable contribution to understanding *how* those works relate to traditions, and what they do to them. In other words, close reading makes traditions dynamic, transforming not a given but an aspect of an ongoing cultural process.

Instead of indicting or endorsing the Zwarte Piet tradition, Fox's images probe many of the tensions it harbours, exploring what it means to hold on to what at a rational level must be rejected. They question what it means for specific individuals to perform, rather than watch, the representation of the very past on which, for better or for worse, contemporary Dutch society rests. From a position both inside and outside the context within which this tradition functions, Fox probes and sympathizes, lingers within positions of identification, then moves out playfully to show the problems, before moving in again.[15] The images take me on a journey to tradition land, where the past sits like a wandering rock in the present, and back again, loaded with new baggage. The images solicit a variety of identificatory moments, all implicating the viewer, who is gently prompted to go, through the detour of that foreign country – the past – to a place in the present where perhaps she has never been before. A place where foreign countries are no longer relegated to the past.[16]

15 Fox thus connects with the 'frog's perspective' inherent in much black British art, a perspective advocated by Gilroy in his essay 'Cruciality and the Frog's Perspective,' in his book *Small Acts* (1993). It is especially the impossibility of appealing to 'authenticity' discussed by Gilroy (also in his book *Black Atlantic*) that is important to me here. The position I am trying to stake out is not based on my 'authentic' Dutchness, but on the ambiguity of any person who is both Dutch and something else (critical, anti-racist, feminist, and a frequent traveller, to mention only those elements of my 'identity' that are relevant for this chapter).

16 The forms of identification I have in mind are varieties of what Kaja Silverman has called 'heteropathic identification,' based on a movement outside of oneself, risking who one is, and 'autopathic identification,' of the cannibalistic sort, where the other is reduced to a simulacrum of the self (1996).

Revisiting Tradition

The reason the Zwarte Piet tradition is really impossible is also the reason it cannot be dismissed too easily. Both Dutch culture and the meaning of Dutchness are changing. To keep in touch with that culture's past, it is no longer enough to be taken to the Rijksmuseum by one's parents and shown what once constituted the glory of Dutch art. What matters most at any present moment – hence, also today – is to watch over, indeed, cherish, a culture's changeability. The past can be neither dismissed nor repressed. Elsewhere, I have argued that if a culture is to fully incorporate constructive changes and to allow for the potential of changing more, it is of vital importance not to eradicate its memories, the traces of its problematic past.[17]

In *Double Exposures*, I develop this argument through a detailed reading of installations in the American Museum of Natural History (AMNH). I analyse the tensions between the museum's desire to address contemporary audiences and its obligation to preserve the past that is the focus of this particular kind of museum. Many of the choices made in that past are today perceived as blatantly racist. Their consequences can be softened, but not quite eradicated. More subtle forms of representation, tainted by racism and often more recent, are harder to frame. Museum representation remains an arena of ongoing adjustment.

That tension was very difficult to negotiate, especially since that museum is a childhood favourite of many native New Yorkers. As I have been told on several occasions, they get seriously nervous whenever cultural critics like myself 'mess with *my* [meaning 'favourite'] museum.' Part of the problem I faced in that analysis had to do with my own background. I acknowledge the implication that, as a non-American, I was touching delicate sentiments. Yet that and similar museums are today facing a predicament structurally similar to the one the Dutch face with Zwarte Piet.

The problem is, indeed, structural. And it is this that justifies the choice of our Dutch case – equally importantly, inflected by an art work from a national of another European country – for the present discussion of travelling traditions. How to present display material from a colonial past – specifically, racially informed visions of Afri-

---

17 See ch. 1 of *Double Exposures*, in contrast to ch. 5 of that book, where I probe the problems of repeating the past under the pretext of critique.

can peoples – to an audience the majority of whom are young, impressionable schoolchildren and many of whom are of African descent? The AMNH, as it is arranged today, although constantly updated and critically rethought, still encourages its visitors to make biological identifications – to literally enter a pact of self-understanding.[18] Like native New Yorkers, the Dutch do not like to be confronted with their inner contradictions. Yet, like them, they must be; forced by social reality and intellectual and moral debate; forced, also, by artistic practices which, like critical philosophy, examine their context.

But, if one wants to deal with the problems that both reside in and 'colour' the social relations of the present, it is as unproductive to forget the past as it is to reiterate it unthinkingly. Recent debates on the importance of keeping the memory of the Holocaust alive and the difficulty of representing that past have made this clear.[19] Memory is not just something that happens passively to people; it is an act that intervenes in the present, gives it shape, body, and direction.[20] Forgetting entails repression, and what is repressed tends to return, often with a vengeance. The Dutch, for example, have not been very good at handling the utterly bizarre chronology of their colonial war in Indonesia, which began soon after Holland was liberated from Nazi-German oppression.[21] Nor have the French dealt well with their *Guerre d'Algérie*. Both cultures would benefit in the present from a serious 'working through' of that past, and from bringing that work to bear on today's ambivalences. They need to revisit the past, not as tourists or frightened children, but as critical ethnographers. Art, like Fox's, can be the best rough guide for such a visit.

For this reason, I see the cultural importance of the portraits in Fox's series not as an uncritical endorsement, or as a finger-pointing,

18 This last sentence was suggested to me by Darby English, who said he was one of those kids. His response, which I gratefully acknowledge, is here coming from a position in relation to the AMNH that is symmetrical to my relationship to the Zwarte Piet tradition.

19 For an illuminating review of positions and strategies pertaining to this issue, see van Alphen (1997).

20 On the cultural function of memory seen as activity, see Bal, Crewe, and Spitzer, eds. (1999).

21 Tom Verheul's sensitive documentary film *Tabee Tuan* (1995), but importantly, also his earlier *Denial* (1993), bear testimony to the ongoing suffering that results from such massive repression.

distance-taking indictment. In the light of the need to neither repress nor simply continue problematic traditions, I see them instead as interventions in a larger European culture, where each country has its own past but today faces similar challenges. Ambivalence characterizes Fox's photographs, just as ambivalence characterizes the Zwarte Piet tradition. But they are two different forms of ambivalence. The former makes the latter less easy to live by.[22] Through images that revitalize the tradition *and* its ambivalences, by making these more explicit through the subtleties of visualization that frame it, Fox's work produces *an act of cultural memory*. An act that the viewers of her work can perform – as a performance of the work's performativity.

The concept that orients my analysis here, then, is double-edged, in two ways. It bears on the tenacity of cultural conservatism, and thus questions the potential for change and the efficacy of cultural analysis; and it explores, simultaneously, the relative social value of specific traditions. The specifics, or contents, of a tradition are neither progressive and wholesome, nor reactionary and harmful, by definition. Moreover, the question is for whom their possible effects are either good or bad. Dictionary definitions do not pronounce on such questions, as the lemma in Longman, quoted above, demonstrates. Looking at the word-use of 'tradition,' one imagines the social cohesion involved in the first definition – the handing down of information, beliefs, and customs – along with the tendency to conservatism in the second – a convention or set of conventions – which makes the break in the Leavis example sound liberating. The third definition – cultural continuity in social attitudes and institutions – can be seen as lending itself to both.

But, unlike such definitions, Fox's photographs draw attention to the *activity* that cultural memory necessitates. Replete with a many-layered history, the images constitute just such an act of cultural memory as any productive engagement with the past for the sake of the present requires. Tentatively, I submit, this 'memory-acting,' or memory-enacting, is the result both of an engagement with a word-concept – tradition – that travels – here, through past and present – and of the wavering attitudes towards tradition itself, whereby the impossibility of an arrogant cultural disentanglement in the name of political progressivity is acknowledged. Fox's images can only be understood in their effectivity as cultural critique on the condition that they are read closely – but not autonomously. They can only be read in relation

22 See, on this issue of double ambivalence, Bhabha (1986).

to the three traditions they deploy and subvert. Let me highlight a few of their aspects.

The images are portraits, indeed. What can that mean? Portraiture in itself is a deeply ambivalent tradition. Like racist typology, portraiture as a visual discourse produces and reflects a long-standing interest in the articulation of human variety. Portraiture foregrounds individuality. But it also provides tools with which to speak of the sameness in difference and the difference in sameness, both at once. This ambivalence of portraiture is what makes it so suitable to offer a 'counterpoint *within*,' to the racism of the Zwarte Piet tradition.[23]

The tradition of portrèaiture critically engages the tradition of black-faced fools, from within a position of productive complicity. The generic character, Zwarte Piet, is decomposed into as many individual faces, each begging to be looked at in detail, named, and understood in terms of what its subject is doing dressing up like this. In the face of a tradition that lumped fantasmatic black men under one generic name as if slavery were still alive, individualizing them according to a class-bound tradition that dates back to the 'Golden Age' of which Dutch culture is so proud is already an act of display that does not simply reiterate. As has been argued, the history of the portrait as a traditional genre is closely linked with specific social historical developments; hence, portraits carry the meanings that, via this context, have accrued to the genre.[24]

In these four photographs (figs. 6.2–5), the specific features of the portrait that stand out are the posing and the dark background. In conjunction with Zwarte Piet's traditional white collar, these features strongly recall traditional Dutch portraiture of the seventeenth century, the period of the joint successes of colonialism, slavery, and capitalism. It is the dark background of the wealth that enabled the bourgeoisie, rooted in an individualism that is still with us today and that underlies the genre's greatness, to rise to power. A power, incidentally, maintained even today, in the name 'Golden Age,' still used, without self-consciousness, by academics.[25]

The photographs as portraits thus refer to – without reiterating – a

23 I am very grateful to Darby English for insisting on this point.
24 See, on portraiture and its meanings today, van Alphen (1996).
25 A new centre for the study of the 'Golden Age' was recently created at the University of Amsterdam. On some of the ironies of the idea of a Golden Age, see Roxann Wheeler's essay 'New Golden Age' in *The Complexion of Race* (2000).

6.2–6.5 Anna Fox, *Zwarte Piet*, Numbers 1, 3, 2, and 14, from colour photographs made in The Netherlands between 1993 and 1998.

tradition in art that was always-already problematic. Portraiture was not, of course, only a Dutch tradition. But it was particularly suitable for the emerging Protestant merchant class in my country. Spain, the country with which the Seven Provinces had been warring for so long at the time of their 'Golden Age' – and not coincidentally the mythical origin of the Zwarte Piet tradition – was also the artistic rival of the Low Countries. This is not only a fact of art history; it is also a demonstration of the intricacies between art and other social and political processes.

Velázquez's 1650 portrait of the black painter Juan de Pareja is alleged to be the first full *portrait* – in the aesthetic tradition of that genre – of a 'man of colour' in Western art (fig. 6.6). Until that moment, black people had only held supporting roles. As servants, of course, but, sometimes even as elements in a still life. Rembrandt's *Two Black Africans* (signed and dated 1661) is a good foil for Velázquez's work (fig. 6.7).[26] The heads in this painting are closer to the kind of racist ethnographic typification of which print and paint media in the nineteenth century were so fond than to the genre that aimed to individualize its subjects. It depicts the figures for their strangeness, their difference from white individuals, and in that function they are both like each other and like innumerable other representations of black people. In contrast, Velázquez's portrait individualizes, also through the pride of pose and facial expression that comes with the genre. It was more than just a portrait; it was the portraitist's business card, an advertisement for the latter's skills in the genre. It is, in other words, the product of Velázquez's steadfast application of his extraordinary skills to the mastering of the variation of human types.

The painting not only served as an exercise and demonstration for the later portrait of Pope Innocent X. In order to obtain the commission for the Pope's portrait, Velázquez devised a ruse that provides us with an extraordinary anecdote. Pareja, also Velázquez's slave, took the painting and showed it to his master's friends, who were able to judge the painter's skills from a comparison of model and representation. The ruse was successful. The master received the commission and, six months later, freed his slave, who became a painter in his own right.[27]

---

26 The date, not the signature, has been contested. It is also not certain whether both heads were painted from life. See Schwartz (1985: 315).
27 Lecture by Victor Stoichita at the University of Michigan, Ann Arbor, 24 February 1999.

6.6 Diego Velázquez, *Portrait of Juan de Pareja*, 1650, oil on canvas

6.7 Rembrandt van Rijn, *Two Black Africans*, 1661, oil on canvas

Forecasting Pareja's future, the painter gave his model the pose he himself had taken in his most famous painting, *Las Meninas*. If we take this case as an allegory, then painting, and tradition, have the power to change themselves from within, and also to change social reality. This is how art can be truly performative, and how tradition can turn against itself. Velázquez, we can thus say within the context of this chapter, revisited the tradition within which he was making his career, to turn it around while also holding on to it. But let's not get carried away here. Idealizing Velázquez's ruse and its subsequent double outcome would blind us to the ambivalence inherent in portraiture. By sending Pareja to Rome with his own portrait, the master offered him up for identification *as* the object of representation; not for identification *with* him. The story remains an allegory, but, as such, demonstrates something that spills over from the confines of individual intention – from the individualism that portraiture, emphatically, labours to promote. The master may have wished to glorify himself, but his act of individualizing was effectively continuous with Pareja's emancipation.[28]

Again: Performing Performativity

In addition to engaging with portraiture, Fox's photographs, like tourists travelling to a neighbouring country, engage with another significant practice of performance: theatre. For, despite the fact that the figures in her images masquerade as powerful, they are not. The casual, less-than-fancy backgrounds that shimmer through the artistic darkness – the radiator, the edge of a formica table – are indexes of the class background within and for which the Zwarte Piet play is staged. They recall the urban school as the theatre for Coleman's children. Yet the subjects are dignified. Not because their portraits are being made, but because, individualized as they are, and unlike the black subjects of the Western artistic tradition who remained confined to their subservient roles, but like Juan de Pareja, they appear masters of their poses. The ambivalence of the genre and its history is thus inscribed in each image.

A well-known portrait of a black man by Henri Regnault, from 1870, titled *Head of a Moor*, offers an interesting parallel example of the intersection of portraiture and theatre (fig. 6.8). The comparison demonstrates the subtleties of such generic allegiances, and the impossibility

---

28 This paragraph engages a more negative argument offered by Darby English, who usefully cautioned me against idealizing Velázquez here.

6.8 Henri Regnault, *Head of a Moor*, c. 1870, oil on canvas

of using concepts as labels. In Regnault's work, the perspective from below makes the figure look heroic. His gaze – directed outside the image, to the wings so to speak, whereas traditional portraits tend to have the sitter look at the viewer – and the red mantle he dons, which has clearly been chosen for its colouristic effect, both strongly suggest theatricality. But, as a portrait, it is emphatically *not* performing an appeal to identification. The way colour is used emphasizes blackness, so that it can only be seen as 'othering,' the opposite of identification. This is done not only by the facial colour itself – which is black in a way that black people rarely are, setting off the whites of the eye, in turn emphasized by the sideward look – but also by the bright yellow on the left and the deep crimson garment, elements that make this a colour picture in more senses than one. Theatrical performance does not come, here, with critical performativity. In this sense, Regnault's work stands in contrast with Velázquez's individualizing portrait, but also with Coleman's deployment of theatricality.

In a move comparable to Bourgeois' 'amendment' of Bernini's *Teresa*, American artist Ken Aptekar revised Regnault's painting *preposterously*. In a show that critically worked over a number of pieces belonging to the collection of the Corcoran Gallery of Art in Washington, DC – as an instance of precisely the double-edged engagement with tradition that I am exploring in this chapter – Aptekar used Regnault's painting twice, as if to compensate for the lack of black subjects in the collection; at first sight, a gesture of identity politics.[29]

This is a portrait, and as a minimal intervention in the tradition for which it stands, it has been reversed (fig. 6.9). The artist has kept only the most essential part of the face, cropping the portrait and eliminating the bright colours. The powerful sense of facing from the self/other portrait can be seen here, quite fully, even though the figure looks to one side. Most important, by way of interdiscursive polemic, the painting has become monochromatic, to avoid the picturesque colouring of the source. By being painted in one colour, burnt umber, the face regains its nuances, and the visibility taken away by the excessive contrast – which recalls the cultural politics of 'invisibility blues' of which Michele Wallace wrote so powerfully – is reinstated.[30]

29 The following remarks on Aptekar's two paintings are based on my earlier article on his Corcoran project (Aptekar 1997).

30 I cannot do justice to the extremely thick concept 'invisibility blues' here. Briefly rendered, it refers to the varied forms of cultural politics rendering black people and black culture invisible. But a full account of this concept is keenly relevant for this chapter. See Wallace (1991).

6.9 Ken Aptekar, *Strength. Determination. Power.* 1997, oil on wood, bolts, sand-blasted glass

In addition to making other slight changes to the source paintings in his show at the Corcoran, Aptekar mounted glass plates over them, on which he wrote short texts. Sometimes these were autobiographical mini-narratives; sometimes they were quotes, for example, from comments made by museum visitors. These words drove the point home that visual images are always overwritten by cultural discourses. The text written over this particular painting was not long, not narrative; it was a snippet from audience responses:

Strength. Determination. Power.
And that's a little like myself.
Carrie Parker, age 15

The text endows the features of the face with the positive feedback that their former invisibility could hardly have been given. Yet the quoted teenager made these remarks in response to Regnault's, not Aptekar's, painting. Heroism, in Regnault's painting, served a purpose that Velázquez's portraiture also did – but not *qua* portrait. The visitor responded to the pose and the perspective, the *mise-en-scène*. Moreover, her statement connects the audience to the figure through the explicit identification, based *not* on skin colour but on the features the figure as a person emanates. The figure in the painting is retrospectively given the 'Strength. Determination. Power.' that he always had, yet could not be given in the *portrait as such* by Regnault, because the use of colour there made his facial features invisible. Carrie Parker, young, female, contemporary, gives the figure these positive features as much as she takes them from him for her own benefit: 'And that's a little like myself.' Her comment demonstrates the importance of the loving gaze that affirms the subject of the interaction that language most basically is. Parker's response demonstrates the way external images 'key' the self to the values presented, to the skin as the shape of the self.

Identification is also the basis of Aptekar's other portrait made after this Regnault, *After his license was suspended* (fig. 6.10). This work was also executed monochromatically, so as not to yield to social pressures to make skin colour a distracting and defining element. The burnt umber of *Strength* has been replaced with an overall blue that denaturalizes colour altogether while alluding to the many senses of the word 'blue.' Aptekar does here to the tradition of depicting back people as emphatically black – ethnographically – what Dutch culture tried to do, and didn't like, when it experimented with Red, Yellow, and Blue Piets. This denaturalizing effect is emphasized by the frame that has been added, and made to 'hang' askew. *After his license* offers one of those autobiographical mini-stories about the artist's past, this time about his adolescence; he can drive and goes out late at night, goes to bars and listens to music:

> After his license was suspended, I drove my older brother to bars in Detroit where whites didn't go. I tried to be cool, sitting down in a booth with my ginger ale. My brother unzipped his gig bag, raised his trumpet, and sat in with the best of the be-bop bands.

The story tells about a Jewish boy delving into black culture on a touristic trip to a tradition hitherto unknown to him.

After his license was suspended,

I drove my older brother to bars

in Detroit where whites didn't go.

I tried to be cool, sitting down

in a booth with my ginger ale.

My brother unzipped his gig bag,

raised his trumpet, and sat in with

the best of the be-bop bands.

6.10 Ken Aptekar, *After his license was suspended*, 1997, oil on wood, bolts, sand-blasted glass

The thrill of transgressing is audible – 'I tried to be cool' – and the pride the boy felt when his older brother managed to participate in 'the best of the be-bop bands' conveys the past 'feel' of the story more than the past tense does. The musical phrase 'the best of the be-bop bands,' with its alliteration and short drumming words, leaves an echo of be-bop as if we had been there too. This is identity poetics, not politics, at least not the kind of politics that separates and judges. The moment puts the autobiographical subject on the threshold of adult-hood, on the threshold of a culture at a time of *de facto* segregation, on the threshold, again, where self and other meet. The threshold is the frame. The question raised here, both poetically and effectively, is: Is a frame a boundary that keeps distinctions in place, or a meeting point where a frame-up yields to an embrace? Here, then, this work harks back to chapter 4.

The various thoughts I have attempted to address to tradition so far converge in this move beyond identity politics. To be or not to be: the question of identity is omnipresent and relative, explored in its tenacious difficulty and made to appear easy. The last chapter of this book engages this question obliquely but at greater length. Here, I allege Aptekar's reworking of Regnault's traditional painting, which suggests an intercourse with the word-concept of tradition and with those dubious values, in the case of race-based cultural distinctions, that are attached to the particular tradition out of which the Dutch Zwarte Piet grew and within which it cannot but remain rooted.

'Good' messages are not available; they are deceptions of simplicity. There are many unsettling, worrying, anxiety-inducing messages running through our culture – and here, I use 'our' in a broader sense, one that connects Dutch with other European and North American cultures. One way or another, these unsettling messages relate to the way the individual's voice is erased by authority both within the family – which, after all, is shaped and confirmed by institutions – and within institutions. The diagnosis is sharp, but full of compassion in the literal and lived sense, too full to be a complaint. The interaction between public institutional pressures and their effect on the personal, private life that comes back to haunt public culture is scrutinized as well as put forward, literally, into the viewer's space. By integrating audience response, it makes explicit what art can do, what even fifteen-year-olds can do to *it*, when they respond to art's performativity by offering their counter-performance.

This, perhaps, makes empowerment the central theme of Aptekar's project. An empowerment that is also the goal of a cultural analysis of the kind I have been trying to put forward through my engagement with this art. But, for art to empower, it must be performative. Using theatricality, not to deceive or to impose sentimental identification by means of these reworkings of Regnault's portrait and the tradition it deploys, Aptekar enlists Carrie Parker as an actor, performing – in the two senses of that word. Performing on the stage – the museum – her speech act of self-empowerment.

Theatrical Portraiture

The two conventions of theatre and portraiture that have now accrued to our concept of image are reactivated in Fox's work. They come together in their working through of this painful tradition informed by moralism. My hypothetical explanation of the Dutch attachment to this tradition is based on the notion that moralism, even progressive, anti-racist moralism, is less a critique of the tradition than an integral part of it. This collusion is inevitable. Aptekar's works acknowledge that fact, and have this aspect in common with Fox's photographs.

By virtue of their emphatic interdiscursive relationship with portraiture, Fox's photographs command an individualizing attention that takes the masquerade as part of the subject's individuality. As part of it, along with other parts; but sometimes, also, as synecdoche, as the part standing for the whole, making the rest of the individuality invisible through figurativity. Masquerade, then, comes to stand for a new, disabused form of individuality, in the way Coleman's theatricality came to embody a new form of authenticity.

Fox's portraits thus become a critique of portraiture from within, a critique of its ruthlessly power-based individualism. But they replace that individualism with one that does not obscure the individual's allegiances and collusions. These updated portraits ask us to look through the disguise, the similarity, the assumption of generic identity that the collective name Zwarte Piet, the costume, and the black-facing offer us – at first sight. The subjects are women, but in the photographs, nothing of their traditional gear helps us to notice their gender; no breasts, no feminine clothing, no ornaments, no poses. We are just looking at faces, painted for disguise, and yet, in most of the photographs, we see women.

We see they are white; many have blue eyes. Still, in some cases I hesitate: is the woman with the blue bonnet, red hood, and white lace collar who looks me straight in the eye, white or black (fig. 6.2)? To me, and to the friends to whom I showed the photographs, she 'looks black.' This commands a closer look. I scrutinize the image with an incurable, acquired, ideological magnifying glass. From my stock of prejudices, I glean all the features I have learned to associate with black people, and here I am, detailing the racist taxonomy learned so long ago in geography books at the age when I was also still a little scared of Zwarte Piet. This is how the photographs implicate their viewers; the past, they say, is not out there; it is here, today. And, to some extent – which I can neither master nor eradicate – it is inside me.[31]

And, while I am doing this, knowing that I am doing it, I also see the whiter edges around the subject's eyes, indexes of racial uncertainty, the hand that refuses to assert racial truth. Then I notice the smudge of black paint on the woman's upper lip. This smudge works like a wink, as if she is pulling my leg. 'I am not who you think I am,' the figure seems to say.[32] Is this a black woman playing a white woman playing a black man? What she is, here, *is not* the point; *that* is the point. The game she plays involves me, who I am, as much as it involves the she that she does not want to reveal herself to be. This is how Fox, by crossing portraiture and Zwarte Piet, and soliciting theatricality, de-naturalizes tradition. The theatrical space opened up here is the space where culture doesn't simply exist – but happens.

What this image does to my awareness of the race-consciousness within me also happens with gender. We see women, all different. Or do we? Is the proud-posing person in the purple mantle, whose wig or bonnet has slipped backwards to reveal, intentionally or by accident, a white hairline, a woman or a man (fig. 6.3)? Through the defiance in her gaze and on her lips, the figure's gender becomes so emphatically ambiguous that I wonder if this is a man posing as a woman posing as a man. And so, again, I realize that sometimes you do not know – and sometimes it does not matter. Sometimes, in other words, it is possible to reject compulsory identification *as*, and to replace it with identification *with*, another. The posing itself, the choice of and the mastery over the way each person is represented in this series, determines whether one is of a particular sex or gender – or whether s/he is playing the in-between. In this series, gender, like race, is emphatically an event, an effect, not a cause or an origin of social positions. Hence it is bound to the subject choosing to act it, and not an excuse to naturalize social positions and the inequities that come with them.[33]

31 I am alluding to my position as having been raised, *schooled*, in this tradition. Schools are productive fields for critical fieldwork. For the example of geography, see Ineke Mok's detailed analysis of the racism underlying geography textbooks in the Nether-lands (1999). This study provides extremely useful insights into geography's map-ping of racial differences and the drill with which an entirely white-invented race-consciousness is instilled in Dutch children.

32 I took this phrase from Ernst van Alphen's relevant analysis of cross-gender transves-titism, so far, unfortunately, unavailable in English (1998).

33 For the conception of gender that underlies this viewing of the photograph, see Butler (1993).

Each woman is different from every other. But this individuality does not entail distance. Despite resembling the paintings in Dutch museums in some way, they are also very close, very personal, looking me straight in the eye, and inviting me to share the pride, boredom, fun, fatigue, resignation, fear, insecurity, comfort, or discomfort that playing the role entails, despite also resisting the precise reading necessary for such identification. The Zwarte Piet in the Italian Renaissance pose – in bright red and blue and pristine white, with a Zwarte Piet clad in yellow in the background – looks the way I dreamed I would look when I knew I would not be chosen to be Zwarte Piet because of my inability to muster that confident prettiness (fig. 6.4).

This woman, who looks so utterly confident in her Renaissance role and who raises the issue of naturalizing role-playing in general, emanates the success which, for me, defined the class identity of those whose station was just a notch above mine. Having been raised with the ambivalent class consciousness characteristic of upward-striving, lower middle-class families (the target audience of Zwarte Piet in an era of the commercialization of tradition), as a child I would not have been aware that the woman emanated for me the successful impersonation of a class position superior to mine. But I would have sensed it. It would have been part of the drill: the learning of categories and power positions that came with them; *that* is the main task of children. Even the well-starched, well-ironed collar and the gold bands decorating the costume demonstrated the perfection I knew I would never achieve. The blue eyes are the most secure symptom of the travesty. But the pose of perfection – the head inclined just enough to be a flattering facial representation yet held proudly and easily at the same time – and the self-confidence of the facial expression are emphatic enough to reveal the artificiality of the pose caught in the act of its success. The acting itself, its visible performance, suggests this is not a wealthy girl from among my classmates, but a lower middle-class woman posing as an upper middle-class woman posing as a lower-class man.

Accordingly, the strategies of this play are different from the two other, ambiguous portraits I have been responding to. While the transvestite undermining of racial and gender identities that creates a space of uncertainty deploys an emphatically artificial conception of theatricality to achieve this effect, this portrait probes the limits of realistic theatre, or of that form of theatre that encourages the audience to forget its own nature and naturalize the spectacle instead. This seems to me to be a highly effective cultural intervention on the part of the artist-cum-model. Subtly approaching class by questioning naturalizing realistic representation, this photograph definitively implicates all viewers – willingly critical or not – in the tensions and ambiguities that representation brings with it, thus undermining its drilling educational effect from within.

My favourite Zwarte Piet in this series looks the way I would have looked given the chance, and seeing her, I know my case was hopeless, even if hers is not. Her hat is as brown as her stained face and eyes. Here, the brown, set off against the shiny, black nylon curls of the wig and the dark background and black costume, recalls that black isn't black, but just a symptom of a dichotomy that barely covers a physical reality (fig. 6.5). The brown has been less than well applied by a brush, the result is as artificial as the colour of the lipstick. Nor is the white white, if the stained collar is any indication. The girl's costume is a bit shabby, her make-up sloppy. This most monochromatic of the portraits – as monochromatic as Velázquez's *Portrait of Juan de Pareja* – is also the most emphatic in its de-naturalizing of colour on the level of representation. Caught up in a whirlwind of maintained and decom-posed traditions, I wonder why this portrait captivates me, and which share of its effect is the woman's, which the artist's, which the charac-ter's, and which my own.

The deep ambiguity here, which holds in its sway all the other ambi-guities, is a psychological one. Her body, clad in black, barely visible, the shoulder with its fraying collar, tells a hundred stories. Straighten your back, her mother must have told her when, growing too tall too quickly and sprouting breasts before her classmates did, she/I tended to hunch her/my shoulders. Hold your head proud instead of looking down, she would have heard, when she didn't know she was soliciting her own status as wallflower that she so dreaded. She looks bravely, lips slightly parted, as if she were about to overcome her shyness and actually speak. Her entire face and body are held back just a fraction, perhaps stiff, expressing both the act of posing for the merciless eyes of the camera and the public, and the pain it inflicts on her. Her face speaks to me of fear and bravery; insecurity and the desire to overcome it. Fear, not of Zwarte Piet, but of playing the part in public. This is what I would have liked to be at one time in my life: a tomboy posing as a good feminine girl posing as an exuberant black man. The middle term is the price to pay for the empowerment of the first and the last elements of this theatrical, triple identity.

Trans-gender, trans-racial, and trans-personality travesty merge inextricably here to perform the kind of intersubjective process that constitutes cultural life. This, then, the least successful Zwarte Piet, is the closest you get to a self-portrait of me as viewer. My own performance as viewer, subjective and unpredictable as it is, thus also belongs to the performance of this work. Tomboy, transvestite, black-faced clown: playing the part of what you are not fulfils a deep desire. Like getting yourself dirty, or doing dirty deeds. Like mastering fear rather than mastering others. Like coping with the entanglements of this tradition rather than *simply* rejecting it, as if you owned it.

Dirty Art

I have been talking about complicity in this chapter. But casting that complicity in the past alone is another form of disingenuous disavowal. Fox's art, again, helps counter that tendency. For it compels me to acknowledge that I enjoy these photographs. This is an effect of aesthetic as 'binding,' and through that aesthetic effectivity the photos hit me, performatively, with something in myself. They confront me with a tradition of which I have been too fond to simply shed the memories of it. Meanwhile, they confront me with a tradition that makes me blush with embarrassment. There is something shameless about these images. How can I negotiate them with the help of a concept – tradition – that itself has dirty hands? The variant of travel involved here seems to me, at best, to be that of tourism. Am I, can I only be, an exploitative, superficial tourist?

Regardless of the contingency of the cultural status of traditions and the value placed upon their historical specifics, it is not easy to determine the attitude of cultural agents today towards traditions that many consider unproductive for a dynamic society. For even harmful traditions cannot simply be wished away. The kind of critique that a politically alert cultural analysis can usefully bring to bear on traditions cannot cleanly disentangle itself from the cultural fabric in which the critique itself is embedded. And this cultural fabric is replete with tradition. To probe this issue, I have critically engaged with an extremely dubious yet perniciously persistent tradition in the country where I grew up and still live – and where the age-old tradition continues to thrive.

My goal was to question, through this example, both the easy dismissal of traditions and their unquestioned maintenance. Avoiding moralizing and partisanship, I discussed the Zwarte Piet tradition as a member of a culture that appears unable to let go of it, even in the face of increasing pressure to do so. I did this through a body of images that present themselves as a critical representation of that tradition, espouse another tradition to do so, and are made from a point of view exterior to the culture of the former (Zwarte Piet), while sharing the latter (portraiture). Taking my standpoint firmly in the present and looking first at the tradition's meanings and effects for contemporary (Dutch) culture, I considered the presence of the past in that present. In addition, I considered the status of traditions – both in art and in Dutch culture at large – that make up the fabric of Dutch society. I argued that traditions are neither dismissible fictions nor acceptable truths. Instead, I seek to understand their workings so that the culture can engage them, critically, where needed.

I said I would suspend judgment. Judgment here is to be understood in the two senses it usually takes – condemnation or valuation. Progressive criticism tends to indict cultural practices such as traditions, for their pernicious political conservatism. The more traditional (!) criticism of the venerable humanistic tradition implicitly or explicitly values the object of study. Any cultural object worthy of attention is by definition 'great,' or at least worthy of attention, according to the standards of the artistic canon and its collaterals or side effects. These two traditions – one of anti-traditional critique and the other of traditionalism – were suspended in this chapter. Instead, I aimed to practise an analysis that is anti-tradtional*ist*, that argues against the two academic traditions that know, or think they know, the outcome of their search. Risking the objectionable position of endorsing yet another dubious tradition, I proposed to act like a tourist, at least in one respect.

Tourists bring souvenirs home, but they are very much aware of the fact that they enjoy from the outside, and are not close enough to judge, the cultures they visit. And, whereas tourism is officially much snubbed by progressive academics, it is what every student of cultural objects practises – all the time. Tourists are superficial visitors, exploitative and contributing to the ruination of the culture they admire. They know it, and they still do it, alleging their contribution to the local economy, which they know to be not so local. The position of the tourist is embarrassing. Maybe it is that embarrassment that makes cultural analysis potentially effective.

In this discussion, I have visited Fox's photographs, and through them, my own past as a foreign country. The four photographs I have discussed in detail here represent for me, in the keenest possible way, the ambiguities and tensions of the Zwarte Piet tradition. Through that tradition, they deploy, decompose, critique, and exploit other traditions, such as photography, ethnography, portraiture, and theatre. Contending, like Aptekar, with a work that itself contended with a tradition, Fox has captured these tensions – not so she can document them, but as a way of working through, and working with, the space they open up. Within that space, the tradition can be used, for better or for worse, to probe a culture in flux, a culture that is tragically locked up in itself yet unable to maintain the illusion of self-identity.

A culture is not condemned to forever maintain – let alone celebrate, in a profoundly nostalgic sentiment – its racist roots. On the contrary, it is, by definition, changing.[34] This changing quality does not mean change is automatic; the direction it takes is the subject of the continuous struggles among the subjects of that culture. Just think of South Africa. Art is not a slavish imitation of reality; that, too, is only too obvious. Nor is it cut off from reality as has sometimes been argued; much of present-day cultural practice is still entangled in the difficulty of articulating a position for art that is socially involved yet capable of doing its own job. It cannot be easily defined. Much recent work on representations of race, artistic as well as academic and critical, has demonstrated the importance of the efforts to keep trying.

Grosso modo, it is fair to say that in the history of Western art, black subjects have been represented the way they were treated in social reality: as marginalized or neglected; made ugly, sometimes monstrous, even comical; or idealized, always a projection screen for white painters' fears and desires.[35] But, as I have argued elsewhere, progressive cultural critics have tended to reiterate such abuse in the very gesture of indicting it.[36] Such representations, including the criticism addressed to them, are neither imitations of, nor disconnected from,

---

34 Nostalgia in relation to racism became painfully apparent in the wake of the release of Nelson Mandela and the turn to the rainbow regime in South Africa. At the time, Dutch television showed yesterday's anti-racist artists, such as Adriaan van Dis, dressed up as a pioneer Boer in sporting boots and a hat and singing 'Sari Mareis,' the white South African song best known in Holland.

35 Fred Wilson's successful exhibition at the Contemporary in Baltimore in 1996 offers one of many examples of how to deal with that pictorial past in and for the present. For a recent collection of essays on the problems of representation in a context that tries to define itself as post-racist – South Africa by way of the 1998 Johannesburg Biennial – see Atkinson and Breitz (1999).

36 See chs. 6 and 8 of *Double Exposures*.

social imagery and traditions. Art today cannot but interact with that embarrassing tradition if it is to be effective in its interventions in changing culture. Only by neither repressing nor reiterating the past can we live with a present brought forth by that past, and that still harbours it, whether we like it or not.

Like Velázquez's, Regnault's, and Aptekar's paintings, each in their own temporal landscape, Fox's photographs are both disabused and optimistic. Humorous and tender, ironic and identifying, they are powerful in the way they offer art as a means to face the need to interact head-on. This is the chief aspect of the interaction that the portrait as genre has become: rather than pretending to settle what an individual is – a lone power broker – the portrait of this postmodern variety proposes the individual as framed by time and history but able to exercise the performativity that a theatrical authenticity solicits. Fox's images stand here for a practice of cultural analysis that manages to avoid the two most predictable attitudes to which a project like this might succumb: the endorsement of reiteration and the moralism of indictment.

To say they 'avoid' is to say they do something. The images' quality that I am implying through that phrase is their performativity. Beyond their artistic work of portraiture alone, beyond their theatrical play, they do something; they act. Like words. One of the many things they do is to take advantage of the ambiguity of images as such, in order to critique a tradition without dismissing it off-hand. For, living in the present and travelling to the past and back again, cultural tourists can no more avoid dirty hands than any other tourists can.

'Dirty' is the word that characterizes both this tradition and its disingenuous disavowal. It is a word that might at some point emerge as a concept. I think it would be a useful addition to the conceptual toolbox of cultural analysis. For, theoretically, it denotes the complicity that inhabiting a cultural situation inevitably entails. It is a gentle rebuttal of both false innocence and hasty distancing. Unlike words such as 'contamination,' which inspire fear of otherness, 'dirt' is not frightening. Dirt sticks to you but can be washed off, although after that washing you get dirty again.[37] It is inevitable, embarrassing too, but not deadly; as long as you take good care of yourself, you can continuously negotiate how dirty your environment can make you.

---

37 On the fear of contamination, see Stallybrass and White (1986).

Fox has played with dirt by selecting a tradition that, by materially playing with dirt, is also ideologically dirty; working with it as an impossible ethnographic project that renounces the illusory pretension that you can 'come clean.' Too close to home – within Europe – but not really home – not in Britain – the Zwarte Piet tradition enables Fox to probe the ambiguities of our, and specifically her, relationship to the traditions that have comfortably shaped us, and that continue to shape us while negatively shaping others. She was also able to establish a connection between the cosy home and festive but dirty street, and 'high art.' The mediating objects are visual images.

Images are readable, but what they say exactly remains subject to debate. In our case – the Zwarte Piet tradition and Fox's photographs of it – this is all to the good. The ambiguities here are indispensable, for, as I have suggested, moralism is part of both the racism and the anti-racism that have coloured Dutch culture in the wake of post-colonial migration. Together with the taxonomies of race, gender, and class, which provide the grids through which children learn to bring order into the chaos of the world, moralism itself is tabled here. For it is moralism that attempts to channel children's affective lives and fill them with ideological interests. Disturbingly – but offering food for thought – moralism also underlies the wish to do away with this tradition.

The tool Fox uses to break this moralism open, while avoiding traps of any simple representation of the tradition, is to appeal to the identif-icatory trajectories that powerful images are able to propose. These allow viewers to travel backwards in time, not on the national but on the personal level, to relive their own childhood, and perhaps to exor-cize the fear that came with the fascination. The bed of the artificial ideological river that channelled childish anxiety through the special-ization of racial othering can be enlarged. Enlarged photographs of today's images infused with pastness as if they were the products of double exposures may, I would like to suggest, serve to trigger, by way of the allegorical exploitation of their medium, an intensification of the reflection on where we can go from here. The emphatic effect of a mas-querade that persuades us there is no real identity to be seen yet no fic-tional mask to hide behind in the face of a disturbing, yet, for the time being, ineradicable tradition: this is simultaneously the photographs' performance, the viewer's liberation, Fox's teaching, and Zwarte Piet's *démasqué*. And, as the next chapter will continue to suggest, teaching as the primary tool of the cultural analyst can only work if it, too, changes, through its 'travelling' practice.

Tradition's Last Word

Tradition, Edward Saïd recently reiterated, is not only a weapon in the service of the state-directed manipulation of cultural memories. It can also, precisely because of the power to empower the people that cultural memory possesses, be turned into a means of communicating and furthering understanding. But only if tradition is de-naturalized and thereby pluralized. With the impressive example of Israeli and Palestinian memories converging around the same symbols – prickly-pear cactus, orange groves, forests – he alleges Carol Bardenstein's sensitive analyses of the tensions, convergences, differences, and above all, conflicting usages of such symbols of 'the land.'[38]

Saïd urges each community to recognize the other's memories, fixed in tradition. But he also points out the different position of each tradition in relation to power inequalities in the present. In the face of the political urgency of these reflections, the playful theatricality of the Zwarte Piet tradition, as Fox's photographs probe it, may appear frivolous. It is not. The presence of a deeply racist tradition in one of the 'postcolonial' societies most proud of its liberal tradition cannot be called frivolous, especially not in confrontation with Bardenstein's examples. Its very playfulness, its theatricality, constitutes its appeal to the children it shapes.

Tradition, as a word we tend to take for granted as expressing a cultural value to be endorsed or rejected, is complicated by *tradition* as a concept, thus serving as a searchlight to illuminate the process, performance, and performativity whose subjects are seduced into realizing that they are doing the acting. No longer tourists, the Dutch and any other people addressed by this series are burdened with the ethnographer's duty to do fieldwork. Travelling to the past and making it a familiar country – one for which one is responsible – and to the foreign country within one's own, in which being coloured is not a theatrical festivity, the spectators of Sinterklaas' entrance fully participate in the tradition, as agents, and are thus themselves framed by that tradition but not passively subjected to it.

Where does that leave the object of analysis here, tradition, and specifically, the two kinds of tradition – the sustaining, identity-shaping

---

38 The examples from popular culture such as posters and shop windows, juxtaposed to poetry and diaries, demonstrate a continuity between tradition and (cultural) memory. The most recent version of Bardenstein's analysis focuses explicitly on the memory aspect of these symbols (1999).

ones, and the invented tools of state power that sustain the nation at the expense of others and of its own historical awareness – that I have distinguished for the sake of this discussion? Artistic traditions (the portrait) and 'popular' cultural traditions (Zwarte Piet) have been maintained and subverted here at the same time. The concrete analytical means was theatricality. Thanks to the wedge that theatricality inserts between these two traditions, they were not handled in the same way. Artistic traditions here served as markers of recognizable forms, through which new perspectives, critical ideas, might be figured. The beauty of the images, their aesthetic quality, was used as a tool, in the same way as the mobilization of tradition was used to increase the affective quality of the images, which is a precondition of their performative effectivity.

The cultural tradition has been transformed only slightly. Art cannot simply change society, and believing that it can is an act of elitist hubris. But, like that smudge of black paint on the lip of that woman whose racial identity remains stubbornly ambiguous, the mirror of self-reflection held up by her photograph helps, ever so slightly, to enhance the painfulness of tradition. Until, that is, one day, the culture concerned wakes up sick of the pain. Only then – perhaps – can this tradition be relinquished, wholeheartedly; not suppressed by moralism, but rejected for the pain it causes to all its members. By that time, another tradition will have been invented, one that fits the culture better – and that hurts less. Until it, too, becomes the culture's backlog, dragging behind the times.

7

Intention

intention
- *a determination to act in a certain way, a resolve*
- *what one intends to do or bring about; an aim*
- *(phil.) a concept; esp. a concept considered as the product of attention directed to an object of knowledge*
- *the purpose or resolve with which a person commits or fails to commit an act, as considered in law*
- *(archaic) import, significance*

A Concept We Hate to Love

The concept *tradition*, central to chapter 6, entailed particularly tenacious political problems. My guess is that many readers are aware of those problems. It seems easy to distance oneself from traditions, especially one that turns out to be so pernicious. Yet, I argued, a tradition should not be too easily rejected because it has a cultural bearing that cannot be wished away. The concept central to this chapter – *intention* – is also problematic. But here, the problematic aspect is less easy to see and disavow. It is a concept closer to home for most of us, and it is problematic primarily for methodological reasons, although also for political ones. Methodology and politics come together in this concept in the sense that it is bound up with *individualism*.

Whatever their explicit positions, both traditionalists and those who think of themselves as progressive are replete with individualist habit.[1]

---

1 As well as being a word that is easy to understand, *habit* is also an important concept

So this concept cannot be wished away either. I am all too aware that our culture is not ready to abandon the individualism that subtends it. How, then, can *intention* best be discussed when it appears to go without saying that artists' intention is the bottom line of all inquiry?

To make the most convincing case and to demonstrate an academic practice that is both common and rarely examined, the argument here will be presented as a polemic: as a debate for and against the use of a particular concept – intention – in cultural analysis. One of my aims is to demonstrate the form such a polemic can take if the issue at stake is truly intellectual and 'trashing' is emphatically considered unproductive. The outcome of this debate will subsequently allow me to reorient rather than reject the concept outright. Lastly, through this reorientation I will open up the question if and how cultural analysis, beyond broadening the scope of particular disciplines, is also *fundamentally* different from the mono-disciplines that constitute the humanities. In other words, by discussing one travelling concept, *intention*, together with its 'foreign' counterparts *agency* and, as I will argue, *narrativity*, I will attempt to assess the nature of cultural analysis as a travelling discipline that cannot settle down.

When we are standing before a work of art, and when we admire it, are touched, moved, or even terrified by it, when a work of art somehow seems to do something to us, the question of artistic intention loses its obviousness, for the artist is no longer there to direct our response. Something happens in the present, while someone did something in the past. That act, we may suppose, was wilful, intentional. What is not so clear is that between the event in the present and the act in the past the same intentionality establishes a direct link. While it would be futile to doubt that an artist wanted to make her work of art and that she proceeded to do so on the basis of that will, the control over what happens between the work and its future viewers is not in her hands. But that later event is still, logically, a consequence of that act – the doing of an agency.

Present – past. It is history's mission to be attentive to change over

---

in Peircean semiotics. The best access to the concept is offered by Teresa de Lauretis' discussion of *experience* in her 1983 article 'Semiotics and Experience,' which opens with an anecdote from Virginia Woolf. This story beautifully demonstrates the combination of understanding, perception, and physical response that is involved in non-reflective responses to the world. By bringing in this concept here, I wish to underscore the near-'instinctive' quality of the appeal to intention in the cultural disciplines.

time. It is a cultural commonplace – in the present – that art, more than other things, has the remarkable capacity to move us in the present. If this contention can be maintained, regardless of the question of what non-artistic objects do to us, then the history of those cultural activities we call in shorthand 'art' has its task cut out from the start: to understand the agency of works of art across time. This task is not predicated upon a universalist conception of 'beauty,' but on the simple fact that all works of art, even those made today, require time and a change of situation to reach their receivers and 'do' things to them. Art 'works' across time, if not eternally. But the artist is involved only part of the way. He disappears, gives his work over to a public he will not know. What happens after the work has been made is not determinable by artistic will.

Reasonable as this view seems to me, I have had ample opportunity to observe that it is not generally accepted as a starting point for the questions about the arts that guide research and analysis in the humanities today. This may be because it still entails two unresolved problems. The first is a theoretical, philosophical one: the nature of the agency that performs the work's effect needs elucidation. The second is a practical, epistemological problem: the methodology of interpretation needs a new standard to replace the documentation that traditionally provides data on the artist's intention. To solve these two problems, I will stage a discussion both between an art historian and myself as a cultural analyst, and between two art works. Through this staging, I will demonstrate how the methodology of cultural analysis, even if practised in relation to the classical objects of a mono-discipline such as art history, differs fundamentally from art history's methodology. My aim is to further strengthen the case for a program of cultural analysis that (at least) supplements the separate disciplines in general and art history in particular.

As I have already stated, the concept of *intention* will be probed, not simply rejected. Owing to the popularity of intentionalism in the cultural disciplines, the task at hand is to offer a satisfying alternative. In terms of analysis, here the object/subject of close reading is triple: old art, contemporary art, and art history. Old art is the kind of art that can demonstrate my case most clearly, because often there is simply not enough documentation to prove intention. Contemporary art, I will argue, is as much in need of *historical* interpretation and as little bound to the artist's intention as old art. Art history, in contrast, *is* bound to intentionalism. It is represented here by someone whom I highly respect as a serious scholar in her field, and from whose work I have often learned. I select her because the quality of her work warrants what I have called, in the following chapter, a 'critical intimacy.' The format of discussion itself – which, of course, I can only approximate in a single-author book – requires such intimacy, if it is not to flounder in pointless and simplifying polemic.[2]

Svetlana Alpers is one of America's leading historians of Old Master painting, the most traditional object of art history. She often takes current responses to these old works of art as a starting point. Yet her work is committed to accounting for the artist's intention. For me, this is paradoxical. In this chapter, I will explore the consequences of her discourse of intention for the understanding of the art work it yields, and for the self-styling of the discipline of art history. I will do this by bringing in an alternative concept to fill the void left by the elimination of intention. The concept of narrativity will be my antidote to intention. Alpers explicitly rejects this concept for visual analysis. For her, as for many art historians, narrativity smacks too much of language.

Taking up what I have learned from her insistence on intention, from her ongoing attentiveness to the visual features of images, and from her resistance to the use of the concept of narrativity for the analysis of visual art, I will engage a dialogue with her work to explore the possibility of accounting for the agency of images over time. This agency can be attributed neither to the artist nor to the viewer, but, as I will conclude, only to the process that happens between these two parties when the product of the former becomes the product of the latter, that is, when viewing becomes a new way of making.

Forms of Abandon

The room smells. The work looks messy. The sculpture drips. Norwegian artist Jeannette Christensen makes sculptures out of Jell-O. Do they keep? No. That's the point. Look at this one (fig. 7.1). What does it mean to say 'That's the point'? That question is the point of this chapter.

Christensen's 1996 installation has an untranslatable title: *Tiden lager*

2 For this reason, and also to make the issue concretely relevant for the study of the humanities' objects, I engage the concept of intention here through a discussion with the concrete deployments of intentionalism in the work of Alpers, rather than taking such theoretical classics as Anscombe (1957), which contains useful logical analyses, or the volume on literary intention edited by Newton-de Molina (1976) as my starting points. For a succinct, useful overview, see Patterson (1995).

7.1 Jeannette Christensen, *Tiden lager alle sår*, 1996 and 1997, installation of seven steel benches with red Jell-O

alle sår, a pun on 'tiden leger alle sår.' 'Time heals all wounds' becomes 'time makes all wounds.' Different, but as ambiguous and ambivalent as the English expression 'killing time.' Elsewhere I have written about the temporality of this installation. Here, I propose it as a companion piece to Rubens' representations of the drunken Silenus, or his sleeping Samson, as analysed by Alpers. Christensen's installation gives form to *abandon*. And abandon is the opposite of intention.[3]

The seven bright red, human-sized Jell-O benches looked gorgeous at first. But their existence was fragile, from the start wavering on the edge of decomposition. During the four weeks of the installation, things happened to them. The suggestion of pleasure and food, light and beauty, yielded to the other association that had been lurking around all along: the association with wounded, fallen soldiers, with decay and death. At one moment, early on in the show, when the

3 On Silenus, see Alpers (1995), ch. 3. On Christensen, Bal (1998, 1999a).

benches were still fresh and brightly coloured, the enigma of sexual and temporal difference came up. This ambiguity remained, hovered around: desire, deadly wounds, feminine voluptuousness, built on happy, slightly nostalgic childhood memories of Sunday desserts, yet already future altars in honour of scarred, disintegrating, sacrificial bodies. Humorous and hyperbolic, deeply serious and mournful. The sweet smell of the traditional dessert would soon become a sickly smell evocative of blood. The moment when the sweet smell turned bad could not be pinpointed.

Early on in the exhibition, visitors touched the benches, sometimes tasting the Jell-O, poking their fingers into it to test its elasticity. Unlike with Old Master paintings, this physical contact was allowed. But then the benches started to grow old, to dry, to harden in some places and liquefy in others, and people stopped eating and touching; instead, they felt disgust. And then something else totally unpredictable and unforeseen happened as well. Some of the benches started to drip and bleed, making gorgeous pools in suggestive shapes on the floor. This separation of colours was an unexpected effect of abandoning the sculpture to time (fig. 7.2). Whereas the entire process of decay was a matter of merging and blurring boundaries, the colours, all on their own, moved in the opposite direction. They split into red and yellow. A golden yellow overlayered and embraced the red, creating erotic shapes that became strong metaphors for erotic desire as imagined inside the body. Red and yellow playing together; blood and urine, voluptuous golden desire.

If history is defined by its attention to change over time, then this work is 'about' history. The question I want to raise here is simple: who did this? The puddles, with their shapes and colour schemes, just happened. The artist did not know they were going to happen. Of course she expected some form of decay, and abandoning her beautiful, sharply cut, translucent forms to that decay was her act, its unmasterable effect, her 'point.' But she was still flabbergasted by the puddles, and happy as well, because they were 'beautiful.' Yet their aesthetically pleasing appearance was not a consequence of her will, or an expression of her subjectivity, a reflection of her authorial intention. Did she make the puddles? She caused them to happen but she did not shape their shapes in the way she shaped the sharply cut benches. The contrast between the sharp cutting of mastery and the appealing, pleasing result of the shapes produced by abandon is structural, not arbitrary. This contrast is what structures change across time. But again, who did this?

7.2 Jeannette Christensen, *Tiden lager alle sår*, 1996 and 1997, installation of seven steel benches with red Jell-O. Detail after four weeks (two coloured puddles)

If this event had happened four hundred years ago, there would have been no photographs to document what happened to it once it was abandoned to time. Today, we have at least that: slides, transparencies, photographs. No documentation of the design, just a few reviews, a catalogue essay – all interpretations. The photographs show that what happened is a change, a transformation of form and colour, not a loss of form, not formlessness. The sharply delineated form of the 'classically' perfect benches became a different, baroque form based on colour and colour distinction.

In contrast, take the *Narcissus* in the Galleria Barberini in Rome, a contested Caravaggio painting from four centuries ago (fig. 7.3).[4] The

4 The attribution is considered uncertain, although I am convinced by Gregori's arguments (1985: 265–8) in favour of it. For further support, see Marini (1974: 162–3, 387–9), Bardon (1978: 94–114), and Cinotti (1983: 518–20).

7.3 Caravaggio, *Narcissus*, c. 1600, oil on canvas

knee of the figure in that painting comes forward with an emphasis that, common sense tells us, *must* have been the artist's intention. The hand that made this picture obeyed a mind that decided to make the most of chiaroscuro, and thus painted flesh out of oil so that it would come forward in a very sensuous way. 'So that': this way of putting it suggests more intentionality than is warranted. The artist *did* paint it in this way, and lest we make more of the historicizing of the concept of the 'artist as craftsman-only' than seems justified, the hand and the mind were working together. The result is the fleshiness of the knee.

But the formulation 'so that' is mystifyingly ambiguous: does it mean 'with the consequence that,' or 'in order that'? Is the causality mechanical or psychic? And is the knowledge of that causality located with the maker or the viewer? These are three important questions with respect to 'intention.' The first differentiates consequence, or effect, from intention. Effect is the state of things as it differs from the prior state, the cause. As deconstructionist criticism has amply argued, causality is only an inference from the later state or event.[5] That inference, logically, is the doing of the person making the inference, a reader or a historian, not of the maker of the work. The second question, which superimposes its doubt on the first, differentiates mechanical from psychic causality. The former can be attributed partly to the maker – still on the basis of inference by the reader – and partly to technical circumstances and material possibilities. Psychic causality is more clearly located in the maker, but there the muddled nature of subjectivity comes into play. We know human subjects are not, as Freud phrased it, master in their own house. Even those averse to psychoanalysis will concede that thought depends on the historical moment and social circumstances, that is, on frames of reference. We also know that even the keenest and proudest of artists are limited in their freedom. Such factors as commissions are only the most overt and clearly limiting elements.[6] To make matters worse, the third question – the location of the knowledge about cause – cannot be resolved. Even if

5 For a lucid explanation of the reversed logic of causality, see Culler (1983: 86–8). In art history, this reversal has been articulated by Baxandall (1985).
6 For a meticulous analysis of a number of other Caravaggio works, based on the relationship between art work and commissioners, see Treffers (1991), in Dutch, and a more recent version, in English (2001). Although Treffers would probably disagree with the position I am defending here, I consider his analyses as strong evidence against intentionalism.

an artist leaves explicit and extensive documentation concerning her intentions, the *questions* that produce the knowledge of intention are raised by the historian, not imposed by the art work.

Caravaggio's *Narcissus* is invoked here to make this point. A feature of this painting that has often been noticed is the knee. It is impossible to prove whether the artist meant that knee to be central to the wheel-shape of the body for reasons of composition only, or for the purpose of 'figurability,' in other words, to produce a meaning 'figurally,' as Hubert Damisch phrases it. In a casual discourse about artistic agency, I can accept that the latter is likely, given the meanings the painting as a whole produces and the insistent way it does so 'figurally.' But what I mean with such a statement would not be covered by 'intention.' Rather, the ambiguity of 'to mean,' about which I wrote in chapter 1, in my view helps to avoid pointless debate. In fact, Damisch and I agree on the notion that the question is relevant, undecidable, yet not completely arbitrary, and that the answer to it 'means something.'[7]

What we know we can never know (but only surmise, or project from our own twenty-first-century perspective, or decide to think against all odds) is whether or not the knee was meant – intended – to look like, as Damisch has it, a hyperbolic, iconic phallus.[8] The phallic shape would be the element that gives this representation of narcissism a strong, psychoanalytic, and hence, 'modern,' reality. This reality is an important reason why the painting 'works,' 'acts' for us in the present. This 'work' is performed even for those who turn their backs on psychoanalysis, simply because that theory and its vulgarized interpretations are around us today, as a frame. They were not around at Caravaggio's time, even if phallic shapes were. Must we feel bad about such projections? Must we make them, and then later disavow them? My answer is an emphatic 'no.' Such meanings are partly responsible for the excitement that makes us admire, like, even love the painting; that is, they are partly elements of agency.

Yet the knee does, without a doubt, have that specific shape which, combined with the fleshiness, signifies 'penis' *now*; the size that makes it 'hyperbolic' is part of that meaning production. As a consequence, 'phallus,' Damisch's word, is descriptively right, even if a particular viewer chooses not to take that (kind of) meaning into account. The shape is 'out there'; the meaning is not, cannot be. It can only come to

---

7 Damisch (1996: 31).
8 Damisch (1996: 32).

mean something when it is instituted as a sign. And that requires a subject willing to attribute meaning to it.[9] Yet without that attribution of meaning, the shape itself, remaining in the shadow as a sub-figure, may not be perceived at all. So positive existence – 'out there' – is doubly meaningless.

One reason for the reluctance to attribute that particular but by no means compulsory meaning to that undeniable shape can be the sense of anachronism: Caravaggio did not know psychoanalysis, hence, had not had the opportunity to develop the habit of seeing sexual things in ordinary shapes. Yet psychoanalysis is the context within which this kind of meaning is most often discussed. The argument of anachronism is quite common, and although I have a number of objections to it, I will only signal one of them. Speculation on what the artist might have known about a postromantic subjectivity is indeed pointless, but we can still safely assume that he knew the difference between a penis and a simple *boule* (Damisch 1996: 31), that he knew what power was (but supposedly without the particular awareness we have of it today), and that he knew there was a link between these two elements. The two elements that make the figuration of a phallus socially meaningful – namely power and male sexuality – were known to him.[10]

I am interested neither in affirming nor denying the possibility that the knee 'was meant to' mean what Damisch says it means. There is something arrogant in such claims. Who are we to assume that people at the turn of the sixteenth century had no *intuitive* sense of such things? And even if we discard meanings we consider anachronistic, we can only do so after the fact, after they have occurred to us in the first place. Thus, by protecting the painting against retrospective impositions, we inevitably do violence to its effect (and to ourselves). I will not discuss this issue of what might be called the 'propriety' of psychoanalytic interpretation, primarily for reasons of the debate I am trying to stage. For Alpers would, I presume, not be interested in this at all.

9 Without discussing its detail, I must cite Peirce's definition of the sign at this point. 'A sign, or *representamen*, is something which stands to somebody for something in some respect or capacity. It addresses somebody, that is, creates in the mind of that person an equivalent sign, or perhaps a more developed sign. That sign which it creates I call the *interpretant* of the first sign. The sign stands for something, its *object*. It stands for that object, not in all respects, but in reference to a sort of idea, which I have sometimes called the *ground* of the representamen' (Peirce 1984: 4–23; emphasis in text).

10 For arguments against the notion that psychoanalytic interpretations of pre-modern artefacts are anachronistic, see Bal (1991b: 227–41).

My claim about intention in this chapter is not contingent upon the acceptance of psychoanalysis as an interpretive frame.

I bring up the knee because there is an aspect to its effect that we definitely know could *not* have been *meant* by the painter in the intentionalist sense of that verb, because, like the separation of colours in Christensen's sculpture, it was, so to speak, out of his hands. Yet that aspect, too, is descriptively 'right.' I am referring to the knee's detachment from the body. The knee, itself bright, is surrounded by darkness, and this makes it come forward as if in isolation. This kind of contrast was part of Caravaggio's stock-in-trade. The reflection in the water reiterates the detachment. *But the contrast has been deepened, radicalized, over time*. The fabric of the boy's clothing has melted away into the surrounding darkness. As a result of the denuding effect of time and the difference between our own time and the thoughts that 'live' today, one can now speculate that the work is 'about' the failure, rather than the success, of narcissism. For what we see is the Lacanian *corps morcellé*, or fragmented body, rather than the imaginary wholeness that narcissism conjures up as a protection against the spectre of that fragmentation.[11]

This interpretation is, of course, also wildly anachronistic. But, unlike the phallic shape Damisch saw in the knee, this detachment, whatever its meaning, while more obviously than ever not intended, is also more undeniably 'there.' It is not a shape in itself but the edge of a shape, a form, in the sense of appearing progressively detached from the indistinct background. When this form crystallizes out into something different from what surrounds it, we cannot prevent it from becoming a *figure* liable to produce meaning. Yet the progressive apparition of the form in a detached figure as the darkness of the background takes over and erases the dark velvet garment that was the tenuous link with the body – that, we know with certainty, is an effect of time. The painter did not 'know' it.[12]

Did Caravaggio cause it to happen? Did he, like Christensen, abandon his painting to time? Strictly speaking, he did. Not, we may suppose, that he knew what time would do to his figure's knee: separate it from the body and open it up to meanings he most probably didn't have 'in mind,' even if he had made an object – this painting – that performed this separation. But nor did our twentieth-century sculptor know that

---

11　See Silverman (1996) and Bal (1999a, ch. 8).

12　I am grateful to Michael Holly, who first drew my attention to the work of time in producing this effect.

her puddles would separate into colours. The difference is, she did know she would not be able to know. She wilfully endorsed the conception of learning that Felman derives from psychoanalytic theory – as knowing that you do not know – and puts it in opposition to knowledge that becomes corrupted into 'opinion, prejudice, presumption.'[13]

This corrupted knowledge is, I contend, the kind of knowledge that underlies intentionalism. The importance of knowing the artist's intention is thus doxic – unarguable, commonplace, dogmatic. Caravaggio did not know *what* he could not know, but, as both the craftsman he is claimed to have been and the artist we have construed him to be since romanticism transformed our sense of the figure of the artist, he knew that what he made would change over time. Whether he knew that consciously or as a habit developed through his work as a technically savvy painter, we cannot know. In contrast, Christensen's sculpture *addresses* this changing of art over time; that is its point. She intended it to do just that, regardless of her lack of knowledge of the outcome. To put the case more strongly in favour of my intentionalist opponents: her abandonment is wilful; his was not.

Paradoxically, Christensen's intention is to let go of intention. Caravaggio's, on the other hand, was overtaken by abandonment; that is, even if we are invested in tracing intentions, we assume he did not *will* abandon.[14] But isn't it the artist's ambition that his work will outlast the time allotted him to master it, even though he knows better than anyone that paint, canvas, oil, even meaning, are not eternal, not stable in time? Clearly, we have reached a shady area where all pronouncements are condescendent, unwarranted, and, in the end, futile.

This futility makes it necessary to carry the question of intention beyond epistemological considerations. For it is the question of intellectual relevance that is of importance here. How far does the notion of intention take us towards understanding pictures? This is the idea that Christensen's work, as a theoretical object, puts forward, in a gesture that links her work to Caravaggio's as commentary is linked to art

---

13 As I mentioned before, Felman discusses learning, and teaching, in the context of Freud's discovery of the value of knowing the limits of knowledge, or of not knowing (1983: 32n15).

14 This paradox resonates with my discussion of mystical experience in ch. 2. The fact that, here, the paradox can be extended to intention in general justifies in retrospect my extension there to eroticism, beyond the metaphorical comparison of mystical to erotic experience.

work. In an exploration of historical subjectivity – of intentionality fragmented and changing over time – the splitting of colours betokens the notion that intention, agency, and subjectivity are not whole, not even in the putative moment of execution, because the work is made to change over time, and thus to slip out of control. Unforeseeable as this event was, the artist endorsed the impossibility of mastering meaning.

Productive Opposition

'As a result [of Roger de Piles' oppositional argument,] even today it is hard to look at Poussin in different terms – to see that to look at him as a philosopher-painter appealing to the mind, rather than to the eye, is a way of seeing him and not the thing itself.'[15] 'Him,' as opposed to 'the thing itself.' The opposition Alpers formulates here, in her explication of de Piles' influence in doing just that, is the one between mind and body, like the one between person, subject, intention, and the work, object, result, or effect. Alpers is opposed to this opposition. So am I. When I read this, I saw what was wrong with a term I once had used to overcome it, namely, *propositional content*. I had used this term to indicate an area of meaning production not causally related to the artist's intention. The argument I made was bound to be misconstrued, and, as a result for which I take responsibility, the debate I conducted with, among many others, Svetlana Alpers, proved to be less productive than it should have been. The present discussion is an attempt to rework this debate, which concerns the issue of the differences between seeing 'him' (the artist) and seeing 'the thing itself' (the painting). Differences, mind you, in the plural.

In a paper to which Alpers once kindly responded critically, I formulated an attempt to make a case for a notion of pictorial narrativity that would take the image not as an illustration of a narrative that is already around, but as the production of a narrative that would necessarily be new, or different, as a result of the pictorial gesture folded into the viewer's compulsion to read. In order to argue for a specifically pictorial narrativity, I was adamant that recognition is not the underlying mode of processing. But Alpers was not quite satisfied. She resisted my invocation of narrative.[16]

---

15 Alpers (1995: 89).
16 The argument is now most easily accessible in Bal (1991a), ch. 5, esp. 198. Alpers responded in a personal communication.

She had written about narrative in painting before. The oppositional structure which, I thought, seemed to underlie much of Alpers' work has often made me feel uneasy: descriptive versus narrative (Dutch art, *Las Meninas*), genius versus business (Rembrandt), nationalism versus transnational humanism (Rubens). While opposition, by virtue of its clarity, is often a helpful tool for communicating complex ideas, it also tends to simplify them.[17] But Alpers then proceeds to complicate the opposition again. A most compelling case of her complicating gesture is her argument that the 'feminization' of Rubens missed the possibilities for gender-bending – she calls it androgyny – in his work.[18] This case appeals to me for a number of reasons, only one of which is my interest in gender and representation. It also appeals to me – I should say, allegorically – because of the gender ambiguity I see in Christensen's work, where the ambiguity is not at all based on the peaceful coexistence of two possibilities, but on the overruling of one by the other through the violence of time. What is at first a camp sort of femininity, in association with 'sweet and beautiful,' later becomes an equally hyperbolic tragic masculinity, when the bodies of Jell-O develop associations with wounded soldiers. Meanwhile, the gender hyperbole in the Caravaggio-according-to-Damisch is strongly gender-specific, even if the psychic condition named after this figure is emphatically not.

But my primary interest in this case stems from a theoretical point. Alpers points out that even when gender roles are reversed in the reception of Rubens, the opposition is maintained, at the cost of understanding Rubens' play with gender as a performance rather than as fixed and ontological (1995: 147–50). I couldn't agree more, especially in view of the intricacies of the relationship between performance and performativity in their impact on the image. Alpers explains the oppositional hang-up as a Saussurian, structuralist bias that makes oppositional thinking a cultural condition. The attention to Rubens' abandonment to flesh as a way around gender opposition has been all but erased by later ways of looking at his work, she argues. Whereas Christensen made me understand Caravaggio better, Watteau, Alpers claims, obscures aspects of Rubens. Her argument, which I find compelling, not only made me think about specific issues – here, Rubens'

---

17 It is the damaging aspect of opposition that I am attempting to neutralize or at least counter as best I can in this chapter. The beneficial effect of complexity lies in its suspending of simplification, not in complexity for its own sake.

18 Alpers (1995: 138).

performance of gender – but also pushes me to revise my own opposition to opposition.

The opposition I would like to revise runs as follows. Alpers is
primarily interested in the making of images – in what motivates,
informs, and impels that making. She attributes her interpretations to
the artist through various terms that I will discuss below, thus securing
'historical weight' for them – her cautious way of stating the case
without overstating her claim positivistically. I prefer to attribute the
interpretation to (my historically embedded reaction to) the image's
semiotic power to produce meaning for and with us, *now*. One implication of this difference is that Alpers' primary concern is historical in the
sense of understanding the past, while mine is historical in the sense of
trying to place present-day viewing within its own historical frame.

I wish to explore opposition – and this one in particular – as constructive, positive, creative, for opposition is also performative. But the
'speech act' it performs is not pre-determined. In order for opposition
to be positive, it must exceed its own binary structure. In the case of
my opposition against intentionalism here, this entails the need to suspend the analogy between the contemporary art work and its old
counterpart. It also requires that the issue of will be superseded by
something else. Hence, instead of trying to understand Caravaggio's
will by reflecting on process in Christensen's sculpture as a user's
guide for it, I wish to understand his performance, his doing – its
result, its effect, and its affect.

Performance is precisely the word Alpers used (1995: 64) to distinguish Rubens' act of making from his unreadable mind ('I was not trying to offer a reconstruction of what might have been in Rubens' mind
when he started the work, but rather the intentionality of the work
itself ...' 65). But rather than seeking historical weight for the interpretation of that performance, I look at it from, or with, Christensen's
experiment, which helps me to disentangle kinds and degrees of doing
through the variable relations between making and time, relations that
harbour the undoing of intention.

Without common ground there is no discussion, no productivity in
debate. Therefore, establishing that common ground is a first condition
for productive opposition. Alpers and I share a keen interest in images
themselves, an interest, that is, in close reading as a form of attention.
This interest in images is not at all obvious, or common, in art history.
On the contrary, a distinct lack of interest in actual images is demonstrated by many art-historical publications. There, images are too often

merely illustrations (called 'evidence') in support of an academic argument, drowned, as the latter are, in precedents, sources, and documents, or strangled by patrons, whose intentions displace those of the
artist. Alpers drew my attention to this years ago, and the observation
shocked me.[19]

I do not think I am misreading Alpers when I claim that, in addition
to this commitment to the image, we also share a commitment to articulating representation in relation to ideology, politics, and aesthetics,
in the belief that these domains cannot be separated. We share this
commitment, even if the kind of politics, and the emphases we place
on it, may differ considerably. This commitment is obvious from the
articulation of abandon in relation to pleasure and aesthetics, flesh and
paint in Rubens, an articulation that can be called, without much distortion, a *politics of abandon*. In a different but even more enriching
way, this commitment leads to the most interesting parts of Alpers and
Baxandall's book on Tiepolo, on which more shortly (1994). Perhaps,
most importantly, we both, in different ways, attempt to get away from
an iconographic concept of narrative images based on their conformity
to, or deviance from, a literary source, that is, away from the idea of
'illustration.'

But against this ground of common interests, we differ on key
points. These stand out as figure does against ground, giving relief to
and thus clarifying the opposition I wish to probe here. I am interested
in intention versus viewing, or 'reading' (my term), overdetermined as
that opposition is by past versus present as the primary frame of reference. Since how we differ on this point has been given relief by Alpers'
writings against (a certain notion of) narrative, against the ground of
my ongoing interest in narrative that so strongly and continuously
benefits from her hermeneutics of suspicion and her focus on the dan-

19 Because, I suppose, the common-sense view of what art history is about would sug-
    gest otherwise. Two almost arbitrarily selected examples – with different thrusts and
    results – of this overruling of the image by documentation, and of the artist by
    patrons, came to my attention in my readings on Caravaggio: Gilbert (1995) and Tref-
    fers (1991). Both studies are excellent in their way, and I learned much from them,
    about Caravaggio as well as about historical analysis. But whereas Gilbert pays atten-
    tion to the images as such in relation to their making and effect, Treffers' exclusive
    interest in the sources informing the iconography all but obscures the visuality of the
    works. He reads the meanings 'off the page,' or rather, 'off the painting,' in the dou-
    ble sense of 'off.'

ger of reducing visuality to literary concerns, 'narrative' is the term I have to bring into the discussion here.

The Logic of Intentionalism

Before doing so, however, I shall first explicate my understanding of Alpers' discourse of intentionalism through a close reading of passages from *The Making of Rubens*. In this book, Alpers' deployment of the concept is sophisticated and challenging. Its deployment is most explicit in the first chapter, whose argument she sums up at the beginning of the second chapter: 'The aim [in chapter 1] was to reconstruct Rubens' intentions – the engendering in the sense of the begetting of the *Kermis*' (65).

What we have here is a move – and the rest of the book goes on to show that it was an intentional [!] one – from intention to origin, then on to genealogy and begetting (as the male's part in it). Thus the issue of intention itself, in a rather biblical mode and choice of idiom, is mythically gendered male. This turns out to be central to the book as a whole. But we do not find this out until we have read the third chapter, where the gender-bending mentioned earlier becomes a central concern. On the same page, we then find the rejection of the mind as the site of intention – 'to see that to look at him [Rubens] as a philosopher-painter appealing to the mind, rather than to the eye, is a way of seeing him and not the thing itself' – and the displacement of intention onto the intentionality of the work.[20]

The argument of the first chapter has it that the representation of Flemishness in the representation of partying peasants is combined, slightly awkwardly, with iconographic allusions to an antiquity that transcends nationalism, and with a pleasure in painting that, moving from 'he wanted to do' to 'he did,' shifts the argument from intention as a state of mind to the performance of pleasure in freedom. To give a sense of the intricacies this shift entails, the following merits quoting:

> Rubens does not *intend* us to separate out his portrait of the Flemish peasants from the aspect under which he presents them – so firmly has he *tried* to bind and so define his view of the state of Flanders and its people to this old, general view of humankind. (41–4; emphasis added)

---

20 Alpers' position here – the primacy of the intentionality of the work – is close to Eco's (1990); in art history, it has become attached to the name of Michael Baxandall (1985).

This passage already suggests that the 'intentionality of the work' is – in the sense Michael Holly might pick up on as a case of prefiguration – its response to later interpretations, among which Alpers' own in its previous phase of unfolding. In this formulation, intentionalism works as a lens through which to focus attention on the work, an attention protected by blinders that keep out any distracting knowledge that has accrued to the image like the dust of time.[21]

Although this focusing of attention is the productive result of the discourse of intentionalism, it also has another side. It lends authority to the spectre of the artist's authority over the vision that is not necessarily, or not entirely, his. Although Alpers points out those visual features of the image that bring in these two views of Rubens, one might also wonder, for example, where the *hierarchy* established between nationalism and a supranationalist humanism should be located: in the viewer or in the maker's will? For, on the basis of the same features, one might instead describe, perhaps even more convincingly, their lack of integration, the messy and conflicted juxtaposition of these two sentiments. My sense that Alpers' own subjectivity is here inevitably intertwined with interpretation and its construction of intentionality suggests a shadow of herself as what literary critics call, with a term I find problematic for the same reasons, the 'implied author.'[22]

This term refers to the author, or maker, as his or her image comes across in the work. It is the personified unification – the unification through turning into a person – of the meanings an interpreter 'sees' in the work. The term was coined to encourage a disjunction between the implied author and the historical person who made the work, a disjunction necessary to account for those fictions with 'unreliable narrators.' Its use, however, demonstrated an unforeseen problem. The concept allowed projections of meaning by critics to be unproblematically attributed to the author, thus, literally, *authorizing* interpretations while obscuring the hand that makes them – the critic's. The tool, again, is the ambiguity of 'meaning' as both 'to mean to' and 'to mean.' I would put this problem forward as a footnote to Alpers' account of Rubens' double allegiance to nationality and humanism, with the latter serving to overcome the limitations of the former.

To mean to, or to mean, that is the question. There is no inherent

21 See Holly (1996).
22 For the first articulation of this concept, see Booth (1961). For a critical assessment, Bal (1997b: 18, 76).

bond between these two usages of the verb. Symmetrically, its double sense plays tricks on the viewer. The question of Caravaggio's detached knee comes up again, this time in terms of readability. Does a shadow obfuscate the image, or does it enhance its relief in the way Rembrandt sometimes obscures a sitter's eye so that we will take a better look?

Further complicating the notion of intention is the intricate mixture of modalities of logic involved in any attempt to pin down intentionality, a mixture I came to discern through Christensen's willed but unmasterable abandon. The metaphor of travelling concepts is again helpful here, as is the practice of close reading through the concept under scrutiny. The methodological issue can be stated as follows: when the itinerary of an intentionalist argument is signposted in terms of the plurality of logics it involves, it seems, at best, to lay out a map that comprises a patchwork of considerations, none of which is bound by necessity to any other.

The following passage demonstrates this (for analytical purposes, I number the argument's structural units):

> Why (1) did Rubens take up the peasant subject in the first place? How can we explain (2) his concern to depict the peasants at this moment (3)? What were the circumstances (4) in Flanders (5) ... and Rubens' attitude (6) toward them at the time he painted the *Kermis*? How far can they take us in viewing the picture (7)? (1995: 25)

This passage leads up to the section 'Circumstances I,' one of three sections that, in the first chapter, alternate with three other sections, all called 'Painting' and also numbered I to III.

I distinguish seven steps above, barely noticeable because they are connected by the common-sense use of ordinary words – by linguistic habit, although not by the necessities of logic. I disentangle them here, not because I object to common sense (which I often do but not obsessively), or because of a craving for neatness, but because their unravelling sheds new light onto the complexity of subjective agency and intention. And this as much for the argument at hand as for the intricacies of the transforming of subjectivity in Christensen's *Tiden* and Caravaggio's *Narcissus*.

'Why' (1) asks for intention, although if it were not for the subsequent attribution to the proper name, it could, ambiguously, refer to a more open causality, as does 'explain' (2), which asks for determining cause. The two do not necessarily overlap. Reference to 'moment' (3), as distinct from subjectivity, refers to historical context positioned in time, diachronically, whereas 'circumstances' (4) position history synchronically, thickening the moment in a suspension of time that allows it to spread out so as to surround the image. This is the question of framing. 'In Flanders' (5) specifies context, or rather, frame, as a moment in national history. This makes sense in the case of a painter who was also a diplomat, but it also narrows down what the frame of reference is assumed to be.

The decisive discursive activity of binding occurs in the final two elements. The word 'attitude' (6) binds 'what happened' to Rubens as a subject, as an individual with his political views, specifying 'circumstances' to mean psychic response. Most pertinently for my analysis, in (7), Alpers' discourse implies that all these questions or considerations pertain to the picture as an object of viewing. This outcome of the itinerary of the underlying concept of intention is illuminating, as it brings Alpers' position within reach of a position that would not put intentionality at the centre. For, as the passage from pages 41–4 (quoted earlier) appears to suggest, the connection between intention and viewing can also be reversed, since the work responds to our response to it. Not only does the object cast a long shadow over us across time, we also cast a shadow over it.

This is beginning to look like a circle that defines the image, a circle that moves back and forth between the seventeenth and twenty-first centuries, encircling the act of making as a performance embracing the act of viewing that has not yet taken place but which it already acknowledges. Is it vicious or hermeneutical, or can this circle be characterized differently? To be better placed to answer that question, I will, for now, connect intentionality to its other side, that is, to the image's relation to subjectivity as viewers construct it through meaning. In other words, I will separate the implied author from its Siamese twin, the critic whose product it is.

The Performance of Thought

The concept of intention is, for Alpers, bound up with her strong commitment – which I share – to avoid subordinating the image to the discourse about it, and of which it can, at best, be seen as an illustration. But we differ on where to look for a more helpful term. Whereas I agree with her resistance to the subordination of images to language, I in turn resist the idea of 'pure' visuality. My commitment to interdisciplinarity stems from the sense, developed in the preceding chapters, that there is no opposition between image and language. Neither linguistic nor visual artefacts can be isolated from their frames or considered dead objects, since they perform in performance and performativity. If we try to avoid thinking in terms of an essentialist opposition between visual and linguistic domains, we are forced to come to terms with the notion that images may be mute. But they are no more stupid, thoughtless, passive, or arbitrary when mute than when subordinated to language.

How, then, do images produce meaning beyond the obvious, word-by-word but rather uninteresting meanings that texts are so much better suited to express? In this sense, an iconographic analysis limited to meanings dictated by theological or political debate, as documented in sources, bypasses the key question of *how* images not only convey the master's message – whether the master is the artist or the commissioner – but also articulate thought visually. In other words, the question is, how do they *think*? How can they be intelligent but at the same time offer ideas for reflection and debate, ideas in which the political and ideological flavour cannot be distinguished from the domain of visuality itself?

In their Tiepolo book, Alpers and Baxandall use the term *pictorial intelligence* to denote this. In my *Reading 'Rembrandt,'* I proposed *propositional content* as an encompassing term for the 'thought' of pictures as distinct from their aesthetic or 'purely visual' aspects. My resistance to an essentializing ontology of the media was the main thrust of that book. But, as I mentioned above, with hindsight and through the rethinking that Alpers compelled me to do, I find the term *propositional content* problematic because of its potential implications, one of which is to maintain the oppositions I sought to avoid.

The most tenacious problem posed by this term is that the word 'content' is predicated upon a form/content opposition, which is again overdetermined by the qualifier 'propositional.' The latter term comes from logic, a rather un-visual domain, one not 'thick' enough to sustain analysis of cultural works, and it means 'content' as emphatically distinct from 'form.' It suggests, moreover, that there is an outside to the image, inevitably construed as prior – which was what I was trying to avoid in the first place. Finally, through its link to logic, it encourages the reaffirmation of precisely that opposition that Roger de Piles put in place, and which the passage quoted earlier, from Alpers' *The Making of Rubens*, describes in all its problematic implications. Logic implies a mind, a 'him' that produces it. I can trace the logic in Alpers' argument in favour of intentionalism, but when it comes to Christensen's and Caravaggio's works, logical analysis will not do. Yet there is thought, there are ideas – and these works produce them. They perform them, visually and temporally, through a necessarily shifting subjectivity.

To be sure, my second thoughts about the association with exteriority should not be taken as a plea for formalism. Exteriority is very much involved in any processing of images, from the social environment of their making to that of their various readings. But the representation the image offers, performs, or *is* can relate to it or respond to it yet not be explained by it, let alone reduced to it. The fundamental untenability of the status of any image as object only – hence, of the formalist or immanent criticism of images – is best assessed when the visuality of the image is respected, including its meanings and the way they are produced. Any separation of form and content will damage such an assessment.[23]

The implications for the notion of intention of meaning and its production, as exemplified by the Christensen/Caravaggio 'debate' with which I began, were brought forward by reception aesthetics.[24] The exteriority, here, consists of the gaps, the discrepancies, and the problematic assumption of causality between process and object, between the muteness of the object and the need to (re-)activate it. But if the activity of filling in the gaps is a matter of reconstructing the maker's intention, then it would be insulting for visual art to suppose that the work needs that effort, just as a solely iconographic reading-off-the-page of meanings is an insult to the work's visuality and its capacity to make meaning through that visuality.

---

23 This is my fundamental problem with Summers' discussion of intentionalism within art history (1985–6). Summers posits a binary opposition that thoroughly manipulates the discussion when he writes, 'If the work of art is truly cut loose from intention, then art becomes autonomous' (308). If this were true, then his conclusion, 'Intention is also thus radically contextual' (311), would be inescapable. My argument goes in the opposite direction. Intentionalism, whereas often compatible with contextualism, leads away from the aspect of 'context' as accounting for art's effective and affective results. I would blame this problem on the concept of context itself. As I have argued in ch. 4, 'context' is a mystifying term for what 'framing' explicates much more adequately.

24 The classic text of this movement is Iser (1978). Kemp is among those art historians who brought these ideas to bear on visual art (1985).

Gaps *are* not exterior; reception aesthetics claims they are *in* the work. But they *produce* exteriority. Better still, they undermine the distinction between exteriority and interiority. Again, Christensen's sculpture helps probe the depths of this insight, having demonstrated that it is indeed not possible to distinguish exterior from interior. The unforeseen, and unintended, later exterior effect was inherently caused by interiority, by the body of the sculpture itself. Exteriority, then, becomes a problem only when it is disavowed.

But if I now understand the potential implications of the term *propositional content* and must therefore abandon it, this is not really very helpful. Giving up that term neither solves the problems of the intentionalist circle suggested by the problem of the concept 'implied author,' nor disposes of the problem of narrative as dangerously hovering between pre-established literary meaning and unmasterable process. In view of the attempt to stage a productive polemic, it makes sense to look to my opponent for an alternative. And, since *pictorial intelligence* was the term Alpers proposed as an alternative to *visual narrativity*, I expect that a further probing of the two terms she put in opposition might help to solve the problem left hanging by intentionalism. So I will examine *pictorial intelligence* first, then see how it could possibly relate to, or even encompass, the more specific term *pictorial narrativity*.[25]

Towards the end of the Tiepolo book, in a close reading of the Würzburg *Treppenhaus* frescoes, Alpers and Baxandall's formulation suggests that *pictorial intelligence* might, indeed, be a satisfying option. For the passage draws attention quite precisely to the tension, in intentionalist accounts, in the relationship between interpretation, meaning, the maker, the viewer, and the effects of time, as highlighted here in the Christensen/Caravaggio cases. The passage comes after a description of the successful adaptation of the depictions of three 'foreign' continents to the circumstances of changing light and moving perspective. The depiction of the fourth continent, Europe, the authors note, does not seem to fit in very well.

There seems to be a certain awkwardness in the *Europe* section when it is compared to the other three, at least when they are compared in terms of the rococo principles of ambiguous dimensionality, horizontal

---

25 Thomas Crow, another well-known art historian, proposes the term 'the intelligence of art' in a sense that comes close to that of Alpers' term. See his book that bears this term as its title (1999).

balance, and the figuration of bodies in movement. However, they write, 'rather than writing off *Europe* as a relative failure, *it is better* to make a case for it by *constructing* a function it can be seen as meeting.'[26] Who would not fully agree that respect for the object requires a suspension of judgment based on pre-established principles? This is how a work of art, or any image for that matter, can become a theoretical object. Such an object 'occurs' when it is *observed* (which implicates the subjectivity of the viewer), and when it *resists* (implicating the 'intentionality of the work') normalization into the theory previously held. Thus, paradoxically, respect for the image as *immutable object* requires acknowledgment of its *transformation*: it demands we see it differently. Hence, the art work is not an immutable object only, but acts over time and across subjectivities. If the art work is to be respected on its own terms, it must be undone and redone again and again.[27]

Alpers and Baxandall's decision that 'it is better' indeed implies taking a position on this holding off of what we think we know. But if holding off is better, what, then, do we do instead? The verb 'constructing' makes clear that the act that follows is a construction from the vantage point of the present, as any psychoanalytic interpretation of Caravaggio would be. However, such a construction of 'a function it can be seen as meeting' begs the question of intentionality so strongly that the term *pictorial intelligence* seems to blur rather than clarify the issue.

Both Christensen's puddles and Caravaggio's detached knee can be seen as fulfilling a function, provided we construct one for them. However, the connection of each to the kind of thought, in relation to making, that the notion of pictorial intelligence suggests remains stubbornly ungraspable and diverse. The puddles fulfil a function, one they entice us to construct for the work as a whole: that of giving a positive account of time as aesthetically productive in its very unmasterability. In other words, *the aesthetics of time entails the limit of intentionalism*. As such, Christensen's puddles can be seen as theoretical objects.

Responding to the question that the puddles address to it, the detached knee fulfils a related but slightly different function. It makes us aware of the bizarre arbitrariness of the effect of time, and, simulta-

---

26 Alpers and Baxandall (1994: 154; emphasis added).
27 I have made a similar claim for the strangely reversed leg of Bathsheba in Rembrandt's painting on that subject, in *Reading 'Rembrandt,'* ch. 6.

neously, of the inescapable meaning-producing machine that figurative art cannot help but be, even if meaning abducts the figures from the image's initial state. Whereas the puddles' 'theory' was primarily a theory of temporality that deployed fragmented notions of subjectivity to make its point, *Narcissus*' 'theory' primarily de-naturalizes the unification of meaning, using time to make that point. Instead of asking whose intention is at work here, we must now ask to whose pictorial intelligence we are responding.

In the *Europe* section, the construction presented in the discussion of Tiepolo's work is a wonderful reading of the image, opening it up to important political and aesthetic concerns. These, in turn, account for what is no longer awkwardness, but without explaining the former 'awkwardness' away. 'Concerns,' but whose? Tiepolo's, I have no qualms about that. But, as in the itinerary of intentionalism in the Rubens passage, both the subject and the nature of 'accounting' remain elusive.

The authors continue their reading, however, by ascribing their construction to the work and its maker: '... its *purpose* and conditions of viewing are different ...' (154; emphasis added). The keenly political analysis could only benefit from a thickening of the subjectivities involved. For it is true that the content of the construction – a certain centralizing of Europe as a compulsory vantage point from which to look at the other continents – can convincingly be seen as part and parcel of the ideology of Tiepolo's time, and – why not? – of Tiepolo himself. On the other hand, though, the interpretation has a distinctly contemporary, postcolonial feel to it, which is what makes it so compelling:

> In fact, perhaps one has no business looking at *Europe* from the same upper gallery from which one looks at *Asia, Africa* and *America*. If anything, one should look *from Europe* ... *Europe* is the rubric, the initial code ... The ostensible frame of reference is Europe with the other three parts of the world as tributary. (154; emphasis in text)

The rhetorical colour of this passage is telling: 'one has no business,' 'one should'; Eurocentrism is presented as a code that presides over meaning production. This is quite clearly both discourse from today – belonging to cultural politics – and a successful attempt to bind that discourse to a visual image from the past. In other words, the awkwardness that set off this thought is itself a construction – carrying meaning, hence, a sign – of the present – of Alpers and Baxandall. Thus, 'awkwardness,' that productive heuristic device, is a tool that helps reposition the work in the present and break it open from its formalist self-enclosure. Why would one wish to disavow this bond, where past and present meet without merging?

This political interpretation cannot be located in the pictorial intelligence of the maker only. It would be a shame, indeed, to detach it from the present, which gives the work the specific appeal for which the Tiepolo book is in fact pleading. But how can such a bond between past and present be theorized without de-historicizing the painting? This is the crux of the argument I am having *with* Alpers – in the strong sense of that preposition. In this theorization, which will also answer the question about the nature of Alpers' circle posed earlier, the idea of narrativity can no longer be avoided. For what I mean can, in part, be understood through a concept – a special form of subjectivity – that is bound up with narrative.

The meeting point where pre-enlightenment politics and postcolonial sensibility come together to illuminate each other is the point where awkwardness and its solution intersect. This meeting point can be construed as a case, or zone, of 'free indirect focalization.' Long ago I coined this term in analogy with 'free indirect discourse,' to describe cases where the point of view or focalization seems to lie with a subjectivity that is a conflation of the narrator and the character, or of the subject and the object of figuration.[28]

But how does this term accommodate not the narrator and the character, both agents interior to the fiction, but the pictorial subject and the external viewer? The details Alpers and Baxandall foreground are infused with meaning and affect; indeed, they have no meaning without affect. And the authors acknowledge this. The analysis is followed by an account of what they call a 'delayed Tiepolo effect' (160). There are two reasons why I propose the term 'free indirect focalization' as a provisional tool to account for this description of Tiepolo's *Europe* section, an account that must include its awkwardness, which is the evidence of the presence of its present-day viewers within it. The first is that the thought – the meaning illuminated and thickened by affect, which the authors rightly describe as pictorial – cannot be attributed to the work's 'intelligence' alone. Therefore, the viewer is brought into

28 Bal (1997b: 159–60). For the concept of focalization and its relation to visuality, see ch. 1 of the present book.

the picture; or rather, the picture, like the dripping benches, reaches outside, into an exteriority across time. There is 'thought,' that is, intelligence; it is pictorial, but not confined to the interior of the work. Nor can the participants in the dance of ideas be merged or neatly disentangled. Abandon is appropriate here – abandon to the process of art, and whatever that may entail.

Narrative Abandon

The second reason for my use of the emphatically narratological term 'free indirect focalization' – and this leads me to the final point I wish to make – is that this instance of response constitutes a narrative. Hence, it seems quite relevant that Alpers and Baxandall's analysis is connected to an act of story-telling. It is a story of viewing and its difficulty, of the temporal deferral inherent in the connection between viewer and image, a kind of Freudian *Nachträglichkeit* to which the characters must abandon themselves.

The description is set in an evasive third person – 'one' – which barely covers the first-person narrative in which the characters are also the narrators. The narrative runs as follows:

> For an hour or two after leaving the Treppenhaus, one is every time teased by a sense of having failed to attend to a dimension of Tiepolo's picture that, in retrospect, registers strongly. The picture has a tart sort of moral after-taste. The effect was not noticed and reflected upon in the presence of the picture. But when one hurries back to the Treppenhaus to attend directly to what must have been neglected, it again becomes elusive on site: the morale still cannot quite be seen or located. There seems a diffused meaning here that condenses only *after having seen* the picture. (160; emphasis added)

This story is a wonderful account of what would be exterior to the image if images were bound to their maker, for the effect it narrates is out of his reach. This ruthless exteriority, however, can only complete the communicative loop, or circle, on condition that the temporal effect of delay is accepted as an integral part of the image. In other words, only if the narrator is willing to become a character *within* the enlarged image – no longer a formal unit but an unmasterable event – can pictorial intelligence perform its work.

Precisely for these reasons, then, *that* work – the work of the work of art – must be defined as narrative, whether the image tells a tale or not. This is what the present chapter adds to the ongoing unfolding of the concept of image in this book. The authors of *Tiepolo and the Pictorial Intelligence* have known this all along. Early on in their book, struggling with an anti-narrative hope, they wrote:

> But in making *visual* sense of depiction we become narratively engaged. [...] If we wish, positively, to give the peculiarity of the pictorial its due, we need some minimalist sense of narrative – we need a sort of para-narrative. Para-narrative would refer to the human elements we infer in making visual sense of a pictorial representation. (42; emphasis in text)

Narrativity is here acknowledged as indispensable, not because all pictures tell stories in the ordinary sense of the word, but because the experience of viewing pictures is itself imbued with process. In this process, interiority and exteriority interact and get entangled without actually merging into a unified stability, so that formalist accounts will inevitably fail, and delayed action must be retrospectively adopted.

'Para-narrative,' if I interpret the term correctly, means something like a sense of narrative but without an eventful, pre-established, and recognizable story; in other words, not a story told 'in the third person.' But, I would suggest, there are other narrative modes not contingent upon such a traditional conception of narrative. The need for a new term stems from underestimating narrative, its possibilities, and its potential for experiment. What I find extraordinarily insightful and sensitive in this passage is that the authors here invoke 'para-narrative' to account for the pictorial itself: 'If we wish, positively, to give the peculiarity of the pictorial its due ...' The Greek preposition *para-* means 'sideways,' stepping aside in order to see.

As a concept, then, *para-narrative* seems to convey the indispensable idea that I am also attempting to articulate here. As a term, with its suggestion of secondarity and marginality, however, it distracts from the central mediating function that narrativity can fulfil in Alpers and Baxandall's attempts to do full justice to the processual visuality of images, as well as to their – not *his* – 'intelligence,' without separating them as if they were different pursuits. Christensen's dripping, smelly, mildewing Jell-O enacts that narrativity. My borrowing of concepts and ideas from literary theory to further articulate this narrative is an attempt to get away from giving hierarchical precedence to language. Here, there is no story outside the image.

The Jell-O has a narrator but not a maker; the materiality of the stuff, in its transformation, tells its own story – 'in the first person.' The sweet smell, the disgusting smell, but also the beautiful shapes and colours throw themselves at the viewer in an attempt to enforce a 'free indirect focalization.' It is the Jell-O turning bad that smells. But without the visitor, it would not, would it? What is a smell but a typical feature of an object penetrating the body of a viewer? My wording here, to all intents and purposes, resonates with Alpers' begetting of Rubens. There is gender-bending going on here as well. As a parody of begetting, the bodily power of the object to get inside the viewer articulates, or embodies, yet another element of the theoretical object's thoughts.

The Jell-O sculpture, ever resourceful in finding new ways of keeping us focused on the vagaries of time, turns the dilemma posed by the two major narrative modes into a productive solution that is not the result of a dialectic with a happy ending but of a further differentiation. In its initial beauty, it posited 'third-person' narrative and its claim to objectivity and distance but with its often-objectifying denigration of characters. Then, when the sculpture began its process of decomposition, it drew attention to itself, as in 'first-person' narrative. But as viewers ate from it and the smell began to turn bad, it enforced a lively face-to-face interaction, as Erving Goffman, that pioneer of close reading of social process, would have it.[29]

Neither 'third-person' and its iconographic version, nor 'first-person' and its subjectivism, which tends to fall back into the authoritarian, elitist claims of connoisseurship, are the final station of Christensen's sculpture's process. When the Jell-O sticks to the visitor's finger, or when the smell hits the body of the viewer, what comes about is not what I would call 'para-narrative' but, more simply and more emphatically, narrative 'in the second person.'[30] It is the unmasterable domain where the 'you,' the viewer, and the 'I,' the allegedly image-internal narrator, meet; that, I submit, is the arena where 'in making *visual* sense of depiction we become narratively engaged.' Such an engagement is historical: in the present, connecting to the past. It is through the concept of second-person narrative that we can theoretically account for an image's agency, which reaches across time, without neutralizing it and the historical differences its passage entails.

29 Goffman (1974).
30 On the ins and outs of second-person narrative in painting, see Bal (1999a, ch. 6).

Understanding this process requires detailed attention to the image, including to that aspect in it that conveys a sense of subjectivity, agency, even intention. It also requires a complex but urgent historical framing. The commitment to understanding this crucial feature of visual art in its full social relevance is where the opposition between Alpers' intentionalism and my interest in narrative melts away, like Christensen's Jell-O. When Alpers wrote, in *The Making of Rubens*, 'This [Alpers' account so far] leaves out what is most puzzling and also what is particularly pleasurable about the painting – or *more properly* what was puzzling and what was pleasurable to Rubens ...' (44; emphasis added), she bridged the gap between two untenable positions through a self-correction that is, perhaps typically, her own stance, a word that appeals to authority – more *properly* – in the very gesture of abandoning herself to the pleasure that she, as an art historian, gets out of art.[31] It is because her writing remains in that tension, because it never resolves its own ambiguities, because it cannot be reduced to a logic she so earnestly pursues, that I will always learn from it, in and on that elusive but crucial domain shared by teaching, social life, and art – of second-personhood.

Abandoning Authority

And so the travel through the discourse of intentionalism and a practice of narrativity has arrived at a point where I must leave it to the reader – say, the participants in the fictive seminar described in chapter 1 – to decide where to go next. They can continue with me, in further search of a concept that can fully grasp the complexities that have accrued along the way, leaving *intention* behind, even if for now there is no definite place for us to go. Or they can remain in Alpers' domain, where intention is common and comfortably recognizable as a concern, yet where teachers like Alpers both provoke and confuse compliance with the discipline of the discipline. The choice, I contend, is the one between moving into cultural analysis or staying with art history. By engaging the same (kind of) objects – works of art in need of historical understanding – these two areas may be compatible, but they are surely in tension.

This tension, I hope to have demonstrated, is not only quite strong, perhaps even radical; it is also productive. It produces insights that

---

31 See Derrida (1982: 1–38) for a deconstruction of 'proper.'

neither my nor Alpers' earlier work quite displayed. If I may take this situation slightly allegorically as a measure of the differences between art history and cultural analysis, the conclusion would have to be that most desirable would be an academy with an explicit place for both disciplines. Mine is an argument, should it be needed, against cutting departments, a threat that emerged in the wake of the merging that came with the turn to cultural studies, the most practical, material drawback of the turn I mentioned at the beginning of this book.

But if we can claim a place for both (because the tension itself – the knowing we cannot know, in the sense of 'own,' the 'truth,' or meaning, of cultural objects – is what makes the debate productive), then debate itself, as the privileged mode of teaching and learning, ought to be the central pedagogical mode in the practice of cultural analysis. This is one reason why, in this chapter, I have been close-reading the work of an esteemed colleague from the other country – art history. But debate, as we all know, is not by definition productive. More often than not, it forecloses any advance in the collective effort to learn that we are better off (un)learning. To allege Felman's view of teaching again, debate, if not truly open, forecloses learning and instead makes the participants, each in their stronghold positions, fall into 'opinion, prejudice, presumption.'

My effort has been to map out a space for intersubjectivity in this sense. A space where the argument of the other (here, in some ways, even, the opponent) can produce its best elements. A space, too, where the argument of the speaker (here, me, as the author of this book) yields maximally to the other position, to produce more knowledge. This would be the 'interminable task' of 'analytical apprenticeship' (to recycle some of Felman's headings in her article on teaching), an apprenticeship where ignorance is not opposed to knowledge but an 'integral part of the very *structure* of knowledge' (Felman 1983: 29).

If I, as the author of this single-author volume, have the privilege of the provisional 'last word' here (Alpers will perhaps respond elsewhere) the emphasis on 'provisional' must be understood as heavy. For I have not remained unaffected by the resistance to my views phrased in the quotes and summaries of Alpers' (and Baxandall's) work. The aftermath of this effect is not in my knowledge-as-possession but rather in the structure of my knowledge, where ignorance belongs too. In other words, I do not know what the concept of intention will look like, even to myself, a few years from now. But I do know it looks different since writing this chapter.

This staged discussion was meant to suggest the kind of discussion between disciplines and cultural analysis, as an inter-discipline (as a discipline that has no existence without *inter*-connections to other disciplines), that would be the most helpful. It has striven neither to a merging nor to an abandonment of disciplines – the latter of which would leave them to their defensive self-protection – but to keep the work being done in both areas vital. As I see it, the key to such productive debates is the concept I will put at centre-stage in the final chapter of this book: *critical intimacy*. Unlike in this chapter, there I will make the case while refraining as much as I can from positioning my own views in the discussion. The case, in other words, pushes the presentation of academic discussion to its extreme, while at the same time reframing the relinquishing of intention so as to include my own. Relinquishing my position as teacher, I will stage another teacher and be her student. For, in Felman's view of pedagogy, the difference between teacher and student is dramatically reduced, since both are guided by ignorance, process, and the collective pursuit of knowing how to not know.

8

Critical Intimacy

critical
- *inclined to criticize severely and unfavourably; consisting of or involving criticism; exercising or involving careful judgment or evaluation; including variant readings and scholarly emendations*
- *of or being a turning point or specially important juncture; of or being a state in which or a measurement, point, etc. at which some quality, property, or phenomenon undergoes a definite change; crucial, decisive; in or approaching a state of crisis*
- *sustaining a chain reaction*

intimacy
- *the state of being intimate; familiarity*
- *(euph.) sexual intercourse*

This openly declared interest makes my reading the kind of 'mistake' without which no practice can enable itself.

Gayatri Chakravorty Spivak[1]

Figuring the Teacher

A teacher needs to know how not to know. I am a teacher. One of the joys of that profession is literally to see thought emerge into clarity and shed its initial fuzziness. The concept I put forward in this chapter is

---

1 In *Critique of Postcolonial Reason* Spivak says this (1999: 39) about her analysis of Hegel, but she could have said it many more times throughout the book. Here I wish to endorse this statement as characteristic of my own reading of her book.

important for such a process. The proximity, indeed, the intimacy of a person, a student, struggling with thoughts struggling to have her think them, to recall Bollas' 'unthought known,' of a person skilled and knowing not to know, is an eminently fertile situation for the combination of creativity and interaction that distinctively characterizes cultural analysis. In such a field, a person's intention is irrelevant; including, of course, the teacher's. So what practice of teaching 'culture' remains, then? The final leg of our travel is an attempt to think, stage, and figure a map that can serve as a provisional answer to that question.

Approaching the end of our travels, we return 'home.' That is, we return to a place in the here-and-now that has lost its routine, its familiar homogeneity, that has been enriched by strangers, strangeness, and self-estrangement. I might be saying this in the literal as well as the figurative sense. Literally, the world has changed, and hence, travel has changed its meaning. In the figurative sense, disciplines are no longer what they used to be before the interdisciplinary 'movement' (an odd but not so inappropriate word) took hold.

The literal and figurative senses join forces when we consider the enormous impact of 'postcolonial studies' on the established disciplines. Tourism, as the pursuit of the thrill of the manageable picturesque, makes no sense in the contemporary world. Not long ago, 'we' used to speak of 'others,' coining words like 'othering' and 'alterity,' together with qualifiers like 'respect' and 'understanding,' 'dialogue' and 'equality,' words that made us feel good – about ourselves. The catchword that stood alone at the summit of such discourse was 'culture.'

No one felt too comfortable when asked to define it. For perhaps this is one of those words we are better off *not* turning into a concept – at least not a clear one, and not too quickly. Because, before we knew it, its uplifting derivatives, such as 'multiculturalism,' were appropriated in the Northern Hemisphere to join forces with unquestionable liberalisms-cum-individualisms, to mean indifference, tolerance, and condescension.[2] Such words and phrases have lost their innocence today. It is no longer possible to say 'we,' or, for that matter, 'other,'[3] because the structure of the thought subtending such words is itself under scrutiny.

2 See Hamacher (1997) for a critique of multiculturalism.
3 For the politics of 'we,' I refer once again to Torgovnick (1994). The discourse of 'the other' has been subjected to critique by many, from de Certeau (1986) to Spivak (1999).

Figuratively, again, in terms of the methodological issues I have attempted to discuss in this book, the lesson this development seems to offer is that now is the perfect time for shedding other innocent words and views as well. The seminar situation I sketched in the introduction will never be the same again. Students will no longer be able to use their normal words like buzzwords, or to fall back on routine procedure, without running the risk of being teased by peers to explain what the point might be. That this happens in discussions may seem excruciatingly clumsy and may seem to imply that lots of time would be spent on 'metadiscourse,' not on 'content.'

But, on reflection, the disadvantage of lost innocence – concerning, among other things, the nature of 'content' – turns the tables on what once seemed to be a clear division between content and fussing in the margins. In an attempt to counteract this common-sense resistance, I proceeded by performing detailed case studies. Through these, I hope to have demonstrated that such fussing heightens the yield of the inquiry, in terms of content and of breaking away from the already-known, even if 'content' has changed its meaning in the process and the 'knowledge' of content is being performed together 'with' the object, not simply 'about' it. Fabian (1990) makes a strong case for such a performative conception of knowledge in ethnography. It might seem easier to understand this concept in ethnography than in the arts, where the object of knowledge is a 'thing,' not other people. But I hope to have made a strong enough case for the extension of the subjectivity of the object as other *with* whom the knowledge is being performed.

But whoever says 'content' is bound to be intrigued by its traditional 'other' – form. Case studies such as I have presented here often meet with the suspicion that they are based on a remnant formalism. I find that suspicion both irritating and helpful. Irritating because it remains stuck in the form/content binary, so that whoever holds the view that 'formalism is bad' tends to fall back on a naïve contextualism once called the 'social history' of, say, art, literature, music, or film, without feeling obliged to rethink the assumptions inherent in such approaches. Helpful because the very *quotation* of 'formalism' invokes the importance of specific human subjectivities. Such resistance obliges the cultural analyst to connect textual to subjective specificity, and singularity to larger groups, issues, and interests.

In light of the above, it seems only reasonable to end this book with the use of a concept and the study of a text both of which in many ways can stand for the changes this book promotes. The concept at stake in this final chapter – *critical intimacy* – reflects the concern for keeping together what only scholars would separate: 'form' (whatever that may mean), 'content,' and 'context'; issues that go by the names of cultural, social, or political. Less abstract, and also less general, less formal, and less academic than any of the other concepts discussed so far, this concept stands for the methodological position I have been advocating. It points to a constructive exchange with the 'others' of cultural analysis: practices, in the earlier chapters; tradition, in chapter 6, and the traditional disciplines, in chapter 7.

As a concept, *critical intimacy* is a neologism I borrow from Spivak. But I could not have been sensitive to its potential without an 'unthought' practice of it, when one of my students engaged in a critical intimacy with me as her teacher, in doing a work that ended up as a book called *The Intimacy of Influence*.[4] Critical intimacy points to a relationship blatantly opposed to (classical academic and pedagogical) 'distance.' It points to a pedagogy and practice whose intimacy has been under fire yet remains crucial: the practice of teaching. And it points to subjectivities – in the plural. In acknowledging this concept's source, I also wish to emphasize that it points to the field of study whose practices and whose very name are subjected to the concept-as-method, 'postcolonial studies.' A field that travels the world, that engages 'otherness' in a critical intimacy so that the concept of 'other' loses its innocence and can make its home wherever it wishes. Such as, for example, in an English department.

After travelling with and through concepts, is it possible to return to an English department, for example, and to call it one's home in the academy? In chapter 7, I made a case in favour of the right to a territory of their own, for both the traditional disciplines and cultural analysis. Having made that case, I will argue here that such divisions on the basis of complementarity and productivity of debate need not even lead to the institutionalization of cultural analysis for its own sake. Nor must the argument in the previous chapter be construed as claiming

---

4 The phrase 'intimacy of influence' rewrites Bloom's term, which locates creativity in misreading, albeit not to the spirit of his term, which puts rivalry at the centre of creativity (1973). Lord (1999) develops a more 'cooperative' sense of misreading 'under the influence.' Her creative vision of 'influence' as not copying by reinventing 'masters,' is doubly effective. The intimacy she stages between later women writers and their predecessors not only goes a long way to explain 'influence' as creative rather than competitive. It also allows the critic to use her own intimate engagement with poetic narrative to inform readings of theoretical texts.

that inhabitants of the traditional disciplines should be exiled. In reply to the question of whether returning 'home' is possible, of course my answer can only be an emphatic 'yes.' On condition that the traditional disciplines, once relieved of *their* 'anxiety of influence,' relax their vigilance around their borders.

One of the best-known academic world travellers I know – Gayatri Chakravorty Spivak – happens to return to just such a place after each trip. I will take Spivak, or rather her most recent book, *Critique of Postcolonial Reason* (*CPR*), as my final case study, in order to examine the productivity for the interdisciplinary practice of cultural analysis of simultaneously working through three concepts: the rhetorical concept of *personification*, the semiotic and philosophical concept of *subjectivity*, and the academic figure/concept of *teacher*. The concatenation of these three concepts, used here as casual-words-turned-concepts and as concepts-fine-tuned-as-words, helps further flesh out the alternative to intention that I began sketching in the preceding chapter. They represent the building blocks for an attitude, or practice, that I think would be most helpful for the current state of the humanities because it would allow all the divides that have developed and deepened during the last decade to be bridged – a state of which my own teaching practice has given me a taste, of which my students and the author of *The Intimacy of Influence*, in particular, have given me the experience, and for which Spivak's work has given me the desire and a name: critical intimacy.

Critical intimacy with something or someone who at least is conceived as 'other': this is what I attempt to discuss, demonstrate, and achieve here. In engaging Spivak's *CPR*, I also attempt to practise that book's injunction to rethink what can be the most felicitous and the most productively critical position for scholars today in the humanities. To experiment in line with Spivak's probing of (im)possibilities, I abdicate the 'we' position and endorse the position of outsider – because postcolonial theory and philosophy, the main areas of her book, are not mine.[5]

---

5 The graphism '(im)possible' is explained in Spivak (1987: 263). Robert Young renders Spivak's position on positions thus: 'rejecting none of them according to the protocols of an oppositional mode, but rather questioning, reworking and reinflecting them in a particularly productive and disturbing way' (1990: 157). Mark Sanders, whose review of *CPR* offers a wonderful testimony to Spivak's teaching, also quotes this passage (1999).

Reading Other-Wise

As many readers familiar with Spivak's earlier work will surmise, *CPR* is not an easy read. Yet reading is what it is about, what it does, and what it teaches. On more levels than one, but beginning with its own accessibility, it teaches how to read – *other-wise*. Indeed, it is perhaps *over*-readable, if such a notion makes sense. By this I mean a form of readerliness based on a multiplicity both of (academic) levels and of lines of argumentation, subjects, and discourses. It can be read in many different ways none of which is adequate and all of which are enriching and useful for whatever area of specialization one is working in – as long as one is engaged in (thinking through) *culture* and the activity of *analysis*.[6]

'My aim, to begin with, *was* ...': beginning in the past tense and ending with the word 'undone,' this book has no beginning and no end. In this respect, it is like its subject matter, which can be summarized briefly as a passage, from its title, to a program of developing 'transnational literacy,' in other words, to a practice of intellectual travel. The phrase 'transnational literacy' is an extremely felicitous synonym for the goal of a productive teaching program in cultural analysis. To pretend that either this book or its subject matter has an end is to closet it.[7] Both have many openings that beckon you in yet leave the doors open so that you can leave when and how you wish. Thus the book sets itself up to be appropriated, and in full awareness of how that makes me complicitous with much of what the author rants on about at times, I feel compelled to do just that: productively misread it.

Thus invited to take the book 'home' – to divert it from its many-branched course but to confirm its multiple readership – I will offer three misreadings of *CPR* all guided by the concept of *critical intimacy.* In reading the book in this way, I aim to offer a pedagogical *supplement* that operates in two ways. The obvious one is that it makes Spivak's book useful beyond its own 'field.' A less obvious but equally important one is that it turns the tables in the traditional teacher-student relationship through demonstrating how I, as a teacher, benefited from

---

6 Sanders traces Spivak's mode of reading in terms of ethics, or rather, 'ethicity.' Although I cannot develop this road in the map of Spivak's book, I urge the reader to read Sanders' text for an understanding of the ethics of reading involved.
7 In the sense used by Patricia Williams to indicate that the righteous, well-meaning, but ineffective desire for colour-blindness 'closets' race (1997: 8).

Lord's work as 'my student.' In other words, I also aim to advocate a critical intimacy between these two positions at the centre of the field of pedagogical practice. In my misreadings I will follow, or spin, three threads, to which the book is in no way reducible, and which are even insufficiently complex to account for the part-issues on which they focus. My goal is to convey one sense in which *CPR* can be read with enormous productivity. Misreading it may be a pre-condition for that productivity. Through my critical intimacy with it, I hope to demonstrate the concept to which this chapter is devoted, and to persuade my readers that critical intimacy is a productive – perhaps the most productive – mode or attitude for reading scholarly texts.

To briefly characterize the 'mis-' in my three misreadings: in a study explicitly allied to postcolonial theory and politics, I will discuss aesthetics; in a practice of deconstruction, I will talk about referentiality; and in a book of intricate and self-reflective writing, I will foreground orality. These paradoxes serve to make explicit the meaning of *critical intimacy* itself and of its bonds with other, related concepts such as *subject, native informant*, and *personification*. They also make explicit this concept's yield for interdisciplinary analysis, where total expertise in all the disciplines concerned cannot be achieved. Most importantly, they serve to demonstrate that suspending (pre-)judgment is itself productive, because it is not the same as repressing, forgetting, or abandoning judgment to become an uncritical follower. These three paradoxical elements are meant to underscore and remedy the profound mis- readings to which those who mistrust, misinterpret, or misjudge the author's triple allegiance to transnational culture studies, deconstructive critique, and teaching have subjected her work and the likes of it.[8]

CPR contains four long chapters, simply titled 'Philosophy,' 'Literature,' 'History,' and 'Culture.' Their *sequence* is clear and significant. Read both forwards and backwards, it is justified as an itinerary and a guideline for an interdisciplinary culture study responsible to each of its components as well as to the objects that can be confined to none. Read forwards, 'Philosophy' examines the arguments, 'Literature' the figurations, and 'History' the archival material in which the arguments and figurations collaborate to determine, and retrospectively leave

8 In this sense, this chapter converges with the ASCA Theory Seminar out of which the present book grew. This seminar has been devoted, in the twelve years of its existence, to the purpose – deceptively simple in its formulation – of reading difficult texts for interdisciplinary work.

traces of, what happened.[9] History also changes the practice of history by interpolating between positive research and philosophy, the need to read, and a way to do it borrowed largely from literature. 'Culture' then opens up to the politics of a world in which culture is a global issue, and for which the ill-fated term 'multiculturality' fails to account and women's representability remains the touchstone. A plea for *transnational literacy* binds the four chapters together.

Read backwards, the critical examinations of theories of (postmodern) culture are critically engaged for the possibilities and impossibilities they offer for representing women. But, at the end of the itinerary, neither 'representing' nor 'women' can be taken at face value, certainly not monolithically. Theories and approaches are faulted for ignoring what Spivak irreverently calls the 'homework' that should be done out of respect for that foreign country – 'the past' – to which the 'vanishing present' is also on its way to belonging.[10]

The next step backwards is from contemporary cultural theories and practices to the archive. By not taking that step, these theories fail to measure up to the diagnosis of the present they claim to provide. Back to 'History,' then. In the process, we get a new sense of history, its importance, and specifically, its *presence*. Now, however, we know that archival research is not fact-finding but fact-reading. It cannot be performed without the specific reading skills that literary studies teaches. 'Literature' provides the examples that demonstrate that literature and the literary belong in the world. Therefore, they must be seriously taken into account, not just by addicts but by everyone. Through a reading of the figurations – the tropes of postcolonial reasoning and colonial writing – the reader arrives at the starting point, Kant-Hegel-Marx, the 'last Three Wise Men of the Continental (European) tradition' (*CPR* 111), whose basic concepts laid the foundations for what is now the object of critique in Spivak's own critical intimacy: postcolonial reason.

Having arrived at the starting point, the traveller is equipped to follow the same path again, but this time without considering those wise men as the hierarchical top, since it is now known they are still standing there but shouldn't be – because the present that holds on to them

---

9 The word 'to determine' is extensively taken apart in Spivak's book. See below.

10 In Spivak's book, especially in the chapter 'History,' the past is, of course, a foreign country, in the literal as well as the figurative sense; and, in her deconstructive thrust, if what I have said is true, the distinction can no longer be trusted.

is vanishing. Philosophy can no longer be read as a master discourse, isolated and superior, even though, or precisely because, it still is a master's discourse, the pervasive 'His Master's Voice' to which it is so hard not to listen. Nor do the Three Wise Men stand alone on that imaginary mountain top. Spivak has joined them there in the *critical intimacy* (425) that is her book's red thread. Critical intimacy: that is what I find most generally productive about *CPR*, and it is just that relationship that I aim to try to achieve with it.[11]

Spivak's first two chapters offer three case studies each. The first takes on Kant, Hegel, and Marx: a perverse reading of passages from Kant's *Critique of Judgement*; a joint reading-for-complicity of Hegel and a canonical Hindu text, the *Srimadbhagavadgita*, which he wrote about; and a concept in Marx tracked throughout his writings. The three parts of the first chapter are complementary and, while structurally hetero- geneous, offer distinct demonstrations of different reasons for, and ways of, reading philosophy today: for transnational literacy, in view of interdisciplinary analysis, and in search of travelling concepts.

The second chapter is made up of three dossiers around a classic text from Western literature, accompanied now by a rewriting, then by a second, more obscure text, and finally by an 'other' – a text that escapes the structure at issue, which is sometimes archival. Here, the question of philosophy remains present while that of history is fore- shadowed. As the book progresses, the chapters loosen this structure and become centred on larger cultural issues – in 'History,' for exam- ple, on two women's lives. They offer Spivak's rewritings of her own earlier, classical, and much-debated texts, here expanded to encompass new issues and to find their place in a truly global philosophy of culture.[12]

CPR's rewriting of Kant's titles, one of which, unsettlingly, comes with the word 'pure' (*rein*), is a bold move through which Spivak draws attention to the book's key element: critique. Her volume exam-

---

11 In this attempt, I am not mimicking Spivak's own posture in her book. An aspect of the difference is, of course, gender. Spivak engages intimately with men – who could only be men – of a different time than hers. Lord staged an intimacy between three women, each situated at a different moment. I engage with two other women, Spivak and Lord, situated in the same moment.

12 As I will mention in the last section of this chapter, the new issues have largely come out of teaching situations. For more on the positionality issue regarding Spivak's reframing of her earlier text, see Sanders (1999).

ines critically the structure of the production of postcolonial reason.[13] But the reason in question is not 'pure,' precisely because it is postcolonial, which is an 'impure' notion anyway. With its compound nature concocting a temporal disorder, and with the prefix 'post-' referring to the 'impurity' that is the colonial situation, which was also Kant's contemporary context, *CPR* rewrites Kant's *Critique* by foregrounding the extent to which it is not what it would like to be. But, lest one expect easy – and anachronistic – rejection, Spivak repeatedly cautions against the temptation to reject that in which we are caught. For, according to her, nothing is less productive than 'unacknowledged complicity.' It is to counter such complicity that she develops, through demonstration, critical intimacy as an alternative. Suggestively playing with the conceptual metaphor of travel, and engaging the problematic of intention, the book offers an 'itinerary of agency in complicity.'[14]

This recurring theme develops into a concept referring to a mindset Spivak relentlessly points to, both in the mystifying complexity of philosophical thought and the simplistic moralism of much of cultural studies, and in feminist, colonial, and postcolonial reason. Moreover, each critique of the Three Wise Men – and of others, such as Freud – comes with an acknowledgment of their value, indeed, of their subtlety, which in all cases is greater than that of their followers or attackers. Paradoxically, then, they do remain 'great,' but the cultural analyst engaging their ideas is responsible for the *critical* part of that engagement as well as for the *intimacy* of it.[15]

On behalf of the participants in the imaginary seminar I described in the introduction, I wish to draw attention to the function of Spivak's book for even the most traditional students of philosophy, history, literature, and culture, in order to counter the tendency to shrug it off as belonging to an 'other' field. I contend that *CPR* engages the core of aesthetics, and of all academic disciplines in which aesthetic objects are studied. I resist the attempt to confine her study to the ghettoized specialization of postcolonial studies and feminism, on which one can then feel at liberty to turn one's back ('it's not my thing'). I see this as similar

---

13 Although focusing on the *Critique of Judgement*, the title rewrites primarily the *Critique of Pure Reason*. The emphasis on (im)purity in what follows is my responsibility, not Spivak's. In a different argument, one might claim that Spivak's title rewrites the *Critique of Practical Reason*, whose emphasis on ethics her book shares.

14 Sanders formulates Spivak's position in these words (1999: 1).

15 This resonates with Lord's view of the way the intimacy of influence allows novelists to critique theorists.

to – to use a tendentious analogy – dismissing rape from general interest (as is often done) because it is a 'women's issue,' thus foreclosing the obvious fact that it is primarily a men's issue. Such dismissal is one of many instances where the us/them binary has pernicious consequences.

Much of the above pondering makes explicit what my earlier case studies have suggested. I propose, therefore, not to look at how one can be an activist and interested in aesthetics at the same time, but how one cannot help being an activist – at least, acknowledging the need to be one – if and when one is interested in aesthetics, academically or otherwise. In a similar vein, I will subsequently argue how Spivak deploys a deconstructive mode of reading to 'read the world' so that she can expose the falsity of the oft-alleged rift between deconstruction and referential reading. Finally, for those, encouraged by dismissive critics, who think Spivak is difficult to read, and for those who read Derrida's work on writing with an (anti-Derridean) literal mind, I will argue that Spivak's text is best read as spoken.[16]

To quote her on her own misreading of Hegel, which serves as the epigraph to this chapter: 'This openly declared interest makes my reading the kind of "mistake" without which no practice can enable itself' (39). The current chapter should not be mistaken for a review of her book. Instead it is, perhaps, an appropriation, which is inappropriate; but even so, I am glad of 'having' it. Or, perhaps for the interdisciplinary travellers addressed here, it is a path among many possible paths, and one that suits some of us. But who, then, is 'us'? At stake in this pronoun is the concept of *subject*.

Aesthetic Activism

'Us' is the subject, the one Kant is at pains to wrestle out of its negative, so that judgment can be a triumph of the will.[17] This is the provisional halting place where Spivak's wrestling with the angel of Western aesthetics appears to lead. After the nightly struggle that transformed Jacob's name into Israel, a name heavy with responsibility, the name 'us' of present academic-speak has turned into a foreign name. This

---

16 Such a literal mind would see Derrida as objecting to the study of oral cultures.
17 This resonance with the title of Leni Riefenstahl's film is intentional, although not meant to suggest a genealogy between Kant and her work. But, reading 'for the present,' in Spivak's spirit, nor is there any point in foreclosing the resonances between romantic and *Aufklährung* philosophy and the trauma of the mid-twentieth century.

new name is neither plural nor singular, neither 'first-person' nor 'third-person' ('them'), but the impossible name between the first and second person of unstable positions in need of each other.

As Spivak states early in her book, she writes in order to track the figure of the *native informant*. Is this latter term a subject or a personification? Importantly, for the use of concepts surrounding personhood, it is both, thus standing as a bridge over the divide between formalist and social approaches. This tracking of a figure – a figuration of an idea – is simultaneously one of many ways in which Spivak frays pathways through her text, and one of its many 'literarizations' or 'aestheticizings,' or, if you wish, fictionalizing devices.[18] In this sense the figure of the *native informant* embodies the concatenation of meanings that have accrued throughout this book to the idea of travelling concept. It is a figure best known from ethnography, where it has been a central trope for anthropology's complicity with colonialism as well as for that discipline's epistemological problems.[19]

But ethnography, an obvious counter-discourse for Spivak's project, is not her primary target of critique, for there the figure of the native informant is, precisely, only too easy to track. Rather, ethnography's helpmate is the antiphrastic vehicle of the concept-metaphor she designs. In the tight methodological program sketched by the four chapters of her book, this discipline 'of the other,' so to speak, is only one of the many fields held up to her methodology. It is not a crucial one either, because there, the native informant is exploited, mistrusted, altered perhaps, but not suppressed. Instead, Spivak's native informant is a figure, a figuration put forward to counter the unfortunate effects of contemporary flirtations with those universalized, idealized, and thereby offensively misused figures of the 'other' – the 'nomad' or the 'migrant.'

This figure of the native informant is so called for a good reason: native as opposed to migrant; informant as opposed to unknowing or 'innocent.' It is an indispensable supplement to the ethnographer. It is, Spivak argues, needed, if the great texts – of Western philosophy in the first place – are to be 'great'; and in those texts it is foreclosed. 'Foreclosure' is taken in the strict sense offered by psychoanalysis, in the words

---

18 But please keep in mind that, for literary folk, fictionalizing is not opposing but specifying and highlighting the real world.

19 See, for example, Fabian's attempt at critical intimacy with his 'native informants' (1990) and my reading of that text (1996: ch. 5).

of Laplanche and Pontalis (1985: 166–9) as they quote Freud: 'Here, the ego rejects [*verwirft*] the incompatible idea *together with the affect* and behaves as if the idea had never occurred to the ego at all' (*CPR* 4). The need for the figure and its foreclosure comes from the desired 'purity' of reason, the effort to keep philosophy clean of politics and other 'dirty' elements. But the reasoning Spivak opposes to this foreclosure demonstrates that such cleansing is impossible. After dirty art, then, we run into dirty philosophy – and we get splashed.

The shift between Kant's foreclosure and Spivak's re-figuration of the native informant happens when she wilfully 'mistakes,' as seriously consequential, Kant's casual and bracketed example of the *Neuhollander* and the *Feuerlander*, alleged by him apropos of man's free will, as the limit of humanity – 'raw man.'[20] In a founding 'mistake,' Spivak takes this example as if it belonged to the 'pure' text of reasoning, infusing both the example and Kant's text with literariness.[21] The philosophical question implied in this move concerns the status of the marginal; the literary-aesthetic question concerns the status of the detail.[22] Invoking psychoanalysis as a speculative theory whose use is an ethical responsibility as well as a technique that helps her read the *pre-emergent* (4), Spivak is then able to identify a symptom of foreclosure that is also a symptom of 'not-pure' reasoning in Kant.[23] The

20 New Hollanders, the aboriginal population of Australia, and Firelanders, the original inhabitants of the southern part of present-day Argentina.

21 In one of those substantial footnotes that make her book rhizomatic, Spivak speculates on the *poetic* reasons for Kant's choice of ex-centric, 'sub-human' examples. Here, the sound of the German names is relevant (27). The footnote forecasts her next chapter, 'Literature,' where she expands on a 'touristic' and silencing use of exotic names, while also enacting loyalty to the object under scrutiny (because responding to Kant's aesthetics aesthetically). The other programmatic 'detail' in this context is Spivak's search for the real existence of the two peoples, which is an act of what I will below call 'archival ardour.' The detail of Kant's example, and Spivak's creation of a native informant out of it, thus works as a *mise-en-abyme* of the book's project, content, and structure.

22 On marginality, see Derrida (1984); on detail, Schor (1987) is a founding study. On the detail as specifically aesthetic, see Arasse (1992), who unfortunately ignores Schor's relevant book.

23 The term 'pre-emergence' is taken from Raymond Williams (1980). I use the term 'symptom' on my own account, but not in the psychoanalytic sense. 'Symptom' in Peircean semiotics is a sign that is involuntarily produced as sign. In fact, in the anti-intentionalist perspective that is Spivak's – and which I fully share – symptoms are everything. But I use the term in the more limited sense of 'small details with unprogrammed significance.'

relation to Kant's aesthetics – the aesthetic that, in spite of the many attempts to criticize it, is still the dominant one in Western culture – is, therefore, central to Spivak's book on many different levels. It is a relation of critical engagement where complicity is acknowledged and endorsed, and a practice of critical intimacy performed so that an ethical relation, foreclosed by 'pure' reasoning, can become possible. Towards the end of her rough guide to interdisciplinarity, this ethical concern becomes crucial.

Spivak reads Kant's aesthetics but only unearths the native informant in a space beyond it, where Kant expands in order to tie up the aesthetics' loose ends. The foreclosed native informant comes (im)possibly in sight at the end of the first part of Kant's two-part book, when aesthetic judgment is left in need of a subject.[24] 'He' becomes visible in the second part, but only in the corner of your eye. The division of Kant's book into two parts – aesthetic and teleological judgment – is a cut that covers over a problem. The aesthetic part is fundamentally incomplete, for the subject is still lacking the subjectivity required for the jubilant outcome of the sublime experience, later explained as the free will to reason.

The second part supplements the first part in a truly Rousseauist-Derridean-Spivakian sense.[25] According to Spivak's reasoning, then, it makes the first fundamentally 'impure.' This part is only too well known, although the key term of the sublime is still often misunderstood, simplified, and distorted. *CPR* rehearses it, not in a simple gesture of repetition – although the inevitability of repetition is part of the book's argument – but to smuggle into the sameness that characterizes Western aesthetics a difference that proleptically undermines this aesthetics' predominance.[26] The analysis foretells the end of the present's vanishing in this sense as well.

Kant's aesthetics comprises two key terms, both of which have aroused a lot of commentary: 'disinterestedness' (for aesthetic experience to be possible, one must cut oneself off from one's earthly interests), and 'the sublime' (which has definitively, but ambivalently,

---

24 For the graphism '(im)possible,' see Spivak (1987: 263).
25 Derrida (1976), a text which is profoundly present in Spivak's writing.
26 This prolepsis announces the vanishing of the present in one of the senses of the book's subtitle. No unproblematic sublimity can be claimed henceforth. The currently fashionable flirtation with a postmodern sublime is mercifully absent from *CPR*.

shifted aesthetics from beautiful objects to the subject's experience).[27] Most contemporary commentaries focus on the sublime, and often try to save that concept for an aesthetics that is not based on disinterestedness, so that sublimity can function in the social world.[28] Even regardless of Kant's exclusive focus on nature, not art, in his discussion of the sublime, contemporary misreadings turn the experience into a feature of the object. They also tend to follow Schiller in his psychologizing of the narrative implied in Kant's description.[29] Spivak's discussion of Kant's text entails a powerful refocusing of the entire aesthetics by way of negotiating a transition between the two parts. And, just as the sublime, then, is of the order of the performative, so the inscription of the 'native informant' is performatively accomplished.

As always at the key junctures of her arguments, Spivak is very clear here.[30] She straddles the gap as follows: 'In the moment of the Sublime the subject accedes to the rational will' (10). Loyal to Kant and her project, in this sentence she dramatizes the foreclosed connection between aesthetics and the call for activism. That this accession should be a sublime experience already points to the self-enclosed narcissism that underlies the experience's gratifying character. Caspar David Friedrich's painting *Monk by the Sea*, with its lone figure casting a potentially mastering gaze over nature, remains the keenest illustration of this moment.[31]

But here is the point of the sublime as Spivak elaborates it: 'It has

27 For a good recent philosophical study of Kant's aesthetics, see Kern (2000). The German word *Interesse* is strongly bound with partiality and partisanship, rather than with what we consider 'interesting.' Thinking of Habermas' famous book helps keep this difference in mind (1972).

28 A recent feminist attempt can be found in Battersby (1998). In my own work on the subject of aesthetics, I am more interested in reinterpreting disinterestedness ('Aestheticizing Catastrophe,' in press). Spivak rightly focuses on the sublime though, because this is the climactic moment for Kant, as well as the hinge to the place where Spivak's figure of the native informant is foreclosed. Not coincidentally, I suppose, the utmost aesthetic experience has neither art nor other human subjects in the scene. In this sense, my book argues for an opposite aesthetic, of 'interest.'

29 Paul de Man (1996) criticizes Schiller for this in a discourse that Spivak critiques with subtlety (16). Here is another case where Spivak's literary reading skills gain philosophical relevance.

30 See, on this, below. It needs spelling out, though, that I insert my own commentary here and there, notably when I develop the incipient suggestions of a fundamental narcissism in this universalistic reasoning around what it is to be human.

31 For an excellent art-historical commentary on this work and others like it, see Koerner (1990).

often been noted that the rational will intervenes to cover over a moment of deprivation' (10). The structure of Kant's work – its divisions – is an icon of that deprivation and its repression.[32] The foreclosed figure will soon – in the next part, though – be called upon to remedy this lack, which causes 'un-pleasure.' Spivak writes: 'The feeling of the sublime is ... a feeling of pain arising from the want of accordance between the aesthetical estimation ... formed by the imagination and the same formed by reason' (10). Here is the rift within Kant's rationality. I see this 'want of accordance' as arousing a kind of perverted narcissism, perverted because it erases libidinal investment. Spivak argues that since this 'judgment of the inadequacy of our greatest faculty of sense' is reasonable and correct, 'a pleasure [is] excited' (10). The superiority of the rational over the sensible 'arouses in us the feeling of our supersensible determination [*Bestimmung*]' (Kant 1951: 96–7).[33]

It is in this process of frustration and the exhilaration at its being overcome that the subject of sublime experience is, in fact, ethically fleshed out. The (im)possible ethics is figurative. The freedom that, according to Kant, is needed for this jubilatory victory over the senses is, Spivak writes, a *trope* of freedom: a clandestine metalepsis (substitution of effect for cause). For it is programmed not by reason but by the pleasure the victory of reason over the senses provides. Kant himself even clandestinely attributes that pleasure to the object. Respect for the object (nature) is substituted for 'respect for the idea of humanity in our *subject*' (Kant 1951: 96, emphasis *CPR* 11). Hence Kant himself scripts his readers' frequently committed error of replacing performativity with constativity. The issue – the deprivation covered over – is the question of human access to rational will. It is in this context that Kant, in fact, wittingly commits the displacement of sublimity from the experience to the object: 'Everything that excites this feeling [of superiority to nature within and outside of us] in us ... is called then (although *improperly*) sublime' (Kant 1951: 104; emphasis *CPR* 12).

32 I use the term 'icon' here strictly in the Peircean sense (most accessible in Peirce 1984).
33 Throughout the book, Spivak devotes a great deal of fine-tuning to the German term *Bestimmung*, enriching it with resonances from Freud and others, including the musical sense of 'tuning.' This is one of the ways in which she is able to keep philosophical and aesthetic/literary concerns and sensibilities connected, if not identical. It is also one of the ways in which she practises the kind of (travelling) concept-building I have been advocating here.

The slippage is significant, indeed, symptomatic, but it is also more than that. Since it is explicit and acknowledged ('although improperly'), it is a fully endorsed abandonment of the possibility of 'pure' reasoning. No alternative formulation intervenes here to correct the error; no 'proper' language is possible. The 'impure' supplement is not lost on Spivak. For this slippage is the moment of Kant's discourse when aesthetics bleeds into the ethical need for exiting the self-enclosure of the subject, leading to what can be called 'aesthetic activism.' The slippage is the *necessary* metalepsis that digs a gap, which in turn will be repaired by the creation and foreclosure of the native informant.

This is where Spivak deploys the concept – the native informant as a figure of methodology – to articulate her critically intimate encounter with Kant. Not only is Kant implying the lack that he needs in order to cover over in the second part – the critique of teleological judgment. His bracketed but real slippage also implies the 'culturedness' of this nature. But by using the term 'human nature' for the agent of 'culturing,' he irreparably muddles the issue of the distinction on which the entire argument rests. For if culture is the product of human nature, nature is cultural, and so is 'human nature' – defined culturally. 'It is not possible to *become* cultured in this culture, if you are *naturally* alien to it' (*CPR* 12, re: Kant 1951: 105).[34]

That the very notion of human *nature* confuses the distinction between *nature* and *culture* is all the more significant because the further attempt to define human nature brings in – and casts out – the figure of the native informant. Standing for a fleeting moment at the boundary of culture and nature, and falling between the cracks of that division, the *Neuhollander* and the *Feuerlander* look on, as *man* defines himself narcissistically. Thus, I venture to add, by an accident of unwitting implication, an accident that has some poetic justice to it, Kant casts *moral* being out of this human being.[35]

Attributing the limit of humanity to the foreigners presented as fictions is a grave act of bringing into reason what Spivak calls the

34 See Figlio (1996) for a psychoanalytically inflected account of the bond between nature and culture.
35 'The moral being is moral only insofar as he cannot cognize himself' (*CPR* 22). Knowing himself was what condemned Narcissus. See Spivak's brilliant 'Echo.' On the implication of the prediction that Narcissus would live long on the condition that he did not know himself, see Bal (1999a: ch. 8). Incidentally, given that the issue for Narcissus was self-love, 'knowing' in this story is closer to the biblical carnal knowledge than Kant's alleged victory over the senses claims.

axiomatics of imperialism. These unargued and unarguable assumptions that structure imperialist thought – and include us/them-speak – are largely present, and active, in disciplinary defensiveness and, indeed, in the 'imperialism' of the current academic scene. Spivak is careful to distinguish Kant's philosophizing of difference from the thought that emerged more directly from European territorial imperialism. But, technically, through the technique of reasoning, this axiomatics is why Kant's two-part *Critique of Judgement* can be considered rationality's continued alibi.[36] Philosophically, that is, the very project of reasoning that Kant's texts exemplify and found is inherently, not coincidentally, bound with imperialism on Kant's own terms: as logic. And so is, potentially, by extension, every aesthetic that – today still – takes Kant's as its unexamined starting point, even if polemically.[37]

Aesthetically, moreover, in Kant's figuration, the three creative acts of detailing, dividing, and staging hang tightly together, to furnish the reasoning with a literary seduction that make it totally irresistible. His aesthetic practice performs what it refuses to state and what it attempts to escape: confusion. He weaves together tightly and inextricably the two foreclosed peoples with their poetically resonating names, the narrative form of the casual limit-example, the division into two parts of the book, and the description of the sublime experience 'improperly' bleeding into the object.

This reasoning – this *critique* in Kant's own sense – is more than the mere retrieval of a figure who should be visible but isn't, indeed, whose trace in the affective life of the foreclosing text is made invisible but can be reconstructed through a critique that remains within its object – an *intimate* critique. In the first place, it is also an act that, by all accounts of the aesthetics or 'literariness' of literature, is itself artistic. Just as Coetzee's *Foe* retrieves foreclosed figures from Defoe's *Crusoe* by side-stepping to one of the author's other texts, making the figure speakable, even if voiceless, so this reasoning is a figurative but also figural intervention of an aesthetic order.

Secondly, therefore, this reasoning foreshadows the methodological program of *CPR* as a whole. It does this in multiple ways, one of which

36 An alibi is a *usage*, which is not the same as a *source*. This is an important distinction in Spivak's anti-moralistic stance.
37 Potentially means neither really nor not-really; taking a Kantian position without endorsing the implicated axiomatics of imperialism, then, requires distancing oneself *reasonably* from the implication of this moment.

is the kind of reading-for-the-detail that is incompatible with earnest philosophy yet indispensable for a full philosophical critique of Kant's *Critique*.[38] This detailing, to the extent that it is also a stylistic feature of the reasoning, is in itself another aesthetic act. Moreover, and as an enactment of the tight connections between her four chapters, reading the literary figure into Kant's text is shown to be possible by way of 'the archive' – here, figuratively, as the site of 'real' history. Spivak went there to look, for the 'literal' existence of the figure that Kant used to foreclose Spivak's figure.

If *CPR* begins with Kant's aesthetics, it is for more reasons than just the overt one of critiquing a founding text of imperialism alone. The way Spivak acts aesthetically in her reasoning returns in the later chapters as a demonstration of critical intimacy, as a practice of it, on the level of composition or intellectual style. To give just one example: the figuration of the foreclosed native informant in the second chapter, 'Literature,' is performed in a neatly constructed dialogue between the three or four texts of each 'dossier.' The author argues the rationale of the sequence of the first two chapters through the figure of antiphrasis ('I am working here with a rather old-fashioned binary opposition between philosophy and literature; that the first concatenates arguments and the second figures the impossible. For both the native informant seems to be unavoidable' [112]). In other words, she rejects ('old-fashioned') and immediately replaces ('For both') the rationale she advances.

Spivak *figures* that double rationale by avoiding literary language altogether, by condensing modes in which the figure of her search shows up, and by re-aestheticizing philosophical moments in the texts. This is a literary intellectual style that fits the kind of interdisciplinary practice exercized in this part of her text. The less-than-full subjectivity of Jean Rhys' character of the black servant Christophine in *Wide Sargasso Sea*, 'technically' – in the criticism – a case of aesthetic failure, thus becomes the figuration of philosophical overhaul:

> Rhys' text will not attempt to contain her in a novel that rewrites a canonical English book within the European novelistic tradition in the interest

---

38 It is primarily Derrida's contribution to the expansion of philosophy that has launched the literary habit of 'detailing' within philosophy, which in turn has laid the groundwork on which a move such as Spivak's can now be philosophically pertinent.

of the white Creole rather than the native. No perspective *critical* of imperialism can turn the other into a self, because the project of imperialism
has always already historically refracted what might have been an incom-
mensurable and discontinuous other into a domesticated other that con-
solidates the imperialist self. (130)

Hence, one might add, the problem of 'we.' Activist reading thus
deploys aesthetics to fight aesthetics: it defends aesthetics against
itself, and by staying critically loyal to or intimate with the Kantian tradition, it gives the lie to easy dismissals in the name of a nominally
anti-elitist anti-aestheticism that is, in fact, deeply elitist.

The intellectual opponent here is the rift between aesthetic and political literary work, also named by the tired and self-indulgently hyperbolic phrase 'culture wars.' This rift is to my mind most ironically
undercut when Spivak follows the straight, upright literary scholar,
chasing him or her straight into the archive. The case is clear-cut literary, in the aesthetic sense, and it accommodates – then, of course,
embarrasses – all those who want to get back to the business of
honouring the great masters. Spivak picks an uncontested masterpiece,
Baudelaire's poem 'Le cygne,' where the figure of the native informant
shows up in the form of the inexplicably evoked, exoticized, silenced,
and abjected 'négresse' (*CPR* 148–57).

Filling a few verses, this figure can be neither ignored nor integrated
into the nomenclature of the poem, which opens with the classical and
classicist words 'Andromaque, je pense à vous!' Spivak tracks critical
responses to the 'négresse,' and shows how this figure has served as a
tease to literary scholarship committed to the 'purity' of the discipline.
The poem-cum-responses 'offer us a mirror of our performance of certain imperialist ideological structures even as we deconstruct the
tropological error of masculinism celebrating the female' (148). This
works quite nicely in the face of attempts by some of humanities' finest
to explain the wilfully unexplainable.

Currently, literary critics are so used to the routine confusion of the
neo-New-Critical attending to the text-alone, today called 'rhetoric,'
with the remnants of a biographism reminiscent of Taine's *race, milieu,
moment*, today called 'the call for history,'[39] that the contradiction keeps

---

39 This is beautifully critiqued by Culler in *Framing the Sign* (1988). Incidentally, this
book is also largely devoted to undermining the rift between aesthetics and politics
through demonstrating the inevitable – systemic – collusion between both.

passing unnoticed. Thus they fall from Baudelaire's phonetic and met-aphoric charms straight into the arms of his African-European mistress Jeanne Duval, whose attraction for critics needs some explaining. In the face of this 'detail' of the negress, literariness fades away.

This is one of many moments where Spivak deploys her orally inclined writing in a teacherly mode of backtracking and forecasting – and knowingly not-knowing. With reference to Derrida's reading of Freud's 'text of life' in *The Postcard*, she explains that 'unlike psycho-biographical criticism, deconstructive reading does not privilege the text of life as an obligatory object of investigation. It is part of the text being read, written otherwise and elsewhere' (154). An appeal to Jeanne Duval, then, is strictly meaningless, tautological; and, worse, it obliterates the obliteration in place in the poem – through anonymity – of the negress.

Spivak exposes three ways of misreading-away both the figure and the problem she poses. One is to appeal to a projected intention, by ascribing to Baudelaire the compassion felt for the abjected figure. A second is to bring in Duval, thus casting out the figure of the negress as the literary figure tenaciously beckoning our interpretive attention. A third, properly psycho- (auto-?) biographical way consists of seeing in this figure the poet's 'dark double.'[40] As we move from intentionalism to anecdotalism to psycho-diagnosing, the problematic use of race increases.

But does it help, even the racism-indifferent aesthete? Not at all: by practising critical intimacy Spivak inexorably leads even the most stubborn 'not-my-thing' litcrit to the conclusion that she is the better aestheticist. The three suppressions of the scandal of the 'négresse' pose problems of epistemology. How can we know authorial inten-tion? And, even within the individualistic humanism that informs such approaches, such problems of discretion, what business is it of ours to probe Baudelaire's socializing habits, or indeed, his dirty mind? But, as these moves help to not-see the figure of the negress, they also most surely fail to read it. All three swirl away from the text-as-such. Spivak prods us back to the poem, and to underpin its reading more meaningfully, she leads us to the question of 'the archive' – its uses and abuses.[41]

---

40 Ahearn (1977).
41 The discussion of this case offers, of course, support to the argument in ch. 7 of the present book.

Many times in the course of *CPR*, Spivak chastises intellectual lazi-ness. One sentence among many gives a sense of her impassioned defence of serious culture study against partisan cultural studies. Her second chapter ends thus: 'The conventional highway of a politically correct single issue is merely the shortest distance between two sign-posted exits' (197).[42] My guess is that both uncritical endorsements and equally unexamined dismissals of the Kantian aesthetic tradition fall under this criticism. But Spivak is loudest in this indictment when plain and simple historical research is on the line.

The decisive step, here, is to bridge the gap dug by recent academic history between traditional standards of scholarship and innova-tive, politically motivated critiques. Coming from Spivak, who has been a leading figure in the latter field, this criticism must not be – defensively – dismissed as attacking her own constituency. Instead, by holding her own line of work up to the common standards, she is breaking away from a condescending and, in the long run, self-destructive indulgence. The ardour to dwell in the archives – the domain some of us tend to fantasize as inimical to commitment to the 'real world' and the present – is, I think, one of the most constructive, almost utopian moves that Spivak-the-Teacher, the theme of my third misreading, performs.

Archival Ardour

> But if, as critics, we wish to reopen the epistemic fracture of imperialism without succumbing to the nostalgia for lost origins, we must turn to the archives of imperialist governance.
>
> *CPR* (146)

Before contemplating teaching, then, I propose to follow Spivak briefly into the dust-gathering archives, where opponents of much innovative work tend to hide out, at the same time as they are busy dismissing such work for lack of 'rigour' or 'historical foundation,' or 'facts,' or

42 Single-issue reasoning is one of Spivak's opponents. The refusal to research is another: 'Traveling around the United States, advising aspiring culture studies pro-grams, I encounter a great deal of resistance to research among faculty, which silences me when, from the other side, I hear the criticism that culture studies undermines the rigor of literary scholarship' (196). The serious, extensive, and always specifically argued references in Spivak's own book demonstrate that she is not involved in moralizing finger-pointing here.

just 'scholarship.' The bad news is that they often seem to have a point. Spivak will not have it, nor will I; no innovative thinking discharges anyone from the work still needed to build a solid case. What does it mean for a deconstructionist to demonstrate an impassioned eagerness to descend into such august but intimidating, exasperatingly unyielding, and decisively foreign, places?

What we are facing, here, is that other dogmatic element of the ethnography that Spivak more or less leaves alone in this book: *fieldwork*. It is well known that she does a lot of work that qualifies as fieldwork, although of an activist, not ethnographic, kind. I would also consider the kind of teaching of which Spivak's book reports affiliated with fieldwork. And, if her book is any indication, she also does a lot of archival research, which is the historian's fieldwork. With gusto she digs up strange documents, such as minutes of company meetings, century-old political pamphlets, or director's directives. Among the many particularities of *CPR*, extensive documentation is one of its most remarkable.[43] I venture to say that my reading of *CPR*, in addition to being a mis-reading, is also a piece or report of interdisciplinary fieldwork, in the specific sense relevant to how I am probing the point of travelling with concepts *in specific fields*.

The turn to the archive is intriguing. Facing the tedium of traditional archival-only publications, this chapter may well be the most exciting of the four.[44] In the chapter 'History,' the archive is central. But, in 'Literature,' its need already shimmers through. Just as the first chapter demonstrates loyalty to the philosophical project through deviation from it, so the chapter on literature ends up in need of an interpretation that wishes to be truly literary, by abandoning the text-only approach in order to serve the text better.

The archival turn is equally paradoxical, and decisively relevant for Spivak's project (as much as for mine), which, it must not be forgotten, is to offer a critique of postcolonial reason in the mode of critical intimacy, also called affirmative deconstruction. In one bracketed half-

---

43 For a future edition, a bibliography at the end heads my wish list. A more complete index is second. Both belong to the tools – of entrance into, and teaching out of, the book.

44 I have had quite a bit of exposure to such works myself, first as a make-believe biblical scholar, then as a not-quite-not art historian. I found the difference between archival work for its own sake and the use of documentation to make a (non-archival) point almost shockingly radical. Spivak's mode of 'reading the world' offers a demonstration of what archival-but-not-only work can yield.

sentence, Spivak defines the spirit of deconstruction as 'unaccusing, unexcusing, attentive, situationally productive through dismantling' (81). Needless to say, through the element 'attentive,' this is again a philosophical-aesthetical way of reading. The element 'situationally' requires a descent into the archive. The critical intimacy itself, specifying the kind of intercourse with the texts found in the archive, is further sustained by a reflection on Freud's *Interpretation of Dreams*.

This reflection is methodological, not analogical; these documents are not (like) dreams. The thrust of Spivak's reading of archival texts is similar to what informs her reading of Kant: to discern the limits of disinterested, 'pure' reasoning, or, as the case may be, reporting. Spivak writes: 'the willed (auto-)biography of the West still masquerades as disinterested history, even when the critic presumes to touch its unconscious' (208). Here, I see another instance of the travel of the concept of (an aspect of) subject, both geographically and between disciplines. For, obviously, the discourse of the unconscious in criticism, thus flawed for its narcissistic self-enclosure, does not sit easily with the project of reading imperialism's archives. What Spivak seeks is not a diagnosis, but traces of an 'aesthetic' that helps imperialist discourse pass off its decisions as 'natural.' This is aesthetic seduction, not unconscious automatism, even if the question of the unconscious of the writers of the documents must remain unresolved. Spivak argues tightly what Freud's (anti-) hermeneutic can do for her project.[45] The point of *The Interpretation of Dreams* is not meaning or its unconscious motivation but the concept of overdetermination.

After first pointing out that the term 'overdetermination' makes both causality and expressionism – two dogmatically defended tenets of many historical approaches to art, literature, and history – completely untenable, let me then lay out Spivak's concept-building work with Freud's concept here. Having recalled the resonance of tuning, she then disassociates overdetermination from its less known and more adequate neighbour: she is less interested in over-determination (*mehrfach determiniert*) than in 'determined otherwise' (*anders determiniert*). What imperialist discourse has in common with 'dream' is merely this: 'The *quality* of the images in the dream-text is determined *otherwise* "by two independent moments [*Momente*]"' (*CPR* 218; SE 4: 330).

45 As I mentioned in ch. 2, Jean Laplanche's argument to the effect that psychoanalysis is fundamentally an anti-hermeneutic, also based on the 1900 book, is central to this argument (1993; 1996).

'Attentive and situationally productive' (81), then, Spivak takes the plural word *Momente* very seriously.

Two moments, then. One is wish fulfilment, 'where the psychical agency seems close to the deliberative consciousness that we colloquially identify as our "self."' The distinction of two moments not only allows her to locate the imperialist self-centredness of the discourse in the archive, but also to sever it from, then re-connect it to, the other, more enigmatic moment. 'With respect to the second moment, Freud uses the word that covers for him when he wants to finesse the question of agency: "work"' (218–19). What kind of work is this that connects some form of self to this *other* determination, or tuning?

Spivak quotes Freud's formulation: 'the greatest intensity is shown by those elements in a dream on whose imaging [*Bildung*] the fullest amount of condensation-work has been made use of' (SE 4: 330). Imaging, making images, is thus the work of agency. It is the work of making things visible. This would be how archival material constitutes the *evidence* of nothing more or less historically real than the work of (the axiomatics of) imperialism, to bind the European self to the other it figures, so that the self can be. That figures.

What Spivak wrests from the archival bits and pieces, then, is not only the fulfilment of her own desire or archival ardour, propelled by her wish to make cultural studies more effective and less limited, more respectful of the object and less negligent; more like what I call cultural analysis. Rather, she invests the bits, through Freud's 'transvaluation of all psychic value,' with a concept-metaphor – of otherwise-determination – that opens them up to readings that do not flounder in the mud of either moralism, relativism, or free-floating pluralism.[46] These readings lead the reader far afield.

For example, from Bertha Mason in *Jane Eyre*, through Rhys' *Wide Sargasso Sea*, to the terrifically difficult question of *Sāti* and the non-*Sāti* suicide of a young woman we know from one of Spivak's most classical pieces, here reworked again. Bhubaneswari Bhaduri, the not-quite and not-quite-not subaltern heroine, is thus awoken from her slumber in 'Can the Subaltern Speak?,' an over-read and hence no-longer-read piece that remains crucial to Spivak's project. The formal analogy with Freud's method – not between dream and imperial text – is, in the end,

---

46 From the latter, the endeavour is rescued by the refusal to see overdetermination as just many determinations. She specifically points to the basis of the pluralism of the New Social Movements, with reference to Laclau and Mouffe (1985: 198).

effective, again thanks to its aesthetic deployment. Spivak articulates the possibility of a 'determination whose ground is itself a figuration: a "determination otherwise."' 'Otherwise' is, here, in the truest possible sense of the word, a displacement, hence, a figure, of rhetoric, of aesthetic, making the two more real than any 'dusty,' reconstructive, archival work could do.

Many readings in this archival-ardour mode could be presented here as evidence of the referential will of deconstructionist reading. They are sometimes aesthetically narrated, sometimes explicitly methodological. They move from archive to anthropology, from literature to philosophy; they move against time, and deploy what Spivak calls *fadeout*, as a way of moving backwards. The reader will see for herself what she wishes to know and remember of this journey to the source of the Nile of the vanishing present. But Spivak is no tourist guide. She does not encourage her readers to just pick and choose, to take snapshots of exotic stories. The project is too intricate and too coherent for that. Her critique of the critique of the subject – which she faults for its indifference to ideology, for example – cannot 'simply' be taken home, for fear that we will fall back into a subject-centredness that remains disingenuous about its geopolitical determinations (but mind the multiple resonances of the latter term; 253). Whatever the field of Spivak's own research, whatever the theoretical argument, the reasoning mercilessly leads back to the test of relevance for the project of transnational literacy.

Speaking of Marx, who – like today's cultural student racking her brains to understand how Foucault and Deleuze can *both* miss the point of the intricacies of interest and desire – 'hears' what happens around him without quite 'seeing' it, Spivak writes:

> Marx's formulations show a cautious respect for the nascent critique of individual and collective subjective agency. The projects of class consciousness and of the transformation of consciousness are discontinuous issues for him. (261)

This remark, again, is not, as some critics seem to think, a facile, ahistorical trashing. On the contrary, it is a careful reconsideration of the way the past is in the present. For the present is where archival ardour leads the author, and ought to lead us all. She continues: 'Today's analogue would be "transnational literacy" as opposed to the mobilizing potential of unexamined culturalism.' The time, then: today. The place:

the classroom. The subject: an (im)possible 'we,' qualified as addressees and listeners who are required to take turns.

Portrait of a Teacher

... and the secret keeps us, not the other way around.[47]

For the classroom is Spivak's site of passion. Much of her writing is
expressly devoted to teaching issues.[48] Although many scholars have
written about the ethical question in literature and the teaching of literature, including in a 'postcolonial' perspective, I know of no colleague
who is so consistent in this endeavour and who also remains so firmly
distanced from moralizing.[49] The secret of Spivak's readability – a
secret she does not keep from us but that keeps us – resides in this
aspect of her writing.

   Allow me to end with the beginning, then, by positioning my reading in terms of the seminar room. For the travelling concepts of subject,
native informant, and personification come together in the figure of the
teacher who advocates agency over intention and whose trade is critical intimacy. For this final chapter, I decided to write about a book that
I found useful for myself, simply saying why this was so, in order to
make, not the gist of it, but its hospitality available to others; a good
halting place on a hectic trip. It may be because of the teacher in me;
but then, it may not be a coincidence that it was the teacherly quality of
Spivak's book that struck me so forcefully. The impulse to put forward
the teacherliness of this book came from the staggering discrepancy
between Terry Eagleton's account of his reading experience – presented as a review – and my own. The difference is one of modes of
reading, in the face of the book's peculiar readability.[50]

   Reading is a practice of intimacy, not of love or passion, nor of
hatred or irritation. For only reviewers actually read – or pretend to
read – a book that rubs them the wrong way. It is an activity in which

---

47 Spivak (*CPR* 245n73), regarding Rigoberta Menchú.
48 Her students go public with their enthusiasm. The letters to the editor following
   Eagleton's review testify to Spivak's effectivity as teacher. Another example is Mark
   Sanders' on-line review of *CPR* (1999).
49 Just a few examples to which *CPR* can be compared: Attridge (1999), Hamacher
   (1989), Buell (1999), Miller (1987).
50 Eagleton's review should be read against my analysis of trashing (1992).

friendship is the motor of response.[51] Those reading otherwise would lay such a book aside. Readability is an irritating but indispensable concept. In interdisciplinary cultural analysis in particular, one is frequently confronted with the question of readability, and with the doubt as to how to impute unreadability. Is it one's own lack of fluency with another field, or is the writer at fault? It is not easy to acknowledge publicly that one finds a particular reading difficult, so it is easier to attribute, Kant-wise, the difficulty to the object. But, for a teacher, something important can be gained if one challenges a convention born out of intimidation.

I, too, found *CPR* difficult to read. Readability *is* at stake, but I propose to pause before the sarcastic dismissal Eagleton feels justified to perform. Readability is best understood when the word refers not to degree but to mode. No two friendships are identical. But all are forms of critical intimacy. Let me be clear here. What is *unreadable* should not be read. In contrast, what is *difficult* may be worth exploring, in order to understand *what* readability is involved in reading it. Degree and mode are not unrelated, but they are discontinuous.

Reading Mallarmé, as Barbara Johnson and Derrida demonstrated for me, is not the impossible and therefore ultimately ungratifying task it seemed to be when I first tried it. Johnson offered me a mode of reading him.[52] Don't try to follow his logic, follow his words, one after the other, chewing on each of them – was the implicit injunction in her own, demonstrative reading. The words multiply, spread out, disseminate, and coalesce again – other-wise. Instead of remaining dispersed, they end up forming a rhizome. Baudelaire, also a great poet, is easier to read, and becomes enjoyable right away. Not that you read everything right out of the poems, not that you don't want to reread them again and again. But, in terms of degree, Baudelaire's readability is greater than Mallarmé's. It is also different in terms of mode: in Baudelaire, the poetic and semantic aspects merge more easily.[53] But it is also similar in that critical intimacy empowers readers to be critical, say, of elements that appear to convey misogyny or racism – the 'négresse' Spivak discusses, the rigidification of female figures in Mallarmé's

---

51 See my earlier remarks on friendship rather than passion, in ch. 1. Emmanuel Loiret is currently writing a book on texts – literary and ethnographical – in which such an epistemology underlies the practice (in prep.).
52 Johnson (1987).
53 See, for example, Culler's reading of prostitution in Baudelaire (1996).

'Hérodiade' – without rejecting the text because of it. One trusts a friend. When you have a good friend, it is in your interest not to lose her or him; you 'discuss' what appears painful or problematic. You are eager to hear an explanation that makes the problematic element more acceptable. Or not; you can forgive a slip. Why would you do that? Because – and this is the important pedagogical moment – once the problem is explained as fully as possible, you can recognize in yourself similar sentiments, or slips. This is the moment when critical intimacy *teaches.* You learn. For learning is always, also, learning something about yourself and the *hic-et-nunc* in which you live.

But I was talking about textual difficulty. What holds for the cultural critique around misogyny and racism also holds for moments of problematic readability. Mallarmé remains the more difficult of the two poets. Does anyone reject the quality of Mallarmé because of it? You may give up trying, alleging that this kind of tough poetry is not your cup of tea. Or you may read Johnson first, then read the texts she interprets, then more Mallarmé. There is no intrinsic merit in either decision. But neither Mallarmé nor Baudelaire is at stake here. The central issue is your interest, your tolerance for difficulty, the sense of what you get out of persevering, your desire before – and pleasure after – stretching your limits and 'going for it.'[54]

In contrast, difficult reading is too often held against writers when they write 'theory.' Not always, though. Some difficult writers have held firm, and the difficulty has collectively been overcome. Lacan, for example, has avoided providing easy reading, wary of the kind of vulgarization that fatally simplified Freud's ideas in the vulgate. In my moments of feeling intimidated, I have tended to suspect that he couldn't write differently, that he simply was not a very good writer. That may be true. I could neither judge nor change that. But it is also

54 Sometimes difficulty is even a measure of quality, sometimes it isn't. Annette Apon's film *The Waves* was unyielding at first viewing; but then, Woolf's novel isn't exactly soap-opera material. Seeing the film a second, third, time makes it riveting. The voices become haunting, the movements poetic, the lack of action gripping as it makes your heart beat from the intensity of time passing so slowly. Marleen Gorris' *Mrs. Dalloway*, starring Vanessa Redgrave, was a blockbuster. Pretty pictures, great acting, and so realistic that Woolf wouldn't recognize it. Adequate to the plot, hence easy, and therefore, successful, but incompatible with the writing. A good but utterly forgettable film. The former film is up to Woolf, the latter is not, and it should not be measured by the standards of Woolf's modernist masterpiece. When judging art and literature, 'difficulty' is not a standard. Not being up to it may translate into not being interested, but as you know, taste is personal, and no one cares either way.

true that his ideas are complex and difficult. They take some training; but once you are ready to understand them, you can. Take another case: Derrida. Sometimes I get bored by yet another word play and wish he would get down to business instead of indulging in his astonishment at words. But his writing is also a demonstration of its content, and since the point is that meaning is never simple, expecting simple writing to convey that idea would be utterly false.

The French language and culture are more tolerant of difficult reading than the English, or the Dutch for that matter. There is an intrinsic connection between that tolerance and the tolerance for 'theory,' or abstraction. The 'resistance to theory' (de Man's phrase) often obscures either a fierce anti-intellectualism or a repression of uneasy psychic material.[55] Or it may cover over a foreclosure of uneasy political dilemmas. Eagleton's review of Spivak's *CPR* reiterates an Anglo-Saxon tradition of resistance to difficulty, compounded by single-issue chagrin and an outward projection of one's limitations. It also reads like a resistance to theory on all three grounds mentioned. The sheer length of the review, its wordiness, and the scarcity of arguments other than that of the text's difficulty, 'demonstrated' through out-of-context quotes, indicate that something else is the matter. Lest I fall into the trap demonstrated by Eagleton's text, though, I will resist the temptation to read a colleague symptomatically. Instead, I will reframe the question Eagleton's review poses and then begs: the question of Spivak's readability.

The question is not: can you read Spivak? As long as reading is the issue, the question is, is it worth (your, my) while *learning* to read Spivak? In the author's own terms, the question concerns learning to read ethically and pedagogically, in the sense of learning not to master. The answer I offer, here, too, is an unqualified 'yes.' And hence the subsidiary question: how? What is the nature of Spivak's readability? Compare Spivak to Lacan and Derrida. I used to come across many people who had stopped trying to read these men, and who reverted to explanatory secondary texts. For some, it is enough to decide they don't want to get involved. But you can also decide to follow the excitement that attracted you in the first place. Once upon a time, I tried that, for I, too, found them difficult to read. I read some of both, didn't understand enough to 'get it,' but did understand enough to want to. So I read Silverman on Lacan, and Culler on Derrida. And I

55 See, on this issue, Chase (1987).

knew I was in for hard work; so many ideas, so different, but so important. Hence, I picked up 'The Mirror Stage'; only six pages long. I read it, and read it again. Then I tried my hand at 'The Instance of the Letter.' The day I gave up trying to 'get it,' but instead let myself be carried away by the flow of ideas, I somehow got something out of it. Something more than the text's argument; something about reading itself. And that was empowering.

Lacan – for me and at the time – read like poetry; something between Mallarmé and Baudelaire. I had to read him again, but then, with poetry you do that all the time.[56] Derrida was different. Reading Culler enabled me, helped and prepared – history's irony – by Spivak's clear introduction, to put more flags in *Of Grammatology*. I tried 'Writing and Difference.' Then I was able to read it, and reread it. It didn't become poetry for me, not Derrida. But, after Lacan, it did seem a little more manageable. It became like a 'difficult' but readable novel whose plot spreads out, say, like a Calvino novel; just as rewarding. Something that can only be read slowly. Managing these few texts definitively enriched my life, and my work. I did not become a Lacanian or a Derridean, but I did stop being uninformed, and therefore anti-; a position too close to anti-intellectualism for comfort, which I have always found unbearably self-demeaning. And Spivak? Read her as if you *hear* her *teach*, and all difficulty fades away.

Teaching has a long tradition as a model for philosophizing. Plato is the generic example in the Western tradition.[57] Teaching, there, is presented through personification, as a love relationship. But I am not convinced, for love entails dependency. Friendship is a better model. Since philosophical activity consists primarily of creating concepts, trying them out, modifying them, arguing on and through them, the teaching mode conceived in terms of friendship seems a more suitable model for that activity.[58] But it is not an easy one to follow.

Teaching is communicative, dialogic; it operates on an authority constantly questioned in its *work* – as in 'the setting to work of deconstruc-

---

56 This is, of course, an idiosyncratic choice of reading mode. The point is not that this particular mode of reading is the recommended one, but that choosing a mode is a way of engaging, instead of rejecting, difficult reading. In fact, Malcolm Bowie (1987: 105) proposes reading Lacan the way I propose reading Spivak: 'Lacan's prose aspires perpetually to the condition of speech.'

57 It is actually worth comparing Spivak's mode of writing to Plato's staging of Socrates (1937).

58 This bring us, together with Deleuze and Guattari (1994), back to the end of ch. 1.

tion'[59] – but also accepted and enjoyed on principle, in critical intimacy. That intimacy, which assumes that the parties remain critical but trusting, could be a helpful model, not only for reading teaching but also for teaching reading. The interaction between students and teacher around the latter's authority could, in fact, offer an alternative model for the academic review. So, what's the point of reading Spivak as a teacher?

Technically, teaching is oral; the teacher talks. Although she does most of the talking, the students know they can always talk back. Even if, riveted by the teacher's expositions, they prefer not to speak, the teacher watches out for the raised brows and silent sighs through which they direct her, like an orchestra conducting the conductor. Digressions constantly intervene whenever students require the teacher to side-track, to clarify or complicate a point, to add information or argue a position. But the good teacher still manages to complete the day's program: the structure of the class may be fleshed out beyond recognition during the session, but it falls into place at the end. The topic, which a written text could only 'treat' systematically, is here endlessly enriched by the small fallout of the oral situation. But there is more. The teacher makes her students so excited that they all want to emulate her brilliance and become inspiring teachers in turn. The teacher is not afraid of self-criticism. On the contrary, she shows her students that without self-criticism dialogue is foreclosed, and hence, knowledge cannot expand. Whatever her field of expertise, the good teacher is also always a teacher of ethics – for the young generation will one day manage the world, and they must do a good job of it.

There is a mistaken assumption about orality: that it is built up out of short sentences. Long sentences appear writerly, a symptom of difficulty, even unreadability. When your lecture is written out, it sounds written, but *not* because of sentence length. On the contrary, teaching, as I know from experience, produces long, often convoluted sentences. For, unlike writing, teaching is constantly engaged in reading faces and adjusting to what they tell you. Whenever a class has been particularly successful, I have caught myself regretting that I didn't tape it. I did once. The sentences were much longer, complex, holding a full argument, including its history, in a 'bracketed' clause. Yet the students found them clear. Their notes were much clearer than my taped sen-

---

59 This is the title of Spivak's short appendix, in which she offers a survey of Derrida's changing ideas. Writing that appendix is a significantly teacherly act in itself.

tences. There is a particular oral quality to Spivak's text that I read as
this teaching quality.

Picture this: 'In this class, we will go over Philosophy, Literature,
History, Culture. It sounds like a lot, but instead of going over them,
we'll go through them, traversing them, on the basis of cases.' And,
suddenly, it sounds feasible. Spivak presents herself as a teacher, as
evidenced by three of her sentences that I will briefly invoke here. As a
good teacher, she is explicit about what will happen in the class.

The preface of her book states the nature of the contract between the
teacher and her students; it states, in other words, her starting point,
which clarifies what she expects of her readers. After recounting an
anecdote demonstrating the global arrogance and lack of logic displayed by the WWB (Women's World Banking), she comments:

> It is my belief that a training *in a literary habit of reading the world* can
> attempt to put a curb on such superpower triumphalism only if it does
> not perceive acknowledgement of complicity as an inconvenience. (xii,
> emphasis added)

The notion of 'training' speaks to the teacher/student interaction that
will follow. The teacher states her discipline: reading the world. Reading is a skill conventionally taught in literature programs, and many
surrounding disciplines would be wise to endorse interdisciplinarity if
only to have their students learn such reading.[60]

'The world' is the area that will be painstakingly defined, refined,
and justified, as the field where (what Spivak calls) 'transnational culture studies' is to be practised.[61] The notion of 'reading the world' is
also programmatic in its reference to reference. As argued in the previous section, although reading is inflected through deconstruction – a
reputedly anti-referential mode of reading – Spivak rigorously refuses
the deconstructive vulgate (mostly existing in the minds of its opponents) that remains within an 'infinite play' of language. Without for a
moment transgressing the logic of deconstruction's philosophy of lan-

---

60 Anthropologists, who come closer than any other disciplinarians to having to 'read
the world,' are but one example. In my own experience, art history is another discipline that could greatly benefit from reading skills, but it is reluctant to develop them,
wrongly assuming that 'reading' implies 'language.' See Bal (1991a).
61 Spivak (1993b) offers this term as an alternative to cultural studies and postcolonial
studies.

guage, *CPR* explains, demonstrates, and argues the need for reading 'mistakenly,' and for 'worlding.'

The sentence cited above posits an agenda that is plainly and openly activist: 'to put a curb on such superpower triumphalism.' And throughout the book, activist reading remains the order of the day. If there is any writer of what is broadly called 'cultural studies' who has been successful in arguing that, and how, reading can be activist and politically effective, it is Spivak.[62] As is only fair, her condition for admission to her much-desired class is also presented beforehand. The condition is modest and open enough. Participants are required to 'not perceive acknowledgment of complicity as an inconvenience.' In other words, students of reading the world must not feel hindered by their participation in the world, with all its lack of justice.[63] For, frustrating as it is to feel forced into complicity, it is also true that denial, disavowal, and bad faith can only lead to condescension, disempowerment, or – the worst sin for Spivak – simplistic one-liner activism. Complicity – historically inevitable, presently fatal – can only be neutralized by working through it. Critical intimacy with an 'other,' someone who is not a clone of oneself, offers an arena where you can do that working through with a measure of safety. Working with my student Catherine Lord on developing her study of 'the intimacy of influence' was my attempt to build such an arena. To read all these things in Spivak's one sentence perhaps makes the sentence difficult. To read them as the 'normal' part of classroom logistics makes it utterly easy.

The second sentence that exposes the teacher's position is the first sentence of the first chapter, on philosophy. The sentence is clear: 'Postcolonial studies, unwittingly commemorating a lost object, can become an alibi unless it is placed within a general frame.' Here, I heard a welcome to people like myself who are not 'into' (specialized in) postcolonial studies, but who feel the need not to accept its ghettoization. The alibi issue speaks to the complicity already mentioned. The general frame, here, is double. 'The world,' as the text to be read through literary training, is compounded with the founding text of Western aesthetics, Kant's *Critique*, which the chapter goes on to read

62 The drawbacks of both terms have been widely acknowledged by now. Spivak's commitment to teaching is the explicit subject of one of her articles (1995), but it is obvious in all her writings.
63 Cannily, this 'condition' defuses the danger of backlash inherent in the disingenuous bad-faith apologetics so fashionable of late, of the order of 'forgive me for being a white male.'

in detail, in the way one might teach this text.[64] The argument implied proposes that 'the world' – the globality that has today overruled and reframed the postcolonial condition – is to be read against Kant's *Critique*, as an example of philosophy's complicity with political and social situations.

The phrase in the subordinate clause of the sentence, 'unwittingly commemorating a lost object,' resonates by contrast with the book's subtitle, 'toward a history of the vanishing present.' It also resonates with current interest in cultural memory, with mourning and melancholia, so that the connotation /the present/ *as* or *is* the past, becomes, through that poetic detour, a vibrant programmatic statement towards the book's ethics. This ethics, painstakingly unpacked throughout the 400-odd pages, is grounded in the (im)possibility of (not) speaking from the vantage point of the past, since it sits, uneasily, within the present. Spivak the teacher, in other words, offers the only kind of history lesson possible in the face of the global condition.[65] The sub-clause also sets the tone of the class. Gentle yet combative, it reassures the students that the teacher knows what their baggage is, and that she still welcomes them, without assigning blame ('unwittingly'). Constructive criticism, isn't that what teachers always try to offer?

The third sentence specifying Spivak's teacherliness follows directly after the previous one, and explains the history lesson further. The issue at stake in this conception of history is that of complicity. Complicity is produced not only because of everyone's 'being' or existing within the global capitalism of the present, but also because it inheres in every student who has been trained too well in what is called 'historical thinking' but what is, in fact, historically extremely problematic:

Colonial Discourse studies, when they concentrate only on the representation of the colonized or the matter of the colonies, can sometimes serve the production of current neo-colonial knowledge *by placing colonialism/ imperialism securely in the past, and/or by suggesting a continuous line from that past to our present.* (emphasis added)

At this point, the students who feel either unable to read this prose,

---

64 As I have argued, the phrase 'in detail' is not an innocent one.
65 The conception of history that underlies her book might be somewhat congenial to the one I have termed 'preposterous' in my book, which I now see as being on an art history of the vanishing present (1999a).

such as Eagleton, or unwilling to be retrained in historical thinking and literary reading, unlearning a lot in the process, are allowed to leave the room. Just count your losses. But if you stay, the contract stipulates that you don't sabotage the class. You can argue, object, raise questions, ask for more information, and the teacher will be more than willing to cater to your whims. Unless you keep thinking you are in the wrong class. At page 197, you would be dismissed anyway ('The conventional highway of a politically correct single issue is merely the shortest distance between two signposted exits').

Spivak's rewriting of Kant's title implies a promise relating to the importance of what she has to say. It also extends the realm of philosophy to include what philosophy, as she argues throughout the first chapter of the book, has been at pains to foreclose. If *CPR* comes anywhere near fulfilling these promises, would we mind that it might also emulate Kant in difficulty? I have never read reviews complaining about the intricacies of the Master's discourse. On the contrary, its intricacies seem to warrant extensive books, full of commentary gloating in the pleasure of explanation. Not only by obedient disciples, but also by people like Spivak: critical but respectful, like a younger friend, engaging seriously with the great thinker, deeming his ideas worth close scrutiny, precisely because they are important, influential, and culturally present. In writing her first chapter, then, Spivak offers a model for the kind of reading her own book deserves. Anything less is self-depriving, even self-demeaning.

Eagleton's review and the likes of it embody the mark of foreclosure: the English gentleman whose amused interest in the rest of the West can only be teased so far. In such a spirit, the native informant is gauged then dismissed, as soon as he turns out to speak a language of his own. Such critics refuse to learn anything that isn't straight: straight Marxism, straight postcolonial victim talk, straight feminism. Any combination, any integration of these is not admitted. Should I do a symptomatic reading of his review, as Spivak does of Kant? If one of my students asked if they should, I would say: don't. I would prefer you spend your time rereading Spivak's book, doing archival research, or reading the works she discusses anew. Even a conservative literary scholar should be glad that Spivak 'saves' the canon, by allowing the needed native informant to become visible. *CPR* connects the Western canon to issues of postcoloniality and neocolonialism. Most importantly, it analyses the present so that its – that is, our – complicity cannot remain foreclosed.

Homecoming

The three misreadings I have committed here are meant to fill out a sketch of a teacher-image, 'imaged' in much the same way as Spivak unpacks other-determination. A teacher-image that also profiles my ideal for students of cultural analysis when they become teachers in the humanities of the present. In the case of the Spivak of my misreading, the sketch consists of three elements: the traces of the native informant as figure; the historicizing and self-critical self-declarations of the transnationally literate 'I'; and the deconstructions (but see also the characterizations above) of the West-and-the-rest opposition in its migrant-idealizing variant. This combination is a reading for the emplotment of *learning* the work of postcolonial critique as learnable and teachable. Spivak, like Lacan, perhaps dramatizes her excellence as a teacher in order to compensate for the difficulty of her writing. Perhaps she doesn't. It doesn't matter. As more than just a compensation for a lack, this strategy turns her writing into a superb form of teaching (teaching-to-teach).

If Lacan became readable for me by being read as a difficult poet, like Mallarmé, and Derrida as by being read as a postmodernist novelist, like Calvino, then Spivak becomes more than readable – engaging, generous, and passionately communicative – by being read as a teacher. Indeed, the many parentheses, the long footnotes, and the convoluted sentences can be absorbed as the painstaking efforts of a teacher committed to being clear without simplification, to being nuanced and fair, and to being responsive to the many 'second-persons' who follow her class. On such a reading, what otherwise might make the text difficult to read becomes something else: an utterly responsible 'second-person' discourse, by a teacher who, you trust, will go out of her way to make difficult things understandable. What kind of critical intimacy can the student – eager to become a 'good' cultural analyst, and painstakingly accumulating the baggage for which no shopping lists are available – mobilize to respond to this teaching? Listening, knowing that you can object to it, argue with it, 'apply' it to your own work. In other words, the best mode of reading this book is going with the current. It is ready to be a source for learning to understand not only concepts but also the kind of activity conceptualization is – working your way through the intricate frayed pathways of the global cultural field and the many quaint disciplines that have examined bits of it. You can travel with some baggage, but, given the restrictions of what you can carry, the baggage will change along the way. You can keep travelling, or return home, whenever you feel the need. But, as all travellers know, after this trip you will never be the same again. Nor will 'home.'

Afterword

'I wondered if there is a place for the "us" to figure in the final section ... figure, that is, as a possibility that perhaps you have finally to undermine in order to sign the text as your "mis-reading," but that in some respect connects the very direct way in which you address your reader at the end with how you specify your situation at the beginning, i.e. as a teacher of a group of graduate students ...' These words are taken from a letter I received from Anna-Louise Milne, a student with whom both Spivak and I worked in graduate seminars. Once upon a time, this student showed me Eagleton's review of Spivak's book, shared her annoyance about it with me, and, unwittingly, made me write the first version of the last chapter of this book. Her letter was a response to the draft of that chapter, then article, that I sent her.

This student, who has now finished her PhD and is an excellent academic teacher in her own right, recalled in her letter how we had talked about academic polemics. She ends her letter as follows:

> For what it's worth, I've recently tended to an isolationist stance faced with that sort of polemics (with far-reaching consequences), but your emphasis on complicity and cooperation has given me a whole other vision of the business. Perhaps that is why I am so keen not to see the 'we,' however unstable, disappear at the end ...

I found this comment extremely stimulating and encouraging. In the face of such a response, I want to reconsider the use of 'we.' The rhetoric of that pronoun requires caution and revision. But what this letter-writer hints at is the loss of community that results from its rejection, that threatens as tenaciously as the false sense of community that potentially and inevitably most certainly results from its unreflected endorsement. I am particularly troubled by the bracketed clause, 'with far-reaching consequences,' which suggests that pressures on students to take sides – precisely, the problem of 'we' – cannot be wished away.

Reconsidering 'we' at length in the face of this response will have to wait for another occasion, but I will keep it on my agenda, because it is the interaction between teachers and students that is on the line here. As I near the end of this book, though, that letter sends me back to this book's beginning. As yet another travel, one within this volume, I look back and notice that the pronoun 'we' may perhaps one day become a word-emerging-as-a-concept. More than of any of the concepts discussed here, the use of 'we' must be provisional. It is dependent, as Benveniste taught us, on the *hic-et-nunc* of the situation in which we speak. It is constantly subject to doubt, suspicion, seduction, and lure. Each occurrence is different. Each, consequently, is a performance in the theatrical sense of the word; a collective subjectivity *ex machina* to be constructed on the spot, to come up, from the wings where it is always hiding, onto the stage, to relieve the tensions and resolve the remaining problems before the curtain falls.

Theatricality has been a recurrent theme throughout this book. It offers the attraction of mediating between many of the issues I have put forward. Initially, I set up a fictitious performance in the guise of an imaginary seminar. That was the stage of the 'we,' however unstable this pronoun must indeed remain. Though artificial, such an imaginary setting – a metaphor for the real situations out of which this book emerged and within which it, hopefully, will be used – provides the freedom to imagine that teaching situations need more than just firmly delimited content. The artificiality of the theatre comes to stand for self-reflection and playfulness, commitment to perform as best one can, and the pleasure of not being held to a rigid authenticity. These meanings of theatricality run like a red thread through all the chapters. They impinge not only on the process of ongoing teaching and learning that cultural analysis is, but also on the level of the cases or objects. The Bernini sculptures discussed here make the theatrical metaphor concrete. For these sculptures, whether religious, erotic, or both, are themselves theatres of lust. The women in them enact *ecstasis*, performing that unrepresentable experience as if with costume and make-up. Teresa displays herself on stage. The concept *mise-en-scène* brings all the latent theatrical elements together.

This concept goes on to enhance the theatricality involved in each of the other travelling concepts discussed here. In writing the report of my one-time experience with a practice (chapter 4), for example, I realized what I had not noticed at the time: that the show I had organized, by being dis-unified so as to foreground a multiplicity of frames, had become a *theatrical* exhibition. It was as messy as the stage during the heat of a play. It kept the audience captive, forcing visitors to play their own roles, and perform their own acts of viewing without a clear and simple script.

Theatricality, in all it meanings, is most obviously present in chapter 5, but there, too, even more aspects accrue to the concept from the object. After all, the central work there concerns the rehearsal of a performance. The children's prospective dance, their ambition for a better life with cultural memory as the stage director, the theatrical voice anonymous and thereby undermining the individualism of a moralizing kind of political correctness: they all affect the theatricality of the photographs, while leaving them literally centre-stage.

By focusing on theatricality explicitly, I am able to present the tradition of Zwarte Piet – thoroughly theatrical, after all – as theatre in the profound sense: playful in appearance only, deeply influential, perhaps cathartic, perhaps merely luring. Neither simply racist nor simply ready to be discarded, but enacted every year, in performances that differ.

The imaginary classroom remains the stage in the final two chapters. Academic debate is *staged*, not real, in a monologic text that only approximates dialogue through quotation and representation of the other voice. It is an instance of prosopopeia, a rhetorical figure that represents an imaginary or absent person as speaking and acting. That representation is an image, in all the aspects that have accrued to this concept throughout this book. In this multilayered sense, the theatricality lingers within the image, enough, hopefully, for the other voices to be imagined. By putting a colleague in the role of main character, in the final travel – if not quite, of course, of 'first-person' speaker – I hope to reveal an element of theatre that is perhaps its most utopian: the relinquishing of the claim to authenticity that sustains the individualistic view of identity. On the premise of theatricality in these senses, then, I am willing to reinstate 'we.'

It is also on the basis of theatricality that the guiding metaphor of this book can be seen to work. Having used the metaphor of travel to convey the adventure of interdisciplinary cultural analysis, the question might arise whether what I have been promoting is not just a silly form of tourism. Tourism is a frequently alleged metaphor for contemporary culture, where the Internet promotes surfing and television zapping. Ours is a world where global capitalism makes the politics of national boundaries and the subsequent policing of migration quaint, unfair, and untenable. As a nostalgic leftover from colonialism, a destroyer of human and natural environments, and the privilege of the wealthier part of the world, tourism is no more than a superficial form of gaining knowledge-as-possession, as embodied in the snapshot and postcard, or rather – video. Obviously, I would not wish to see an interdisciplinary travel with concepts mistaken for this kind of tourism.

Yet the metaphor of travel evokes tourism, and so it must. For only in the acknowledgment of what is close but must be resisted can the intellectual thrust of interdisciplinarity be maintained – defended, held up, continued. A 'touristic' approach to the study of culture 'beyond' traditional disciplinary boundaries would be recognizable through the two features I have tried to oppose here: superficiality and colonialism. One way I hoped to counter the first danger was by proceeding through detailed case studies. Another was by engaging concepts. If this book has one central contention, it is this: superficiality can be countered by bringing well-thought-through concepts to bear on specific objects. In terms of theatre, the analysis of culture is not a performance, or even a dress rehearsal, but the production itself, a constant working with a script, which can only come to life through that working.

The colonialism inherent in going out and taking possession presents territorialism as its major 'personality trait.' In my experience, the boundary policing carried out in the name of traditional disciplinary thoroughness is more territorialist than any 'invasion' – to use the opponent's vocabulary – of those disciplines could ever be. But the dangers of colonization work in both directions. If interdisciplinary students of culture take for granted access to the 'other' field, they are also stuck with the civil duties in force out there, in that field. Spivak-the-teacher gets upset when her students shrug off the need to do research. I get equally upset when my students allege images, for example, as illustrations of a theoretical or political point, turning a blind eye to what the image itself has to say. But turning around, I see many inhabitants of the safely guarded discipline of art history doing precisely that. Hence, simply 'becoming' an art historian doesn't help much in overcoming the limitations of that field, nor does the abuse of visual material for the sake of an argument that remains alien to it.

Far be it from me to pronounce moralistically and anachronistically against surfing and zapping. What I wish to do is uphold the notion that a good quality of *attention* to the subjects and objects that make up a culture does more for an understanding of why these objects affect its users than a hasty assessment. But, regardless of the issue of speed, the kind of travel I have been alleging here really is different from surfing and zapping – in other words, from armchair tourism. The travel I have been designing – as an adventure of learning not predicated upon the conception of knowledge as taking possession – requires more time, more baggage, and more willingness to change oneself.

Each of the preceding chapters has proposed a dynamic intercourse between one or more concepts and objects. The dynamic of that intercourse of necessity affects the student doing the analysis, hence, making the trip. The travel aspect underlying each chapter lies in the radical unfixing of all traditional certainties. The loss of methodological guidelines of the sort built into disciplinary paradigms – with the dogmatic or at least axiomatic status of the methods – is compensated by the travel itself. For, in addition to the depth, complexity, and revision of earlier-held assumptions, knowing that one does not know opens many possibilities. These, in turn, yield new insights and facilitate new skills. 'Travel' stands for a commitment to that unfixing. The difficulty in the kind of analysis I have been advocating here is to keep a balance that is never stable.

At this point I wish to emphasize the single most important point these chapters have been collectively trying to make. Because of the perpetual uncertainties cultivated by cultural analysis, the latter can be neither confined to nor separated from existing disciplines. But the opposite is also true. I do not hesitate for a moment to contend that the perspective, the method of travelling through a field both larger (for example, 'culture' instead of 'Dutch painting') and smaller (for example, single objects instead of 'periods' or 'genres') than what the disciplines prescribe, with *indeterminate* concepts as one's baggage, is indispensable for the revitalization, perhaps even survival, of the disciplines in the humanities today.

I have often been told that what I do is not 'really' biblical scholarship or art history, but literary study. To which I reply, it was not meant to be. Funnier still is the moment when I was told it was not 'really' cultural studies; to which I cheerfully replied, I am ever so happy not to be policeable by what appears to be just another disciplining discipline. Not that I mind being held up against standards. In fact, this whole book argues to the contrary. But no one owns such standards; and such standards are not, and never can be, beyond doubt, beyond dispute.

Finally, the most irritating claim this book might be accused of making is that it overstates its innovative quality. True, if the insights-cum-knowledge – that specific knowledge that knows its own ignorance – are to make sense beyond the boundaries of the old institutions, they must be relatively *new*. This innovative quality may not necessarily be radical, but at least it unsettles tired routine procedures based on unexamined methods and presuppositions. Without claiming interdisciplinary analysis to be, by definition, innovative, or that the traditional disciplines are unable to be innovative from within, I firmly believe that responsible interdisciplinary inquiry is likely to offer new combinations of insights, or – to shift the metaphor one last time – new *bricolages*.

By selecting somewhat classical objects – most recognized as artistic – together with well-known concepts, I have wanted to take the risk of being told there is not much new in these analyses. But the innovative quality it was my ambition to advocate is not bound to objects or concepts. It is through the intricate exploration of their combination – say, their critical intimacy, which I have called 'travel' – that I seek to renegotiate the fragile, tense, but indispensable intimacy between tradition and innovation. Reaching back from a poststructuralist perspective to the tradition of New Criticism, for example, as many literary scholars have done all along, may allow me to make a modest claim to innovation, but only if that innovation resides in a revision of formalism and a displacement of intention, a recasting of practice and a recombining of distinct concepts.

Today, in an era of backlash, and in the wake of affairs such as, most famously, the Sokal spoof, I see the primary critique of pioneering cultural studies as suggesting that it leads to a rehearsing of disciplinarity on a somewhat larger scale, where disciplines are grouped together according to disciplinary affiliations: languages, literatures, the media, the arts, philosophy and religion, the various linguistics. In my view, such grouping can at best claim only multidisciplinarity. Beyond administrative streamlining, I see no intellectual gain in such reorganizations. In contrast, I believe that interdisciplinarity, precisely because it is under attack for its difficulty in maintaining methodological standards, can open new directions. Directions in which intellectual rather than administrative possibilities can be explored, and the search continued for a methodology flexible enough to facilitate experiment yet trustworthy in its intersubjectivity. In the first place, because it yields awareness of the limits of knowledge – and hence, of unlimited learning.

Bibliography

Ahearn, Edward. 1977. 'Black Woman, White Poet: Exile and Exploitation in Baudelaire's Jeanne Duval Poems.' *French Review* 51: 212–20

Alcoff, Linda, and Elizabeth Potter, eds. 1993. *Feminist Epistemologies*. New York: Routledge

Allen, Suzanne. 1983. 'Petit traité du nœud.' In *Figures du baroque*, ed. Jean-Marie Benoist. Paris: PUF

Alpers, Svetlana. 1995. *The Making of Rubens*. New Haven: Yale University Press

Alpers, Svetlana, and Michael Baxandall. 1994. *Tiepolo and the Pictorial Intelligence*. New Haven: Yale University Press

Alperson, Philip A. 1998. 'Performance.' In *Encyclopedia of Aesthetics*, ed. Michael Kelly. Vol. 3, 464–6. New York/Oxford: Oxford University Press

Alphen, Ernst van. *See* van Alphen, Ernst

Ankersmit, F.R. 1993. *De historisch ervaring*. Groningen: Historische Uitegverij

Anscombe, G.E.M. 1957. *Intention*. Ithaca: Cornell University Press

Appadurai, Arjun, ed. 1986. *The Social Life of Things*. Cambridge: Cambridge University Press

Aptekar, Ken. 1997. *Ken Aptekar: Talking to Pictures*. Washington, DC: Corcoran Gallery of Art (exhibition catalogue)

Arasse, Daniel. 1987. *La guillotine et l'imaginaire de la Terreur*. Paris: Flammarion (English: 1989. *The Guillotine and the Terror*. Trans. Christopher Miller. London/New York: Allen Lane/Penguin Press)

– 1992. *Le détail: pour une histoire rapprochée de la peinture*. Paris: Flammarion

Ashcroft, Bill, Gareth Griffiths, and Helen Tiffin, eds. 1998. *Key Concepts in Post-Colonial Studies*. New York: Routledge

Atkinson, Brenda, and Candice Breitz, eds. 1999. *Grey Areas: Representation, Identity and Politics in Contemporary South African Art*. Johannesburg: Chalkham Hill Press

Attridge, Derek. 1999. 'Innovation, Literature, Ethics: Relating to the Other.'
   PMLA 114 (1): 20–31
Augé, Marc. 1999. *An Anthropology for Contemporaneous Worlds*. Trans. Amy
   Jacobs. Stanford: Stanford University Press
Austin, J.L. 1975 [1962]. *How to Do Things with Words*. Cambridge: Harvard
   University Press
Bal, Mieke. 1987. *Lethal Love: Literary Feminist Readings of Biblical Love Stories*.
   Bloomington: Indiana University Press
– 1988a. *Death and Dissymmetry: The Politics of Coherence in the Book of Judges*.
   Chicago: University of Chicago Press
– 1988b. *Murder and Difference: Gender, Genre and Scholarship on Sisera's Death*.
   Trans. Matthew Gumpert. Bloomington: Indiana University Press
– 1991a [1994]. *Reading 'Rembrandt': Beyond the Word-Image Opposition*. New
   York: Cambridge University Press
– 1991b. *On Story-Telling: Essays in Narratology*. Sonoma, CA: Polebridge
   Press
– 1992. 'Narratology and the Rhetoric of Trashing.' *Comparative Literature* 44
   (3): 293–306
– 1994a. *On Meaning-Making: Essays in Semiotics*. Sonoma, CA: Polebridge
   Press
– 1994b. 'Telling Objects: A Narrative Perspective on Collecting.' In *The Cultures of Collecting*, ed. John Elsner and Roger Cardinal, 97–115. London:
   Reaktion Books
– 1996. *Double Exposures: The Subject of Cultural Analysis*. New York: Routledge
– 1997a. *The Mottled Screen: Reading Proust Visually*. Trans. Anna-Louise Milne.
   Stanford: Stanford University Press
– 1997b. *Narratology: Introduction to the Theory of Narrative*. 2nd ed. Toronto:
   University of Toronto Press
– 1998. *Jeannette Christensen's Time*. Bergen, Norway: Center for the Study of
   European Civilization
– 1999a. *Quoting Caravaggio: Contemporary Art, Preposterous History*. Chicago:
   University of Chicago Press
– 1999b. 'Narrative Inside Out: Louise Bourgeois' *Spider* as Theoretical Object.'
   Oxford Art Journal 22 (2): 101–26
– 2000. 'Religious Canon and Literary Identity.' *European Electronic Journal for
   Feminist Exegesis* 2 (no page nos.)
– 2001a. *Louise Bourgeois' Spider: The Architecture of Art-writing*. Chicago: University of Chicago Press
– 2001b. *Looking In: The Art of Viewing*. Ed. and with an introduction by Norman Bryson. Amsterdam: G & B Arts International

– 2001c. 'Voix/voie narrative: la voix métaphorée.' In *La voix narrative: cahier de narratologie*, vol. 1, ed. Jean-Louis Brau, 9–36. Nice: Centre de Narratologie Appliqué

– 2001d. 'Mission Impossible: Postcards, Pictures, and Parasites: In *Religion and Media*, ed. Hent de Vries and Samuel Weber, 241–68. Stanford: Stanford University Press

– In press. 'Aestheticizing Catastrophe.' In *Charlotte Salomon: Gender, Trauma, Creativity*, ed. Monica Bohm-Duchen and Michael Steinberg. Ithaca: Cornell University Press

Bal, Mieke, ed. 1999. *The Practice of Cultural Analysis: Exposing Interdisciplinary Interpretation*. Stanford: Stanford University Press

Bal, Mieke, Jonathan Crewe, and Leo Spitzer, eds. 1999. *Acts of Memory: Cultural Recall in the Present*. Hanover, NH: University Press of New England

Bardenstein, Carol. 1999. 'Trees, Forests, and the Shaping of Palestinian and Israeli Collective Memory.' In *Acts of Memory: Cultural Recall in the Present*, ed. Mieke Bal, Jonathan Crewe, and Leo Spitzer, 148–68. Hanover and London: University Press of New England

Bardon, Françoise. 1978. *Caravage ou l'expérience de la matière*. Paris: PUF

Barthes, Roland. 1975a. *Pleasure of the Text*. Trans. Richard Miller. New York: Hill and Wang (French: 1973. *Le plaisir du texte*. Paris: Editions du Seuil)

– 1975b. *S/Z*. Trans. Richard Miller. New York: Hill and Wang

Battersby, Christine. 1998. *The Phenomenal Woman: Feminist Metaphysics and the Pattern of Identity*. Cambridge: Polity Press

Baxandall, Michael. 1985. *Patterns of Intention: On the Historical Explanation of Pictures*. New Haven: Yale University Press

– 1991. 'Exhibiting Intention: Some Preconditions of the Visual Display of Culturally Purposeful Objects.' In *Exhibiting Cultures: The Poetics and Politics of Museum Display*, ed. Ivan Karp and Steven D. Lavine, 33–41. Washington and London: Smithsonian Institution Press

Becker, W. 1998. 'Garden, Night and Farewell.' In *Michel Huisman: Garden, Night and Farewell*, 7–12. Aachen: Ludwig Forum für Internationale Kunst

Beger, Nico. 2001. *Que(e)rying Political Practices in Europe: Tensions in the Struggle for Sexual Minority Rights*. Amsterdam: ASCA Press (PhD dissertation)

Benezra, Neal, and Olga M. Viso, eds. 1999. *Regarding Beauty: A View of the Late Twentieth Century*. Washington, DC: Hirshhorn Museum and Sculpture Garden, Smithsonian Institute in association with Hatje Cantz Publishers

Benjamin, Walter. 1968. *Illuminations*. Ed. and with an introduction by Hannah Arendt. Trans. Harry Zohn. New York: Schocken

– 1977. *The Origin of German Drama*. Trans. John Osborne. London: New Left Books

– 1980. *Gesammelte Schriften. Werkausgabe*. Vol. 2, 1. Frankfurt am Main: Suhrkamp

Bennett, Tony. 1995. *The Birth of the Museum: History, Theory, Politics*. New York: Routledge

Benveniste, Emile. 1966. *Problèmes de linguistique générale*. Vol. 1. Paris: Gallimard (English: 1971. *Problems in General Linguistics*. Trans. Mary Elizabeth Meek. Coral Gables: University of Miami Press)

Bersani, Leo. 1989. 'Is the Rectum a Grave?' *October* 43 (Winter): 197–223

Bettelheim, Bruno. 1976. *The Uses of Enchantment: The Meaning and Importance of Fairy Tales*. New York: Knopf

Bhabha, Homi K. 1986. 'The Other Question: Difference, Discrimination and the Discourse of Colonialism.' In *Literature, Politics and Theory*, ed. Francis Barker et al. New York: Methuen

Biezenbos, Lia van de. 1995. *Fantasmes maternels dans l'œuvre de Marguerite Duras: dialogue entre Duras et Freud*. Amsterdam/Atlanta: Rodopi

Bilinkoff, Jodi. 1989. *The Avila of Saint Teresa: Religious Reform in a Sixteenth-Century City*. Ithaca: Cornell University Press

Bleeker, Maaike. 1999. 'Death, Digitalization and Dys-appearance: Staging the Body of Science.' *Performance Research* 4 (2): 1–8

– 2002. *The Locus of Looking: Dissecting Visuality in the Theater*. Amsterdam: ASCA Press (Ph.D. dissertation)

Bloom, Harold. 1973. *The Anxiety of Influence: A Theory of Poetry*. New York: Oxford University Press

Bois, Yves-Alain, and Rosalind Krauss. 1997. *Formless: A User's Guide*. New York: Zone Books

Bolland, Andrea. 2000. '*Desiderio* and *Diletto:* Vision, Touch and the Poetics of Bernini's *Apollo and Daphne*.' *Art Bulletin* 82 (2): 309–30

Bollas, Christopher. 1987. *The Shadow of the Object: Psychoanalysis of the Unthought Known*. New York: Columbia University Press

Booth, Wayne C. 1961. *The Rhetoric of Fiction*. Chicago: University of Chicago Press

Bowie, Malcolm. 1987. *Freud, Proust and Lacan: Theory as Fiction*. Cambridge: Cambridge University Press

Bryson, Norman. 1983. *Vision and Painting: The Logic of the Gaze*. London: Macmillan

– 2001. 'Introduction' to *Looking In: The Art of Viewing*, ed. Norman Bryson, 1–39. Amsterdam: G & B Arts International

Buchloh, Benjamin H.D. 1999. 'Memory Lessons and History Tableaux: James Coleman's Archaeology of Spectacle.' In *James Coleman*, 51–75. Barcelona: Fondació Antoni Tapies

Buci-Glucksmann, Christine. 1994. *Baroque Reason: The Aesthetics of Modernity*. Trans. Patrick Camiller, with an introduction by Bryan S. Turner. London and Thousand Oaks, CA: Sage Publications (French: 1984. *La raison baroque: de Baudelaire à Benjamin*. Paris: Galilée)

Buck-Morss, Susan. 1989. *The Dialectics of Seeing: Walter Benjamin and the Arcades Project*. Cambridge: MIT Press

Buell, Lawrence. 1999. 'Introduction: In Pursuit of Ethics.' *PMLA* 114 (1): 7–19

Butler, Judith. 1990. *Gender Trouble: Feminism and the Subversion of Identity*. New York: Routledge

– 1993. *Bodies That Matter: On the Discursive Limits of 'Sex.'* New York: Routledge

– 1997. *Excitable Speech: A Politics of the Performative*. New York: Routledge

Careri, Giovanni. 1995. *Bernini: Flights of Love, the Art of Devotion*. Trans. Linda Lappin. Chicago: University of Chicago Press

Caruth, Cathy, ed. 1995. *Trauma: Explorations in Memory*. Baltimore: Johns Hopkins University Press

Certeau, Michel de. *See* de Certeau, Michel

Chase, Cynthia. 1986. *Decomposing Figures: Rhetorical Readings in the Romantic Tradition*. Baltimore: Johns Hopkins University Press

– 1987. 'The Witty Butcher's Wife: Freud, Lacan, and the Conversion of the Resistance to Theory.' *MLN* 102 (3): 989–1013

Cinotti, Mina. 1983, *Michelangelo Merisi detto Il Caravaggio: tutte le opere*. Vol. I of *I pittori berghamaschi. Il seicento*. Bergamo: Edizioni Bolis

Code, Lorraine. 1991. *What Can She Know? Feminist Epistemology and the Construction of Knowledge*. Ithaca/London: Cornell University Press

– 1995. *Rhetorical Spaces: Essays on Gendered Locations*. New York: Routledge

Crow, Thomas. 1999. *The Intelligence of Art*. Chapel Hill and London: University of North Carolina Press

Crowther, Paul. 1989. *The Kantian Sublime: From Morality to Art*. Oxford: Clarendon Press

Culler, Jonathan. 1983. *Roland Barthes*. New York: Oxford University Press

– 1986. *Ferdinand de Saussure*. Ithaca: Cornell University Press

– 1988. *Framing the Sign: Criticism and Its Institutions*. Norman and London: University of Oklahoma Press

– 1994. 'What's the Point?' Introduction to *The Point of Theory*, ed. Mieke Bal and Inge E. Boer, 13–17. Amsterdam: Amsterdam University Press; New York: Continuum

– 1996. 'Prostitution and *Les Fleurs du Mal*.' *ASCA BRIEF: Issues in Cultural Analysis*, 11–26. Amsterdam: ASCA Press

– 2000. 'Philosophy and Literature: The Fortunes of the Performative.' *Poetics Today* 21 (3): 48–67

Damisch, Hubert. 1996. 'Narcisse baroque?' In *Puissance du Baroque: les forces, les formes, les rationalités, Ouvrage Collectif*, 29–42. Paris: Galilée

Davidson, Donald. 1984. 'On the Very Idea of a Conceptual Schema.' In *Inquiries into Truth and Interpretation*, 183–98. Oxford: Clarendon Press

de Certeau, Michel. 1982. *La fable mystique, I, XVI–XVII siècle*. Paris: Gallimard

– 1986. *Heterologies: Discourse on the Other*. Trans. Brian Massumi, foreword by Wlad Godzich. Minneapolis: University of Minnesota Press

Deleuze, Gilles. 1993. *The Fold: Leibniz and the Baroque*. Trans., and with a foreword, by Tom Conley. Minneapolis: University of Minnesota Press

de Lauretis, Teresa. 1983. 'Semiotics and Experience.' In *Alice Doesn't: Feminism, Semiotics, Cinema*, 158–86. London: Macmillan

Deleuze, Gilles, and Félix Guattari. 1972. *Anti-Oedipus: Capitalism and Schizophrenia*. Vol. 1. Trans. Robert Hurely, Mark Seem, and Helen R. Lane. London: Athlone Press (1984)

– 1976. *Rhizome: Introduction*. Paris: Editions de Minuit

– 1980. *A Thousand Plateaus: Capitalism and Schizophrenia*. Vol. 2. Trans. Brian Massumi. London: Athlone Press (1992)

– 1994. *What Is Philosophy?* Trans. Hugh Tomlinson and Graham Burchill. London: Verso

de Man, Paul. 1979. *Allegories of Reading: Figural Language in Rousseau, Nietzsche, Rilke, and Proust*. New Haven and London: Yale University Press

– 1982. 'The Resistance to Theory.' *Yale French Studies* 63: 3–20

– 1996. *Aesthetic Ideology*. Minneapolis: University of Minnesota Press

Denaci, Mark. 2001. 'Bloodletting.' *The Thick of Things: Framing, Fetishism, and the Work of Art History*, 77–101, Rochester, NY: University of Rochester, Visual and Cultural Studies

Derrida, Jacques. 1976. *Of Grammatology*. Trans., and with an introduction, by Gayatri Chakravorty Spivak. Baltimore: Johns Hopkins University Press

– 1978a. *La vérité en peinture*. Paris: Editions du Seuil (1987. *The Truth in Painting*. Trans. Geoff Bennington and Ian McLeod. Chicago: University of Chicago Press)

– 1978b. *Writing and Difference*. Trans. Alan Bass, 196–231. Chicago: University of Chicago Press

– 1982. *D'un ton apocalyptique adopté naguère en philosophie*. Paris: Galilée

– 1984. *Margins of Philosophy*. Trans. Alan Bass. Chicago: University of Chicago Press

– 1985. *The Ear of the Other: Otobiography, Transference, Translations (Interview with Christie McDonald).* Ed. Christie McDonald, trans. Peggy Kamuf and Avirall Ronell. New York: Schocken Books

– 1987. *Psyché: Inventions de l'autre.* Paris: Galilée

– 1988. 'Signature, Event, Context.' In *Limited Inc.,* trans. Samuel Weber, 1–23. Evanston: Northwestern University Press

– 1990. 'Force of Law: The "Mystical Foundation of Authority."' *Cardozo Law Review* 11 (919): 921–1045

– 1999. *Donner la mort.* Paris: Galilée

de Vries, Hent. 1992. 'Anti-Babel: The "Mystical Postulate" in Benjamin, de Certeau and Derrida.' *MLN* 107: 441–77

– 1999. *Philosophy and the Turn to Religion.* Baltimore: Johns Hopkins University Press

Didi-Hubermann, Georges. 1992. *Ce que nous voyons, ce qui nous regarde.* Paris: Editions de Minuit

Drew, Leder. 1990. *The Absent Body.* Chicago: University of Chicago Press

Dupont-Roc, Roselyne, and Jean Lallot. 1980. *La poétique: Aristote.* Trans. and annotated by Roselyne Dupont-Roc and Jean Lallot, with an introduction by Tzvetan Todorov. Paris: Editions du Seuil

Durham, Scott. 1998. *Phantom Communities: The Simulacrum and the Limits of Postmodernism.* Stanford: Stanford University Press

Dyer, Richard. 1997. *White.* London and New York: Routledge

Eagleton, Terry. 1999. 'In the Gaudy Supermarket.' *London Review of Books* 13 May (3): 5–6

Eco, Umberto. 1976. *A Theory of Semiotics.* Bloomington: Indiana University Press

– 1990. *The Limits of Interpretation.* Bloomington: Indiana University Press

Eliot, T.S. 1975. 'Tradition and the Individual Talent.' In *Selected Prose of T.S. Eliot,* ed. and with an introduction by Frank Kermode, 37–44. London: Faber and Faber (first published in *Egoist,* September and December 1919)

Elkins, James. 1999. *On Pictures and the Words That Fail Them.* New York: Cambridge University Press

Fabian, Johannes. 1990. *Power and Performance: Ethnographic Explorations through Proverbial Wisdom and Theater in Shaba, Zaire.* Madison: University of Wisconsin Press

– 1999. 'Remembering the Other: Knowledge and Recognition in the Exploration of Central Africa.' *Critical Inquiry* 26 (Autumn): 49–69

Felman, Shoshana. 1982. 'Psychoanalysis and Education: Teaching Terminable and Interminable.' *Yale French Studies* 63: 21–44

– 1983. *The Literary Speech Act: Don Juan with J.L. Austin, or Seduction in Two Languages.* Ithaca: Cornell University Press

Feyerabend, Paul. 1993. *Against Method*. London/New York: Verso

Figlio, Karl. 1996. 'Knowing, Loving and Hating Nature: A Psychoanalytic View.' In *FutureNatural*, ed. George Robertson, Melinda Mash, Lisa Tickner, et al., 72–85. London and New York: Routledge

Fisher, James. 1992. *The Theater of Yesterday and Tomorrow: Commedia Dell'Arte on the Modern Stage*. Lewiston/Queenston: Lampeter Edwin Mellen Press

Foster, Hal. 1995. 'The Artist as Ethnographer?' In *The Traffic in Culture: Refiguring Art and Anthropology*, ed. George E. Marcus and Fred R. Myers, 302–9. Berkeley: University of California Press

Freud, Sigmund. 1965. *New Introductory Lectures on Psychoanalysis*. Ed. and trans. James Strachey. New York: Norton (or. 1933)

– 1982. *The Interpretation of Dreams*. Trans. and ed. James Strachey. New York: Avon Books (or. 1900)

Genette, Gérard. 1972. *Figures III*. Paris: Editions du Seuil (English: 1980. *Narrative Discourse: An Essay in Method*. Trans. Jane E. Lewin, with a foreword by Jonathan Culler. Ithaca and London: Cornell University Press)

– 1982. *Nouveau discours du récit*. Paris: Editions du Seuil (English: 1983. *Narrative Discourse Revisited*. Trans. Jane E. Lewin, with a foreword by Jonathan Culler. Ithaca and London: Cornell University Press)

Gilbert, Creighton E. 1995. *Caravaggio and His Two Cardinals*. University Park: Pennsylvania State University Press

Gilroy, Paul. 1993. *Small Acts: Thoughts on the Politics of Black Cultures*. London: Serpent's Tail

– 1995. *The Black Atlantic: Modernity and Double Consciousness*. Cambridge: Harvard University Press

Giraud, Yves F.-A. 1968. *La fable de Daphné*. Geneva: Droz

Goffman, Erving. 1974. *Frame Analysis: An Essay on the Organization of Experience*. With a new foreword by Bennett Berger. Boston: Northeastern University Press

Goggin, Joyce, and Sonja Neef, eds. 2001. *Travelling Concepts: Text, Hybridity, Subjectivity*. Amsterdam: ASCA Press

Goldberg, Roselee. 1996. 'Performance Art.' In *The Dictionary of Art*, ed. Jane Turner, 403–9. London: Macmillan

Greenberg, Reesa, Bruce W. Ferguson, and Sandy Nairne, eds. 1996. *Thinking about Exhibitions*. London and New York: Routledge

Gregori, Mina. 1985. 'Narcissus.' In *The Age of Caravaggio*, ed. Mina Gregori, 265–8. New York: Metropolitan Museum of Art and Electa/Rizzoli

Greimas, Algirdas Julien. 1966. *Sémantique structurale*. Paris: Larousse

– 1976. *Maupassant. Exercices pratiques*. Paris: Editions du Seuil (English: 1988.

Maupassant: The Semiotics of Text, Practical Lessons. Trans. Paul Perron. Amsterdam and Philadelphia: J. Benjamins, Publishers and Co.)

Habermas, Jürgen. 1972. [1968]. *Knowledge and Human Interests.* Trans. Jeremy J. Shapiro. London: Heinemann

Halbwachs, Maurice. 1992. *On Collective Memory.* Chicago: University of Chicago Press

Hamacher, Werner. 1989. 'LECTIO: de Man's Imperative.' In *Reading de Man Reading*, ed. Lindsay Waters and Wlad Godzich, 171 201. Minneapolis: University of Minnesota Press

– 1997. 'One 2 Many Multiculturalisms.' In *Violence, Identity, and Self-Determination*, ed. Hent de Vries and Samuel Weber, 284–325. Stanford: Stanford University Press

Hartman, Geoffrey H. 1996. *The Longest Shadow: In the Aftermath of the Holocaust.* Bloomington and Indianapolis: Indiana University Press

– 1997. *The Fateful Question of Culture.* New York: Columbia University Press

Hirsch, Marianne. 1997. *Family Frames: Photography, Narrative, and Postmemory.* Cambridge: Harvard University Press

Hirsch, Marianne, ed. 1999. *The Familial Gaze.* Hanover, NH: University Press of New England

Hobsbawm, Eric, and Terence Ranger, eds. 1983. *The Invention of Traditions.* Cambridge: Cambridge University Press

Holly, Michael Ann. 1996. *Past Looking: Historical Imagination and the Rhetoric of the Image.* Ithaca and London: Cornell University Press

Huisman, Michel. 1998. *Michel Huisman: Garden, Night and Farewell.* Aachen: Ludwig Forum für Internationale Kunst

Huntington, Patricia. 1998. *Ecstatic Subjects, Utopia, and Recognition: Kristeva, Heidegger, Irigaray.* Albany: University of Albany Press

Huyssen, Andreas. 1995. *Twilight Memories: Marking Time in a Culture of Amnesia.* New York: Routledge

Innis, Robert E., ed. 1984. *Semiotics: An Introductory Anthology.* With introductions by Robert E. Innis. Bloomington: Indiana University Press

Irigaray, Luce. 1977. *This Sex Which Is Not One.* Trans. Catherine Porter and Carolyn Burke. Ithaca: Cornell University Press

Iser, Wolfgang. 1978. *The Act of Reading: A Theory of Aesthetic Response.* Baltimore: Johns Hopkins University Press

Jacques, Francis, and Jean-Louis Leutrat. 1998. *L'autre visible.* Paris: Presses de la Sorbonne Nouvelle

Janssens, Ann Veronica. 1999. *Ann Veronica Janssens: une image différente dans chaque œil/ADifferent Image in Each Eye*. Ed. Laurent Jacob. Liège: Espace 251 Nord

Jay, Martin. 1998. *Cultural Semantics: Keywords of Our Time*. Amherst: University of Massachusetts Press

Johnson, Barbara. 1987. *A World of Difference*. Baltimore: Johns Hopkins University Press

Kant, Immanuel. 1951. *The Critique of Judgement*. Trans. J.H. Bernard. New York: Hafner Press

Kelly, Michael, ed. 1998. *Encyclopedia of Aesthetics*. 4 vols. New York/Oxford: Oxford University Press

Kemp, Wolfgang, ed. 1985. 'Death at Work: A Case Study on Constitutive Blanks in Nineteenth-Century Painting.' *Representations* 10: 102–23

Kern, Andrea. 2000. *Schöne Lust. Eine Theorie der Ästhetischen Erfahrung nach Kant*. Frankfurt am Main: Suhrkamp

Kirschenblatt-Gimblett, Barbara. 1998. *Destination Culture: Tourism, Museums, and Heritage*. Berkeley: University of California Press

Koerner, Joseph Leo. 1990. *Caspar David Friedrich and the Subject of Landscape*. New Haven: Yale University Press

Korsten, Frans-Willem. 1998. *The Wisdom Brokers: Narrative's Interaction with Arguments in Cultural Critical Texts*. Amsterdam: ASCA Press (PhD dissertation)

Krauss, Rosalind. 1993. *The Optical Unconscious*. Cambridge: MIT Press

– 1999a. *Bachelors*. Cambridge: MIT Press

– 1999b. 'First Lines: Introduction to *Photograph*.' In *James Coleman*, 9–25. Barcelona: Fondació Antoni Tapies

Kristeva, Julia. 1986. *About Chinese Women*. Trans. Anita Barrows. New York/London: M. Boyards

– 1998. *Vision capitales*. Parti Pris. Paris: Museé du Louvre, Réunion des musées nationaux

Kuhn, Thomas S. 1962. *The Structure of Scientific Revolutions*. Chicago: University of Chicago Press

– 1986. 'Objectivity, Value Judgment, and Theory Choice.' In *Critical Theory since 1965*, ed. Hazard Adams and Leroy Searle, 383–93. Tallahassee: University Presses of Florida (or. 1977. Thomas S. Kuhn, *The Essential Tension: Selected Studies in Scientific Tradition and Change*. Chicago: University of Chicago Press)

Lacan, Jacques. 1975. *Le Séminaire, Livre XX, Encore*. Paris: Editions du Seuil

Laclau, Ernesto, and Chantal Mouffe. 1985. *Hegemony and Socialist Strategy*. Trans. Winston Moore and Paul Cammack. London: Verso

Langeler, Arno. 1994. *Zwarte Piet: een Moor in dienst van Venetië*. Amsterdam: Jan Mets

Laplanche, Jean. 1993. 'Court traité de l'inconscient.' *Nouvelle Revue de Psychanalyse* 48: 69–96

– 1996. 'Psychoanalysis as Anti-Hermeneutics.' Trans. Luke Thurston. *Radical Philosophy* 79: 7–12

Laplanche, Jean, and Jean-Baptiste Pontalis. 1985. *Fantasme originaire: fantasmes des origines, origines du fantasme*. Paris: Hachette

Lauretis, Teresa de. *See* de Lauretis, Teresa

Lavin, Irving. 1980. *Bernini and the Unity of the Visual Arts*. New York: (for) Pierpont Morgan Library (by) Oxford University Press

Lecercle, Jean-Jacques. 1990. *The Violence of Language*. London: Routledge

Lehmann, Hans-Thiess. 1997a. 'From Logos to Landscape: Text in Contemporary Dramaturgy.' *Performance Research* 2 (1): 55–60

– 1997b. 'Time Structures/Time Sculpture: On Some Theatrical Forms at the End of the Twentieth Century.' *Theaterschrift* 12: 29–47

Lentricchia, Frank, and Thomas McLaughlin, eds. 1995. *Critical Terms for Literary Study*. 2nd ed. Chicago: University of Chicago Press

Loiret, Emmanuel. In prep. *Sur le terrain*. Amsterdam: ASCA Press (PhD dissertation)

Lord, Catherine. 1999. *The Intimacy of Influence: Narrative and Theoretical Fictions in the Works of George Eliot, Virginia Woolf and Jeanette Winterson*. Amsterdam: ASCA Press (Ph.D. dissertation)

Lowenthal, David. 1985. *The Past Is a Foreign Country*. Cambridge: Cambridge University Press

– 1989. 'Nostalgia Tells It Like It Wasn't.' In *The Imagined Past: History and Nostalgia*, ed. Christopher Shaw and Malcolm Chase, 18–32. Manchester: Manchester University Press

Maleuvre, Didier. 1999. *Museum Memories: History, Technology, Art*. Stanford: Stanford University Press

Man, Paul de. *See* de Man, Paul

Marin, Louis. 1983. 'The Iconic Text and the Theory of Enunciation: Luca Signorelli at Loreto (ca. 1479–1484).' *New Literary History* 14 (3): 253–96

– 1988. 'Towards a Theory of Reading in the Visual Arts: Poussin's *The Arcadian Shepherds*.' In *Calligram: Essays in the New Art History from France*, ed. Norman Bryson, 63–90. Cambridge: Cambridge University Press

– 1993. *Des pouvoirs de l'image: gloses*. Paris: Editions du Seuil

Marini, Maurizio. 1974. *Io, Michelangelo da Caravaggio*. Rome: Studio B Bestetti e Bozzi York: Metropolitan Museum of Art and Electa/Rizzoli

Michel, Régis. 2000. *Posséder et détruire: stratégies sexuelles dans l'art d'occident.* Paris: Musée du Louvre (exhibition catalogue)

Miller, J. Hillis. 1987. *The Ethics of Reading: Kant, de Man, Eliot, Trollope, James, and Benjamin.* New York: Columbia University Press

Mitchell, Juliet, and Jacqueline Rose, eds. 1982. *Feminine Sexuality: Jacques Lacan and the École Freudienne.* Trans. Jacqueline Rose. London: Macmillan

Mitchell, W.J.T. 1985. *Iconology: Image, Text, Ideology.* Chicago: University of Chicago Press

Mok, Ineke. 1999. *In de ban van het ras. Aardrijkskunde tussen wetenschap en samenleving, 1876–1992 (Under the Spell of Race: Geography between Science and Society, 1876–1992).* Amsterdam: ASCA Press (PhD dissertation)

Morse, Margaret. 1998. *Virtualities: Television, Media Art, and Cyberculture.* Bloomington: Indiana University Press

Moxey, Keith. 1994. *The Practice of Theory.* Ithaca: Cornell University Press

Nederveen Pieterse, J. 1990. *Wit over zwart: beelden van Afrika en zwarten in de westerse populaire cultuur.* Amsterdam: Koninklijk Instituut voor de Tropen/ Stichting Cosmic Illusion Productions; The Hague: Novib

Neef, Sonja. 2000. *Kalligramme. Zur Medialität einer Schrift Anhand von Paul van Ostaijens* De feesten van angst en pijn. Amsterdam: ASCA Press (PhD dissertation)

Newell, William H., ed. 1998. *Interdisciplinarity: Essays from the Literature.* New York: College Entrance Examination Board

Newton-de Molina, David, ed. 1976. *On Literary Intention.* Edinburgh: Edinburgh University Press

Niranjana, Tejaswini. 1992. *Siting Translation: History, Post-Structuralism, and the Colonial\Context.* Berkeley: University of California Press

Ovid. 1994. *Metamorphoses.* Ed. and trans. Frank Justus Miller, rev. G.P. Gould. Cambridge: Harvard University Press (Loeb Classical Library)

Patterson, Annabel. 1995. 'Intention.' In *Critical Terms for Literary Study*, ed. Frank Lentricchia and Thomas McLaughlin, 135–46. Chicago: University of Chicago Press

Parker, Rozsika, and Griselda Pollock. 1995. *Old Mistresses: Women, Art, and Ideology.* London: Pandora Press (revised edition of or. 1981. New York: Pantheon Books)

Pavel, Thomas. 1984. 'Origin and Articulation: Comments on the Papers by Peter Brooks and Lucienne Frappier-Mazur.' *Style: Psychopoetics at Work* 18 (3): 355–68

Pavis, Patrice. 1998. *Dictionary of the Theatre: Terms, Concepts and Analysis.* Toronto: University of Toronto Press

Paz, Octavio. 1988. *Sor Juana or, The Traps of Faith.* Trans. Margaret Sayers

Peden. Cambridge: Harvard University Press (expanded version of 1982 *Sor Juana Inéz de la Cruz, o, las trampas de la fe*)

Peirce, Charles Sanders. 1984. 'Logic as Semiotic: The Theory of Signs.' In *Semiotics: An Introductory Anthology*, ed. and with introductions by Robert E. Innis, 4–23. Bloomington: Indiana University Press

Perlove, Shelley Karen. 1990. *Bernini and the Idealization of Death: The Blessed Ludovica Albertoni and the Altieri Chapel*. University Park: Pennsylvania State University Press

Plato. 1937. *The Dialogues of Plato*. 2 vols. Trans. B. Jowett. New York: Random House

Pollock, Griselda. 1999. *Differencing the Canon: Feminist Desire and the Writing of Art's Histories*. London: Routledge

Popper, Karl. 1972. *The Logic of Scientific Discovery*. New York: Harper and Row

– 1982. *The Open Universe: An Argument for Indeterminism from the Postscript to The Logic of Scientific Discovery*, ed. W.W. Bartley. Totowa, Ill: Rowman and Littlefield

Porter, Gaby. 1991. 'Partial Truths.' In *Museum Languages: Objects and Texts*, ed. Gaynor Kavanagh, 103–17. Leicester/London/New York: Leicester University Press

Potts, Alex. 1999. 'Louise Bourgeois – Sculptural Confrontations.' *Oxford Art Journal* 22 (2): 37–54

Propp, V. 1966. *Morphology of the Folktale*. Austin: University of Texas Press

Reynolds, Teri. 2000. *Case Studies in Cognitive Metaphor and Interdisciplinary Analysis: Physics, Biology, Narrative*. New York: Columbia University (PhD dissertation)

Rogin, Michael. 1996. *Blackface, White Noise: Jewish Immigrants in the Hollywood Melting Pot*. Berkeley: University of California Press

Rorty, Richard. 1979. *Philosophy and the Mirror of Nature*. Princeton: Princeton University Press

Saïd, Edward. 2000. 'Invention, Memory and Place.' *Critical Inquiry* 26 (Winter): 175–92

Saleci, Renata, and Slavoj Žižek, ed. 1996. *Gaze and Voice as Love Objects*. Durham and London: Duke University Press

Salomon, Nanette. 1991. 'The Art Historical Canon: Sins of Omission.' In *(En)Gendering Knowledge: Feminism in Academe*, ed. Joan E. Hartman and Ellen Messner-Davidow, 222–36. Knoxville: University of Tennessee Press

– 1998. *Jacob Duck and the Gentrification of Dutch Genre Painting*. Doorspijk: Davaco

– 1999. 'Vermeer's Women: Shifting Paradigms in Midcareer.' *The Practice of*

Cultural Analysis: Exposing Interdisciplinary Interpretation, ed. Mieke Bal and Hent de Vries, 44–59. Stanford: Stanford University Press
– In press. *Shifting Priorities: Gender and Genre in Seventeenth-Century Dutch Painting*. Stanford: Stanford University Press
Sanders, Mark. 1999. 'Postcolonial Reading.' In *Postmodern Culture: An Electronic Journal of Interdisciplinary Criticism* 10 (1) (Sept.) 1–13
Sayre, Henry. 1995. 'Performance.' In *Critical Terms for Literary Study*, 2nd ed., ed. Frank Lentricchia and Thomas McLaughlin, 91–104. Chicago: University of Chicago Press
Schaeffer, J.M. 1997. *Les célibataires de l'art*. Paris: Editions du Seuil
Schneider, Rebecca. 1997. *The Explicit Body in Performance*. New York: Routledge
Schor, Naomi. 1985. 'Restricted Thematics.' In *Breaking the Chain: Women, Theory, and French Realist Fiction*. New York: Columbia University Press
– 1987. *Reading in Detail: Esthetics and the Feminine*. New York and London: Methuen
Schwartz, Gary. 1985. *Rembrandt: His Life, His Paintings*. Harmondsworth: Penguin
Schwenger, Peter. 1999. *Fantasm and Fiction: On Textual Envisioning*. Stanford: Stanford University Press
Sedgwick, Eve Kosofsky. 1990. *Epistemology of the Closet*. Berkeley and Los Angeles: University of California Press
– 1993. 'Queer Performativity.' *GLQ* 1 (1): 1–16
Sherman, Daniel J., and Irit Rogoff, eds. 1994. *Museum Culture: Histories, Discourses, Spectacles*. Minneapolis: University of Minnesota Press
Silverman, Kaja. 1983. *The Subject of Semiotics*. New York: Oxford University Press
– 1988 *The Acoustic Mirror: The Female Voice in Psychoanalysis and Cinema*. Bloomington: Indiana University Press
– 1996. *The Threshold of the Visible World*. New York: Routledge
Spivak, Gayatri Chakravorty. 1987. *In Other Worlds: Essays in Cultural Politics*. New York: Methuen
– 1993a. 'Echo.' *New Literary History* 24: 17–43
– 1993b. 'More on Power/Knowledge.' In *Outside in the Teaching Machine*, 25–52. New York: Routledge
– 1995. 'Teaching for the Times.' In *The Decolonization of the Imagination*, ed. Bhikhu Parekh and Jan Nederveen Pieterse, 177–202. London: Zed
– 1999. *A Critique of Postcolonial Reason: Toward a History of the Vanishing Present*. Cambridge: Harvard University Press

Stallybrass, Peter, and Allon White. 1986. *The Politics and Poetics of Transgression*. Ithaca: Cornell University Press

Steinberg, Michael. Forthcoming. *Listening to Reason: Music and Subjectivity in the Long Nineteenth Century*. Princeton: Princeton University Press

Steiner, Wendy. 1982. *The Colors of Rhetoric: Problems in the Relation between Modern Literature and Art*. Chicago: University of Chicago Press

– 1988. *Pictures of Romance: Form against Context in Painting and Literature*. Chicago: University of Chicago Press

– 1995. *The Scandal of Pleasure: Art in an Age of Fundamentalism*. Chicago: University of Chicago Press

Stengers, Isabelle, ed. 1987. *D'une science à l'autre: des concepts nomades*. Paris: Editions du Seuil

Stengers, Isabelle, and Judith Schlanger. 1991. *Les concepts scientifiques: invention et pouvoir*. Paris: Gallimard

Summers, David. 1985–6. 'Intentions in the History of Art.' *New Literary History* 17: 305–21

Teresa of Avila. 1988. *The Life of Saint Teresa of Avila by Herself*. Trans. J.M. Cohen. New York: Penguin USA

Torgovnick, Marianna. 1994. 'The Politics of "We."' In *Eloquent Obsessions: Writing Cultural Criticism*, ed. Marianna Torgovnick, 260–78. Durham, NC: Duke University Press

Treffers, Bert. 1991. *Caravaggio: genie in opdracht. Een kunstenaar en zijn opdrachtgevers in het Rome van rond 1600*. Nijmegen: SUN

– 2001. 'The Arts and Crafts of Sainthood: New Orders, New Saints, New Altarpieces.' In *The Genius of Rome: 1592–1623*, ed. Beverly Louise Brown, 338–71. London: Royal Academy of Arts

van Alphen, Ernst. 1992. *Francis Bacon and the Loss of Self*. London: Reaktion Books; 1993 Cambridge: Harvard University Press

– 1996. 'The Portrait's Dispersal: Concepts of Representation and Subjectivity in Contemporary Portraiture.' In *Portraiture: Facing the Subject*, ed. Joanna Woodall, 239–56. Manchester: Manchester University Press

– 1997. *Caught by History: Holocaust Effects in Contemporary Art, Literature, and Theory*. Stanford: Stanford University Press

– 1998. 'Duchamp in travestie.' *De Witte Raaf* 76 (Nov.–Dec.): 14–15

– 2000. *Armando: Forms of Memory*. Rotterdam: NAi

– 2001. 'Imagined Homelands: Remapping Cultural Identity.' Lecture, ASCA soirées on the Politics of Place (org. Ginette Verstraete). Amsterdam: ASCA

– 2002. 'Caught by Images.' In *Image and Remembrance: Representation and the*

Holocaust, ed. Shelly Hornstein and Florence Jacobowitz, 133–57. Bloomington: Indiana University Press

Venuti, Lawrence. 1994. 'Translation and the Formation of Cultural Identities.'
Current Issues in Language and Society 1: 214–15

– 1995. *The Translator's Invisibility: A History of Translation*. London: Routledge

– 1996. 'Translation, Philosophy, Materialism.' *Radical Philosophy* 79: 24–34

Vries, Hent de. *See* de Vries, Hent

Wallace, Michele. 1991. *Invisibility Blues: From Pop to Theory*. London and New
York: Verso

Weber, Samuel. 1982. *The Legend of Freud*. Minneapolis: University of Minnesota Press

Weigel, Sigrid. 1996. *Body- and Image-Space: Re-reading Walter Benjamin*. Trans.
Georgina Paul, with Rachel McNicholl and Jeremy Gaines. New York and
London: Routledge

Wheeler, Roxann. 2000. 'New Golden Age.' In *The Complexion of Race: Categories
of Difference in Eighteenth-Century British Culture*. Philadelphia: University of
Pennsylvania Press

White, Hayden. 1973. *Metahistory: The Historical Imagination in Nineteenth-
Century Europe*. Baltimore: Johns Hopkins University Press

Williams, Patricia J. 1997. *Seeing a Color-Blind Future: The Paradox of Race*. The
1997 BBC Reith Lectures. New York: Noonday Press/Farrar, Straus and
Giroux

Williams, Raymond. 1980. 'Base and Superstructure in Marxist Cultural Theory.' In *Problems in Materialism and Culture*, 40–2. London: Verso

– 1983. *Keywords: A Vocabulary of Culture and Society*. New York: Oxford University Press

Wuthnow, Robert, et al. 1984. *Cultural Analysis: The Work of Peter L. Berger, Mary
Douglas, Michel Foucault and Jürgen Habermas*. Boston and London: Routledge
and Kegan Paul

Young, Alison. 2000. 'Into the Blue: The Image Written on Law.' Lecture. International conference (*Of Languages and Laws*) of the Law and Literature Association, Sydney, Australia, 7 July 2000

Young, Robert. 1990. *White Mythologies: Writing History and the West*. London:
Routledge

Index of Names and Titles

Index of Terms and Concepts